The Women of
Renaissance Florence

Power and Dependence
in Renaissance Florence
Volume 2

The Women of Renaissance Florence

Power and Dependence
in Renaissance Florence
Volume 2

Richard C. Trexler

Medieval & Renaissance texts & studies
Binghamton, New York
1993

© Copyright 1993
Center for Medieval and Early Renaissance Studies
State University of New York at Binghamton

Library of Congress Cataloging-in-Publication Data

Trexler, Richard C., 1932–
    Power and dependence in Renaissance Florence / Richard C. Trexler.
        p. cm.
    Includes bibliographical references.
    Contents: v. 1. The Children of Renaissance Florence—v. 2. The women of
Renaissance Florence—v. 3. The workers of Renaissance Florence.
    ISBN 0–86698–156–X (v. 1). —ISBN 0–86698–157–8 (v. 2).
ISBN 0–86698–158–6 (v. 3)
    1. Florence (Italy)—Social conditions. 2. Children—Italy—Florence—History.
3. Youth—Italy—Florence—History.   4. Women—Italy—Florence—History.
5. Working class—Italy—Florence—History. I. Title.
HN488.F56T74 1992
306′.0945′51—dc20   92– 44785
                                                                                CIP

Printed in the United States of America

Contents

For my sister and friend

Catherine

Achiever

Introduction

PERUSING THE NEW YORK REVIEW OF BOOKS FOR 20 DECEMBER 1990, MY attention was caught by the title of Amartya Sen's essay, "More Than a Hundred Million Women Are Missing." It deals with the fact that in many present-day populations, far fewer than the expected number of females are to be found. The more things change, the more they remain the same. The three essays in the present collection were in fact originally inspired by a similar problem: where were the missing women of Renaissance Florence? For researchers in the 1970s and early 1980s studying the history of Florence had begun to see that within the general population, a disproportionate number of females were missing at certain points in the female life cycle. What could explain this? And equally important, what was it like for females to live day to day, given that they obviously had to withstand particular pressures to survive?

The three essays I bring together in the present volume describe three links in the chain of women's experience in this urban world. They are quantitative in nature, and readers encountering them may ask how a quantitative approach, even of the finger-counting type used here, can open up the world of women's qualitative experiences. One of the main goals of this collection of essays is, in fact, to demonstrate just how the student can become qualitatively attuned to persons in the past by pursuing quantitative questions. At the same time, reading these studies will acquaint the student with one of the central problems of contemporary women's history: was women's fate in the medieval and early modern world a generally dismal one? Or was there a redemptive quality about their existences? Or indeed, did they have a separate sphere of independence? And if there was, how is one to unearth this heroic sociology from sources that were largely written by men? I put these questions to three types of Florentine women of this age: nuns, prostitutes, and widows.

The first essay here, on nuns, is the most exotic of the three for today's reader. For it is not easy for people today to imagine a girl entering a convent with the clear knowledge that she might remain there for the rest of her life, with no sexual experience and without the experience of bearing children. My study of the population of Florentine nunneries from the early fourteenth century until the middle of the sixteenth century was undertaken to gain some insight into that exotic world.

Recall that this was the age of all those (male) intellectual and artistic giants for whom Renaissance Florence is famous. It was an age in which, as Jacob Burckhardt claimed in his *Civilization of the Renaissance in Italy*, and as mostly male professors long taught legions of students of both sexes, women had the same opportunities as men. And yet, even before the computer age, the merest glance at the Florentine landscape revealed that something was wrong with this picture because Renaissance Florence obviously held many nuns, and their convents were hardly hotbeds of Burckhardtian "equality." When in the late 1970s the computer made its entry into Florentine studies, the matter became pressing because some things could no longer be doubted: women, at different ages, were indeed missing from the population, and there were in fact a mass of nuns in Florence. A study of the demography of the nunneries over time would begin to reveal the nature of life in these houses.

The picture that emerged from my finger-quantification of the nuns proves quite amazing. Clearly, the percentage of Florentine women living behind the walls of urban convents increased radically in these two centuries, until something between eleven and thirteen percent was reached, even while the number of Florentine women living in nunneries outside the walls of the city, in its so-called dominion, was also increasing radically. Like today's prisons, physical plants made to hold just a few persons now bulged with humanity. These women usually came from the better, if not the very richest, levels of the population, and so it soon became evident that the convents provided a solution to a pressing problem of a particular segment of the population: those families whose fathers, lacking the assets to properly dower their daughters in marriage, married off fewer and fewer daughters and built more and more nunneries to house the surplus.

The details of the social pathology evident in these crowded prisons of women await the reader, and indeed, await the future researcher, since this essay no more than cracks the door into this little known world. Yet the very size of the female religious contingent in the city, combined with the fact that female religion in Florence was overpoweringly affected by families' dowry considerations, meant that the pool of marriageable females in this segment of the population had decreased, so that a corresponding decrease in the rate of marriages of young Florentine men must also have occurred. Two results of this situation seem certain. Postponing marriage, young men must have engaged in a significant amount of heterosexual behavior with prostitutes and homosexual behavior with adolescent males.

One of the historian's strategies for archival research is to search out a compact written source to answer particular historical questions, such as that at the heart of the second essay in this volume, the experience of prostitution. Clearly, my interest in the problem of heterosexual prostitution in Florence had become part of a larger inquiry, a certain type of history of women that would link nuns with prostitutes as elements of a broader crisis of females in this fabled city. This interest was greatly stimulated when I discovered in the Florentine State Archives a large volume of the Florentine Office of Decency (*Onestà*). Covering the period 1441–1523, it summarized judicial sentences against those female prostitutes and their male clients who had violated laws governing brothel prostitution. Relying on this compact source meant that mine would necessarily be a limited inquiry, since the brothel prostitutes this source describes were foreigners and not Florentines. Florentine women who sold sex made up a whole other group who, so far as they continued to reside in Florence, lived scattered about in other parts of the city, in shops, private homes, and convents. The Office of Decency did not protect or supervise them.

Still, a study of these foreigners in their brothels, located in the very center of Florence in today's Piazza della Repubblica, could, as I hope the reader will agree, not only bring to light the daily life of these women, a matter of no small importance. It could also, I hypothesized, help us understand the sexual activity of the young men mentioned above—those who were not marrying the girls who had become nuns—because the city's stated aim in fostering brothel prostitution in the early fifteenth century was to dissuade just such decent young Florentine males from homosexuality.

The actual results of my research brought out a great wealth of information about women's experience, but also some surprises. To begin with, the brothel prostitutes themselves were indeed almost never from Florence, but from abroad. Amazingly, in the early fifteenth century a good half of them and a third of their pimps were from distant Flanders and Germany. In the course of that century those figures declined, until the percentage of north-Italian prostitutes and pimps finally reached almost 100 perecent in the early sixteenth century. The women who sold sex in the center of Florence, alongside the Old Market, had no ties at all to Florentine families or societies.

A second surprise came when I calculated the vital statistics of the women's clientele. As far as occupation, these men were mostly simple artisans and, as regards status, only rarely people of substance. Here was a first tip-off: these were males from a social class beneath that of those boys who, in other times, would have married the monachized girls of Florence. Then followed the greatest surprise of all: more than half of the women's clients came from outside Tuscany, while another full quarter were Tuscans, but not from the city of Florence. Only one in four clients of the brothel prostitutes of Renaissance Florence was a native!

In short, the centrally located public brothels in this great capital of the Renaissance were filled by women who were never Florentines, and served men who were foreigners in two of four cases, and non-Florentine Tuscans in one of four cases. These brothels in fact served lower class visitors. What then had become of all those Florentine young men whose "decent" heterosexual behavior had been the stated aim of the brothels? They must have taken their pleasure elsewhere, presumably with those women who sold sex in parts of the city away from the brothels. One of the hypotheses with which I had entered this research on brothel prostitution had in fact proved false: the young men who could not marry the girls placed in convents did *not* instead frequent the city's stewhouses.

In the meantime, however, I had learned a valuable lesson regarding the study of women's institutions in the Italian Renaissance, and that is that female domestic institutions, including the nunneries but also Florentine families, were significantly affected by the movements of other women and their pimps arriving from all parts of Europe. Whatever future students may discover about the use of private and part-time prostitutes by the Florentine males who were not marrying, the fact was that a major female institution like that of the nunneries could not be understood only in relation to another domestic institution such as marriage dowries. One day other researchers, perhaps in Siena and Lucca, will find all those Florentine women driven abroad to engage in brothel prostitution. Now we know that an international pool of unwanted women tuned the forks of Florentine female institutions.

It goes without saying that the Florentine fathers' fear that their daughters, denied marriage, would prostitute themselves was the cultural factor that more than any other fueled citizens' zeal to found and fund the city's social institutions. As I explain in the volume on children in this series, nowhere is that concern more evident than in the history of Florentine foundling institutions.[1] Because they feared that young *Innocentine*, that is, girls raised from infancy in the foundling home of the Innocenti, would perforce turn to prostitution if they could not marry at a convenient age, the city fathers provided small dowries to help the matter along (they did this not only for foundlings, but also in other contexts where young girls were at risk of prostitution). In a serious manner, the city fathers—who were commonly the biological fathers of many illegitimate girls in the homes and thus had a major interest in preserving not only their daughters, but their family honor—sought to maintain legitimate nuclear family units and to generate new ones out of the disgrace of bastardy.

This civic inspiration lies at the heart of a third essay in Florentine women's history, a study of the Orbatello home for widows. Though the house was founded around 1370, here the concentration is on the first two-thirds of the sixteenth century, for which documentation is both concentrated and relatively abundant. The Orbatello was a two-story apartment house or welfare asylum, taking up the better part of a city block, whose approximately 58 dwellings were bestowed on widows by city officials. These widows commonly brought children with them, the idea being that the boys among them would be raised there until put out at twelve years of age, while the girls would be reared until they married—with dowry aid from the government—and thus started new, legitimate nuclear families. Given the available documentation, what I wanted to retrieve was a sense of what it was like for the women living there.

The picture that emerges is truly impressive. Here was a welfare institution

---

[1] *The Children of Renaissance Florence* (*Power and Dependence in Renaissance Florence*, volume 1) (Binghamton, N.Y.: Medieval and Renaissance Texts and Studies, 1993).

that, as far as one can tell, was run on a day to day basis by the senior women who lived there, even though male officials had formal authority. To a remarkable extent, the occupants tended to stay in one apartment over long periods of time rather than move about. Perhaps most impressive, the main goal of this communal existence seems to have been fulfilled: after maturing, many young girls did in fact marry, in the Orbatello chapel, to then leave the home and start new families. To a gratifying extent, this research provided an intimate look into a world of women living in community, and the image left behind is positively life-affirming.

Or so it was until later in the sixteenth century, when signs of collapse began to appear in the Orbatello as in many other institutions for Florentine women. Three thousand nuns crammed into half a hundred convents; hundreds, perhaps a thousand or more *Innocentine* unable to find husbands; and the inhabitants of several other homes for unwanted women forced into the streets, so to speak, their institutions no longer able to support the cost of this overflow of seemingly unwanted humanity. Many of these women in internal exile swept down on the Orbatello, effectively ending its function of producing new nuclear families. Instead, Orbatello became a house of prostitution, or so was the allegation. The story is gruesome, but cannot be told until much more research has been done on Florentine women in institutions.[2]

What does need to be noted in closing this introduction is that some students contest what they see as too negative a reading of the female condition in Renaissance Florence—a negativity that is admittedly heightened by the fact that these are studies of disadvantaged and not advantaged women. The claim of redemption that some make for the females of Renaissance Florence, even including its nuns in their convents, is a point of view that will need to be tested in years to come. Readers of these essays can begin to judge the matter.

Finally, keep in mind that Florence is but one European city. Alas, in-depth studies of female institutions in many other individual Italian cities would be necessary before any generalizations could be hazarded about the female condition in Renaissance Italian welfare institutions. For instance, it appears from recent research, referred to at the end of this volume, that even in nearby Venice, so similar to Florence at so many levels, the female condition was significantly different, some would say better. Thus intense research into local historical conditions does not guarantee the scholar any global wisdom in these matters. Still, by counting fingers, these essays do allow the student to identify and have solidarity with some women of the past. That is a small gift of Clio.

---

[2] See now S. Cohen, *The Evolution of Women's Asylums Since 1500: From Refuges for Ex-Prostitutes to Shelters for Battered Women* (New York, 1992).

Celibacy in the Renaissance: The Nuns of Florence[*]

WRITING THEIR FISCAL DECLARATION TO THE COMMUNE OF FLORENCE IN 1478, the nuns of San Piero Martire humbly insisted that because of the strict observance of their rule and their continual prayers for the city, their house had always been exempt from city taxes. "Which prayers," they continued, "coming as they do from persons of such great religion, are more useful than two thousand horses."[1]

Some years earlier, a burgher of Florence had drawn up a list of all the houses of *vergini sacrate* in the city. "They spend day and night praying for the most worthy Signoria of Florence. Open your eyes and appreciate that!"[2]

It is difficult for a person of the late twentieth century to understand how reassured a burgher of late medieval or early modern Europe felt about the state of his city by vast congregations of religious. The acts of piety that were part of the strict rituals of monastic communities seemed the opposite, the *alter ego* so to speak, of the mundane preoccupations of the merchants and artisans. In this vale of tears, the good state of the commune appeared guaranteed as long as the area within the walls and in the nearby environs contained the incorporated City of God.

It is banal for a medieval historian to say that in the course of the thirteenth century the monastic movement ceded right of place and religious interest to the urban and evangelical creations of the Mendicant friars. But there is another side to this picture. Clare, the friend of Francis of Assisi, did not preach in the highways and byways. The thousands of nuns who followed

---

[*] This essay appeared previously, in French, in *Annales E.S.C.* 27 (1972): 1329–50.

[1] *Archivio di Stato, Firenze* (hereafter *ASF*), *Catasto* 989, fol. 711v.

[2] *Biblioteca Riccardiana, MS. Moreniana* 103, fols. 62r–63v: "Stanno e giorni e notte in orazione a far preghe per la dignissima signoria di Firenze. Apri l'occhio a questo, e gusta."

her appeared to be a new avant-garde of the old monastic movement. While the nuns of previous times had sown and woven, those in Florence at the end of the Middle Ages devoted themselves to prayer and cult.[3] The city created a new type of monasticism. In its role as an inspiration for urban society, monasticism did not disappear. Rather, it changed sex.

The purpose of this article is to study the demographic aspects of female vocations in thirteenth- to sixteenth-century Florence. My conclusions will be provisional in character, but I do hope to sketch out the convents' secular trends of recruitment during a period of some three centuries. One may surmise that what a great merchant city like Florence did with its women holds the greatest interest for the social history of the Italian commune in general. This study also begins with the hypothesis that the composition of the ecclesiastical estate in a city of this type in part determines the tone of that society's religiosity. These working hypotheses make demographic research such as this indispensable. Once the changing proportion of the populace which the nuns made up is determined, we can evaluate more realistically their position in it and their influence.

Anyone visiting Florence at the time of the *Primo Popolo* (1250–1260) would have experienced a religious excitement that was common to many European cities of the time. While the Mendicant orders consolidated their positions, our visitor could have seen the churches of the Franciscans and Dominicans rise up; he or she would have been struck by the laity's largesse in building them and impressed as well by their enthusiasm in listening to sermons of the great preachers. The religious zeal of the women would have been equally evident. In the city streets, the visitor could have seen hundreds dressed in the robes of the Franciscan and Dominican third orders. It would seem in effect that religious vocations had expanded outside even as religion had renounced its natural habitat in the convent. There were female monasteries in the city—perhaps five at the time[4]—but their census was small and their spiritual influence on the city weak.

During the next half century, however, the picture changed radically. Numerous houses of women—traditional Benedictines or nuns in the new Mendicant orders—were established in the city. In 1336, Giovanni Villani counted 24 nunneries in the city or in its immediate surroundings.[5] At about the same date, the free circulation of the tertiaries of the Mendicant orders began to change into a more and more sedentary life where the nuns were cloistered within stable establishments.

Three factors caused these convents to move toward the city: wars, incomes, and family considerations. The security of rural monastic establishments had always been problematic, and would remain so for years to come.

---

[3] This passage from production to ritual was noted by L. Eckenstein, *Women under Monasticism* (New York, 1963), 356.

[4] At the time the following nunneries were definitely active: S. Andrea, S. Ambrogio, S. Michele, S. Felicità, and S. Piero Maggiore.

[5] *Croniche di Giovanni, Matteo e Filippo Villani* (Trieste, 1857), book XI, chap. 94.

Soldiers of fortune and communal armies often used the spacious rooms, halls, and grounds of the convents to quarter their troops. But a second factor proved still more decisive in pushing the convents toward the city: the nunneries of the *contado* or suburbs and the more distant *distretto* witnessed the decline of potential sources of revenue. G. Volpe calls our attention to the massive attacks on ecclesiastical holdings in the area around Volterra during the thirteenth century.[6] The monastic establishments tried to parry these attacks by appropriating rural churches and their different revenues, but this proved an unsatisfactory solution, given how poor these churches themselves were and how much difficulty they had in collecting their own rents and tithes. Further, living in rural areas, the nuns could not count on regular alms, and became more and more dependent upon *elemosine* originating in the city and from the commune. Lastly, family ties seem to have been a factor for migration toward the city. It may be assumed that the greater the number of nuns coming from the Florentine bourgeoisie, the greater pressure to have their houses relocated closer to the city, so that they would be close to their families. Davidsohn believed that reasons of this type masked one single and fundamental motivation, the desire to be near the exciting life of the city.[7]

Whatever the reasons, the migration of so many communities toward the city brought new sources of revenue. The moves stimulated an increase in the populations of such houses, a phenomenon that can be related to the foundation of several new nunneries in the city at the end of the duecento. Finally, such displacements indicate that the function of these establishments was changing. If it is true that the earlier female monasticism in Florence had been important in the development of the wool industry,[8] the economic importance of the nunneries at the end of the Middle Ages is less evident. From the economist's point of view, the convents were becoming agents of consumption rather than of production. But from the point of view of the normal layperson of the Middle Ages, they continued to produce spiritually. That production, however, must be the subject of future study.[9]

Let us now broach the demographic models that result from these transfers and these new foundations.

The movement toward the city was undertaken between 1250 and 1350. It affected convents tucked away in the depths of the *contado* and *distretto*, but also many others that had been built close to old walls. This movement tended to proceed by agglomeration: in the following period, that is, nuns from Florence are found installed within the city and when not, in a convent situated close to an important city of the *distretto*.

The disorganization brought on by these transfers was often serious. Two of the best known monasteries in Florence owed their origins to dissentions that the choice of their new domicile brought on among the nuns of Ripoli

---

[6] G. Volpe, *Toscana medievale* (Florence, 1964), 98f.

[7] R. Davidsohn, *Storia di Firenze* (Florence, 1965), 7:85.

[8] Ibid., 1:137f.; 6:163.

[9] See the conclusion of this article for some ideas for such a study.

after they had decided to move to the city.[10] Sisters who could move directly into a new residence from the country were, in fact, fortunate. More frequently they had to take up quarters in private homes while promised permanent residences were constructed.[11] At other times they had to rent a part of another nunnery while they waited for their permanent quarters.[12] The nuns' moves seem to have caused much anxiety. The ideal remained to isolate, to avoid associations. But the chastity of the spouses of Christ was difficult to preserve in the midst of all this disorganization.

When they finally settled in, the nuns followed the tendency, common to most medieval professional groups, to live in the same area. The concentration of nunneries in Florence is a striking phenomenon. They are found gathered near the gates and the lengths of certain streets, along two axes in particular: in 1552, from the Piazza San Piero Maggiore, the site of an old nunnery, four houses were strung out along the present Borgo Pinti.[13] Then from the church of San Lorenzo up the street that for most of its length is called via San Gallo, out to the gate of the same name, hundreds of nuns lived in convents which lined both sides.[14] At least seven nunneries housed these women, while the side streets hid still other institutions.[15] No wonder that the Florentine erudite Richa called this street "less the Holy Street than the Street of Confusion."[16] Other concentrations of nunneries could be found at the Prato around Ognissanti,[17] on the via Ghibellina,[18] and around the Porta San Piero Gattolino (the present Porta Roma).[19]

What led to such agglomerations is not completely clear. One might think that they were intended for self-defense, but the documentation does not confirm such an intention. Only in the sixteenth century does it become evident that nuns were being concentrated into contiguous building complexes so as to facilitate their isolation from secular eyes. Why then did the nuns buy and patrons give over to them areas along the walls or in certain streets? Keeping in mind that Italian cities dressed up their gates with statues of their patron

---

[10] S. Orlandi, *Necrologio di Santa Maria Novella* (Florence, 1955), 1:338f.

[11] Cf. *ASF, Provvisioni* 25, fols. 56r–v (24 September 1333); ibid., 40, fols. 64r–v (19 February 1352 stilus florentinus [hereafter sf]).

[12] That procedure was used each time that war forced nuns to move to the city. Thus in 1529, several houses located near the walls were forced to move inside the walls and live with other nuns.

[13] Toward the north: S. Piero Maggiore, S. Maria Candeli, S. Maria Maddalena, S. Salvestro, S. Giuseppe. In the small nearby streets: S. Maria degli Angeli and the nuns of the Crocetta.

[14] Going north: S. Apollonia, Regina Coeli (Chiarito), S. Lucia, S. Luca, S. Chimente, S. Agata.

[15] S. Orsola, S. Barbara, S. Caterina da Siena.

[16] G. Richa, *Notizie istoriche delle chiese fiorentine* (Florence, 1757), 5:157; and E. Viviana Della Robbia, *Nei monasteri fiorentini* (Florence, 1946), 7.

[17] S. Maria sul Prato, S. Anna.

[18] S. Jacopo and San Lorenzo, S. Annunziata (le Murate).

[19] S. Piero Martire, Annalena, S. Chiara, le Convertite.

saints,[20] and that every year the Florentines exorcised the demons from each of the city gates,[21] I would suggest that occult considerations played a role in the monasteries' selection of their sites. Certainly financial reasons played a role, lands located around the gates costing less. Areas that had not been built up were ideal for the nunneries' gardens and, even in the mid-sixteenth century, Varchi noted that with one exception all the convents had a *grandissimo e bello orto*.[22]

How many of these establishments were there? The information we have is brought together in the following table:

Table 1[23]
The Number of Convents

	1336	1368	1376–78	1415	1428–29	1470	1543–45	1552
Inside the walls		16	18	26	20	30	42	47
Within four miles		2	6	3	2		9	9
Total	24		24				51	56

Though these figures are imperfect, they do permit some generalizations. The number of convents remained the same before and after the Black Death of 1348 and up to mid-fifteenth century. A slow increase in the second and third quarter of the latter brought their number within the city up to 30 in 1470. The growth accelerated at the end of the fifteenth and, despite the pest of the 1520s, during the early sixteenth century until 1543–1544, when the number of nunneries in and around Florence reached 51. In the eight fol-

[20] H. C. Peyer, *Stadt und Stadtpatron im mittelalterlichen Italien* (Zürich, 1955), 19.

[21] Davidsohn, *Storia*, 7:112f.

[22] B. Varchi, *Storia fiorentina di Messer* ... (Milan, 1803), 3:103f.

[23] 1336: G. Villani, *Croniche*, XI, 94.
1368: *ASF, Capitoli, Appendici* 27 ("Registro di atti di processo e di mandati fatti di monache di alcuni monasteri fiorentini, 1368"), fols. 1–15v. This list is not complete.
1376–78: *ASF, Beni ecclesiastici* 19 ("Libro di tutte quelle persone che comperorono beni della chiesa, 1375–1378"); this list should be complete.
1415: *Statuta populi et comunis florentiae* (Fribourg, 1783), 3:779–85. The number in the table represents all the nunneries within the four miles from city center that are covered by the *statuta*.
1428–29: *ASF, Catasto* 184, 185. This number represent those nunneries that made a fiscal declaration in these years; it is partial.
1470: *Zibaldone di Benedetto Dei, Bibl. Riccardiana, MS. Moreniana* 103, fols. 62r–63v.
1543–44: *ASF, R. Diritto* 4892, fols. 45–46 (complete list).
1552: *Biblioteca Nazionale, Firenze* (hereafter *BNF*), *Fondo principale* II, i, 120, fols. 102v–206 (census).

lowing years, between 1544 and 1552, five new convents were founded in Florence.[24]

The increasing number of nuns at the beginning of the cinquecento troubled both the lay and ecclesiastical authorities. In 1515, a communal notary noted that "the nuns in the convent of the *Convertite* are very poor; at present there are 162 of them, and their number multiplies every day."[25] Two years later a provincial council of the Florentine church published a constitution aimed at remedying these excesses:

> Item. Although the law requires that no more nuns should be allowed to enter a convent than can live from the house's income, it has nevertheless come about that because certain people insist, the majority of convents in Florence have admitted such a large number that, their income being insufficient, they are faced with famine. Then in order to obtain subsistence, they are forced to associate with lay and ecclesiastical persons and are thus seduced into dangerous friendships which in turn engender the most infame events. This is why the said synod ... orders that from now on no nun can enter into a convent without the license of the ordinary, under penalty, etc.[26]

While the number of houses increased, the number of religious in each house grew still faster. Although acquisitions and donations had at times increased the material support for the houses,[27] the problem of assuring subsistence for those in cloisters had been only partly resolved. As an example, the 162 *convertite*, fallen women who had set about bettering themselves, could not count on the help of families or friends, as could their more fortunate sisters in other convents.

Let us examine now the average number of nuns in each institution over the course of these three centuries.

---

[24] Cf. Table 1.

[25] *ASF, Balia* 40, fol. 77v: "Le monache del munistero delle Convertite sono poverissime e al presente di numero 162 et ogni dì multiplicano."

[26] "Item quia licet jure cautum sit in monasteriis non debere poni nisi tot moniales, quot ex redditibus vivere possunt, tamen in plerisque monasteriis Florentie ob aliquorum importunitatem assumuntur tot moniales, ut fame eas confici contingat, redditibus non sufficientibus, propter quod coguntur postea pro victu habendo saecularium et religiosorum hominum frequentare consortis, et amicitias inire periculosas, ex quibus postea nefandi sequuntur eventus; ideo praefata synodus praecepit ... ne deinceps aliquam monialem admittere possint sine ordinarium suorum licentia, sub poena ..." (J.-D. Mansi, *Sacrorum Conciliorum nova et amplissima collectio* [Florence and Venice, 1759–98] vol. 35 col. 262).

[27] More often, city functionaries acted to limit the use that could be made of neighboring properties, assuring a suitable isolation over the long term; see for instance *ASF, R. Diritto* 4892, fols. 5–6.

Table 2[28]
Average Number of Nuns Per Convent

	1336	1368	1377	1428	1478	1515	1543–44	1552
Suore, otherwise undifferentiated	21		14.5	20	32.8		60.9	72.7
Consecrated Nuns and Novices		11.2		13.7			49.8	64.6
Bocche (total of nuns and laity in the convent)				20		97.8		

What were the different types of "professions" found in the convent? First of all, there were the *sagrate*, usually called *suore*.[29] These were professed nuns, since they had taken the vows of poverty, chastity, and obedience and been consecrated by the bishop. Then came the *converse* or *servigiali*, that is, lay sisters who participated in the spiritual benefits of the convent. Often also listed as *suore* along with, though after, the *sagrate*, they can be identified by their more rustic origins.[30] Next came the novices, usually also called

---

[28] Loc. cit. at note 23 unless otherwise indicated: 1336 (24 units); 1368 (18); 1377: *ASF, Estimo* 338, 340 (10); 1428 (18, 10); 1478: *ASF, Catasto* 989 (11); 1515: *ASF, Balia* 40, fols. 76v–77v (15); 1543–44 (50, 50); 1552 (47, 47).

[29] In what follows, I describe those belonging to the second and not to the third order. Certainly in general, the documentation used in this article refers to both categories. The difference between the two groups was largely marginal, the more so since the tertiaries continually tended to adopt the rule of veiled *sagrate*. See for example the case of a group of tertiaries passing to the second order in A. Gherardi, *Nuovi documenti e studi intorno a G. Savonarola* (Florence, 1887), 68f. The book of M. de Fontette, *Les religieuses à l'âge classique du droit canon* (Paris, 1967) did not help much when we sought to determine the differences betweeen tertiaries and second order nuns. Naturally, the fundamental distinction was that the *sagrate* took formal vows. The inability of the commune of Florence to maintain its own ad hoc definition of second order nuns shows how difficult it was to distinguish between the two. On 16 May 1437, the Signoria proposed a law permitting women of marriage age who "professa fuerit sub perpetua clausura in monasterio clare et bone fame et spiritualis et honeste vite et approbate religionis" to reacquire the capital destined for their marriage which had been deposited in the commune dowry fund, even though they failed to marry; *ASF, Prov.* 128, fols. 31–32. But this attempt at making a distinction between nuns was no sooner law than the tertiary houses began to ask the government to consider them as meeting the above description. A typical example of a request of this type which was approved is in *ASF, Prov.* 142, fols. 62–63 (15 April 1451).

[30] In the necrology of S. Niccolò, the *converse*—identified as such—are included (*Bibl. Riccardiana, MS. Moreniana* 3, passim).

suore.[31] The novices were members of the community who either were on probation, or were professed but awaiting episcopal consecration. The list of types of nuns concludes with the *fanciulle accettate*, young girls sworn to the veil, but not yet novices. They owed their status either to their very young age, or to the fact that the regulation *numerus clausus* limiting the number of nuns had been reached. Thus they awaited the death of a professed nun so that they could pass to the status of novice.

Many people who were not nuns lived in the convent, and their growing number became a source of concern for those responsible for the spiritual life of the houses. First there were widows. In exchange for the gift of all or part of their goods, the nunnery promised support and lodging to these *commesse* for the rest of their days.[32] While the *commesse* were usually there in perpetuity, another group of young girls and often of women were there *ins-serbo*, that is, they simply roomed there. If not on their own, such females could presumably leave the nunnery at the wish of their tutor or protector. An annual provision assured their subsistence.[33]

A convent was normally supposed to have as little contact as possible with the outside world. But the presence of young girls and of lay women (including wives at odds with their husbands) ran counter to this ideal. Theoretically the factors, that is, secular persons who took care of the outside affairs of the convent, lived close to it, but not inside its walls. Now it often happened that a *commessa* filled this role of *fattoressa*, and if she had entered the house not as a widow or single, but accompanied by her husband, this man could thus assume the function of a factor.

The female categories of a nunnery included therefore consecrated nuns, lay sisters or servants, *commesse*, novices, young girls who had been "accepted," and women being lodged. The male contingent was reduced to a minimum. Each house had a chaplain and confessor, functions assumed by two different persons in the richer institutions. These members of the clergy often lived within the nunnery walls, but others lived outside.[34] Then came the diverse factors, often *commessi*, who administered outside affairs, and sometimes, a gardener or a muleteer.

Most of the other needs of the house were assured by the *bocche di fuori*, people from the outside like doctors, barbers, or legal proctors. It is not

---

[31] The legal condition of those identified as novices seems to have varied. Here are some examples taken from the *ASF, R. Diritto* 4892 (1543–1550): novices called *suore, accettate e non vestite* (fol. 111v); novices (12) *non vestite ma acceptate*: seven of them designated *suore*, but the rest simply "la" (fol. 150). "Novitie professe che non sono anchora sachrate" (fol. 322); "Le professe, cioe sagrate" (fol. 323).

[32] The lawsuits of these *commesse* against the convents are legion, for they often tried to recoup their "gifts" to the houses if, for example, they found themselves able to remarry; see the examples in V. Della Robbia, *Nei monasteri*, 15.

[33] Perhaps there was a distinction between *insserbo* and *insservanza*; cf. *ASF, R. Diritto* 4892, fol. 29.

[34] Typical examples for Florence and Pisa can be found, respectively, in Orlandi, *Necrologio*, 1:49, 113f., 160, and *ASF, R. Diritto* 4892, fol. 415.

unusual also to find servants and gardeners coming in from outside at a salary, but without any other support from the convent.

It would be helpful to quantify this typology to some extent. Here are some examples from the years 1428–1429.

Table 3[35]
Typology of the Members of Convents

	Consecrated Nuns	Converse	Others
1. Living in the nunnery of: S. Verdiana	13	4	1 chaplain 1 *cherico* 1 novice
S. Maria della Disciplina	27	–	2 factors
S. Domenico di Cafaggio	27	4	1 chaplain 2 factors

2. *Bocche di fuori*
   S. Giovanni Vangelista: 1 legal proctor, 1 physician, 1 barber.
   S. Maria Monticelli: 1 factor and legal proctor, 1 physician, 1 chaplain, and 1 *cherico*

These examples show that a chaplain could live outside or reside within a convent. The absence of *converse* in the convent of the *Disciplinate* would seem to indicate that the nuns there were from the lower classes, and in fact, the list of nuns is limited to their first names, while in other nunneries the family name is added. Let us however be cautious: documents from 1544 contain two lists of nuns from the house of *Poverine* of S. Girolamo and from that of S. Giuliano.[36] Both are known to have recruited their members from established families, yet neither nunnery had lay sisters.

Taken together, the nunneries that did have *suore converse* are shown in Table 4.

Thus while the number of lay sisters increased in those houses having them, the domestic help made available to each nun decreased some 31.4% in 125 years. The influx of nuns at the end of the quattrocento and during the cinquecento, which was accompanied by strong pressure on the disposable incomes of the community, was compensated in part by a diminution of domestic help. One may also note in this context that in all, 16.1% of the nuns of Florence had no *converse* at all in 1552.

---

[35] *ASF, Catasto* 184, respectively fols. 6r, 14v, 18r, 41, 1 r–v.
[36] *ASF, R. Diritto* 4892, respectively fol. 13 and fol. 136.

Table 4[37]
Ratio of Lay Sisters in the Nunneries

	Average Number of Lay Sisters per Community	Number of Nuns per Lay Sister
1428	3.3	5.1
1552	10.1	6.7

We can now represent the total contingent of nuns, including lay sisters, for the whole of our period. The information at our disposal at present permits the following summary:

Table 5[38]
Total Numbers of Nuns in Florence

Year	1336	1428–29	1552
Nuns	500	440	3419

These figures are truly striking: once again we take note of the growth in the population of nuns which, as shown in Table 2, began in the last quarter of the fifteenth century and continued to increase at the same high rate until about 1515.

The full force of these figures can only be appreciated once we compare the population of nuns in the city and its suburbs to the total population (see Table 6).

The first line of Table 6 represents simply the proportion of the female population interned in the nunneries. The second line, for the year 1552, has a particular value. Assuming that the *sagrate* generally came from the city, while the *converse* came from the countryside, the figure of 11.5% represents the proportion of the female population *of the city* that was recruited by the nunneries. Two points should be made promptly. Since many young Florentine girls lived in convents outside the city and even beyond the suburbs, perhaps one should add four or five points to the figure of 11.5%. Second, since the overwhelming majority of the nuns in 1552 belonged to well established families, recruitment from this specific class of the female population can be studied.

---

[37] Loc. cit. in note 23. 1428: 8 cases; 1552: 47 cases.

[38] Ibid. The number for 1428 is an extrapolation. In 18 cases the average size is 20 persons; there being 22 houses in all, one arrives at 440 persons. See now, however, the higher and more reliable figures for 1427 in D. Herlihy and C. Klapisch-Zuber, *Les Toscans et leurs familles* (Paris, 1978), 157–58.

Table 6[39]

Number of Nuns in the City of Florence in Relation to Its Female Population

Year	1336	1428–29	1552
% of the Female Population	1.2	2.25	13 (lay sisters included) 11.5 (lay sisters excluded)

In a talk given at the 1967 meeting of the American Historical Association, R. Burr Litchfield indicated that the 21 old-line Florentine families that he had followed from the sixteenth century on had placed a good half of their daughters in convents. The breadth of this phenomenon, he added, was maintained into the eighteenth century, when the grand duke put strict limits on recruiting.[40] While awaiting a broadly based study of the social backgrounds of Florentine nuns, we may use Litchfield's estimates as a working hypothesis. For our study of the convents' *bocche* from 1368 on immediately revealed two facts. Firstly, the nuns overwhelmingly came from the established families whose names they bear. Secondly, just as high a percentage of the nuns were born in Florence. Further, we are just as well informed as to the origins of the lay sisters: they came from the lower classes and very often from the countryside.

Perhaps an example is apropos. In 1428 there were 28 nuns and 4 *converse* in the Dominican convent of S. Jacopo di Ripoli, in the via della Scala. The following families were represented among them: Abate, Albertini, Ardinghelli, Benvenuti, Bonavolti, Bonisi, Cicalini, Dati, Fei, Gucci, Gori, Giandoni, Guidalotti, Manovelli, Rondinelli, Sersanti, Viviani, Strozzi, and Torrigiani.[41] These 19 families had 21 daughters in the house. Thus three-quarters of the nuns came from families with surnames. In the convent of S. Domenico di Cafaggio, this percentage was still higher, 24 of the 25 nuns coming from such families.[42] In neither of the two houses, incidentally, were the lay sisters identified by surnames.

---

[39] 1336: This figure was obtained by estimating the total female population from G. Villani's proportions for male and female baptisms (*Croniche*, XI, 94).

1428–29: This figure was obtained by relating the total number of nuns to half of the population of 40,000 estimated for 1427 by J. Beloch, *Bevölkerungsgeschichte Italiens* (Berlin, 1937–65), 2:148.

1552: This figure was obtained by comparing the total number of nuns to the total female population cited by Battara, *La popolazione di Firenze alla metà Cinquecento* (Florence, 1935), 9f.

[40] Cf. R. Burr Litchfield, "Demographic Characteristics of Florentine Patrician Families," *Journal of Economic History*, 29 (1969): 191–205. For this later legislation, see Viviani Della Robbia, *Nei monasteri*, 223–26.

[41] ASF, *Catasto* 184, fols. 65–68v.

[42] Ibid., fols. 16v–18v.

Though the majority of families putting their daughters in nunneries represented well established lineages, they can not be counted among the richest families in the commune. To find out something about their wealth, let us take as a sample the nuns of S. Jacopo di Ripoli in 1428–1429. Of 28 nuns, only 8 had members of their immediate family among the 150 families with the highest tax assessment in their quarter. They occupied respectively the 5th, 11th, 82d, 94th, 111th, 124th, 140th, and 143d spots in that list. The rankings in this sample thus eliminate the very richest families and lean rather toward the middle; this suggests, in turn, that as regards the economic position of the families, recruitment for the nunneries was done among girls whose fathers or brothers were not generally counted among those who played a central economic role in the city. For four nunneries in 1428–1429, the median economic level occupied by those parents among the 150 highest assessed households in each quarter, was only 66, that is, 264th in the whole city.[43]

Why did so few of the girls in 1428 come from the richest families? My hypothesis is purely economic in nature. The richest girls appear to have been the more desirable as partners because of their high dowries, which matched the social position of their families; these families, furthermore, were able to marry more of their daughters. To realize a good marriage alliance, families of more modest income, on the other hand, were ready to put together a significant sum in dowry for one or perhaps two daughters, but the rest were put in convents.[44] In the end, many of these families proved incapable of marrying any of their daughters. The merchant Niccolò di Tommaso di Francesco Giovanni, for example, put his two daughters, aged 13 and 9 years, into the convent *senza dota alcuna*, as family documents attest.[45] As for Niccolò's brother Francesco, he seems to have carefully decided the fate of his first two daughters. Negotiations with suitors for the hand of the older girl, Nana, went on parallel to negotiations with the nunnery of Monticelli so that the latter would accept his second daughter, Costanza. It cannot be mere coincidence that the contract for marriage and the one offering a daughter to God were both concluded on the same day.[46]

---

[43] Cf. *ASF, Catasto* 184, fols. 65–68v with the assessment tables for 1403 and 1427 drawn up by L. Martines, *The Social World of the Florentine Humanists* (Princeton, 1963), 353–78.

[44] The forces at work here are quite clear in one testamental clause of a Venetian noble, who left to his daughter a dowry that would allow her to enter a nunnery, but left open the possibility that she might receive a larger sum permitting her to marry "if it pleased God that, the position of the family having become stronger, she would be able to marry" (J. Davis, *The Decline of the Venetian Nobility as a Ruling Class* [Baltimore, 1963], 66). This type of "paternal love" was of course found among rich families as well, and I am not suggesting here that in Florence the attitude of fathers toward daughters was different in different social classes. Rather more simply, in the political class, economic pressure decreased as one ascended the social ladder. My thanks to David Herlihy for his help on this point.

[45] *ASF, Carte Strozziane* II, xvi, fol. 28v.

[46] Ibid., XVI bis, fol. 4v.

The documentation for 1428–1429 would thus seem to indicate that recruitment was done among families with medium financial power. For the whole period 1368–1552, however, the documents indicate that nuns from "honorable" families, or ones with patronyms, made up about 75% of those recruited. Taken together, these facts clearly hint that such families had to consign their daughters to convents if they wished to safeguard their uncertain economic position. The antiquity of the family name would not render any more attractive the hand of meagerly dowered daughters. The latter themselves often refused a marriage "of little honor."[47] Thus social and economic pressures played out in such a way that the daughters of old but poorly dowered families were a heavy burden for their parents. The percentage of *sagrate* among the total female population (11.5%)[48] is certainly far below that of the population in that social group whence came the majority of the nuns.

Convents also proved themselves useful to these families because of the modest price the father had to pay to matriculate and support his girls in them. Theoretically, nuns' dowries were limited by canon law, but in practice, their size depended on circumstances, no matter what the convents' constitutions ordained.[49] Nevertheless, they remained far below those necessary for a marriage. Something around 100 florins was customary in the fifteenth century, at a time when matrimonial dowries went from 300 to 1000 florins for a girl of the same social class.[50] To be sure, these numbers come from an unsystematic sample, and they do not take into consideration the perpetual charges which had to be paid by the father (or his estate) of a girl living in a convent, charges which a daughter who married did not entail. That is, the differences in the size of such dowries provide only the most general indication of the sums actually spent by a father or his estate.

The pressure of the middle classes on the convents had several consequences. One was that monasteries that had traditionally welcomed poor girls were transformed little by little into institutions reserved, like most others, for the daughters of the bourgeoisie.[51]

While the majority of nuns in the convents had family names, it seems that none of the convents required recruits to belong to the nobility or to the citizenry, a clause that was not unusual in the nunneries of other regions. The nunnery with the closest ties to the *grandi* in the records for 1428 was that of S. Maria a Rosano, some 11 kilometers up from Florence; its sisters came from the Da Castiglionchio, Agli, Tedaldi, Altoviti, Albizzi, and Salterelli fami-

---

[47] One may guess that fathers "incapable" of marrying off their daughters played on the daughters' class pride to dissuade them from resisting consignment to a nunnery.

[48] See Table 6 above.

[49] Cf. for example the constitutions of S. Giusto in Orlandi, *Necrologio*, 1:612f.

[50] In 1425–27, a marriage dowry of a thousand florins put one in the social group representing the top 9% of those assessed in the city; see Martines, *Social World*, 115.

[51] Note the change in the character of the *bocche* of the *Disciplinate del Portico* between 1428 (ASF, *Catasto* 184, fol. 14v) and 1543–44 (ASF, *R. Diritto* 4892, fols. 321–22). The *Convertite* had similar difficulties trying to remain a house for repentant women (ibid., fol. 209).

lies.[52] But if in this one case the houses exercised control over the social quality of their members, it was above all by means of the dowry required that they effectively closed their doors to families of lesser standing. For them there remained only a chance to put their girls in as lay sisters, that is, as servants for their better born sisters.

Until now we have limited our explanations for entry into religion to demographic and economic factors. But doubtless, some girls chose this life on their own, like Lena, the daughter of Luca di Matteo Da Panzano: "... the *Bianchi* having been in the area once more about a month ago, this girl donned their habit and went out with them, flagellating in unison with several hundred women and men." She begged her father to let her become a nun and beseeched him till he gave in and consented. She was twelve years old at the time.[53] Many others, however, decided without really having a choice, like the daughter of Francesco di Tommasso Giovanni who being fully at ease—if we are to believe her father—"entered the nunnery completely contented and of her own free will."[54] Tuscan legend swarms with stories of girls wrenched from their young lovers to be thrown into God's abode. Fear of an unwanted marriage, perhaps even fear of marriage itself, might be a powerful incentive to become Jesus' bride. Such reasons were not demographic or economic in nature, and anyone wanting to know how important free will was should consider them carefully. The church itself prescribed that the nun pronouncing her vows be asked if she took them of her own free will. But one can talk of free will only when other options are available. Even a cursory examination of the sizes of the dowries given for marriages and for taking the veil shows that the economic alternative was so limited that the question of consent had in effect lost all significance by the early sixteenth century.

The practice of putting more than one daughter in the same nunnery also attests to the force of circumstance. Indeed in the 1428 record I found only one case in which a father put daughters in different houses;[55] more often,

---

[52] *ASF, Catasto* 183, fol. 275. The founders of nunneries often required that candidates for entry be examined by members of their families. The following is an indication that at least one nunnery in the cinquecento was founded for nobles: at no. 64 Borgo Pinti one can read an inscription commemorating the foundation of S. Silvestro in 1539 for "noble Florentine virgins." The *bocche* of this convent in 1543–44 lists members of the following families: Ridolfi, Borghini, Bonsi, Da Verrazano, Medici, Sostegni, Giugni, Sassetti, Da Panzano (*ASF, R. Diritto* 4892, fols. 114r–v).

[53] "Sendosi di pochi mesi innanzi ito di nuovo attorno pe' Bianchi, detta fanciulla si vestì, et andò a chompagnia con ... detti Bianchi, battendosi, insieme con parechi centinaia di donne e di huomini ..., io Lucha Da Panzano vi fu', adì detto di sopra, e fu' d'achordo e con lei e co'le monache, elle fusse monaca in detto monastero: e rimessino in me la dota. E detto dì [4 April 1448] io diè loro fiorini trenta. E detto dì quattro d'Aprile 1445 si messe lo schapolore, ch'è di bigio, de l'ordine di Valombrosa." She died 26 July 1449 (C. Carnesecchi, "Un Fiorentino del secolo XV e le sue ricordanze domestiche," *Archivio Storico Italiano,* ser. 5, 4 [1889], 160).

[54] *ASF, Carte Strozziane* II, xvi bis, fol. 5.

[55] Scholaio Salterelli's daughters were at Rosano and in S. Giusto (*ASF, Catasto* 184, fols. 60–61v; 183, fol. 275).

they were put in the same house. In records for nine nunneries in 1428 are found thirteen fathers who had each placed two daughters in the same convent.[56] Two sets of sisters lived in Ripoli, at S. Domenico, three, etc. The 1543–1544 documents have a case of three sisters in the same house—something rare or unknown in 1428—and a single case of four sisters under the same roof.[57] An extreme example of this process of duplicating comes from the nunnery of San Friano (Frediano) in 1543–1544: eight pairs and two trios of sisters lived there, meaning that the 58 nuns in this convent represented only 46 families.[58]

This practice had a monetary side to it. Upon accepting a first daughter, convents at times promised to take in others later, and this agreement was often accompanied by a reduction of the dowries for the subsequent girls.[59] Thus a solution which would allow an older girl to act as the protector of a nine-year-old sister also assured the fortunes of such younger sisters, and that often at less cost. Since the ecclesiastical authorities, including the abbesses, were theoretically required to observe a *numerus clausus* whose size depended on the house's economic strength, such an arrangement had the effect of creating a waiting list, even as it reduced the sources of revenue—that is, the number of families—that the convents had under their wings.

Personal problems obviously followed in the wake of such practices. An establishment that limited itself to only one girl per family ran less risk of the private wars that such family blocks might engender. In 1517 the archbishop forbade nunneries to accept more than two nuns "of the same blood and family . . . , for experience shows that factions and divisions are often engendered by the multiplicity of family ties in the nunneries."[60] The synod was quite right. Just thirteen years later, at the height of the siege of Florence, the convent of the *Murate* was torn into two camps supporting the Medici on the one side, and the *popolo* on the other.[61]

The edict of the church of Florence was not always obeyed: groups of three sisters appeared frequently among the *bocche* of 1543–1544. Families exerted great pressure, and there is no absence of cases in which an abbess or prioress complained that her chapter, acceding to their insistence, accepted sisters only *per istanza*.[62] Before 1545, the only recourse a mother superior had was to raise the amount of the dowry, or to create a "superdowry"

---

[56] *ASF, Catasto* 184, fols. 16v–18v, 19–25v, 47r–v, 48–54v, 57–58v, 65–68v, 75r–v; 183, fols. 275, 331.

[57] Unfortunately, I have lost the precise reference to these *bocche*, in *ASF, R. Diritto* 4892.

[58] Ibid., fols. 34–35.

[59] This is only one of the means fathers used to arrange the futures of their daughters in nunneries. Another was to make a donation to the house with an accompanying clause which would permit a younger girl to enter as the student or servant of an older sister.

[60] Mansi, *Sacrorum Conciliorum*, vol. 35, col. 263.

[61] Varchi, *Storia*, 5:108f.

[62] *ASF, R. Diritto* 4892, fol. 111v.

(*sopradote*) that came into effect when the *numerus clausus* was passed,[63] a practice which gave birth to often sizable groups inside as well as outside the convents of "girls who have been accepted to definitely wear the habit" (*fanciulle accietate sicuramente a vestire*). Complications in this procedure led fathers to bribe prelates, and the synodal fathers in 1517 thought it necessary to forbid any ordinary to accept money in exchange for consecrating a nun *ex pacto*.[64]

Let us try to throw some light on the question of the age at which girls were destined for the religious life, and that at which they actually entered it. One remarkable source can provide a partial answer to the first question, which might seem to be difficult by its very nature. The officials of the public debt or *Monte* kept in a separate annual ledger a list of all the sums fathers had invested in it as marriage dowries for their daughters. Each entry left a blank space so that at a later time one could record what happened to the deposited sum. In the entry details recorded for the girl in question were noted her date of birth and, of course, the date of the deposit. With these facts, I have been able first to calculate that in 1471, for instance, fathers made the deposit when their daughters were, on the average, six years old. Second, it is evident that an insignificant number of girls whose dowries had been deposited in such accounts later entered convents. The overwhelming majority married or died single. The number of those who, in this year 1471, took the veil was far below the percentages of Florentine females we have seen living in nunneries at the time. This would seem to show that in general, fathers investing in the *Monte delle doti* had already decided which of their daughters they would marry by the time the latter were six years old. In other words, girls destined to serve Christ were chosen before their sixth birthday.[65]

After our sample year of 1471, the number of nuns began to spiral upward. This situation reflects the growing number of girls already dowered for marriage, who however could not find a husband, in part because the commune showed itself less and less able to pay out the whole matured dowry investment.[66] One request after the other made its way to the chancery asking that the sum deposited for the dowry of one girl now be entered for that of

---

[63] A 1597 example is in Viviana Della Robbia, *Nei monasteri*, 196f.

[64] Mansi, *Sacrorum Conciliorum*, vol. 35, col. 267.

[65] These figures were derived from *ASF, Monte* 1220 (1 March 1470sf–28 February 1471sf). See now A. Molho, "*Tamquam vere mortue*: Le professioni religiose femminili nella Firenze del tardo Medioevo," *Società e storia* 12 (1989): 1–44. In discussing my stance on this point, Molho unfortunately uses the age of profession to dispute the age of entrance I calculated. But evidently, children remained a long time in the convents before professing, at a fixed minimum age, as I note here, determined by each order.

[66] Cf. L. Marks, "The Financial Oligarchy in Florence under Lorenzo," in E. F. Jacob, ed., *Italian Renaissance Studies* (London, 1960), 123–47, esp. 128f. During this forty-year financial crisis, those running the commune came out better than the mass of people investing in the fund, because they realized an interest of more than 12% on the sums that had not been reimbursed. This is another example of the greater ability of this thin class at the top to marry its daughters (ibid., 130f.).

one of her sisters, since the first had decided to take vows to Christ.[67] Many of these petitions also give the real reason for the change, and almost always, the girl is said to be ill or devoid of charm.[68]

At what age did girls actually enter the religious life? The age of nine years appears frequently in the records, and is perhaps not far from the average. The age at which the nun could pronounce her vow depended on the order, but thirteen years of age was typical. This is precisely the case with Suora Angelica, the daughter of Francesco di Tommaso Giovanni who, having entered at nine years of age, did not profess until she was thirteen.[69] Still, just a year in the cloister might suffice for one to take the title "sister." In 1328 in S. Maria di Candeli in the Borgo Pinti, there were sisters of eight and ten years of age, and two of twelve.[70] But in the three other nunneries in which ages have been preserved for 1428, no "suore" of less than thirteen years were enclosed.

Custom dictated that even *converse* or lay sisters enter at a very early age. In fact it is difficult to give an average age for these servants because they were either very young or very old. In the convent of San Giusto in 1428, for example, the *converse* were 7, 15, and 52 years of age;[71] at Candeli 90, 85, 55, and 53 years;[72] at San Giuliano 98 and 88 years;[73] while the only *conversa* of San Giovanni Battista was a mere 10 years old.[74]

One reason for such early beginnings has normally been neglected: to make future nuns part of the cloistered life before they were exposed to the "puderitia" of life in the world. The founder of the convent of S. Giuliano

---

[67] One of the first such petitions is in *ASF, Prov.* 158, fol. 88v (18 June 1467). The last I found is in *ASF, Prov.* 204, fol. 79v (about 1 April 1519).

[68] Some examples: "Quamvis sit forma honesta decrevit Deo servire"; ibid., 174, fols. 9r–v (22 April 1483) ("Although she has a decent shape, she has decided to serve God"). "Sed postea cum ipsa Marietta non esset bene sana, et cognosceret se non esse aptam ad matrimonium, deliberavit se monacari, sponteque intravit in monasterio . . ."; ibid., 159, fols. 14v–15 (9 April 1468) ("But later, this Marietta not being very healthy, and knowing she was not apt for marriage, she decided to enter a nunnery, and spontaneously entered one"). "E venuta tale malattia e accidente nella persona che a nessun modo non è da marritarla"; ibid., fols. 278r–v (23 March 1468sf) ("She became so sick and unbecoming in her person that there was no way to marry her"). "Impedita et corpore debilita"; ibid., 167, fols. 8v–9 (2 April 1476) ("Impeded and weak in body"). "Et quod quando dictus Bartholomeus constituit dictam dotem pro Iuliana filia sua sperabat illam posse locare viro, veluti est omnium parentum. Nunc vero prefacta Iuliana adeo est effecta informa, ut nullo pacto sit tradenda viro. Et propterea dictus eius pater intendit illam monacare, quam rem ipsa etiam optat"; ibid., 167, fols. 170v–171 (19 October 1476) ("When the said Bartolomeo stipulated the said dowry for his daughter Giuliana, he hoped to be able to place her with a man, as do all parents. Now however the said Giuliana is so deformed, that there is no way a man will take her. And thus her said father intends to put her in a nunnery, and she also chooses this").

[69] *ASF, Carte Strozziane* II, xvi bis, fol. 5.

[70] *ASF, Catasto,* 184, fols. 48–54v.

[71] Ibid., fol. 60.

[72] Ibid., fol. 52.

[73] Ibid., fol. 33.

[74] Ibid., fol. 63.

stipulated that the entry age should be no more than ten years.[75] And did not the diocesan legislation of 1517 forbid any female, "saecularem etiam virginem," who was more than twelve years old to live in a nunnery, unless she was destined for the veil?

> The zither and the psalter do not go well together. Conversations about marriage and about boys, quickly corrupt the virgin heart. Thus worldly gossip of this type gives rise to preoccupations and enjoyments.[76]

Erasmus, a secular spirit if ever there was one, saw in girls' shame and shyness in public a motivation pushing them toward entering the convent.[77] Perhaps then the concerns that accompany puberty helped determine the early age at which girls did enter.

To define the religiosity of the convents, one would, therefore, have to search out the relation between the average age of the nuns in any given house and its particular tone. For example, in a convent full of young nuns we would expect to find a more erotic notion of their "engagement" or "marriage" to Christ, than among women who had passed menopause. What was then the average age in these convents? In 1428, three convents located in and around the city had a median age of 24, 26, and 27 years.[78] Since their average ages were higher (respectively 31.7, 35, and 33.2 years)[79] it is clear that the balance weighed predominantly toward the younger nuns, their older sisters being in very advanced age. In periods of plague (1400 and 1417 in Florence) one especially expects to find very young nunneries. The necrology of the convent of S. Niccolò gives a good notion of the effects of plague: in 1348 the chaplain died on 22 May, a nun on the 25th. In June a lay sister passed away on the 8th, three nuns on the 10th, another on the 20th, and three more between the 22nd and the 27th. In 1363, two nuns died on 15 May, another on the 18th, then the 20th, followed by one more on 1 June. In 1400, three sisters drew their last breath on 18 June, one on 4 July, three on the 8th and one on the 9th, while two others died on 2 and 3 August.[80]

Such precariousness of existence obviously decreases the value of statistics regarding the longevity of convent populations. We have seen that ages leaned toward the extremes. The oldest nun among the *bocche* we have described in 1428 was 78 years old,[81] with several others being almost as old. A study of the ages furnished by the nunnery of S. Niccolò shows that the nuns there in 1543–1544 might hope to have a total of some 30 years of resi-

---

[75] Orlandi, *Necrologio*, 1:612f.

[76] Mansi, *Sacrorum Conciliorum*, vol. 35, col. 260.

[77] "The Girl with No Interest in Marriage," in *The Colloquies of Erasmus*, trans. C. Thompson (Chicago, 1965), 107.

[78] In, respectively, the nunneries of the *Disciplinate del Portico* (ASF, *Catasto* 184, fol. 14v, 24 ages), S. Giovanni Battista (ibid., fol. 63, 4 ages), Candeli (ibid., fol. 52, 15 ages).

[79] Ibid.

[80] *Bibl. Riccardiana, MS. Moreniana* 317.

[81] This honor belonged to Suora Ysabetta di Bililozzo, from the *Disciplinate*; ASF, *Catasto* 184, fol. 14v.

dence on average.[82] If we assume that the average age on entry was 12 years, that would mean that the life expectancy of a nun of this convent came to approximately 42 years, a bit beyond the life expectancy of 40.8 calculated for the whole population of Pistoia at this time.[83] But was their longevity substantially different from that of women from their same social classes? We do not know. However studies done in the United States have shown that nuns as a group actually do live longer than any other group of women.[84]

If we compare what we know about female vocations in Europe with the results of the present study, we will have to admit that the case of Florence is exceptional, perhaps even for Italy. Let us look at some data that permit comparisons.

Florence exerted pressure on its territories in religious as well as in political matters. A quick glance at the origins of male religious residing in Florence shows that the majority came from distant regions. With women it was completely different. They came essentially from Florence, and the concentration of nunneries around this particular city is truly striking:

Table 7[85]
Distribution of Nunneries in the Florentine Dominion, 1545

Arezzo	20
Pescia	4
Pisa	4
Borgo San Lorenzo	6
San Miniato	5
Cortona	10
Pistoia	13
Prato	10
Fiesole	4
Florence	42
Di fuori	9

Of the 127 nunneries in the Florentine dominion, 55 were, therefore, situated in Fiesole, in Florence, and within four miles of the latter's walls. But just as noteworthy, many of the other nunneries in the dominion were stocked

---

[82] I arrived at this figure by comparing their death dates (cf. note 80) to the *bocche* of 1543–44 found in *ASF, R. Diritto* 4892, fol. 28.

[83] D. Herlihy, *Medieval and Renaissance Pistoia* (New Haven, 1967), 283. For life expectancies, see also R. Trexler, "Une table florentine d'espérance de vie," *Annales E.S.C.* 26 (1971): 137–39.

[84] A. P. dispatch in the *Los Angeles Times*, 14 November 1967. The average age of death of American nuns was 77 years.

[85] *ASF, R. Diritto* 4892, fols. 162r–v.

with Florentines,[86] certainly an impressive deployment of women "praying day and night for the well-being and victory of our most illustrious lord duke."[87]

Did other convents in northern Italy experience the same influx? The limited information at our disposal makes comparisons dangerous. In Venice, for which we do have some data, the situation seems to be generally similar: the families of the *Libro d'Oro* sent a significant number of their daughters to the convent, and the predominantly fiscal motivation of these vocations brought problems comparable to those of Florence in their wake. The sixteenth-century chronicler Priuli mentions 25 nunneries in Venice, "public brothels ... which are a disgrace for Venice and ... an affront to God."[88] Till now, only such usually tendentious assessments by chroniclers have found their way into print, and in them, demographic data are only incidental. In the Franciscan province of Milan, an inspector of the order's nunneries counted some 500 virgins in 1482, including well over a hundred, he said, who were there "to avoid the dangers of marriage."[89] This figure would indicate that the total population of nuns in the Mendicant and traditional monastic orders was probably quite high.[90] Twenty years later, in 1502, the statutes of Milan limited to fifteen the number of women who could group together as a religious body.[91] Even if this rule represented an anachronism taken from previous legislation, an ordinance with such a low *numerus clausus* would have been unthinkable in contemporary Florence. Do such figures indicate that the number of nuns in Milan was limited? Cattaneo, our principal authority regarding the religious life of this city, does not express an opinion. He does mention a convent that had 106 nuns in it in 1476, a figure comparable to the size of some nunneries in Florence.[92] But on the other hand, he chronicles the long and monotonous history of the merging of convents in the fifteenth and sixteenth centuries due to a lack of novices. This was also happening in England and in Germany, but it was quite rare in Florence.[93]

---

[86] For example, the nunnery of S. Agostino alla Ginestra, near Montevarchi, where more than half the nuns were incontestably Florentines (ibid., fols. 66r–v), and that of S. Giovanni Vangelista di Pratovecchio, where nine nuns and two of the three novices are identified as "of Florence" (ibid., fol. 331).

[87] Ibid., fol. 5; a typical example of the flattering phrases accompanying such censuses.

[88] P. Paschini, "I monasteri femminili in Italia nel Cinquecento," *Italia Sacra* 2 (1960): 45.

[89] E. Cattaneo, "Istituzioni ecclesiastiche milanesi," in the *Storia di Milano* (Fondazione Treccani degli Alfieri), 9, part 2, 582.

[90] The figure of 500 is comparable to the total number of Franciscan nuns in the Florentine dominion at about the same time.

[91] Cattaneo, "Istituzioni," 581.

[92] Ibid., 629 (nunnery of S. Chiara in 1476).

[93] Ibid., 603–29. One great wave of combining nunneries took place in this period. It happened in 1435: Archbishop Corsini had died, and, with Pope Eugenius IV residing in Florence, the diocese was placed under the control of a pontifical administrator. In the via di San Gallo alone, seven nunneries were reduced to two. But later in that same year, the Signoria determined that such a large number of nuns could not live chastely in so little space, and it reached an accord with the pope allowing the reopening of the other

Can one make any comparisons to convents north of the Alps? Authorities like E. Delaruelle[94] and G. Le Bras[95] believe that the "recruitment crisis" which hit the male Mendicant orders also extended to the nuns. But only the English convents have been the object of a general study, and long range comparisons will have to be limited to that kingdom. There, declining numbers had irrevocably diminished the convents during the fourteenth century. Eileen Power notes that after Edward III, only one new foundation was made, and that at the behest of the dynasty.[96] Five convents disappeared between 1300 and 1500, while in the forty years before the first Act of Suppression of 1536, eight others closed.[97] Far from enjoining people to remain under the *numerus clausus*, as in Florence, the bishops and abbesses of England tried to raise numbers. While the bishop of Florence required a license to enter into an overpopulated nunnery under his authority, the prior of Sheppey in 1511 wanted to raise the number of nuns from 10 to 14 "at least if someone can be found who wants to enter religion."[98] There were hardly 200 nuns in the diocese of London in 1500.[99]

What importance should be attached to the data presented in this study? What was the cause of this secular increase, and what its consequences? I will offer some suggestions by way of conclusion.

The cause of the continuing increase in census? Doubtless the financial situation, and especially the rising cost of dowries, is part of any answer. Perhaps more important still was the communal fiscal crisis which kept girls of

---

five nunneries. Pope and Signoria were each to furnish 100 florins to finance the reopenings (*ASF, Prov.* 126, fols. 264r-v [24 October 1435]).

[94] *Histoire de l'Église* (Fliche and Martin), 14, part 2 (Paris, 1964), 1039, 1059, 1067.

[95] Ibid., 12, part 1 (Paris, 1959), 192.

[96] E. Power, *English Medieval Nunneries* (New York, 1964), 215f.

[97] Ibid., 602-4.

[98] Ibid., 216.

[99] This figure comes from a paper on the population of English nunneries done in my seminar (Univ. of Illinois, Champaign-Urbana) in 1975 by Sarah Lewis. She counted 141 nuns in 7 houses, or an average of 20; the actual number of 11 houses would, then, have held about 200. Note also that the percentage of the female population living in nunneries was always substantially lower in England than in Florence. Calculations by Howard Liebman in the same seminar allow comparison to those in Table 7.

1086	0.027%
1300-1348	0.24%
1377-1381	0.18%
1540	0.11%

These figures were obtained with the help of the data on the general population and on the female religious population compiled by J. C. Russell, *British Medieval Population* (Albuquerque, 1948), chap. 10, and in his "Clerical Population of Medieval England," *Traditio* 2 (1944): 177-212. My thanks especially to the students in the aforementioned seminar for their contribution.

marriage age from receiving upon its maturation more than a fraction of the dowry invested in the communal bank.[100] These financial difficulties run corollary to trends in marriages. In his work on the decline of the Venetian nobility, Davis attaches great importance to the decline in the number of men prepared to marry or financially capable of doing so. This reduced the number of marriages in the nobility, which had the effect of increasing the number of female vocations in the lagoon city.[101] The computerized demographic data on Florence compiled by David Herlihy shows that the women who gave birth during a twelve-month period of 1426–1427 had an average age of 26.5 years; the average age of the fathers in this same period was 39.75 years.[102] Given low masculine longevity, this meant that there were few men ready to marry. We may conclude from this that many women had to either stay at home or enter a convent. Further, it is evident that the number of widows in the city was very high, and in the quattrocento widows often took Christ as their second and last spouse.[103]

Did religious fervor play any role in the increasing numbers of vocations? Is it just an accident that the curve of vocations climbed during the same period when Savonarola exercised such influence in the city? I found no indication that would allow me to suggest such a link, but it would be worthwhile to study the matter further. Eileen Power's view that the long decline of vocations in England proves that convent life had "gone out of style" is problematic, for it assumes that the girls or their fathers had chosen a style of life, a dubious hypothesis at best and one which, in Florence, is out of the question. The decline in England has often been attributed to moral laxity, but to reverse this and explain the increase in Florence by way of religious zeal would be simplistic, if not totally wrong. That a girl's virginity would have been safer at home than in the convent is a complaint that is heard as often in the warm Mediterranean countries as in those north of the Alps, yet vocations were jumping in the south, at least in Tuscany. Neither style nor morality would seem to explain the phenomenon.

As to the effects of this numerical increase, there can be no doubt that withholding from biological reproductive functions some 11.5% of the female population—and as a consequence a much higher percentage of the girls of solid middle class background—had to hamper population growth in mid-sixteenth century Florence. Further, the very size of the movement had to help reaffirm certain attitudes toward women and their own conceptions of themselves. Commenting on the decline of vocations in northern Europe, Eckenstein suggested that the ideal of virginity was giving way to an ideal of maternity.[104]

---

[100] For the history of the decline in value of investments in the dowry funds, see Marks, "Financial Oligarchy."

[101] J. Davis, *Decline*, 62, 67.

[102] D. Herlihy, "Vieillir à Florence au Quattrocento," *Annales E.S.C.* 24 (1969): 1341.

[103] For the practice of widows becoming *pinzochere*, see the descripton of G. Boccaccio, *Corbaccio*, in *Opere*, edited by C. Segre (Mursia and Milan, 1966), 1235f.

[104] Eckenstein, *Women under Monasticism*, 431.

Can one say the same about this Tuscan culture, with its 13% level of virginity?[105]

Certainly a more detailed study of convent customs would be revelatory. Elsewhere, for example, I put forward the hypothesis that the old ideal of the abbess was yielding to the authoritarianism of the mother superior.[106] One would like to know what types of Marian images our nuns favored in the decoration of their common rooms and their cells. Was the erotic girl popular, ecstatic in Christ's presence? Or were the sweet mothers of Perugino favored, or perhaps the sage mother superior of Mantegna, or finally the asexual virgin of Desiderio da Settignano? And what about the saints they revered? Eric Erikson has put forward the idea that a church dominated by a father needs a maternal religion.[107] What type of church—or society—produces a virginal religion?

Is it possible that a well established predominance of religious of one sex or the other could give rise in a medieval or Renaissance city to a different type of religiosity in the lay population? Giovanni Villani says that in 1336, there were 1050 male religious in Florence compared to 500 nuns;[108] two centuries later, in 1552, there were about 750 males compared to some 3419 females.[109] The further one gets into the sixteenth century, the more feminine becomes devotional literature. The religious whose spiritual exercises were described so as to be imitated by the lay world were often women. Miracles were very common in nunneries, and thousands of relics bearing witness to these miracles were kept in the houses. No longer were relics belonging to the Mendicant friars the common subject of conversation in Florence, but rather the latest miracle in one of the city's nunneries. Dramatic representations of sacred stories, performed by nuns, became a typical form of entertainment in Florence. But before all the questions we have raised can be answered, the religious behavior of medieval and early modern peoples will have to be studied much more extensively.

We have not, however, mentioned one obvious result of the increase in vocations: the introduction of lay and communal control into the convents of Florence. In 1421, the republic established a special office of nine persons charged with the "reggimento, governo, amministrazione e cura" of all the

---

[105] Herlihy's article (see note 102), contains some interesting suggestions on the "force of [maternal] female influence," a force substantially encouraged, he thinks, by the fact that statistically, mothers lived much longer than fathers.

[106] Trexler, *Synodal Law in Florence and Fiesole, 1306–1518* (*Studi e Testi*, no. 268: Città del Vaticano, 1971), 100. I have not, however, found the ages of abbesses in mid-sixteenth century; those found in the *Catasto* of 1428 are: 38, 45, 56, 65, and 66 years. The 1517 Florentine synod required that abbesses under episcopal control be over 40 years of age (Mansi, *Sacrorum Conciliorum*, vol. 35, col. 259.

[107] E. Erikson, *Young Man Luther* (New York, 1963), 263.

[108] *Croniche* XI, 94.

[109] The figure for the male religious comes from the census of 1552 (*BNF, Fondo principale* II.i.120). It is composed of 595 "frati grandi e piccoli," 109 priests of all types not living the *vita comune*, 46 chaplains and confessors of nunneries.

convents of the city and four miles around.[110] Then in 1543-1544, a new commission of *deputati* was established by the Medici: they were given truly complete control over *temporalia*, and in cases where the ordinary did not exert his authority, over *spiritualia*.[111]

This is not the place to describe the extent of lay control. It suffices to say that in mid-sixteenth century, the Florentine convents were thought of as state welfare institutions, whose purpose was to preserve the city's *casati* and, at the same time, the state of the grand duke. Even as men came together in confraternities to build and monopolize the nunneries to their daughters' benefit,[112] so the state, for its part, opened them only to the "best" of its subjects, exempted them from taxes even at the worst of times, and placed them to the extent possible under its direct patronage.[113] The nuns simply emphasized that their incessant prayers were useful to the state. The state, for its part, saw things clearly.

An old woman with a life of virginity and religion behind her was an amazing thing for a medieval burgher. Once the solemn rites in the nuns' cemetery were over, and even as the abbess readied the admission of a new *fanciulla* who would replace the dead sister, and perhaps even as the good sisters anxiously awaited to see if the body of their colleague in Christ would reveal its sanctity by performing miracles, family members of the dead nun could take some comfort from the letter that the abbess sent them to announce the death. Our demographic study as a whole lacks human sentiment. Let us conclude therefore with a different tone. Suora Angelica, the second daughter of Francesco di Tommaso Giovanni, died in the convent of Monticelli on 27 January 1509. She was 72 years old, and had lived the holy life of a nun for almost 62 years. Here is the letter that the mother superior wrote to her surviving brother:[114]

---

[110] *ASF, Prov.* 111, fols. 45r-v (23 June 1421).

[111] L. Cantini, ed., *Legislazione toscana* (Florence, 1800), 1:200-206 (*Prov.* of 17 April 1545).

[112] Two excellent examples are in *ASF, R. Diritto* 4892, fols. 293-97, 279.

[113] At the time of the census of nunneries in the 1540s, the normal procedure consisted in determining whose daughters the nuns were, and then assigning as *operai* for each institution from among "coloro che hanno interessi se di parentela" (ibid., fol. 245). One example of many showing such relations is ibid., fols. 217-19.

[114] *ASF, Carte Strozziane* II, xvi bis, a loose sheet attached to fol. 5: "Honorando etc. Con grande passione e amaritudine scrivo questa a vostra humanita dandovi per epsa avviso chome egli e piaciuto a dio di chiamare ad se oggi a hor 19 la benedicta anima di Suora Angelica vostra cara sorella e annoi madre nel signore. La quale speriamo che lei sia in quella superna patria a godere cogli spiriti beati mediante la gratia del nostro redemptore e ancora mediante lopere sue le quale sono state di tale perfectione e examplo in sino all ultimo che noi presumpmiano di dire che veramente epsa sia collocata in luogo di reposo e di gloria. E pero vi pregho pigliate conforto e stae contento alla volonta divina pero che lei a facto quello passo che abbiamo affare tucti e a dio piaccia lo facciamo in nel modo che la facto lei. Non altro per quella se non che vi conforto a patientia per parte di tucte Jesu Christo sia in vostra protectione. A dì 27 di Gennaio, 1508 [sf]. Madonna in Monticeli."

It is with great sadness and pain that I herewith notify your Humanity that today at the 19th hour, God has been pleased to recall to himself the blessed spirit of sister Angelica, your dear sister and our mother in the Lord. We hope that she is now in the celestial fatherland of delights in the company of blessed spirits, through the grace of our savior and through her own works. Until the end, these were of such a perfection and example that we dare to say that she will in fact from now on live in a place of repose and glory. And I beg you to be comforted and to show yourself satisfied with God's will, for she has completed that journey that we all have to make. Let us pray that we finish ours in the same style that she has done. I have nothing further to say, except that I urge you to resign yourself. May Jesus Christ protect you. January 27, 1509.

Madonna in Monticeli.

Florentine Prostitution in the Fifteenth Century: Patrons and Clients

La città mercatrice,
ma che dico, meretrice!

—Aeneas Sylvius describing Florence[*]

I N APRIL 1403 THE GOVERNMENT OF FLORENCE ESTABLISHED THE OFFICE OF
Decency (*Onestà*), the first standing magistracy in the city's history exclusively charged with enforcing public morality.[1] Its specific duty was to wean
men from homosexuality by fostering female prostitution, and this was to be
accomplished by building or acquiring an edifice suitable for a brothel,
recruiting foreign prostitutes and pimps to work in it, and assuring them a
remuneration and protection which would induce them to come and stay.[2]
This article examines the demography of these immigrants and their support-

---

[*] "The merchant city, or rather say: the whore city" (Pope Pius II, *I commentari*, ed.
and trans. G. Bernetti [Siena, 1973], 1:15 [bk. 4, chap. 7]). I would like to thank Bernice
Trexler, David Ransel, Christiane Klapisch-Zuber, and Vernon Burton for their critical
reading of a draft of this paper. This essay appeared previously, in French, in *Annales
E.S.C.* 36 (1981): 983–1015.

[1] *Archivio di Stato, Firenze* (hereafter *ASF*), *Provvisioni* 92, fols. 9r–10r (20 April). The
texts of this and all laws regarding the magistracy are conveniently contained in *ASF,
Ufficiali dell'Onestà*, 6, fols. 3r–7v and passim. The law was then incorporated in the 1415
Statuta populi et communis Florentiae, 3 vols. (Fribourg, 1778–83), 3:41–45.

[2] "Construi et deputari facere unum locum aptum ad postribulum retinendum in
civitate Florentiae.... Et possint dicti offitiales imponere pretia solvenda meretricibus
venturis, prout eis videbitur.... Et quod dicti offitiales ... valeant punire ... quascumque
personas ... molestiam inferentes alicui dictarum meretricium" (*Statuta*, 3:42, 44).
"Officiales ... pro conducendo et conduci faciendo feminas et meretrices ad civitatem
florentinam, servatis servandis dederunt ... salvum conductum ..." (*ASF, Miscellanea
Republicana*, 33, n. 6 [Records of the Onestà of April–October 1436; hereafter 1436], fol.
13v [5 October]).

ing hostelers and clients in the brothel; the world of the baths and of prostitution outside the brothel is beyond our scope.[3] We shall open and close this article by considering prostitution, as did contemporaries, within the context of urban society and culture.

Like other Italian cities of the fifteenth century, Florence believed that officially sponsored prostitution combatted two other evils of incomparably greater moral and social import: male homosexuality—whose practice was thought to obscure the difference between the sexes and thus all difference and decorum—and the decline in the legitimate population which resulted from an insufficient number of marriages.[4] At a time when Florence's own women did not reproduce the legitimate population in part because, as it was believed, men preferred boys, city-sponsored prostitutes arrived from abroad to assist their sisters.

Upon the charms of these foreign women, therefore, rested the welfare of a political and social order. Equally important, their success or failure would affect the fate of all the other segments of the female population, the wives and widows, nuns and nubiles, servants and slave girls of the Tuscan metropole. For the history of prostitution and the history of women were joined. In the early quattrocento, the state of Florentine manhood and womanhood led contemporaries to cherish Graziosa's morality, and her procreative force. Only in the sixteenth century, when the population had increased and Florentine women were becoming nuns and whores at an unprecedented rate, would another generation suggest that Graziosa'a carnality rivalled Sodom's in its wickedness.

For now, men reasoned as follows: lascivious prostitutes free to dress as they liked stood the best chance of keeping men away from boys. By trumpeting their gender upon a discrete city stage, resident prostitutes proclaimed

---

[3] See P. Larivaille, *La vie quotidienne des courtisanes en Italie au temps de la Renaissance (Rome et Venise, XVe et XVIe siècles)* (Paris, 1975); and now M. Serena Mazzi, *Prostitute e lenoni nella Firenze del quattrocento* (Milan, 1991).

[4] For Lucca's (1348 et seq.), Venice's (early quattrocento), and Siena's (1421) use of prostitution as a weapon against homosexual behavior, see T. Compton, "Sodomy and Civic Doom," *Vector*, n. 2 (1977): 57; G. Rezasco, "Segno delle meretrici," *Giornale Liguistico* 17 (1890): 162, 187ff., which also shows how prostitution and the birth rate were the subjects of the same laws in Lucca. Most recent literature on prostitution refers to homosexuality, and thus to population problems, only by allusions; see V. Bullough, *The History of Prostitution* (New Hyde Park, N.Y., 1964), 67; J. Brundage, "Prostitution in the Medieval Canon Law," *Signs* 1 (1976): 830. On the other hand, J. Rossiaud ("Prostitution, jeunesse et société dans les villes du sud-est au XVe siècle," *Annales E.S.C.* 31 [1976]: 289–325), found his city fathers solving population problems caused by rape, not homosexual behavior; see ibid., 298, 307ff., and 324, n. 83 for the one possible allusion to homosexuality in the article. The fear of rape is not used to justify prostitution in the Florentine sources. Thus in 1427 Bernardino of Siena told his Sienese listeners that it was safe to send their daughters on errands, but not their sons, who might be abducted by homosexuals (*Le prediche volgari*, ed. P. Bargellini [Milan, 1936], 908). A reversal is observable at the end of the fifteenth century, when Savonarola warned citizens not to let servant girls go out, for they might prostitute themselves (*Prediche sopra Amos e Zaccaria*, 3 vols. [Rome, 1971–72], 3:233). See also E. Pavan, "Police des moeurs, société et politique à Venise à la fin du Moyen Age," *Revue historique*, 264 (1980): 241–88.

the delectable differences between the sexes and afforded a continuing representation of "natural" sexual behavior: the devil was meant, so ran the contemporary metaphor, to be put into hell.[5] Once cured of their "unnatural" associations with other males, married men would be more likely to have children by their wives, while bachelors would more readily marry.[6]

Doubtless a coordinated attack on Florence's moral and demographic problems required other measures as well. Bachelors should not be allowed to hold political office if they were over 30 years of age;[7] fathers would invest for their children so that their sons would have the capital to support marriage when they reached age 25, and their daughters would have a dowry at about 18 years of age;[8] sumptuary laws would restrain wives' outlays on clothing, the cost of which frightened men away from marriage;[9] punitive laws against homosexual behavior, finally, would deter practitioners of the "unmentionable sin."[10] But prostitution remained a necessary part of the package, or so it was believed. In an elusive yet palpable fashion, the preachers and elders who practically never denounced prostitution but always denounced homosexual behavior were forced to entertain the frightening idea that male love was more attractive than love between the sexes, and that only the wanton female could compete against it.[11] The very first words of the law establishing the Office of Decency spoke

---

[5] Franco Sacchetti, *Il trecentonovelle*, ed. V. Pernicone (Florence, 1946), 227 (nov. 101). In 1425, Bernardino of Siena said God had brought the "soup of the Flood" because men had mixed sexes and relatives (*Le prediche volgari* [Florence, 1425], ed. C. Cannarozzi, vols. 3-4 [Florence, 1940], 4:46). He denounced those involved in homosexual behavior, and not prostitutes, as the greatest enemy of good women (Bernardino-Bargellini, 410, 910). Bernardino's and Savonarola's sermons on sexual problems are examined in Trexler, *Public Life in Renaissance Florence* (New York, 1980), 399ff.

[6] Married men of course could practice anal intercourse or other "unnatural acts" with their wives, and thus be guilty of "sodomy" with them as well; in the stricter sense, sodomy referred to all sexual acts outside the vagina. But generally speaking, moralists meant male homosexual acts when they said "sodomy," and were less concerned with the heterosexual variety. See D. Herlihy and C. Klapisch-Zuber, *Les Toscans et leurs familles. Une étude du catasto florentin de 1427* (Paris, 1978), 439-42.

[7] The government tried unsuccessfully to effect such a law in 1421; *Biblioteca Nazionale, Firenze* (hereafter *BNF*), *Conventi Religiosi Soppressi*, C-4-895 (Priorista Pietrobuoni), fol. 105r. Bernardino continued to urge such a law in 1424; see *Le prediche volgari* (Florence, 1424), ed. Cannarozzi, vols. 1-2 (Pistoia, 1934), 2:47. Lucca passed a similar law in 1454, and Città di Castello in 1465 (Rezasco, "Segno," 188f.).

[8] On these funds, see A. Molho and J. Kirshner, "The Dowry Fund and the Marriage Market in Early *Quattrocento* Florence," *Journal of Modern History* 50 (1978): 430-38.

[9] The sumptuary law of 1433, for example, said that although women were "created to replenish this free city," their expensive clothing was dissuading young men from marrying (cited in G. Brucker, ed., *The Society of Renaissance Florence* [New York, 1971], 181).

[10] In its original form, the constituent law of the Office of Decency contained such coercive measures. Later, such laws against homosexual behavior were separate and distinct.

[11] Some listeners tried to convince the preachers that homosexual behavior was licit, and for proof pointed to the evidence that Christ had not condemned but rather praised it; see Bernardino-Cannarozzi, 2:143, and Bernardino-Bargellini, 410. Bernardino responded that even the devil, being a natural creature, detested such behavior

of sodomy, not prostitution. It begins: "Abhorring the filth of the nefarious [and] unnatural evil and enormous crime which is the vice of sodomy, and wanting to extirpate this crime. . . ." Like so many outsiders, the prostitutes of Florence were to mediate insiders' values and institutions.[12]

Our starting point, then, is the positive interrelation between public prostitution and the broader values and institutions of urban culture. In Florence the world of prostitution was not at the heart of the world of crime, as the narrow optic of the modern censor sometimes imagines; it was an institution of the *salus publicus* which furthered the ethical goals of the community. When in December 1415 the Florentine clergy issued a broadside of writing and sermons against homosexual activity, the government approved their efforts and promptly commanded that two new brothels be built in other quarters of the city to supplement the one great walled brothel downtown.[13] Nor did the establishment in 1432 of an Office of the Night to detect and prosecute males engaged in homosexual behavior obviate the need for the office of Onestà, which continued to foster and regulate prostitution in Florence far into modern times.[14]

Donne cortesi arriving from pest-infested areas might be turned away from Florence; pimps as a whole could be banished from the city.[15] But not once in the history of republican Florence were prostitutes as a group driven out. And when the dwindling food supply of besieged Florence in 1530 prompted the banishment of thirty-some aged prostitutes, the historian Varchi regarded it as a singularly cruel act, as if he believed that these old and helpless women

---

(Bernardino-Bargellini, 902). Preachers said "good women" dressed like prostitutes to keep men from men—not from other women; see my *Public Life*, 380, and Rezasco, "Segno," 214, who cites Franco Sacchetti to the effect that prostitutes and "good women" emulated each other in their dress.

[12] "Nefandi facinoris ipsique naturae contrarii, et enormis criminis putredinem abhorrentes, quale est vitium sodomiticum, et volentes in hoc pro extirpatione huiusmodi criminis in augmentum aliorum ordinamentorum possetenus providere, decernimus quod . . ."; *Statuta*, 3:41. On prostitutes' beneficial mediation of the virtue of virginity among "good girls," see Rossiaud, "Prostitution," 298–301.

[13] City Council discussion of the priests' activity is cited in Brucker, *Society*, 201. The law is in *ASF, Prov.*, 105, fols. 248r–249r (23 December). These brothels in the quarters of Santo Spirito and Santa Croce were never built.

[14] The *Ufficiali della Notte* were constituted by *ASF, Prov.*, 123, fols. 31v–36v (12 April), a law excerpted by Brucker, *Society*, 203f. He omits the prologue, which warned the new officials that unless homosexuality was repressed the city was threatened with godly extinction; see also Compton, "Sodomy," 97.

[15] The term *donne cortesi* is in *ASF, Catasto*, 79, fol. 303r. Contemporaries distinguished "femine meretrici, di partito et cantoniere"; see *ASF, Acquisti e Doni*, 292 (hereafter Carnesecchi Spoglio), *Otto di Guardia, Bandi* (6 July 1504). *Donna di partito* in the strict sense meant a parlor whore, while the *cantoniere* was a streetwalker; see *La vita del beato Ieronimo Savonarola*, ed. attrib. P Ginori Conti (Florence, 1937), 92. In 1504 prostitutes who had recently arrived from certain cities touched by the plague had to leave Florence; Carnesecchi Spoglio, *Otto di Guardia, Bandi* (6 July 1504). All pimps were ordered out of the city and dominion on 6 February 1520 (*stilus florentinus*)/1521 (*stilus communis*) (ibid., at date).

who had served the commune deserved much better.[16] No less a personage than a sixteenth-century archbishop of Florence urged the government to establish a home for abandoned prostitutes—doubtless similar to the other asylums for the commune's elderly subjects.[17] Who were these women who levied such claims of sentiment and support upon the city?

The Immigrants

Demographic questions about the prostitutes and pimps of Florence are best answered by examining a 1436 roll call of the contingent, and especially by studying a parchment *Book of Sentences* of the Office of Decency starting in 1411 and ending in 1523.[18] In succinct fashion, more than 150 notaries regularly listed, in addition to crimes and sentences, the names, provenances, occupations, and places of residence of those involved in each of the 1720 cases brought before the Onestà during these 82 years. Table 1 summarizes the origins of the prostitutes and their supporting male personnel.

The result of simply counting as one unit each name occurring in each case, the tabulations after 1436 are no more a census than the judicial record itself. Their purpose is rather to highlight comparative immigration patterns, and in this the table succeeds admirably. Not surprisingly, the majority of the total units of prostitutes in the *Book of Sentences* came from Italian areas surrounding Florence, stretching from Piedmont in the north to Rome in the south. Very few Florentines worked the brothel, as we shall see; instead, they went abroad as their sisters came to the Arno.[19] On the other hand, few prostitutes or pimps came to Florence from southern Italy, and those who did were outnumbered by the Spanish contingent in the record.[20] Further, very substantial numbers of women came from outside Italy. It may be true that some of those from the second largest contingent area—the south Slavic group commonly said to be from "Slavonia"—were Italians living in the cities of the Dalmatian coast; but there can be no such qualification about those from across the Alps:[21] women from the Low Countries, Spain, France,

---

[16] "Le più vecchi e schife . . . , le quali s'erano ragunate a Santa Caterina. . . . Fu da molti questa pietà empia e crudele riputata" (B. Varchi, *Storia fiorentina* [Florence, 1963], bk. 9, chap. 99). See Rezasco, "Segno," 172, for a Mantuan example of driving prostitutes from the city because their presence was thought to have angered God.

[17] *ASF, Onestà*, 6, fol. 44v (Archbishop Alessandro de' Medici).

[18] 1436, fols. 4v–5v (9 May); *ASF, Onestà*, 2 (*Libro di Condannazioni*; hereafter *LC*).

[19] So did Florentine hostelers: to Avignon, where the Buzaffi ran a whorehouse (Rossiaud, "Prostitution," 314 n. 10), and to Lucca, where Checco of Florence operated in 1416. A Florentine wanted 30 florins to consign his wife to Checco, but the latter offered 16 florins at most, "for she is poorly clothed and I will have to furnish her with a new wardrobe" (Brucker, *Society*, 199).

[20] The Spanish women may have come through Naples, which was ruled by the house of Aragon.

[21] I found only a Magdalena called a slave (*schiava*), and another entry (*Magdalena vocata Ischiavetta*) suggests this was a nickname (*LC*, fols. 61r, 64r).

Table 1
Provenience of the Prostitutes and of Male Personnel[22]

Provenience		Census (%) 1436	Units by Decade (%) 1441-1451	1451-1461	1461-1471	1471-1481	1481-1491	1491-1501	1501-1511	1511-1521	Totals of Units
North Italy	F	18.3	24.2	26.9	41.7	49.1	77.6	67.5	88.9	96.2	539
	M	33.3	33.3	30.5	44.1	27.8	60.0	100.0	0.0	0.0	47
South Slavic	F	5.6	11.6	23.1	17.7	14.4	6.9	2.5	0.0	0.0	96
	M	3.7	8.3	0.0	0.0	0.0	0.0	0.0	0.0	0.0	1
Low Countries	F	36.6	17.9	6.5	3.1	14.4	7.8	5.0	6.7	3.8	79
	M	29.6	16.7	11.1	5.9	22.2	20.0	0.0	0.0	0.0	15
Germany	F	22.5	12.6	14.8	11.5	5.9	3.4	3.7	4.4	0.0	63
	M	18.5	8.3	55.6	44.1	0.0	6.7	0.0	0.0	0.0	37
France	F	9.8	20.0	9.3	4.2	1.7	2.0	3.7	0.0	0.0	45
	M	3.7	33.3	0.0	0.0	27.8	13.3	0.0	0.0	0.0	11
Spain	F	1.4	5.3	2.8	5.2	11.0	0.0	8.7	0.0	0.0	33
	M	0.0	0.0	2.8	2.9	16.7	0.0	0.0	0.0	0.0	5
North Slavic	F	0.0	0.0	11.1	5.2	0.0	0.0	0.0	0.0	0.0	17
	M	0.0	0.0	0.0	0.0	0.0	0.0	0.0	0.0	0.0	0
Greeks[a]	F	0.0	1.0	1.8	3.2	2.5	1.1	5.0	0.0	0.0	17
	M	0.0	0.0	0.0	0.0	0.0	0.0	0.0	0.0	0.0	0
South Italy	F	0.0	4.2	0.0	0.0	0.0	0.6[b]	3.7	0.0	0.0	9
	M	0.0	0.0	0.0	0.0	5.5	0.0	0.0	0.0	0.0	1
British Isles	F	1.4	1.0	0.0	5.2	0.0	0.0	0.0	0.0	0.0	6
	M	3.7	0.0	0.0	2.9	0.0	0.0	0.0	0.0	0.0	1
Sardinia and Corsica	F	0.0	2.1	1.8	0.0	0.8	0.0	0.0	0.0	0.0	5
	M	0.0	0.0	0.0	0.0	0.0	0.0	0.0	0.0	0.0	0
Miscellaneous	F	4.2	0.0	1.8[c]	3.1[d]	0.0	0.6[e]	0.0	0.0	0.0	7
	M	7.4	0.0	0.0	0.0	0.0	0.0	0.0	0.0	0.0	0
Totals of Census and Decades	F	71	95	108	96	118	348	80	45	26	916
	M	27	12	36	34	18	15	3	0	0	118

a. Including Constantinople and the Greek Islands; b. Sicily; c. Gypsies; d. 1 Gypsy and 2 Circassians; e. 1 Russian and 1 Hungarian.
Sources: 1436: ff. 4v–5v; Decades: LC

---

[22] All women were counted, but the only men counted were pimps, hostelers, and brothel cooks. Geographical areas correspond for the most part to present political and cultural areas; thus Brabantines are included under the Low Countries. The table overstates the number from present day Germany, for the words "tedesco" or "Alamannia" could designate a Brabantine or Fleming; see M. Battistini, *La confrérie de Sainte-Barbe des Flamands à Florence* (Brussels, 1931), 6 and passim. Most north Slavic prostitutes were Polish. Those from the south Slavic areas were mostly from present day Croatia. Each decade starts on 13 November (1441, 1451, etc.), and ends 12 November (1451, 1461, etc.).

Germany, and Poland together made up a quarter of all the units in the *Book of Sentences*. Finally, a comparison of the census of 1436 with the later information from the *Book of Sentences* shows that the national population was dominated by Ultramontanes in the early period, but by the 1480s north Italians ruled the roost. In the first forty years of the sentences, German women still accounted for 11 percent, and Low Countries women for 10.5 percent of the total, but in the later decades that contribution almost disappeared.

The male personnel from beyond the Alps were just as prominent, and generally represented a higher percentage of their gender than did their countrywomen of theirs. Italians comprised 39.8 percent of the total male units over the life of the *Book of Sentences* as against 58 percent of the women, but German men accounted for almost one-third of their sex as against German women's 6.9 percent.[23] There was one German man for every two German prostitutes, one Frenchman for every four Frenchwomen, but only one north Italian male for every 11.5 Italian women. Does this numerical disparity stem from fact, or from the nature of the record? The practical disappearance of men from the last 30 years of the *Book of Sentences* gives us room for pause. Perhaps women were more often pimping, but still being listed as whores; we shall allude to the emergence of procuresses in the late quattrocento later in this paper.[24] Perhaps more native Florentine males were pimping, but were more difficult to prosecute than were foreigners. We cannot be sure. But for the bulk of the record, the impressive number of non-Italian pimps and prostitutes is the most striking result of these tabulations.

We now turn our attention to a more exact study of the origins of north Italian prostitutes, for it is obviously important to know from what distance they had travelled to Florence. The roll call of 1436 provides us with one census, while a peculiarity of the *Book of Sentences* allows us to treat the years 1486–1490 as the equivalent of another census.[25] We may therefore compare these two points in time with absolute numbers (see Table 2).

At this point we may calculate the total number of prostitutes in the brothel during the five years 1486–1490 by adding the 35 foreigners we found to the 115 Italians; the resulting figure of 150 corresponds closely to the 148 we obtain by assuming the 115 Italian women represent 77.6 percent of the total, as Italians do for the whole decade 1481–1491. Confident that we are in fact dealing with the equivalent of a census, we may rely on what the table

---

[23] The presence of German textile workers in the city might explain this; see Battistini, *Confrérie*, and below, at n. 29. Yet no pimp was identified in the *LC* as also being involved in the wool trade; a 1406 regulation prohibited any pimp "from Brabant, Cologne, or Asia" from being a weaver; see A. Doren, *Deutsche Handwerker und Handwerkerbruderschaften im Mittelalterlichen Italien* (Berlin, 1903), 131.

[24] Below, at n. 131. It is unclear whether the *padrona* mentioned in Panormita's poem was a procuress or a governess.

[25] During this period, each group of semi-annual officials of the Onestà preventively sentenced all prostitutes for not appearing at roll call (*la mostra*), a sentence which was then cancelled if they appeared on time.

Table 2
Provenience of the Prostitutes from Northern Italy

Transapennines			Tuscany			Central Italy		
	1436	1486–1490		1436	1486–1490		1436	1486–1490
Ferrara	1	11	Pistoia	0	7			
Milan	0	9	Lucca	0	6			
Bologna	0	8	Pisa	1	4			
Parma	0	6	Siena	0	3			
Venice	5	5	Peretola	0	2			
Padua	1	5	Florence	1	2			
Modena	0	3						
Mantua	0	3						
Treviso	1	3						
Forlì	0	2						
Verona	1	2						
Misc. (IX)	2	11	Misc. (IX)	0	18	Misc. (IX)	0	5
Totals	11	68	Totals	2	42	Totals	0	5

Sources: 1436: ff. 4v–5v; *LC*, ff. 126r–172v.

tells us about the north Italians. Certainly the few prostitutes from central Italy is striking; presumably women from this area went to Rome, a recognized center of prostitution at the time.[26] Conversely, the high number from the areas north of Tuscany is no less striking, half again as many as the Tuscan women migrating to the metropole. For of a total of 150 prostitutes documented during these five years, only 28 percent spoke Tuscan. From Table 1 we surmised that proportionate to their sex, Ultramontane prostitutes travelled a shorter distance than pimps from beyond the Alps. Yet Table 2 shows unequivocally that the majority of the prostitutes in the Florentine brothel did not come from the hills and valleys surrounding Florence. More probably the average unattached female from the *contado* or *distretto* came to Florence as a domestic servant, formally if not always factually distinct from her prostitute sisters. As we shall see, these servants ultimately gave prostitution a bad name and, in the end, severely limited the professionals' ability to fulfill the mandate with which they alone were charged.

Our sources do not allow us to reconstruct the company of the prostitute on her arrival in Florence. We know the Onestà, "conducting and causing prostitutes to be brought to the city of Florence," licensed foreign pimps to come to the city with their women, but we know as well that the prostitute

---

[26] Rezasco, "Segno," 194f., summarizing the famous accounts of Aretino and others.

did not need a pimp.[27] The only way to form some notion of the couples who did arrive in the city together is through studying the national affinities and disaffinities of different pairs once they were already in the city. Some pairs arrived together, perhaps having left home when she became pregnant, selling her services wherever they went. Gualtiere and Maie of Ireland probably arrived together, as well as Solisus and Solisa from Lodeto, Spain.[28] Other couples just as surely met for the first time in the city, the large contingent of Flemish and German cloth workers providing a pool from which co-nationals could pick a pimp.[29] Globally, national affinity predominates in the 1436 records, being three times more likely than disaffinity, yet even in that year there were five couples who spoke disparate tongues. In the later period of the *Book of Sentences*, disaffinity was twice as likely as affinity.[30] The lesson of this variety is clear: as the arriving prostitute now found her residence in Florence, love and professional compatibility were as important as language in choosing a partner.

Housing

If you think little of your father, oh [my] little book, I urge You go, go ahead and flee, but toward the walls of Florence.

That city has a delectable place in its center; Go there, and this is how you can find it.

Look for the magnificent temple of Santa Reparata, or the other [of San Cristofano], of him who has the angel of God in hand.

Arriving there, take a right; proceeding a little, Stop and ask, oh [my] tired book, for [directions to] the Mercato Vecchio.

Near it is the obelisk, the genial bordello is right there, the place betrays itself by its odor.

---

[27] A woman could not have a pimp unless he was licensed by the office (*Statuta*, 3:43), and many did not; see below, at n. 62. The text of the quote is above, n. 2.

[28] See Panormita's use of the topos below, at n. 110. The Irish are in 1436, fol. 5v; the Spaniards in *LC*, fol. 92v (1474).

[29] The lack of evidence for this point is mentioned above, n. 23. Nor could I find any evidence that brothel prostitutes were the daughters of this resident work force. A comparison of the membership lists of the German confraternity of St. Barbera with the prostitutes whose fathers are named in the *LC* was without issue (Battistini, *Confrérie*, 65f., 73ff., 82–85, 101–47). For more on the German colony, see Herlihy and Klapisch-Zuber, *Toscans*, 311f., and S. Cohn, *The Laboring Classes in Renaissance Florence* (New York, 1980), 102, 110–13.

[30] In 1436, for example, 5 couples came from Italy, 4 from Flanders, 3 from Brabant, but in the *LC* I could not find more than one couple speaking the same language (1436, fols. 4v–5v, and *LC*).

Enter, and say "Hello" to the procuresses and whores for me; You will be welcomed by all to its delicate bosom.

Elena the blond will approach you with the sweet Matilda, Gifted in stimulating, both the one and the other really have it!

Giannetta will come, and behind her Cagnolina. The Latter is gracious with [the former,] her patroness; with men she is dear.

Clodia will come running quickly, her nude breasts painted, Clodia, a girl valued for her caresses.

Galla will reach with her hands for your penis and her cunt, without blushing, So that you can have both together.

Anna will come up to you and offer you a song in German; In her singing her mouth breathes recent wine.

Pitto, she too, will come, who is unequaled at humping; Ursa, joy of whoring, will be with her.

So that she can greet you, Taide will tell you to come up the nearby Street, which has its name from the slaughtered cow.

All the whores of this so famous city Will come to you, swarming joyfully together because of your arrival.

Here you can say and do whatever pleases you, Nor will a refusal ever redden your cheeks.

Since you've lusted for so long a time, here, as much as you can, You can fuck, oh [my] book, and have yourself fucked.[31]

Written in 1425, these lines from Panormita's *Hermaphroditus* form a worthy humanist introduction to an area which the incoming prostitutes and their pimps saw in much sterner light. Stopping first at the Servite church to pray to its famed Virgin, they might have seen a prostitute doing the public penance the Onestà had assigned her, kneeling with a candle at a Mass she paid for; the alternative was 20 days in jail.[32] Continuing on to the church of San Cristofano, as did Panormita, the new arrivals saw the candles which lit the statue of the Virgin on its facade, candles which had been bought by

---

[31] A. Beccadelli (Il Panormita), *Hermaphroditus* (Coburg, 1824), bk. 2, chap. 37. The verses were dedicated to Cosimo de' Medici, whose family was identified with the brothel area; see below, at n. 47.

[32] *LC*, fol. 150r (1488).

prostitutes as fines for their torts.[33] They entered the rectorate next door to obtain license and information on housing, for the parish rector who lived upstairs rented the downstairs to the Officials of Decency, as he would until the eighteenth century in spite of episcopal displeasure with the arrangement.[34] Outside this house after 1464 was the pillory, put there to punish subjects of the Onestà for a wide variety of crimes, but especially for "the whore who in depraved fashion and unnaturally lends her body."[35] The immigrants exposed to all these admonitory symbols of the punishments which awaited transgressors soon saw the colors of the brothel. San Cristofano lay on the eastern edge, the church's west side closing on the first of the main hostels, the Macciana. *La città meretrice* opened to the newcomers.

Standing in front of the entrance of the Macciana and facing west, the viewers saw just how centrally located the main brothel was, for to the left was the Mercato Vecchio or Old Market—center of business activity—and to the right was the archepiscopal palace and the Baptistry of San Giovanni. Quite as stunning were the number of church towers which seemed to crown the walls of the area like so many bastions. The viewers first saw San Cristofano, then in a circle to the left the church of San Tommaso, Sant'Andrea, the *Torre* or tower of the great Della Tosa palace in the market (to which Panormita obscenely referred),[36] then San Piero Buonconsiglio, Santa Maria in Campidoglio, and San Leo on the opposite, west side, of the brothel; then came the episcopal curia, and the churches of San Salvadore and San Ruffilo to the viewers' right. Now crossing the street from the Macciana and walking due west into the Frascato—as the heart of the main brothel was called—the newcomers passed the "mouth of the Frascato," traversed the Chiasso della Malacucina (Alley of the Bad Meals)—a name familiar to them from brothels in other cities—until they came to the Piazza del Frascato, sometimes called the "cradle of the Frascato," at the intersection of the Chiasso Grande running north and south.[37] It was at that corner that the Macciana's two sister hostels were located, called indistinguishably Al Frascato.

Panormita knew the newcomers would then want to visit the other part of the Florentine brothel area, the Chiasso de' Buoi or Alley of the Cows. To reach it, one left the Frascato on the northwest and walked some hundred yards to the Piazza Santa Maria Maggiore, perhaps passing on the way the penitenial procession of a whore punished by the Onestà by being forced to

---

[33] Ibid., fols. 2r, 3r, 5v (1441–42).

[34] 1436, fol. 3r; *Archivio Arcivescovile, Firenze* (hereafter *AAF*), Z-IV-3 (Visitation of 1514), fol. 7v; *BNF*, II. IV. 505, fol. 89r (Ecclesiastical Catasto of 1427).

[35] "Quecunque meretrix que turpissimo modo et contra naturam prestiterit corpus suum"; *ASF, Onestà* 6, fols. 13v–14v (14 March 1463/4). The first case of its use I located was on a man who had beat a woman (*LC*, fol. 144r [1483]).

[36] On this famous Palagione, see G. Carocci, *Studi storici sul centro di Firenze* (Florence, 1899), 64. Its tower is referred to in *ASF, Catasto*, 79, fol. 170r.

[37] For the cradle, see *ASF, Catasto*, 79, fols. 346r–v; for the mouth, ibid., 55, fol. 475r; for the Piazza del Frascato, ibid., 79, fols. 87v, 330r. Perugia's whores also lived in a Chiasso della Malacucina (Rezasco, "Segno," 175).

walk through the Frascato to the Chiasso de' Buoi with the mitre of ridicule on her head.[38] In 1440 part of this alley had been walled up so that the activities of its whores would not shame so-called decent folk, and so that the prostitutes would not extend their quarters further west toward the Baths and Piazza of San Michele Bertelde.[39] The problem of prostitutional urban sprawl had to be faced again in 1452 and 1454, when *femine mondane* living in this stretch of street were summarily ordered back into the Chiasso by archbishop Antonino Pierozzi.[40] The area between the two main sections of the brothel area, in short, as well as whole areas to the west and north of them, were constantly in danger of being converted into brothel areas. But throughout our period, the majority of the prostitutes subject to the Onestà came from the areas we have just outlined: the Chiasso de' Buoi and the three hostels in the *postribulum maius*.[41]

The property and rental character of the Alley of the Cows remains obscure but intriguing, clearly distinct from the housing in the main brothel area. Despite a search in the commune's Catasto records, for example, I was unable to find any of the main families of the area claiming ownership of a whorehouse there, and in fact in the whole *Book of Sentences* I could locate only one mention of a "hostel," and one other of a "hosteler in the brothel of the Cows," while the official census of 1436 refers to hostels in the Frascato area but not in the Chiasso de' Buoi.[42] Presumably the area consisted of a series of individual hovels, some of which may have been owned by the individual prostitutes; in one case of 1485, Margherita of Brabant lived "in the house of Margherita of Flanders in the brothel of the Cows."[43]

The property in the main brothel area to the southeast was historically associated with some of the most illustrious of Florentine families, and presents fewer problems. Great bankers and papal finance officials, the Pecori lived here and owned properties used for prostitution.[44] The "hostel of the Brunelleschi" served that same trade.[45] Venerable *vicedomini* of the see of Florence, the Tosinghi or Della Tosa profited from the properties they rented to

---

[38] *LC*, fol. 118v (1484).

[39] Carnesecchi Spoglio, no page, references to vol. 5, n. 87 of a *spoglio* by Carlo Strozzi.

[40] Antonino had been appointed binding arbitrator by concerned property owners and the Onestà (*LC*, fol. 25v [6 September 1452], fol. 31r [19 June 1454]).

[41] "Una stalla atta a becchai, posta . . . sul Chiasso de' Buoi" (*ASF, Catasto*, 79, fol. 8r [Carnesecchi family]). Cf. *ASF, Notarile Antecosiminiano*, G 284 (1433–53), fol. 186, for what may be the same property. The latter was brought to my attention by Brenda Preyer.

[42] *LC*, fol. 74r (1446), fol. 188v (1499).

[43] Ibid., fol. 123v.

[44] They had a controlling interest in the Macciana; see *ASF, Catasto*, 79, fols. 302v–303v (1427); 625, fol. 305v (1442); 1019, part 1, fol. 345r (1480).

[45] Ibid., 79, fols. 346r–v, 378r (1427); *LC*, fol. 39v (1457). The famous architect was not of the Brunelleschi family. There are further details on the hotel management of the Brunelleschi in Brucker, *Society*, 191.

the whoremasters.[46] And from the "Piazza de' Medici, there where is the public bordello," the first family of the city did not lag behind: the "hospice of the Medici" quartered prostitutes far into the sixteenth century.[47] No matter that some of the owners were members of important magistracies and of the city's most distinguished religious confraternity. They took their ownership of whorehouses for granted and furnished communal property assessors with exact information on how these places were rented—often on a monthly basis—and on their profits.[48]

To hear the landlords tell it, these properties were a losing proposition. One place had not been rented for three years, and another house for *donne cortesi* was sometimes rented, sometimes not. A third could not be rented at any price.[49] One owner told the officials that the only time his property in this area was rented was when the pope was in town:

> When the court of the pope is here, [the shops] are rented ... , but when the pope is not here they stand unrented, for they are in an evil area.[50]

The commune recognized the peculiar problems of this area, and granted a 20 percent tax break to at least one owner.[51] As the landlords saw it, the source of their difficulties lay not so much in the nature of the trade practiced in the area, as in the low quality of people who rented from them:

> A hostel at the Frascato which whores inhabit ... is rented to Germans, vicious people without any faith. Not three years ago one [of them] left

---

[46] *ASF, Catasto*, 79, fols. 170r–174r, 329r–331r; 52, fol. 399v; 54, fol. 475r (all 1427); 1018, part 1, fols. 120r–121v, and part 2, fol. 393r (1480). Another family in the brothel was the Ghezzo Della Casa (ibid., 79, fol. 72v).

[47] *LC*, fols. 122r, 127v (1485–86). Benedetto Dei in 1470 identified the Piazza de' Medici; see G. Romby, *Descrizioni e rappresentazioni della città di Firenze nel XV secolo* (Florence, 1976), 57. In 1482 Lorenzo de' Medici assigned his property bordering "on the Chiassolino [Malacucina] by which one goes to the Frascato" as dowry for religious services; see *ASF, not. antecos.* M 565 (1481–84), fol. 79v, and R. Trexler, "Lorenzo de' Medici and Savonarola, Martyrs for Florence," *Renaissance Quarterly* 31 (1978): 298f. It is not clear from an examination of *ASF, Catasto*, 826, 827, that Cosimo de' Medici's many properties in the area included whorehouses: *ASF, Catasto*, 79, fol. 79, fols. 87r–93r, and 52, fols. 317r–322v (Bernardo d'Alamanno di Salvestro, 1427); 55, fol. 760r (Rosso di Giovanni, 1427), translated by Brucker, *Society*, 190; *ASF, Catasto*, 625, fol. 355v (heirs of Jacopo di Bartolomeo de' Medici, 1442).

[48] Monthly rentals are mentioned in *ASF, Catasto*, 1019, part 1, fol. 345r. Beltramone Della Tosa and Bernardo d'Alamanno had been members of the Signoria. The latter was an Official of Decency, the one clear case of a property holder of the brothel also being an official; *LC*, fol. 24r (1450–51). He was also a leading member of the Confraternity of the Magi; see R. Hatfield, "The Compagnia de' Magi," *Journal of the Warburg and Courtauld Institutes* 33 (1970): 132, 156f.

[49] Respectively *ASF, Catasto*, 1019, part 1, fol. 345r (1480); 79, fol. 303r (1427); 52, fols. 396r–399v (1427).

[50] "E quando ci è cortte dil papa, cie instanno apigionati ... , ma quando non ci è il papa, instanno spigionati, perchè sono in chattivo luogho" (ibid., 625, fol. 355v [heirs of Jacopo di Bartolomeo de' Medici, 1442]).

[51] Beltramone Della Tosa (ibid., 1018, part 1, fols. 120r–121v [1480]).

with 300 florins in goods and rent he owed [me]. Then [the hostel] went unrented for over a year....[52]

Consider what type of people we have to deal with: German pimps, Spaniards, the most novel people you ever saw. Most of the time they leave us holding the bag.[53]

The nationality of the hostelers was not quite as exotic as the owners made out. Just a few years after these statements of 1427, two of the three persons renting the main hostels of the brothel were Italians, and Italian domination of prostitutional housing increased over time. Between 1436 and 1523 11 of the 14 hostelers identifiable by nationality spoke that language.[54] Nor was their stay always as short as the owners asserted. Of the 19 hostelers whose houses were said to be in the brothel, 12 held their position for more than two years, a respectable degree of residential persistence.[55]

From the Catasto statement of perhaps the most durable of the lot (17 years), we can gain some sense of their operations and the investment in whoring which made the hostelers' departure unprofitable. Betto di Zanobi was hosteler at the Macciana, but also identified himself as a wood carver, the only innkeeper to list a second occupation.[56] At 40 years of age, he was a family man, living in the hostel with his five-year-old son Zanobi and his 28-year-old Italian *femina* Bresciana, who probably functioned as its governess (*madrona*).[57] Betto was an entrepreneur. In addition to the Macciana, which he rented from the Pecori family, he had an interest in a hostel in the Frascato which he shared with a Milanese cook, in another house "usable as a hostel to hold women," and in still another with ten *botteghe* or shops for as many ladies.[58] Then came the investment he had in the girls themselves, to whom he extended credit for clothing and rent, as well as money to bail them out of jail.[59] All told, the apparently illiterate Betto told the scribe who wrote his Catasto statement, some 13 prostitutes owed him a total of 147 1/2 florins, ranging from 24 florins owed by Margherita del Magredino to the mere £5

---

[52] Ibid., 52, fol. 317r; 79, fol. 87v (Bernardo de' Medici, 1427).

[53] Ibid., 52, fol. 399r (Beltramone Della Tosa, 1427).

[54] Two each came from Ferrara, Venice, and Lucca, one each from the remaining cities; 1436, fols. 4v–5v; *LC*.

[55] The longest stayed, in descending order, 17, 14, 10 (3X), 5 (3X) years. One of these was Arrigo di Giovanni delle Fanciulle da Colonia ("of the Girls from Cologne"), on whom, see Doren, *Deutsche Handwerker*, 143.

[56] "Legnaiuolo e abergattore" (*ASF, Catasto*, 52, fols. 497r–498v; 79, fols. 406r–v).

[57] Prostitutes were permitted to have a "matronam, seu unam dominam cum commissione, ... et cum provisione ... et emolumentis, prout visum fuerit, et placebit dictis offitalibus ..." (*Statuta*, 3:43) ("matron, or a lady with commission, ... and with a salary and emoluments, as it will seem good to the said officials"). But the term is not used in the *LC*.

[58] *ASF, Catasto*, 52, fols. 497r–498v.

[59] The *LC* contains many cases of hostelers bailing their girls out. For an example of a client doing so, see below, at n. 84. Advances for clothing were mentioned above, at n. 20.

which Giannaia had to pay.[60] His was a substantial operation, in short, and Betto was not one of those crude Germans who were there one day and gone the next.

The hosteler of the Macciana and his colleagues in the public brothels of the Frascato provided a total of 54 rooms or shops in their three buildings, as a count of the 1436 roll call shows. Adding the 16 prostitutes who lived in the Chiasso de' Buoi at the time, we obtain a total registration of 70. The following table gives a vivid sense of the babel of languages and dress in all these four units:

Table 3
Population of the Hostels and of the Alley of the Cows, 1436

		Hostels							
	Betto di Zanobi of Germany		Agostino di Niccolò of Ferrara		Giovanni di Marco Stornato of Venice		Chiasso de' Buoi		Totals	
	F	M[a]	F	M	F	M	F	M	F	M
Low Countries	8	1	5	3	10	3	3	1	26	8
Germany	2	1	1	0	4	2	9	2	16	5
Italy	6	4	2	2	1	2	4[b]	1	13	9
France	1	1	3	0	2	0	0	0	6	1
South Slavic	1	0	2	1	1	0	0	0	4	1
Spain	0	0	0	0	1	0	0	0	1	0
British Isles	1	1	0	0	0	0	0	0	1	1
Others	0	0	2[c]	2[d]	1[e]	0	0	0	3	2
Totals	19		15		20		16		70	

a. That is, those pimps including the hostelers themselves whose *femine* are identified as being in each hostel and area; b. Includes one Florentine; c. Constantinople and Ganbera; d. Origins not given; e. Lausanne.
Source: 1436, ff. 4v–5v.

In Panormita's poem of 1425, we found evidence that some of the prostitutes had "patronesses," a fact which we cannot verify in the *Book of Sentences*

---

[60] *ASF, Catasto,* 52, fols. 497r–498v.

until the end of the quattrocento.[61] Yet how few of them had full-time male pimps! Since the 1436 roll call lists not only all the personnel but the woman for whom each man pandered, we can be sure that in the hostel of Betto, for example, only 8 of the 19 whores had professional pimps, and that on the whole only 27 of 70 prostitutes were so served.[62]

Though nowhere in our records do pimps say they lived in the room with their women, it seems clear that they did so. I could find no case in which any man was said to pimp for more than one woman, and in itself this suggests that the relationship between pimp and prostitute was not merely profession-al but also domestic.[63] Further, every pimp whose residence was specified in the *Book of Sentences* lived in the brothels rather than elsewhere in the city.[64] The circumstantial evidence suggests, in short, that Table 3 provides not only a census, but a map of residence for prostitutes and pimps.

At Work

Entering the parlor or streets to practice her trade, the prostitute had to know her clients, their origins and occupations, and their behavioral peculiari-ties. Who were these men? No account book of a prostitute, pimp, or hosteler has yet surfaced which might provide an exact answer to this question, and we must rely on the *Book of Sentences* for now. Table 4 gives a general idea of the nationality of clients from 1441 to 1523.

If we assume that justice was blind to national origins, this table allows us to generalize about the provenience of the prostitutes' clients. About one in five of them came from outside Italy, about half that contingent being Ger-man. Among the majority Italians, two of five came from north of the Apen-nines, but very few from the area south of Tuscany. Thus more than half (53.8 percent) of the clientele were non-Tuscans. Adding the quarter of the total who were Tuscans but not Florentines, we find that 74.2 percent of all the clients came from outside the city.

This preponderantly foreign clientele was certainly a strong argument for having a brothel even in the eighteenth century, but it was *not* the govern-ment's justification for expanding prostitution in the quattrocento.[65] To be

---

[61] It is not clear what exactly the term meant, especially since in *LC*, fol. 97r, the prostitute Solisa is called the *patrona* of Ferrando of Spain, who was clearly *not* her pimp; cf. ibid., fol. 92v (1474).

[62] Cf. the information on southeastern France in Rossiaud, "Prostitution," 301ff.

[63] See the information below.

[64] Only nine pimps' residences were listed, however. On the other hand, in many cases where pimps and prostitutes are listed together, the residence of the latter but not the former is given, suggesting that the former were understood to live with their *femine*.

[65] Peter Leopold "abolished ... the public women" of all Tuscany except Livorno, "where the flow of foreigners and fleets merited some special consideration" (*Relazioni sul governo della Toscana*, ed. A. Salvestrini [Florence, 1969], 1:141).

Table 4
Provenience of Non-Professional Males Accused by the Office of Decency[66]

Foreign Areas			Transapennine			Tuscany			Central		
		(%)			(%)			(%)			(%)
Germany	17	(47.2)	Bologna	11	(20.8)	Florence	34	(44.2)	Gubbio	3	(75.0)
Low Countries	10	(27.8)	Venice	9	(17.0)	Prato	7	(9.1)	Rome	1	(25.0)
France	4	(11.1)	Milan	4	(7.5)	Mugello[a]	6	(7.8)			
Spain	4	(11.1)	Brescia	3	(5.7)	Chianti[b]	6	(7.8)			
Albania	1	(2.8)	Ferrara	3	(5.7)	Pisa	4	(5.2)			
			Modena	3	(5.7)	Pistoia	3	(3.9)			
			Other[c]	20	(37.7)	Other[c]	18	(23.4)			
Totals	36	(100)		53	(100)		77	(100)		4	(100)

a. Towns north of Florence; b. Valleys south of Florence; c. Two or one persons.
Source: *LC.*

sure, some of these outsiders were resident aliens rather than transients, like the domestic servant of the philosopher Pico della Mirandola whom we encounter in the records.[67] But few had such an exalted station, as an examination of these clients' occupations from 1441 to 1523 makes clear in Table 5.

This was a clientele of petty shop owners, artisans, and day laborers, and a study of the 46 cases where both occupations and origins are given shows that most of the owners were Italians, most of the laborers Germans and Flemings. Bernardino of Siena once called those who visited the brothels *villanacci*, and that characterization would seem valid.[68] No foreign gentlemen were hailed before the Onestà, and no members of the liberal professions. While preferential treatment may in part explain this neglect, it is more easily accounted for by supposing that these finer people visited courtesans outside the brothel, while also having at their disposal the free and slave servant women of their hosts.

---

[66] The nature of the crime usually indicates when a client was involved. But since clients are not named as such, I compiled this table by counting all individual men except those known to be pimps, hostelers, officials, or brothel cooks, all men who lived in the brothel area, and all those who were cited to appear to obtain licenses.

[67] "Matteus famulus domini Johannis della Mirandola" (*LC*, fol. 171r [28 September 1490]).

[68] Bernardino-Cannarozzi, 4:211.

Table 5

Occupations of Non-Professional Males Accused by the Onestà[69]

Shoemakers[a]	25	Furnace or Bath Tenders	6
Weavers[b]	22	Doublet Makers	5
Butchers[c]	18	Bakers	4
Barbers	15	Hat Trimmers	4
Wool Purgers	10	Others[d]	55
Old Clothes Dealers	8		
		Total	172

a. Includes cobblers; b. Of both silk and wool; c. Includes pork butchers; d. Three cases or less.
Source: *LC.*

Closer attention is due the one in five clients who was a native Florentine. Only 13 of 34 of them listed their occupations, and they were typical of occupations as a whole.[70] Only nine of those remaining had surnames recognizable to students of Florence, and only three of those occurred at random in the *Book of Sentences.* The other six were all accused in one case of 4 May 1458. The latters' eminence, together with their common political affiliation, leaves little doubt that the accusation brought against them was unique in being politically motivated.[71] In light of the reputation of Florentine adolescents and *giovani* for hounding public prostitutes, the low number of name-Florentines in the *Book of Sentences* suggests that the latter were protected from publicity by officialdom.[72]

The motivation for fostering prostitution in Florence had been to diminish homosexual comportment among Florentines in order to increase the population. Having shown that the majority of clients in the brothel during the quat-

---

[69] Five painters were mentioned in the *LC*, but are not included in the table because two of them were not sentenced on criminal charges. They were: Filippo (see below, at n. 98); Baccio called Baccionino (*LC*, fol. 96v [1474]); the well known Leonardo di Giovanni called Lo Scheggia (ibid., fols. 172v, 185v [1490, 1497]); Leonardo d'Antonio da Pisa (ibid., fol. 203r [1505]); Biagio (ibid., fol. 213v [1516]). See also a certain Mariotto di Filippo de' Lippi (ibid., 186v [1497]). The only Jew was Angelo Musetto Da Pesaro, sentenced for wanting to bed with a (Christian) whore (ibid., fol. 25r [1451]).

[70] Two each goldbeaters, dyers, butchers, weavers, and barbers; one each shoemaker, furrier, purger.

[71] The accusation against the six was not specified, and the sentence was later cancelled. Bernardo di Bartolomeo de' Gherardi had been Standard Bearer of Justice several times; he and the coppersmith Francesco di Buonaccorso de' Corsellini were old *accoppiatori*. The belt-maker Andrea di Lapo Guardi and Battista di Berto de' Filiciaia were *arroti* in the extraordinary commission of 1458. Piero di Tommaso de' Minerbetti and Antonio di Guido Giuntini were also in the *reggimento*. On them see N. Rubinstein, *The Government of Florence under the Medici (1434 to 1494)* (Oxford, 1966), 282, 284, 288, 290.

[72] Giovanni Cambi tells how the Eight of the Watch reacted when complaints against citizens or their whores were brought to them: "When I am finished my term in office, I want to be able to go home at nights without being wounded or murdered" (*Istorie fiorentine*, in *Delizie degli eruditi toscani*, ed. I da San Luigi [Florence, 1780], 21:254).

trocento were not Florentines, we may now try to isolate that information in the *Book of Sentences* which comments upon the problem of homosexual behavior. Two practices catch our attention: female transvestism and clients' sodomy with whores. Both violated the whole system which the government of Florence had meant to establish.

Transvestism was against the law for all males and females, and as early as 1260 prostitutes were disciplined for wearing men's short hair and clothing.[73] Little wonder then that the *Book of Sentences* contains 24 cases of prostitutes sentenced for transvestism (Table 7). It is true that two of these cases stemmed from such behavior during Carnival—a time when such reversal practices were common among contemporary Roman courtesans—but all other torts were perpetrated at times of the year having no apparent association with reversal customs.[74] The prostitutes' transvestism was a workaday habit. It withstood a new prohibition of 1506, one whose moralistic tenor could not have been much different from a Venetian law of 1480: women wore their hair in a male fashion so that they would entice men, that law said; female transvestism was just another type of "sodomy."[75]

Implicit in such fears was the idea that some men preferred women who not only looked like men, but acted like them: female transvestism could have been an invitation to types of sexual relations common among homosexual partners and other "unnatural" types, especially anal intercourse and oral stimulation or coitus. Contraception might be the result, but could not have been the purpose of transvestism. Were Florentine prostitutes, in short, attempting to seduce Florentine men away from each other by the very practices common to males practicing homosexuality? We have seen that in 1464 a pillory had been erected in the courtyard of San Cristofano to punish just this "depravity."[76] Did the prostitutes in men's hats, copes, and robes offer their clients a way of avoiding the shame of being caught in homosexual anal intercourse by the Officals of the Night?

The quattrocento records would suggest that clients of this type eluded the Officers of Decency, for with the exception of one man accused in 1474 of acting "against nature" with a prostitute, the practice was not registered until the early sixteenth century.[77] At that point, however, a whole series of such accusations appear in the records. In the *Book of Sentences* two cases of 1516 and 1517 concerned "sodomy" with prostitutes, one of them involving two

---

[73] R. Davidsohn, *Geschichte von Florenz* 4, part 3 (Berlin, 1927), 322f. The law against transvestism is in *Statuta*, 2:271.

[74] "Quia in diebus carnisprivii tulent berrectinum maschilem" (*LC*, fols. 127r, 128r [1486]) ("Because they take away the masculine hat during carnival time"). On the Roman practice, see Rezasco, "Segno," 201.

[75] "Quod est species sodomie" (Rezasco, "Segno," 182). The 1506 decree is referred to in *LC*, fol. 202r.

[76] See above, at n. 35.

[77] "Intentavit suponere contra naturam Solisam spagniolam" (*LC*, fol. 94v) ("He meant to unnaturally mount [and anally penetrate] the Spaniard Solisam").

men.[78] And the records of the Eight of the Watch, who by now were also heavily involved in morals enforcement, contain several cases of "sodomitic" acts with prostitutes. The most common of these was anal intercourse (which Niccolò Machiavelli among others was said to practice), followed by cunnilingus.[79] In two cases of the Eight of the Watch, prostitutes denounced their clients' actions or demands to the authorities without saying that they had suffered bodily harm; but in almost all other cases, the prostitutes protested when their anus had been injured by the "sodomy."[80] Clearly, prostitutes at that time and earlier had not insisted on the distinctions between the sexes with all the fervor demanded of them.

There may be another reason why prostitutes dressed like men, however: wearing a man's clothes compromised the individual to whom they belonged. A glance at Table 7 will show that six prostitutes were sentenced for having knocked men's hats off their heads, and if we follow two of these cases we will see that these hats might then be worn by the prostitutes. Pellegrina of Verona in 1476 first ripped a hat off, and then told its owner she would not give it back until he had intercourse with her; the hat was a form of extortion. When the potential client refused to cooperate, Pellegrina kept the hat.[81] Santa of Padua did the same thing to another client, but she then put the hat on her head, with unfortunate consequences. For as the sentence informs us, Santa's seizure of ser Antonio's beret was the reason another prostitute attacked Antonio when he returned to his shop.[82] As in the Venetian *ballo del cappello* of the time, having a man's hat meant wielding power over him; and inversely the modern Italian *scapellata* by a male of a female was equivalent to

---

[78] "Perchè sodomita contra a natura La Domenica . . . contra la sua voglia" (ibid., fol. 218v) ("Because he unnaturally [anally] sodomized Domenica against her will"); "per sodomiti" (ibid., fol. 219v).

[79] Carnessechi Spoglio, kindly brought to my attention by Elaine Rosenthal. Machiavelli was secretly denounced because he "fotte La Lucrezia vocata La Riccia nel culo" (ibid., *Tamburazioni*, 27 May 1510). Presumably, the same Machiavelli was mentioned in *LC*, fol. 213r (26 February 1516) when "Ipolita del Machiavello" was sentenced by the office.

[80] The normal damage was "anum fregit." The notion that anal intercourse was denounced mainly when bodily harm was done is strengthened by an amusing story of the Piovano Arlotto. A man complained to the anti-homosexual Officials of the Night about another man who had sold him a mule so rough to ride that it had "ruined his posterior" (*Motti e facezie del Piovano Arlotto*, ed. G. Folena [Milan and Naples, 1954], 182f.).

[81] The victim was a servant of Lorenzo Segni—perhaps the father of the famous historian (*LC*, fol. 104r [1476]).

[82] "Quia dicta Sancta extulit de capite ser Antonii berretum, et fuit causa suprascripti malificii commissi per dictam Lodovicam [contra ser Antonium]. Et [eam condemnavit] etiam quia . . . fuit indutus panibus virilibus" (ibid., fol. 113r [1482]) ("Because the said Santa removed the hat from ser Antonio's head, and was the cause of the said crime committed by the said Lodovico [against ser Antonio]. And [he sentenced her] also because . . . she was dressed in men's clothes"). I take this to mean that she was sentenced for wearing men's clothes because she had put on the beret.

binding him to her.[83] In our context, a male without his hat was prima facie evidence that he had been with a prostitute, an indication that a prostitute had gotten the best of him. We do not know that the good women of Florence watched the prostitutes to see if they were wearing their husbands' clothing. But it is a safe assumption that for the authorities, women in men's clothing were women on top.

Such assertive behavior was not what the officials of Decency had had in mind when they first began to regulate prostitution, but it was the very condition of survival for the women themselves. They would mime the male in bed if that was good for business, mock him with headgear if that was necessary to establish their right to support. Before all, they had to treat their clients as the men treated them: as marks whose claim never extended beyond the bed. Pressed to return ten florins which a client had advanced her, Cimellina of Flanders did not let sentiment disarm her:

> I don't want to hurt Antoniello at all, for he has intercoursed with me for three years or more. He did good things for me, and got me out of jail twice and paid [fines of] ten florins or more for me. But I want to sleep with whom I please, [and] he is not my man.[84]

In Court

At some time during her stay in Florence, the prostitute stood a good chance of appearing before the Onestà as either plaintiff or defendant in a legal suit. Like any brothel, Florence's had its gambling and drinking, fisticuffs and knifings, the *effusio sanguinis* common to the oppressed and desperate. But the Office of Decency made Florence different. Prostitutes were presumably employed to solve a structural problem of communal identity—rather than merely to pander to the weakness of individual fleshes—and the government found that success at recruiting and retaining prostitutes who might solve that problem depended on the protection these women could expect while performing their civic task. It had therefore established the Onestà as a special court which was required to take women seriously; in Poggio Bracciolini's words, this magistracy was not only to decide disputes between prostitutes, but to "see to it that they are not molested in the city."[85] The gates of

---

[83] L. Duchamp passed on the information about the *ballo di cappello*, and C. Klapisch-Zuber that on the *scapellata*; see R. Corso, "Gli Sponsali Popolari," *Revue des Études Ethnographiques et Sociologiques* 1 (1908): 493f., and his *Patti d'amore e pegni di promessa* (Palermo: Edikronos, 1991), 67–75.

[84] 1436, fols. 29r-v. Note the reverse situation where a prostitute admitted that a local artisan who had fathered her child was not her husband (*vir*) as she had been claiming (*ASF, not. antecos.* M 569, III, Piero Migliorelli [1458–60], fol. 170v [2 May 1450]).

[85] Poggio Fiorentino, *Facezie*, edited by F. Cazzamini Mussi (Modena, 1927), 75f. Cf. the duties of the normal official elsewhere charged with administering justice over prostitutes in A. Terroine, "Le Roi des Ribauds de l'Hôtel du Roi et les Prostituées Parisiennes," *Revue d'Histoire de Droit Français et Étranger* 56 (1978): 253–67.

justice would be open to the prostitutes as they were to few other women. How well did the Onestà discharge its duty to protect them?

Over the course of 82 years, the Onestà tried the following number of cases:

Table 6
Sentences Rendered by the Onestà, 1441–1523[86]

	Accused				Accused	
	F	M			F	M
1441–1451	87	58	1491–1501		134	53
1451–1461[a]	103	106	1501–1511		65	40
1461–1471[b]	90	81	1511–1521		66	60
1471–1481[c]	103	65	1521–1523		6	3
1481–1491[d]	442	158				
			Totals		1096	624

a. Peak period of 147 cases between 1457 and 1460; b. 48 cases in 1462; c. 133 cases between 1473 and 1475; d. 417 cases between 1487 and 1490, 152 of which in 1487.
Source: LC.

This table shows that women were accused more often than men, and this is not surprising, since the prostitutes formed the majority of those subject to the Onestà. They could be cited to appear before the court ex officio, while males would normally appear only if charged by the whores in a petition to the court. To pursue the question of sex-specific justice, therefore, we should attempt to distinguish between those notorious torts (excluding contumacy) whose prosecution might be initiated by the Onestà ex officio, and crimes of violence and theft which by their private nature were usually denounced by victims. Superfemininity in the former category and a more balanced picture in the latter would tend to show that the Onestà took its duty to the prostitutes seriously.

Thus of 98 cases of this type, 78 involved female defendants, and more than half (43) of the latter resulted from women's assumption of male dress. When we add to this superfemininity the large number of cases where prostitutes were sentenced for contumacy because they did not appear at roll call or in answer to a charge, plus the very high number of cases which did not specify a charge, but clearly involved contumacy, the reason for the superfemininity is clear. It stemmed from ex officio administration of the prostitutes.

[86] As in Table 1, counting starts on 13 November 1441, 1451, etc. Under each sex is listed the number of *cases* (not individuals or events) where that sex was accused. The inflation in the 1480s was explained above, at n. 25. In the following years pimps were prosecuted, but not prostitutes: 1454, 1467, 1469, 1472, 1477, 1501, 1519, 1521, 1523; prostitutes but no pimps: 1441, 1452, 1480, 1496; neither: 1468, 1503, 1508–10, 1512–13.

Table 7
Notorious Crimes, 1441–1523

		Documentation
Dress		
Prostitutes dressed as men	24	1476–1506
Prostitutes wearing hats	13	1482–1516
Housing		
Men abducting prostitutes	12	1459–1490
Prostitutes living in illegal areas	12	1452–1486
Prostitutes' shop a gambling den	6	1483–1490
Prostitutes corrupting girls	6	1483–1499
Men holding prostitutes in illegal areas	4	1488–1489
Irreverence		
Prostitutes prosecuted for:		
—blasphemy	6	1442–1488
—seizing men's hats	6	1466–1487
—obscene gestures	2	1485
—carrying arms	2	1476, 1486
—eating eggs in Lent	1	1474
Sex		
Men prosecuted for:		
—rape	1	1459
—sodomy	2	1516–1517
—acts against nature	1	1474
Total	98	

Source: *LC.*

When the Onestà adjudicated cases *ad instantiam* of others, however, the picture changes radically. Table 8 totals all those cases in which the accused and accuser are both known for the numerically preponderant torts of common violence and theft.

These records of the Office of Decency show without any doubt that its court existed primarily to do justice for the prostitutes, for around 80 percent of all plaintiffs were prostitutes. Just as convincingly these records demonstrate that the prostitutes did not act only against their professional sisters, for on the whole they sued their pimps and clients almost as often as their colleagues (179–207). This was no ideal *città meretrice*, of course. Table 7 shows a low number of sex and rape charges, for example, while Table 8's mere two cases of theft between prostitutes must be unrepresentative of reality. It is just as clear that by the very nature of violent crime, males would not have needed to sue very often against women. Does anyone doubt that the

Table 8

Cases of Common Crimes, 1441–1523

Physical Violence[a]

Aggressor	Victim		
F	F	101	(83.7)
M	F	114	
F	M	28	(16.3)
M	M	14	
		Total: 257	(100.0)

Nonphysical Violence[b]

F	F	52	(83.5)
M	F	34	
F	M	5	(16.5)
M	M	12	
		Total: 103	(100.0)

Theft

F	F	2	(25.9)
M	F	5	
F	M	19[c]	(74.1)
M	M	1	
		Total: 27	(100.0)

a. Includes hitting, whipping, wounding, ear boxing, hair pulling, etc.;
b. Includes "crimes," delicts, threats, stone throwing, "injuries" and
"offenses" otherwise unspecified, and disputes; c. There are many other cases
where prostitutes were accused of theft, but the victim was not named.
Source: LC.

system of prostitution was based on the exploitation of women? Whores
doubtless avoided suits because they feared the consequences of publicizing
the damage done them, and at other times did not seek redress because they
had no witnesses to the crimes perpetrated against them. The low number of
Florentines of good family accused by the Onestà suggests that "good people" were favored, to the detriment of the prostitutes. All that having been
said, however, the evidence that the officials did defend the prostitutes and
give them access to justice is persuasive. The Onestà did not completely dis-
miss the "squabbles of women" or the disorders caused by the males who
used them.

Their task was often difficult. There was the great siege of 1459 when Pope
Pius II was in town, where 18 pimps armed to the teeth marched with servants of the Onestà to the door of the episcopal palace, and cried out to the

other pimps who held a prostitute against her will inside: "Give us back our women!"—before launching their attack.[87]

Nor could the assertiveness of the prostitutes be ignored any more than the irreverence of other subjects. There was the whore Anna of Poland who sent her German pimp to assassinate another Polish prostitute.[88] Maria di Francesco of Pavia was heard to spit out at a sister in a dispute:

> May dysentery plague you and your pimp Giovanni Ciecco, who sells his sisters![89]

And Giovanna of Piacenza showed no more respect for the Onestà than for her colleague from Ferrara:

> "You and the officials can stick it up your asses!" And raising her skirt, she said: "I shit on you and the officials!"[90]

Finally, one cannot ignore political intrigue. One worthy citizen informed the Eight of the Watch that he had heard news of treason when, "moved by the order of nature," he had slept with a prostitute:

> After a lot of conversation—[you know] how little most women can keep a secret entrusted to them—, she confided to me as a sign of the love she bore me. Perhaps the divine will moved her [to do so]. Considering the import of what I [now] reveal, just think how great her confidence was![91]

In most cases, however, the morals police held court for lesser matters, ones which threatened neither the commune, the office, nor even the rule of males. The daily fare of the Onestà was a round of violence, most often by men against women, but not infrequently between colleagues, a situation which was not peculiar to prostitution, but no less depressing for that.[92] These officials took their job seriously because the prostitutes were thought to be so important to the commune at large. It makes one wonder how long these women and their pimps could bear both the responsibility and the tensions of brothel love and hate.

---

[87] *LC*, fols. 46r–v (18 May). Archbishop Antonino had just died. Cf. the *pax* between the two trios of pimps "and their followers" in 1454 (*ASF, not. antecos.* M 569, II [1453–58], fols. 1r–v [27 March]).

[88] *LC*, fol. 31v (1455).

[89] "Che vengha il cacasanghue a te e a Giovanni Ciecho tuo ruffiano che a arofianate le sue sirocchie" (ibid., fol. 17v [1447]).

[90] " 'Eycazo t'in culo a te e agli ufficiali,' et alzando pannos, dixit: 'Io rincato te e gli ufficiali' " (ibid., fol. 45v [1459]).

[91] The news was that Filippo Strozzi was acting on his own and corresponding with the pope (Carnesecchi Spoglio, *Tamburazioni*, 6 February 1527/8).

[92] Everything short of homicide was adjudicated by the Onestà; that crime was handled by higher magistracies.

Resilience

In the records of even the most transitory group one can find plans for the future, and even cases where those plans were realized. We have seen that several of the hostelers invested in the city and remained there; it need not surprise us that pimps and prostitutes also sought a measure of stability and security. Determined to be sure of their men in an unsure world, prostitutes like Margherita d'Arnoldo of Liège took their pimps before the lords of the Onestà and made them vow fidelity:

> Giovanni Ceppi of Liège ..., her pimp ..., in the presence of the [Onestà's] notary ..., makes ... an alliance and agreement.... Namely, Giovanni ... promises ... the said Margherita that up to this day he has not known any woman carnally in any place at any time. And he promised to hold to the said promise and obligation [in the future].[93]

On completing a stretch together as a professional and domestic couple, the prostitute and her pimp might appear before the same officials to amicably sever that relationship:

> Matteo Lovis a purger of Florence and Gianetta of France appear.... The said Matteo asserts he has been and is the pimp of the said Gianetta, and the said Giannetta asserts she has been and is the woman of the said Matteo. And thus they have remained together for about two years, each sharing the other's living and clothing expenses. [Now] both want to separate from each other on cordial terms, so that each can do whatever s/he wants without being reprehended by the other. [Thus] they have unanimously and agreeably separated and freed each other, and have promised that neither of them will dispute with or bother the other. And as a goodbye gift, and as [the final payoff of] any vow by which one could ask or demand anything [from the other], the said Giannetta of her own free will gives, pays, and grants ten gold cameral ducats to the said Matteo, present and accepting....[94]

With the support of the Onestà, therefore, prostitutes and pimps could hope for some measure of interpersonal stability based on human sentiment. Another type of stability was offered by having an institutional identity, and both the hostelers and pimps possessed such a moral face apart from their individual fates. Hostelers could belong to the guild of innkeepers.[95] As parishioners of the churches which surrounded the brothel areas, they shared the duties encumbent on the faithful, and in 1467 Giovanni of Siena and messer Angelo the German, identified in the official ecclesiastical document as

---

[93] 1436, fol. 64 (21 May).

[94] Ibid., fol. 11v (16 August).

[95] Early fourteenth-century statutes only forbid prostitutes from keeping a hostel, which would seem to indicate that whoremasters could, and thus could be members of the guild; see F. Sartini, ed., *Statuti dell'arte degli albergatori della città e contado di Firenze* (Florence, 1935), 151, 238.

hostelers of the Frascato and of the Brunelleschi inn, joined with the Brunelleschi, Torrigiani, Boni, Dello Strinato, and Rinaldi families to elect a new rector for their parish of San Leo.[96]

This same church hosted a "confraternity of pimps" (*societas lenonum*), first documented in a testament of 1429. In it the Flemish brothel hosteler Leone d'Arrigo left money to a German Dominican at Santa Maria Novella for his death masses; to four prostitutes living in his hostel; and to his woman, Margherita of Flanders, whom he made his universal heir. Then he provided for his fellow pimps:

> Item. Since he loves charity, [Leone] left two gold florins to the confraternity of pimps and panders, of which he is a member, so they could enjoy themselves and have a good time.[97]

A delightful testamentary bequest indeed! Yet this confraternity combined religion with fun like other Florentine associations, and commissioned a painting to embellish the confraternal meeting place:

> It is known that many months ago in the presence of the said officials [of Onestà], the painter Filippo ... recognized having received a certain quantity of money given him by certain public pimps. They have their [meeting] place in [the church of] San Leo of Florence, namely, a confraternity titled Of Santa Barbara, and these pimps wanted the said Filippo to paint figures of Santa Barbara in the said church. And [since then] he has not done the figures, violating the pimps' wishes. And to the end that the said Filippo gets on with the said work, [the officials] have fined and sentenced the said Filippo ... to £25 ..., with this reservation: if by next March 12 he finishes and completes the said figure of Santa Barbara such that in the judgement of the said officials it is properly finished, then and in that case they will cancel the fine and sentence.[98]

Finally, even the prostitutes were not without some type of institutional identity, for the nunnery of repentant prostitutes, the Convertite, was both peopled and financially supported by them.[99] A sixteenth-century abbess of

---

[96] *AAF, Beneficiali Paganucci*, VIII (1527–28), fols. 449r-v (*fides* of a document of 3 April 1467).

[97] "Item amore charitatis reliquit societati leonum seu ruffianorum, de qua ipse testator est, florenos duos aureos, pro gaudendi, et bonum tempus facere"; copied by Manni in *Biblioteca Riccardiana, Firenze, MS. Moreniana*, II, 230, doc. iii.

[98] *LC*, fol. 67r (1465). The space in the text for the rest of the artist's name is blank. It will be recalled that there was another confraternity, of "Germans," named for Santa Barbara, at the Servite church; see Battistini, *Confrérie*.

[99] Elsewhere such nunneries were called "Magdalenes" (Bullough, *History*, 115f.). In the cinquecento, the Lenten sermon of Mary Magdalene was used to exhort the prostitutes to convert, and provided a setting for the official census (*ASF, Onestà*, 1, fol. 15v [about 1568]). On the Convertite, see now S. Cohen, "Convertite e malmaritate, Donne 'irregolari' e ordini religiosi nella Firenze rinascimentale," *Memoria. Rivista di storia delle donne* 1 (1981): 46–63.

this house told the authorities that without prostitutes swelling the rolls of the Onestà, without the licenses they purchased, and without their constant prosecution by the officials, the house would immediately collapse, a fate which would have struck Florentine self-righteousness to the quick.[100] For the true function of the Convertite, as distinct from its stated purpose, was to serve as a warning to the women of Florence: the hundreds and hundreds of "good" Florentine girls who were put in convents because their fathers could not afford a marriage dowry knew that a decent life in their convents was better than the shame of the Convertite.[101] Not only were the nuns of San Lisabetta often on the brink of starvation; not only did their census include a much greater percentage of Florentine whores than could be found in the brothel population, but the nunnery often housed Florentine laywomen who were imprisoned there as a punishment for sexual misdeeds.[102] Like the "good" nunneries, that of the Convertite was a warehouse for outcasts, but without servants.

Prostitutes left an institutional imprint on other areas of Florentine life as well, less palpable but not less significant.[103] But what of their and their pimps' individual longevity in the city? How commonly were a whore's children nursed in Florence for as long as two whole years?[104] How many prostitutes stayed in Florence long enough to adopt that young foundling who through her prostitution would support an aging "mother"? How often did the investment whores made to raise young girls in the Convertite to the same end actually pay off?[105] How often, finally, did prostitutes attain that

---

[100] *ASF, Onestà*, 1, fols. 14v, 18r, 26r, 33v–35v; 6, fols. 36v–37r, 41v. Cf. also I. Galligo, *Circa ad alcuni antichi e singolari documenti inediti riguardanti la prostituzione, tratti dall'archivio centrale di stato di Firenze* (Milan, 1869), 7f.

[101] Starting about 1470, the number and census of Florentine nunneries exploded. By 1500 perhaps 1200 women lived in them, and by 1552, 13% of the female population of Florence (3419 nuns and lay sisters) were celibate; see R. Trexler, "Celibacy," in the present volume.

[102] In 1458 the nuns said they were dying of hunger (*ASF, Prov.* 148, fols. 441r–442r [20 February 1457/8]). In a list of almost all the nuns of 1460, 7 of 17 were *de Florentia* (*ASF, not. antecos.*, reference lost). Examples of "lecherous" Florentines confined to the Convertite are brought together in the Carnesecchi Spoglio, *Partiti*, 29 September 1503; 2 and 20 March 1503/4; unnumbered: 24 December 1517.

[103] The records seem to indicate that prostitutes generally provided sex without bearing children. Thirty-four of the first 100 entrants to the new foundling home of the Innocenti in 1441, for example, had slave mothers, but in all the records I examined no foundling was said to have a mother who was a prostitute (Trexler, "The Foundlings of Florence, 1395–1455," *History of Childhood Quarterly* 1 [1973]: 270f.). Probably contraception was common, as were abortions (girls came to Florence from the countryside to procure them [Carnesecchi Spoglio, *Tamburazioni*, 30 January 1511/12]), and infanticide, though I was unable to find any cases of prostitutes prosecuted for the latter ("Infanticide in Florence: New Sources and First Results," *History of Childhood Quarterly* 1 [1973]: 103).

[104] *ASF, not. antecos.*, M 569, III (1458–60), fol. 121v (20 December 1459).

[105] In 1516 the prostitute Laura of Ferrara was sentenced for putting her young daughter in the Convertite, then financially supporting her there with the intention of reclaiming her when she arrived at maturity, "and [then] teaching her streetwalking" (Carnesecchi Spoglio, no heading, 5 January 1515/16). Aretino says it was customary for

age when it was time to repent, and retire to the Convertite or another nunnery to do so?[106] The *Book of Sentences* gives a somber assessment of the stability of pimp and prostitute. Not one of the 15 pimps listed in the decade 1481-1491 could be located before or after their one appearance before the Onestà, and the story is little different among the prostitutes. Searching the census of 1436, for example, besides Betto di Zanobi's woman I found only one of the thirteen girls indebted to Betto in 1427. A search in the *Book of Sentences*, departing from those years when it is most like a census, yields much the same picture. Among 115 Italian prostitutes in the class 1486-1490, only 15 can be identified in the previous records with certainty or probability, and only 8 in the later records.[107] And of 27 prostitutes from the Low Countries named in the same source between 1481 and 1491, only 6 could be found before or after with the same certainty or probability.[108]

By its nature a judicial source cannot adequately measure residential persistence. It is a fact, however, that when prostitutes appeared in the *Book of Sentences*, they often appeared repeatedly to answer for separate transgressions. There would seem to have been no great number of prostitutes who steered clear of the law, therefore. When prostitutes were not in the record, they were not in a town, and this is our reason for believing that the public prostitutes and pimps of Florence were a transient lot. What could have caused this evanescence? Was it the "innumerable disputes, lawsuits, scandals . . . , partialities, divisions, and antagonisms" which whores could cause among their competing friends, or were there other reasons?[109] It is difficult to say. But one thing is certain. Few were the whores, Flemish or Italian, who as in Panormita's fancy decorated their graves with an inscription like this:

> If you want to stop a bit and read this verse,
> You will know which whore is buried beneath.
> In my green years, I was taken as a girl from the fatherland;
> With plaint and prayer my lover led me to do it.
> Flanders gave me birth, then I travelled the whole world,
> [And] finally settled in tranquil Siena.
> My name was Nichina, a name well known. In the bordello
> I settled, and I was a jewel of whoring.[110]

Roman whores to adopt foundling girls for this purpose; see *I Ragionamenti*, ed. A. Toschini (Milan, 1960), 294.

[106] Presumably retirement age was a common point for prostitutes to convert, as it was for some men, who sometimes joined religious orders at that date.

[107] The longest certain residence before this date was 4 years, the longest probable one 13 years. The longest probable residence period after 1490 was 10 years (*LC*).

[108] The longest certain residence before this date was 8 years, after only 1 year (*LC*).

[109] For a description of what a prostitute caused in the Florentine countryside, see *ASF, Prov.* 119, fols. 241v-242v (22 October 1428).

[110] Beccadelli, *Hermaphroditus*, bk. 2, chap. 30.

Climacteric

To this point we have studied the structure of prostitution more than its history. But there came a moment in the early sixteenth century when the men and women of Florence came to regard prostitution as almost the equal of homosexual behavior in its affront to the divine and social order. Part of an international reappraisal of prostitution, that shift in Florentine mentality deserves special attention at the conclusion of this chapter.[111] Analyzing the changing social facts from which the new mentality flows, we will see in high relief what prostitution had been, and would become.

The year 1511 was the turning point in Florence, and the contemporary Giovanni Cambi explains why:

> At this time there was a very large number of prostitutes. And ... no prostitute wanted to remain any longer in the separate places where the laws of the city permitted them. Instead, they did everything to be able to stay in the streets of the good and moral people. So they asked their lovers to get this approved, with the result that a little at a time, they had spread all over the city.[112]

This geographical expansion can be followed in the *Book of Sentences*. We have seen that the government originally intended to concentrate all prostitutes around the Mercato Vecchio, and that when a subsequent plan of 1415 to build additional brothels in other sections of the city was abandoned, this centralization remained official policy.[113] It was not, however, vigorously pursued, and the attempt to contain the prostitutes of the Chiasso de' Buoi, to which we referred earlier, remained the exception rather than the rule. From its first page in 1441, the *Book of Sentences* contains occasional references to prostitutes, subject to the Onestà, who practiced their trade outside the main brothels without official interference. In later years the number of such cases increased, without there being any evidence that the Onestà ever officially sanctioned prostitution in other areas of the city.[114] Two of these locations attained particular prominence. The large area north of the Chiasso de' Buoi, flanked by the new Medici palace and a row of nunneries, and

---

[111] On the reappraisal see Rossiaud, "Prostitution," 311 and Bullough, *History*, 126f. There is also a new rigor evident in Florentine synodal law; see R. Trexler, *Synodal Law in Florence and Fiesole, 1306–1518* (Vatican City, 1971), 123.

[112] This is the first substantive statement on prostitution in the whole Florentine historical tradition; *Istorie*, 21:253.

[113] See above, at n. 13.

[114] There was a spate of forced moves from the via della Scala in 1475 (*LC*, fols. 99r–100v), but otherwise little evidence that the Onestà acted to keep other areas of the city free of prostitutes. Only when more Deliberations of the Office are located will we know more about this question.

centered in the Streets of the Priests and of the Nut, is documented in 1442;[115] the Baldracca, near City Hall and behind the present Gallery of the Uffizi, first appeared in the *Book of Sentences* in 1462.[116] But many lesser centers emerged ever more frequently in the later years of the fifteenth century.[117]

Attracted in some cases by dancing schools run by the whores, the prostitutes' clientele entered these several small centers in search of pleasure, while from these nuclei the whores invaded the streets of the "good people."[118] The government did little to stop this activity, and the few signs of a backlash which appeared at the turn of the century stemmed from neighborhood, rather than communal, initiatives. A remarkable document of 1498, for example, shows that the parishioners of San Remigio had banded together to expel prostitutes from a wide area around the church, while a still more exceptional initiative of 1502 constrained a group of contracting landlords not to let their rooms to prostitutes within specified parishional and administrative sections of the city.[119] Thus in 1511 Cambi articulated a pressing popular concern to which the government had not yet responded. Yet that moment was not far off, for in the most forceful fashion, the preachers had now made the popular cry their own, as we learn from another source of March 1511:

---

[115] *LC,* fol. 2v (Gomito dell'Oro near Borgo La Noce). Other common references in this immediate area were the German baths (ibid., fol. 29r et seq.), the popular via Porciai off Borgo La Noce which by 1487 is called the *postribulum Porciai* (ibid., fol. 103r et seq., fol. 143r et seq.), Borgo Panicale (ibid., fol. 49v), Alle Marmeruche (ibid., fol. 101r et seq.), and via Nuova (ibid., fol. 86v et seq.). This latter was an ancient area of *malavita,* and in 1329 there had been talk of using a place in the parish of San Lorenzo but outside the city walls for a brothel (*ASF, Libri Fabarum,* 14, fol. 19r [27 July]).

[116] *LC,* fol. 56r et seq. In 1483 it was called the *lupanario Baldache* (ibid., fol. 113v).

[117] In 1487 the Chiasso San Jacopo (*LC,* fol. 143 et seq.), in 1500 the Canto dei Quattro Pagoni (ibid., fols. 192r–v), etc. For the matured geography of the cinquecento neighborhood brothels, see *ASF, Onestà,* 6, fols. 33v–34r (residence *bando* of 1547). The 1569 census of the prostitutes in these areas is in Galligo, *Circa ad alcuni antichi e singolari documenti inediti,* 13–20; see also P. Battara, *La popolazione di Firenze alla metà del '500* (Florence, 1935), 15–19.

[118] The dancing schools were condemned by Savonarola and then regulated in the early sixteenth century by the Eight of the Watch; see *ASF, Otto di Guardia,* 222, fol. 16r. In the early seventeenth century they were in the brothels, were auctioned to the highest bidder by the government, and were taxed (*ASF, Onestà,* 4, fols. 89r, 104v, 159v; 1, fols. 5r, 32r).

[119] "Poste in Firenze e nel gonfalone del Carro e nel popolo di San Piero Scheraggio o San Stefano di Firenze o nella via del Chiasso d'Oro, Baldracca, o de' Castellani," etc. (copied in the Carnesecchi Spoglio, *Partiti,* 24 July). The law of 1498 is in *ASF, Prov.* 189, fols. 100v–101v (18 November 1498). The only earlier regulatory documents of the quattrocento I could find were: (1) a law of 1454, at the time of Archbishop Antonino, forbidding prostitutes' residing within 300 yards of any nunnery (*ASF, Prov.* 145, fols. 2v–3r [10 April]), with a marginal note to a similar law of 1418/19 (cf. *ASF, Prov.,* 108, fol. 219r); (2) a decree of 14 March 1493/4 restricting the churchgoing of prostitutes, and the hours they could leave the brothels, and insisting that their heads and shoulders be covered when they did (Carnesecchi Spoglio, unnumbered).

The preachers shout every day from the pulpits: "Castigate the procuresses, whores, and sluts, for they are causing many of God's creatures to end badly!"[120]

We come now to a second popular preoccupation, the fate of Florence's own women. On 8 March 1511, the Eight of the Watch read a secret accusation which they had received. It spoke of one Caterina who in her house behind the cathedral chapter had for weeks

> kept a public brothel of servant girls and [of the] wives of poor artisans of your city. Further, she keeps destitute widows. Further, when one of their kind works for her, she wants a profit of a *grosso* from every servant girl. And further I report that the said servant girls do great harm to their patrons. Further, day and night the said Caterina runs every possible type of illegal gambling operation. And further, if you look into the matter you will find disreputable things of lechery and sodomy, depending on the money paid. And further, she hires daughters of poor persons and similar things.[121]

There is a structural reality underlying this document which transcends the historical moment, and points the way toward understanding prostitution in two epochs. In the crisis which had led to the creation of the Office of Decency in 1403, the talk was that men were not marrying, not that many women were unmarried. The fundamental issue then had been the absence of heirs, but now it was the lack of marriages. Population had in fact been depressed; now it was rising. In the early quattrocento relatively few Florentine fathers put their daughters in the nunneries, and neither politicos nor moralists talked much about the morality of servant girls.[122]

By 1511 much of that had changed. Beneath our document's unexceptional evidence of poor women supplementing their meager subsistence through prostitution, and beneath the contemporary economic and political difficulties which exacerbated their fate, lay the secular fact of an enormous population of unmarriageable females who, as Florentines well knew, were prime candidates for prostitution.[123] Widowed young women and their daughters living in the widows' asylum of Orbatello or in the neighborhoods;[124] the servant and slave women who filled the foundling homes with

---

[120] Carnesecchi Spoglio, *Tamburazioni*, 8 March 1510/11.

[121] Ibid. If the Eight punished Caterina, the anonymous denouncer promised, they would be praised by the preachers. On such servants, see C. Klapisch-Zuber, "Célibat et service féminins dans la Florence du XVe siècle," *Annales de Démographie Historique, 1981*, 289–302.

[122] On the population of the nunneries in the earlier period, Trexler, "Celibacy," in the present volume. The rise in population is graphed by Herlihy and Klapisch-Zuber, *Toscans*, 182f.

[123] On occasional prostitution in France, see Rossiaud, "Prostitution," 303f. On prostitution as the only alternative to monastization, see Trexler, "Celibacy."

[124] R. Trexler, "A Widow's Asylum of the Renaissance: The Orbatello of Florence," in the present volume.

their offspring;[125] the foundlings themselves, who on reaching puberty often left the homes without any stable domestic situation: all this unwanted womanhood was used by the male population of Florence as a source of cheap labor and sex.[126] Meanwhile, the politically powerful males of the city built monastic warehouses to "conserve" their daughters, protecting their family honor by locking their children in convents much as they preserved other men's honor by locking the latter's wives in the nunnery of the Convertite.[127]

The increase in population in the later fifteenth and early sixteenth centuries, and the institutions which the political class created to deal with it, seem in effect to have fostered a change in the nature, and explanation, of crisis. For now preachers declaimed as never before against what appeared a new evil—the corruption of resident Florentine women—and they blamed the malady on prostitutes, a group which at an earlier time had been positively valued for its contribution to urban population and morality. Cambi was sure he knew why thousands of girls 18 to 30 years old could not find a husband, and that reason was *not* sodomy. High dowries explained the crisis, he believed. Men were willing to marry, he said, but they would look only at girls with vast dowries. Despite their beauty and virtue, Cambi continued, girls with less substance were ignored, and in their despair they soon fell prey to the lure of prostitution.[128] In short, the city turned many of its own women into whores. Nuns or streetwalkers, *femine* of God or man, it came to the same thing. Women of the spirit or of the flesh were for sale to the winning bidder.[129]

It is not surprising that in these circumstances, madams such as Caterina took a leading role in the organization and administration of prostitution, and the *Book of Sentences* documents their emergence in the brothels proper. In 1483 women, rather than men, were the first accused of organizing gambling in the bordello.[130] The same year saw the first reference to a female pimp, and she was the mother of the girls for whom she procured.[131] When in 1484 the Onestà expanded beyond its strictly Florentine regulation and launched a sweeping attack on Pratese prostitution, the primary objects of

---

[125] Trexler, "Foundlings," 270f.

[126] The Carnival songs of Florence often refer to the girls' and women's plight; see C. Singleton, ed., *Canti Carnascialeschi del Rinascimento* (Bari, 1936), 29f., 56f.

[127] The anger of the girls was deep and widespread. Bernardino of Siena has a young nun say: "They put me here so I wouldn't have babies, but I'll do it to spite them" (Bernardino-Cannarozzi, 5:204f.).

[128] "E agiunto in vicinanza le meretricie, faceva, che ogni charne era chorrotta, se none in atto, almancho in mente" (Cambi, *Istorie*, 21:253) ("And approaching whoredom, it happened that all flesh was corrupt, if not in the act, at least in thought").

[129] Cambi on marriage negotiations: "E facievasi chom'è merchatare drappi, e lane" (ibid., 257) ("And they acted as they do while trading cloths and wool"). On the bargaining to get one's daughters into nunneries, see Trexler, "Célibat," 1339–42. Families and corporations also built nunneries specifically for their members.

[130] *LC*, fols. 114r, 165r, 166r–v.

[131] Ibid., fol. 115v. For a female *hospes* in the Baldracca, ibid., fols. 154v, 155v (1488).

their zeal were the women of the nearby town who were selling their daughters and "publicly exercising the trade of pimping."[132] In 1490, finally, enormous scandals rocked the nunneries of Florence, and some of them were branded by contemporaries as little more than brothels.[133]

Cambi and his contemporaries criticized the geography and economics of prostitution because it dragged good women down. That was their moral conviction. Yet at a deeper level they feared that prostitution raised women up, just as in earlier times men had condemned homosexuality but secretly feared that it excited an irresistible charm. The third criticism of prostitution in 1511 was, consequently, that it destroyed differences, for prostitutes looked the same as other women. One could not tell a prostitute from a "good woman":

> All these prostitutes wore long rose-colored gowns, and [each] went accompanied by a seemingly modest woman in widow's cloth, such that they conformed to the good women of the neighborhood, and were indistinguishable [from them].[134]

It was the phenomenon of grave and austere prostitutes in public, so lethal a challenge to the presumption that moral worth and high society were one, which proved too much for the government, and led to new legislation. After a century-long reluctance to regulate any part of the prostitutes' dress—as long as it was not masculine—, the Signoria of April 1511 instituted a new dress code for whores intended to make them distinguishable from moral women. Strict laws of residence were not long in coming, and a new era in the public attitude toward prostitution had begun.[135]

Beginning in 1403, the Officials of Decency had imported foreign prostitutes into the brothel to halt homosexual behavior among Florentine men: the gaudy harlots from abroad would represent the principle of "natural" sexuality to an audience of potential Florentine fathers. Our study has suggested that in fact, the majority of those who communed with the prostitutes subject to the Onestà may have been from the lower-middle and lower classes, and non-Florentines. If that in fact was the case, the reason is not far to seek: the

---

[132] Turning their homes into brothels, these women corrupted "even adolescents," the officials pointed out (ibid., fols. 116r, 119v, 120r). See the similar case of 1382 in Brucker, *Society*, 130. The emphasis in these later records on female entrepreneurs indicates at least a male concern with women's power, at most a de facto increase in their visibility.

[133] One such nunnery was S. Caterina in Cafaggio; see *Archivio Capitolare, Firenze*, parchments nos. 1028, 910, 360, 1066. The records of inquest are preserved in the *Archivio Vescovado, Fiesole*.

[134] Cambi, *Istorie*, 21:253.

[135] "La legge de' fazzoletti di colore," *ASF, Prov.* 201, fols. 14r–v. (11 April); fols. 23v–24r (28 April); ibid., 206, fols. 14r–18r (16 June 1527). These laws are copied in *ASF, Onestà*, 6, fols. 22r–v, 24v, along with a 1514 law against male and female sodomy (ibid., fol. 23r). Purchaseable exemptions from these new dress and residence laws and from submission to the Onestà resulted, however, in an institutional class division between rich and poor prostitutes, whatever the interest of the Convertite in having the rich whores and their estates under the authority of the Onestà.

foreign professionals simply found themselves outnumbered by the resident female population of slaves, servants, foundlings, and nuns, a desperate sorority of more local vintage.

Did the professionals discourage homosexual behavior, as the authorities hoped they would? That question is difficult to answer. Since we do not know how much homosexual activity there was in Florence, we have little way of knowing how responsible "sodomy" was for the low fertility rate of the early fifteenth century. Contemporaries certainly thought its impact was massive, and it was only in the midst of the population upswing of the later fifteenth century that Savonarola initiated a rethinking of the problem. Determined to devote a part of his social critique to prostitution, he was willing to challenge the notion that homosexual comportment was widespread. Florence's notoriety in that area, he told his massive audiences, "perhaps comes from your talking and chattering about the vice so much. For maybe there actually isn't as much of it as one says."[136]

In the early fifteenth century preachers and statesmen had deeply believed that no city could long endure in which females and males seemed the same, and each played the other. A century later, *Firenze meretrice* wondered if it could survive when class women could not be distinguished from brothel prostitutes. Which was to be the primal sign of an ordered society? Differences of gender ... or class?[137]

---

[136] Savonarola, *Prediche sopra Aggeo* (Rome, 1965), 219 (in the midst of a sermon demanding a law against homosexuals). For the Dominican's comments on prostitution, see *Prediche sopra Amos e Zaccaria*, 1:322f., 325f.; 2:71; 3:233.

[137] Brotherhood, like sisterhood, also provided a source of class ideology; see R. Trexler, "Charity and the Defense of Urban Elites in the Italian Communes," in F. Jaher, ed., *The Rich, the Well Born, and the Powerful* (Urbana, 1973), 103ff.

A Widows' Asylum
of the Renaissance:
The Orbatello of Florence[*]

OUR CONTEMPORARY ATTITUDES TOWARD THE ELDERLY ARE POTENT mixtures of historical myths and conventional classifications. In the good old days, we would like to believe, the organic or kin family took care of its own; historians know, on the contrary, that early modern European welfare institutions interned thousands upon thousands of disadvantaged persons including elderly parents. The asylum is a modern discovery, we are told, a product of heartless statism which is the inexorable enemy of kin affections;[1] this article will show that, in fact, communal asylums existed in Renaissance Florence whose intent and function was to maintain and augment nuclear families. And finally, if we have trouble thinking of the state as a benevolent father, we encounter no less difficulty in considering the elderly as sexual creatures. The story I tell demands, on the contrary, that we examine the care of elderly women as part of the history of women. Historical reveries, misconstrued concepts of the family, and an historically asexual image of the elderly in history, are the problems which the study of the widows' home of Orbatello addresses.

Built after 1370 by a merchant who envisioned some four or five dozen old women praying his soul into heaven in the lonely comfort of stately individual quarters, the great asylum of Orbatello passed at the turn of the century to the tutelage of the commune of Florence, which revised its function and population in the light of the total welfare needs of the city. What was that historical context? First, through its guilds and other agencies, the city government administered numerous hospitals and homes filled with dependents without

---

* This essay appeared previously in *Old Age in Preindustrial Society*, ed. P. Stearns (New York, 1982), 119–49.

[1] D. Rothman, *The Discovery of the Asylum* (Boston, 1971), examining nineteenth-century America.

functioning fathers. The commune called itself the "father" of these dependents, and, like any father, it aimed to marry off the younger part of that population when it came of age while providing long-term care in hospitals for single surviving elders.

The commune was a father not just to those in institutions, however, but also to its own servants or *familia*. As early as 1378 the Florentine government not only saw to its familiars' hospital bills, but through a type of retirement system kept its "sons" from begging and thus kept them in their nuclear families once they left communal service, so that, in the law's words, the fathers of government would not be ashamed and dishonored.[2] Thus both the rhetoric and the institutions of the time show a complex relationship between the kin family and the family of the commune, each informing the concept and actuality of the other, both supported by the union of male masters and servants we call patronal government.

All elders are not created equal; contextualizing Orbatello involves understanding the particular state of Florentine women which the commune addressed as it reshaped the asylum. First, Florentine marriage patterns insured that, on an average, older husbands died when their wives were still fairly young; in a society where wealth was controlled by men, this meant that caring for the elderly usually meant caring for women.[3] Next, these youngish widows, their ranks swollen by women "widowed" by runaway husbands, usually had children to care for, and the females among those were again the most enduring problem. Wealthy widows might profit from the special investment fund which the fourteenth-century commune, ever the father, had instituted to prevent widows' pauperization and thus their desertion of children; and the daughters of wealthy men might survive with honor in half a hundred urban nunneries.[4] That left the mass of poor widows and their daughters, the latter unable to enter nunneries and also difficult to marry, especially once they lost their "honor." It is this world of nunneries; of superfeminine found-

---

[2] *Archivio di Stato, Firenze* (hereafter *ASF*), *Provvisioni* 66, fols. 37r–38r (12 June 1378); 136, fols. 15r–v (22 April 1445). See further ibid., 119, fol. 268v (27 November 1428); 120, fol. 401r (1429); 121, fol. 168r (1431); 122, fol. 156v (1431); 125, fol. 193v (1434 Florentine style/1435 modern style); 143, fols. 250r–251v (30 October 1452); 153, fol. 160r (27 October 1462); 166, fol. 266r (1470); 185, fols. 37r–v (1495). Also *Statuta Populi et Communis Florentiae* (Fribourg, 1778), 2:352f.; G. Brucker, "The Ciompi Revolution," in N. Rubinstein, ed., *Florentine Studies* (London, 1968), 324 n. 2; B. Varchi, *Storia Fiorentina* (Florence, 1963), bk. 6, chap. 11. On the short-lived communal retirement system, see now G. Brucker, "Bureaucracy and Social Welfare in the Renaissance: A Florentine Case Study," *Journal of Modern History* 55 (1983): 1–21.

[3] The marriage pattern is studied in D. Herlihy and C. Klapisch-Zuber, *Les toscans et leurs familles* (Paris, 1978), 323f., 393–404, 488. See also C. de La Roncière, "Pauvres et pauvreté à Florence au XIVe siècle," in M. Mollat, ed., *Études sur l'histoire de la pauvreté (Moyen Age–16e siècle)*, (Paris, 1974), 666–69.

[4] R. Trexler, "Une Table Florentine d'Espérance de Vie," *Annales E.S.C.* 26 (1971): 138; *ASF, Prov.* 113, fol. 229v (13 December 1423). R. Trexler, "Le Célibat à la fin du Moyen Age: Les religieuses de Florence," *Annales E.S.C.* 27 (1972): 1329–50; a translation of this essay is included in the present volume as "Celibacy in the Renaissance: The Nuns of Florence."

ling homes whose girls, unable to find spouses, grew old among ever-new classes of "innocents"; of desperate mothers in the streets hoping to land a position as some man's servant, nurse, or lover; of the public brothels and "shops" which were often their ultimate recourse; and of young girls in families who cultivated their own desperation at ever marrying, that, taken as a whole, so forcefully argues for viewing the problem of the Florentine elderly as sororal.[5]

Orbatello would be used by the commune to attack one aspect of this immense problem in a highly creative fashion: it would be an asylum where widows and their children would live together. Different from the charities of neighboring Venice, where the care of widows generally remained a parishional obligation,[6] different also from the nunneries and beguinages of Europe, where religious persons and the occasional converted laywoman lived out their lives in community, and different as well from the monasteries and hospitals which provided occasional rental properties to the old,[7] the Orbatello of Florence was a secular establishment providing free housing for large numbers of older laywomen in common life. It may have been the only widows' asylum in Europe, yet Orbatello was more: this was a house whose matrons took in mother-led families, preserving these family segments and creating new solidarities.[8]

The stage is thus set for a dramatic confrontation of two types of paternalistic care of the poor, that which was intended to preserve family segments and that which sought to care, like a father, for those who had none. Our study is about a house for women run largely by the women themselves, and about how this institution faltered when its matrons were attacked by parentless children who defied mothering. The history of Orbatello through the sixteenth century is part of a crisis history of the Renaissance Florentine female.

---

[5] C. Klapisch-Zuber, "Célibat et service féminins dans la Florence du XVe siècle," *Annales de Démographie Historique 1981*, 289–302. See also R. Trexler, "The Foundlings of Florence, 1395–1455," *History of Childhood Quarterly* 1 (1973): 259–84, and my "La Prostitution Florentine au XVe siècle: Patronages et clientèles," *Annales E.S.C.* 36 (1981): 983–1015; a translation of the same is included in the present volume as "Florentine Prostitution in the Fifteenth Century: Patrons and Clients."

[6] B. Pullan, *Rich and Poor in Renaissance Venice* (Cambridge, Mass., 1971), 253, 425. R. Mueller, "Charitable Institutions, the Jewish Community, and Venetian Society," *Studi Veneziani* 14 (1972): 54, says many Venetian hospitals were reserved for widows; I could not verify this.

[7] See R. Trexler, "Une Table Florentine," 138, for monasteries with quarters for the elderly. A mid-fifteenth-century description of the male and female branches of the great hospital of S. Maria Nuova shows them providing such cottages: "E apresso a' detti spedali vi sono case molte belle nelle quali v'abitano donne vechie e huomini vechi" (*Codice Rustici, Seminario Maggiore, Firenze*, fol. 50v).

[8] N. Zemon Davis could find no cases of subsidized housing outside hospitals and beguinages except for the early-sixteenth-century Fuggerei (Augsburg) for elderly workers (*Society and Culture in Early Modern France* [Stanford, 1975], 281).

The Foundation

Located to this day in the northeast section of Florence in the parish of San Piero Maggiore and the ward of the Keys, Orbatello was founded by Niccolò di Jacopo degli Alberti, perhaps the richest man in Europe, familiar of princes and head of Florence's premier banking establishment. About two-thirds built between April 1370 and 24 September 1376, the date of his testament, Alberti's Orbatello was finished and filled by his son Antonio after the father's death on 7 August 1377, and before summer 1378, when a crowd of Ciompi in revolt attacked the place and its allegedly "whoring" inhabitants.[9] After Antonio Alberti's expulsion from the city in 1400, the commune turned the asylum over to the Parte Guelfa for administration, a position which that organization of Florence's finest families kept until the eighteenth century. We gain an idea of its cloistered state, complete with church, from an illumination done in the first half of the fifteenth century (Plate 1); of its total walled structure during the sixteenth century, focus of our study, from the Bonsignori city map of 1584 (Plate 2); of its internal design from an eighteenth-century plan of the Orbatello which preserves the founder's basic architecture (Plate 3). Alongside terrain where, as Niccolò had wanted, "the inhabitants can promenade and accomplish seemly exercise," were three rows of houses, the two nearest the church on a "lower street" whose single units were numbered 1 through 20 in the sixteenth century, the third on the "upper street" with units numbered 21 through 29, which was the last house in Orbatello at that time.[10]

For all the abstract coldness of the plan, examination of the separate apartments reveals units designed for intimate life experience. Each of these houses was divided between an upper and lower floor (hereafter *s* for superior and *i* for inferior), as a 1431 document explains, each apartment being partly divided by an internal wall.[11] Sixteenth-century documents make it clear that there was a *sala* or livingroom on the kitchen side of the partition (no. 4 on the plan), a *camera* or bedroom being on the other side (6).[12] The terminology indicates the domestic intention even if that was not always maintained in practice. Some of the houses also had a *palcuccio*, or loft, above the

---

[9] The testament is in L. Passerini, *Gli Alberti di Firenze*, 2 vols. (Florence, 1869), 2:156–85 (hereafter T). G. Richa's description of an Alberti testament is unreliable (see *Notizie istoriche delle chiese fiorentine* [Florence, 1754], 1:296). A document of 1425 shows the house was finished before the apartments were filled (*ASF, Parte Guelfa, numeri rossi* [hereafter *PGR*], 6, fols. 31v–33r [5 March]). The Ciompi reference is in *Diario d'Anonimo Fiorentino dall'anno 1358 al 1389*, in A. Gherardi, ed., *Cronache dei Secoli XIII e XIV* (Florence, 1876), 365.

[10] T, 161. For the street distinctions see *PGR*, 16, fols. 62r, 117r–154v. Houses 4–11, 13, 14, and 20 (*PGR*, 16, fol. 122v) are on the prior or lower street in the 1540s. "No. 29 supra, videlicet in ultima domo" (*PGR*, 13, fol. 63v). Houses 23–25 and a later house 30 are on the upper street in the 1540s. Records of assignments to designated houses start in 1511.

[11] *PGR*, 27, fol. 14r ("Beni della Parte, 1431").

[12] E.g., *PGR*, 16, fol. 123r (15 May 1549).

Plate 1. Codice Rustici, Seminario Maggiore, Florence.

second floor where a single person lived, but we do not know how intimate the relations between that person and those on the second floor had to be.[13] The staircases shown on the plan, however, indicate that the residents of the ground and second floors could live apart from each other.

The Parte Guelfa and Orbatello

For most of the first century of its stewardship, the only surviving Parte records regarding Orbatello are legislative rather than deliberative in nature, dealing with general objectives and guidelines rather than with the day-to-day

---

[13] The documents are sparing of information on actual living arrangements. Note this description of 15 November 1550: "Tutte le habitante in dete case, che sono a numero xxviiii. Et in ciascheduna habita almancho 2 famigle: una in terreno et l'altra in palcho. Et alchuna casetta in è che ha el palchuccio dove habita una persona sola" (*PG, numeri neri* [hereafter *PGN*], 698, no. 13). There is one hint of more than one loft per house, a document speaking of the "primo palcuccio di sopra" of 21-s (*PGR*, 14, fols. 12v–13r).

Plate 2. Nova pulcherrimae civitatis Florentiae Topographia (detail).
[The cathedral is at the center; Orbatello is the right hand block at the top.]

administration of the asylum. Precise administrative records begin in 1511, and they continue with that precision until around 1550. What the legislative records of the fifteenth century do tell us in no uncertain terms is that the

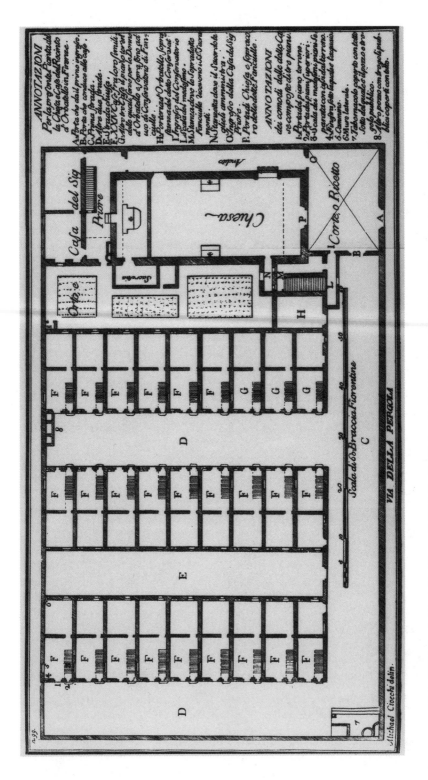

Plate 3. Michael Ciocchi, Plan of 1754. In G. Richa, *Notizie Storiche delle Chiese Fiorentine* I (Florence, 1754), at p. 298.

Parte corruptly used the Alberti funds to finance its own affairs instead of Orbatello's.[14] They tell us that the Parte had not established the lay administration which the founder had mandated, but had instead thrust upon the church rector all the day-to-day financial and social responsibilities.[15] Finally, these legislative records give us our first detailed idea of the composition of the house, both ideally and in reality.

A 1461 Parte declamation comes to the point:

> While it is clear from the words of the testator and from his houses that they were intended for persons of good social status who by some bad fortune have become Shamed Poor, [they have been taken by] a truly brutish bunch who are unsuited [to them].[16]

The Parte captains who described this situation in 1461 pointed directly at the types of "brutes" they did not want in Orbatello. "Slave women, who whenever they enter disquiet and perturb the whole house, [and] Corsican women ... usually have different customs, and this [variety] is not suitable in such a pious place."[17] These legal and geographical disqualifications for entry stayed in force through the remainder of the period, taking on a racial taint in 1520 when the captains spelled out the colors they did not want there.[18] In 1509, meanwhile, the Parte introduced a fiscal qualification which it could never enforce: from then on, it said, only those persons could enter whose ancestors had been subject to taxes in the city for at least 25 years.[19]

The captains of 1461 also addressed another axis of population control, the matter of males. "The places are badly distributed, and in one and the same house men and women are mixed together," they complained. The solutions were two, the first of which was already on the books, and simply needed enforcement: no male relative (usually a son, grandson, or nephew) twelve years of age or over could live with his kin in Orbatello. The second was apparently new: no unrelated men and women could reside together in

---

[14] E.g., *PGR*, 4, fols. 47v–48v (Parte statutes of 1420); 6, fols. 31v–33r (5 March 1424/25); 7, fol. 50r (14 July 1447); 9, fol. 57v (14 January 1459/60); 9, fols. 36r, 61v–62r, 66v, 76v (1461, 1509).

[15] T, 158, 163ff. "Sacristam et rectorem et gubernatorem dicte ecclesie et habitantium" ("Sacristan and rector and governor of the said church and its inhabitants"), the priest was required to prepare inventories "de bonis ecclesie et domibus eiusdem" (*PGR*, 11, fol. 193r [13 February 1514]).

[16] "Il quale chiaramente et per le parole del testatore et per le habitationi d'esso più ornato et meglio aconcie, che a quella tanto bruta gente non si conviene, s'intende essere suto facto per persone di buona conditione, per alcuna mala fortuna divenuti vergognosi miserabili" (*PGR*, 9, fol. 61v [19 March 1460/61]). On the difference between "the poor" and the "miserable poor," and on the legal status of the *vergognosi*, see de La Roncière, "Pauvres," 685–704. See also R. Trexler, "Charity and the Defense of Urban Elites in the Italian Communes," in F. Jaher, ed., *The Rich, the Well Born, and the Powerful* (Urbana, 1973), 67–74.

[17] *PGR*, fol. 61v (19 March 1460/61).

[18] On "ghesse o bigie" or "nere" see *PGR*, 12, fols. 232r, 234v (January).

[19] Vs. persons "di diverse sangue et costumi et forestieri" (*PGR*, 9, fol. 36v [17 January]).

the house.[20] While both rules had significant moral intentions, the former is important from a demographic point of view as well, for it established the classical model of young males' movement out of Orbatello: from no later than 1461, the Parte had an established policy of expelling boys once they reached twelve years of age.

No such policy pertained to adolescent girls. Indeed the "girls of Orbatello," as nubile females were soon called as a group, were expected to remain there until they married, at which time they would be helped by a dowry subvention from the Parte. In 1504 a new ordinance required that these girls live in Orbatello for five continuous years before claiming that dowry.[21] Such was the general administrative policy toward young girls.

The *mulieres Orbatelli*, finally, were presumably in Orbatello for life: the Parte offered no aid for widows to remarry, and none seems to have done so. The chastity of these women was assumed, whatever the reality. Boys would leave before they seduced girls or women, but girls would stay, the Parte regulations seem to assume, to be schooled in abstinence even while the matrons prepared them for marriage. Ideally, the house was without sexual activity.

The Population of Orbatello

On certain feast days during the year, the Parte Guelfa provided a stipend of seven shillings for each "soul" in Orbatello. The total of the alms given on any such feastday, combined with two official Florentine censuses, tell us how many people lived in Orbatello during the first two-thirds of the sixteenth century:

Table 1
General Population[22]

1511	1512	1513	1518	1519	1520	1521	1522	1552	1562
203	195	193	221	254	248	221	259	154	178

Alone among our documents, the census of 1552 gives us a precise idea of the distribution of the inhabitants among the residences, and tells us who these souls were. There were thirty houses in that year, the newest one having

---

[20] *PGR*, 9, fol. 61v (19 March); further *PGR*, 12, fol. 3r (5 March 1517/18); 13, fol. 13v.

[21] This was to prevent fraud; *PGR*, 9, fol. 30v (2 February); further 13, fols. 211v, 213v, 230r, 233r (1520–22), for the "girls of Orbatello."

[22] The payments were made per "persona sive anima" on the following feastdays: Annunciation, Easter, All Saints, and Christmas. They were gathered from *PGR*, 11–13. The census figures of 1552 and 1562 are respectively in *ASF, Miscellanea Medicea*, 223, fols. 151v–153v (hereafter C), and ibid., 224, fol. 119r. All these figures exclude the priest.

appeared in the Parte records for the first time in 1549; and the census taker occasionally distinguished between those living on the first and second floors: an average of 2.6 persons lived on each floor and 5.1 persons in each house.[23] The total population of 1552 was, however, unrepresentatively small, and the more representative largest population figure of 259 in 1522, distributed among twenty-nine houses, yields an average of 8.9 souls in each house and 4.5 on each floor.

The census taker distinguished between children and adults in Orbatello in 1552 by naming the latter but only counting the former. Thus the 11 males among the 154 residents were not named, they obviously being those boys less than twelve years of age who were permitted to live there.[24] This omission of name allows us by a process of elimination to determine the young female component of the house as well. Our counter named the heads of all 30 hearths plus 66 other women, 62 percent of the residents in all. These 96 women were further identified as follows: 86 were called "mone" or adult women ("domne" or "donna" in the Latin sources); two others had the prefix "la" before their name, indicating nubile unmarried women; there was one "suora," (an elderly *pinzochera* leading a saintly life); one woman living with the priest; and six women with no title or designation. The 47 unnamed females were evidently dependents of those who were named, both of the 30 heads of hearths and of the other named women living with them. The preponderance of unnamed girls over unnamed boys (47 compared to only 11) is explained by boys twelve years of age or over having to leave Orbatello. We may therefore, positing a comparable age profile, suggest that of the girls, some 36 were that age or older, only 11 being cohorts of the same number of boys. Finally we should point out that 58 children living with 96 women has its own significance: that meant that there was only one child per floor, and only 0.6 children for every mature woman in the house. This was a predominantly older population of women.

How old? Before pursuing that question, let us recall that to be "old" in traditional European society meant to be over 40 years of age, a literary convention quite in keeping with actual life expectancy. Further, we must recall that bearing children was hazardous in this age, so that whatever ages we find among this population will be significant partly in relation to their generational passivity or activity.[25] That having been said, we must admit that none of our sources gives us any exact means for determining the age of the women of Orbatello. The 68 years of the mona Piera we meet in the 1427 *Catasto*, the

---

[23] The pollster divided the first and second floors of houses 22 and 24 by a line. For no. 30, see *PGR*, 16, fol. 140v.

[24] No males other than the priest were named in the census, perhaps indicating that no other male adults lived there. Note that in the 1562 census, there were 174 females but only 4 males excluding the priest.

[25] On aging in Florentine society, see D. Herlihy, "Growing Old in the Quattrocento," in Stearns, *Old Age*, 104–18. Also C. Gilbert, "When Did a Man in the Renaissance Grow Old?" *Studies in the Renaissance* 14 (1967): 7–32; K. McKenzie, "Antonio Pucci on Old Age," *Speculum* 15 (1940): 160–85.

one sexagenarian who gave her age when she matriculated, and the 35 and 40 years of two women involved in a sex scandal in 1559 are suggestive of the age range, but scarcely of any calculable value.[26] To get a clearer idea of the age profile, we must proceed in other fashions. The stated ages of the children entering Orbatello will help, as will a study of the longevity of particular women in Orbatello.

Since the boys of Orbatello had to leave on their twelfth birthday, the average age of 6.7 years for 15 such boys is less significant than that of the girls, who constituted 77 percent of the 1552 young population in any case. Nineteen girls who entered Orbatello with their mothers between 1511 and 1530 averaged 9.6 years when they entered, while in the same 20 year period, 21 other young females giving their age who were not accompanied by their mothers had a similar average age of 10 years.

These ages, taken from the licenses to enter Orbatello conceded by the Parte during that time, permit us to make a rough calculation of the ages of the mothers who accompanied many of the children once we recall the peculiar Florentine marriage pattern. At the end of the fifteenth century, women with an average age of 21 years married men who were much older; in 1427 that age gap was 18 years for women of the social condition we shall find in Orbatello![27] This meant that women were widowed at a relatively early age. Take a typical woman entering Orbatello: she would have borne her first child at age 22 and, assuming that she had one child each year and entered Orbatello promptly after being widowed, she would have been approximately 42 years of age when she entered with her average 10-year-old. We may go one step further, hypothesizing an average age of 47 for those many mothers whose daughters were dowered by the Parte after the family had been there for five years.[28] Thus there were certainly some premenopausal women in Orbatello, even if I could find no case of a woman marrying after entering there as an adult. But among the 157 donne we can identify in the records between 1511 and 1530, the 39 whose children lived with them quickly passed that landmark. Almost all the other donne, we shall find, were older than these mothers.

Let us first concentrate on the women called "donne." We noticed that in the census of 1552 such women made up almost all those whose names were given, and the same is true for the females mentioned in the Parte records from 1511 to 1530: once the children are eliminated, almost all the other females, 157 in all, were called "donna," and they were mostly laywomen who had been or still were married. This was the case not only with the 43 among them who were identified as widows, but with most of those donne whose

---

[26] The 60-year-old was donna Mea, widow of Domenico of Sesto (*PGR*, 11, fol. 93r). The 1559 case is in *PGN*, 707, no. 104 (11 March).

[27] A Molho and J. Kirshner, "The Dowry Fund and the Marriage Market in Early Quattrocento Florence," *Journal of Modern History* 50 (1978): 433; Herlihy and Klapisch-Zuber, *Toscans*, 207; Klapisch-Zuber, "Célibat," n. 21.

[28] This would apply only after 1504, of course, when that requirement was introduced.

proper name is followed in the records by the Latin genitive of a male name, such as "domna Maria Bartholomei." When we can identify this male through another source, he almost invariably turns out to be the husband of the woman, and not her father.[29] The fact that females without the appellation "donna" before their names regularly follow their Christian names with the term "the daughter of," whereas donne do so only when they also say that they are "a one-time wife and now widow," is significant; the donnas had almost all been married.

We may quickly add: "and mostly widowed." To be certain, donna Lodovica of Ferrara's Savonese husband had fled her and their 10-year-old daughter Maddalena, but he was not dead; donna Lucrezia, with her 14-year-old daughter Francesca and 7-year-old son Giovanmaria, "[did] not live with her husband," but she evidently had one.[30] Nineteen donne among the 39 living in Orbatello with their children between 1511 and 1530 were not named as widows, and there were definitely some wives among them. But 2 of these 19 had children with them who were themselves called "donne," and one of the latter was herself called a widow.[31] It is altogether probable that this widow's mother, like most of the donnas whose genitive male we can identify, was also a widow. It is in this period, in fact, that Orbatello was first identified as a place where "poor widows without a house [were] received."[32]

From the death books which have survived from the contemporary Florentine nunnery of San Niccolò, I have elsewhere calculated that its celibate population—comparable to the women of Orbatello who, as we see, had survived the childbearing years—had a life-expectancy of 42 years.[33] Orbatello was in every respect, therefore, an old women's home; but, like the nunnery, a certain proportion of its population had not only defied the odds of general life expectancy, but had even gone beyond the life-expectancy of about 60 years for those who reached menopause.[34] These women were the matrons of Orbatello, their very longevity claiming our attention even as it gave them authority among their colleagues. Let us look at two biographies.

Twice-widowed donna Antonia was the longest resident of Orbatello we know of. Antonia entered the house in 1513 with her three children: Silvestra

---

[29] "Domna Juliana Tomasii Bartolomei de Businis" (*PGR*, 13, fol. 184r) is actually "domna Juliana vidua uxor olim Tomasii Bartolomei Businis" (*PGR*, 12, fols. 217r–v). "Domna Agnioletta Antonii gualchieroni" (*PGR*, 13, fol. 159r) is really "domna Angioleta vidua uxor olim Antonii gualcherarii" (ibid., fol. 63v). "Domna Magdelena Pieri Muchini" (*PGR*, 11, fol. 176v) is "domna Magdelena vidua uxor Pieri Muchini" (*PGR*, 13, fol. 186v). Several other cases of this type emerge from a comparison of C to *PGR*, 16.

[30] Respectively *PGR*, 11, fols. 23r, 155v.

[31] Donna Angela is the mother of "domna Margherita vidua uxor olim Rafaelis battilani" (*PGR*, 12, fol. 71v).

[32] "Illud vero, quod Orbatellus nuncupatur, in quo pauperculae viduae domo carentes recipiuntur" (Mariano Ughi [fl. 1518], cited in Richa, *Notizie*, 1:297).

[33] Trexler, "Célibat," 1344.

[34] D. Herlihy calculated a life-expectancy of 15.5 years for a 45-year-old Pistoian woman in early fifteenth century; see *Medieval and Renaissance Pistoia* (New Haven, 1967), 287.

(age 12), Goro (13), and Lisabetta (8 months old). It was Antonia's mother-in-law, donna Cucca, who accepted the four into apartment 13-i, and as a part of the same transaction, Cucca also took in her own daughter Maddalena with the latter's sons, Geri (7) and Domenico (5).[35] Antonia must have lived at Orbatello throughout the 1520s, for in 1530 she returned to Orbatello's apartment 7-s with one Pasquino, probably her grandson, from the hospital of the porters of Florence, where all the women had lived during the siege of Florence while Orbatello was garrisoned with troops.[36] Those 17 years since her matriculation would prove less than half her total stay at Orbatello, however. For in 1549 Antonia was still living in apartment 7, now with an unmarried girl who may have been caring for the matriarch in her old age.[37] The following year the Parte captains inspecting Orbatello queried "four old widows of commodious presence" on the state of the house, and few women could have given the perspective which Antonia must have afforded, for in 1549 she had been in Orbatello for 36 years.[38] Recalling that she had been twice widowed when she first entered Orbatello, we may be sure that this matron had now passed her seventieth birthday. She probably died by 1552. In the census of that year, someone else was living upstairs in apartment 7.

Then consider the rich history of Maddalena the widow of Piero di Meo Muchini of Novoli in the Mugello north of Florence, the youngest of the long-term residents I can trace. She must have entered Orbatello before 1510, so as to justify the Parte's dowry paid her daughter Maria in 1515.[39] In 1513 Maddalena accepted as her companion an apparently unrelated 18-year-old girl from Strada south of Florence, and that girl's presence may explain why in 1519 the Parte was so insistent that Maddalena's over-age son leave her apartment and Orbatello instantly.[40] In the meantime Maddalena had married off another daughter, Lucrezia, with the Parte's help (1517), and she must subsequently have bowed to the threat of expulsion and sent her son packing, for Maddalena was living in apartment 17-i with another woman in

---

[35] *PGR*, 11, fol. 155v. Silvestra married with the help of the Parte in 1518 (*PGR*, 12, fol. 195v).

[36] *PGR*, 14, fols. 12v–13r. Silvestra's husband was Bartolomeo di Pasquino; their son could have been our Pasquino. On the Orbatello full of troops, and the "hospitali portitorum situato in via S. Galli, in quo hospitali ad presentem habitent mulieres solite habitare in domibus Orbatelli," see ibid., fol. 3r (23 March 1529/30).

[37] *PGR*, 16, fol. 142r.

[38] "A maggior parte vi sono entrate col partito, et sono vedove povere co lloro figliuole et nipote et qualche nipote maschio minori d'anni 12, et di assai honesta aria. Et vi è infra l'altre quatro vedove vecchie et di commoda presenza. Le quale, chiamate in disparte et dimandate dei costumi e i portamenti delle altre . . ."; *PGN*, 698, no. 13 (15 November 1550) ("The majority entered as the result of a vote. They are poor widows with their daughters and nieces and an occasional nephew below 12 years of age. [The widows] have a decent enough air about them. Among them there are four elderly widows of suitable presence who, taken aside and asked about the customs and behavior of the others . . .").

[39] *ASF, notarile antecosiminiano*, Leoni 140 (1500–1517) fol. 142v. (hereafter Leoni).

[40] *PGR*, 11, fol. 176v; ibid., 12, fol. 112r.

1522, about 12 years after she had entered.[41] Maddalena must have been well beyond 50 years of age. These biographies indicate therefore that a substantial number of elderly women lived in Orbatello a good part of their adult lives, and—a point to which we shall return—that many of them lived in the same apartment for years on end.

Where had these women come from? They were not, first of all, mostly natives, as the Parte regulation of 1509 wished to make them, but to a significant extent came from outside Florence. If we examine the provenance of the dead husbands or rare fathers of the 58 donne among the 157 mentioned in Parte records from 1511 to 1530 who listed that information, we find that only four said they came from the city. Three others were from distant places outside the dominion of Florence, two from Naples and one from Bruges. The remaining 51 women (that is, their husbands or fathers) came from the dominion. A majority of them came not from the nearby *contado* but from the more distant *distretto*, with no noticeable locative concentration. The attention recent authors have drawn to such dominion women, often "bathed ... with tears ... , coming toward the city with their tiny children, some hanging from their necks, some carried in their arms," springs to mind.[42] At least one-third of the donne of Orbatello came from the countryside.

A completely distinct source confirms this finding, and suggests that a majority of these outsiders came more or less directly to the Orbatello rather than entering after a lengthy sojourn in the city. From 1500 to 1517, the Parte notary Bartolomeo Leoni recorded in one of his registers 74 marriages which had been partially dowered by his masters.[43] Twenty of the girls' fathers, who were all deceased, were identified by their origins, and all were originally from the dominion rather than from Florence, again indicating that a minimum of 27 percent of the girls were not Florentines. It is when we turn to the new husbands of these same girls, however, that we begin to suspect that several of the latter had come directly to Orbatello from outside of Florence. Twenty-four of the husbands, about one-third of them, were themselves identified as coming from outside the city. Only 5 of this group of 24 were also said to *live* in the city, their parish of residence being given, and 3 of these 5 were identified as natives of distant Lyon, Genoa, and Bologna. Only 2 husbands from the Florentine dominion were said to also live in the city, therefore; and thus only they were possibly of the type who in Florentine records listed their native area but had actually lived in the city for some time. We may look at the matter from another angle: of the 19 husbands from outside the city for whom no Florentine residence is given, all but one had origins in the dominion. Since the scribe otherwise scrupulously included the parish of residence in the city, there can be no doubt that practically none of the husbands from that dominion had a Florentine residence; they came to Orbatello

---

[41] Leoni, fol. 147v; *PGR*, 13, fol. 168v.

[42] See nos. 3, 5. The quote is from Giovanni Cavalcanti's description of events in 1440; cited in my "Foundlings," 266.

[43] Leoni. Samuel Cohn was kind enough to bring this volume to my attention.

from their homelands, married one of the "girls of Orbatello," and returned home.

Why then were there so many grooms from the countryside, almost all making such quick trips to the city? One simple, arguable, but perhaps less probable explanation would be that the £50 dowry assistance normally provided by the Parte to its girls made these girls attractive. The more probable explanation runs like this: many of these dominion girls had come almost directly to Orbatello from their homelands. Under the supervision of their elders, they had preserved their "pudica honesta" in Orbatello as they would have had trouble doing if they or their mothers had worked in the city as domestics. They were thus in a moral and financial position after five years to contract an honorable marriage, occasionally, be it noted, with the boy back home.[44] Whatever may be the truth of the matter, we have discovered one further element about the asylum of Orbatello: girls not only came to it from the countryside, but left it to return to the countryside from Florence. The Orbatello favored a counter-migration from the city to the countryside.

A final vital statistic about the *miserabili vergognosi* of Orbatello is their social condition of occupation and wealth. First, the occupations of 79 distinct fathers or prematriculation husbands were compiled from the dowry records of 1500 to 1517, and from the Parte deliberations of 1511 to 1530. In Table 2 I add for future reference the occupations of the husbands of the girls who married after their mandatory residence in Orbatello.

Two points seem worth making about these occupations. First, only five in the lot of seventy-nine were farm laborers; the women did not come from a peasant background. Second, the Florentine industrial occupations were as important as the land was insignificant: one in five of these men had labored in Florence or its immediate environs as a salaried woolworker, while one in nine had been in the economically superior position of dyer or weaver in the wool or silk industry.

We have in Orbatello, then, a population roughly one-third of which came from the dominion of Florence, another third whose husbands or fathers had been part of Florence's industrial labor force, and a final third whose husbands and fathers had been artisans not involved in the wool and silk industries. Not surprisingly, the daughters and wives of the Florentine elite of merchant-industrialists rarely landed in Orbatello;[45] and there is almost no indication of eventual occupations of the women themselves.

---

[44] For a girl's father and her new husband both from the Mugello: Leoni, fol. 41v; from S. Maria Contigiono: ibid., fol. 101r; from the Casentino: ibid., fol. 120v. The *pudica honestas* (*PGR*, 9, fol. 30v [2 February 1503/04]) possible at Orbatello may be compared to the many girls of the Innocenti sprung from mothers who were domestics; see Trexler, "Foundlings," 270f.

[45] Single individuals of the following families were encountered: Biscioni, Busini, Cardini, Gerini, Gori, Migliori, Redditi, Ricciardi, and Schiatti. There were two Medici women and two Alberti, for whom see below.

Table 2
Occupations of Fathers and Husbands of the Women of Orbatello

	Merchant Industrialists	Weavers	Dyers	Wool Workers[46]	Chiselers	Masons	Metal Workers	Leather Workers
Pre-Orbatello	2	6	3	16	3	4	4	3
New Husbands	4	13	2	16	0	1	5	0

	Shoe and Hatmakers	Eyeglass Makers	Wood Workers	Spicers	Butchers	Bakers	Poulterers	Used-Clothes Peddlers
Pre-Orbatello	11	3	4	2	1	2	0	2
New Husbands	4	1	1	1	0	2	1	0

	Hostelry	Millers	Agricultural Workers	Barbers	Writers	Painters	Tax Collectors
Pre-Orbatello	0	4	5	1	1	1	1
New Husbands	2	2	6	1	0	0	0

[46] Included are battilani, pettinatori, purgatori, and schardassieri.

A vital question of social origins is that of wealth, and another source of information leaves no doubt that the women did not come from the penniless, destitute population so often encountered among domestics. We know the total makeup of thirty-seven of the dowries which the notary Leoni recorded between 1500 and 1517, and they turn out on inspection to be small but not unusual for girls with fathers in the range of occupations we have documented.[47] They ranged first of all from 15 1/2 to 52 1/2 florins (£64 to £215); but the more significant figure is the contribution the girl herself ("or rather her mother," one document clarifies) made to the dowry.[48] While not one girl seems to have drawn her part from the commune's dowry investment fund, a sure indication of these girls' relative poverty, the average girl's contribution to her dowry, including money and goods, was a respectable 18 florins, £3 (£4, s.2 per florin):

Table 3
Dowries of the Girls of Orbatello, 1500–1517, in £

Average Dowry	Parte Contribution	All Others' Contributions	Daughters' Contributions	Third Parties' Contributions[49]
134, s. 8	50, s. 4 (37.4%)	84, s. 4 (62.6%)	76, s. 16 (57.1%)	7, s. 10 (5.5%)

The thirty-seven dowries averaged in this table include all those dowries which can safely be designated "total," and every one of them includes some contribution by the girl; I could find no certain case of a girl whose total dowry was constituted by the Parte.[50] The girls of Orbatello therefore usually had mothers or relatives who made a significant contribution toward their marriage. This was a population which might be miserable, but was not destitute.

Making Orbatello Work

The Orbatellan administrative records of the first half of the sixteenth century leave the reader with two strong impressions. The first is that there was no

---

[47] See Molho and Kirshner, "Dowry Fund," 418, for comparisons. Herlihy and Klapisch-Zuber characterize households with a taxable estate of from 10 to 100 florins as "de fortunes médiocres" (*Toscans,* 287).

[48] Leoni, fol. 105r. In the following I use a conversion rate of £4, shillings 2 per florin, that used in the midst of the period 1500–1517 by the Parte authorities.

[49] The third parties contributing in 8 cases were the Buonomini di San Martino who catered to the *poveri vergognosi* (3X), the confraternity of the wool weavers (1X), the hospital of S. Maria Nuova (1X), and three private individuals.

[50] There are four cases where the wording would indicate a whole dowry, but they had to be eliminated because of the notary's evolving terminology, which made these cases more probably *pro parte dotis* than *pro dote.*

civil war in the house: not one recorded conflict or case of violence of the type so common in the Florentine nunneries! Second, mobility within Orbatello was remarkably limited. Only 22 of the 157 donnas named in the comprehensive Parte records from 1511 to 1530 showed up in two different apartments, and none lived in more than two. Since few donnas seem to have vacated Orbatello willingly and not many more unwillingly, it seems safe to estimate that five of six donnas stayed in one place until they died. The picture is no different for children, who almost never moved from one apartment to another without their relatives; 5 of the 22 women who moved took children with them, comparable to that proportion of the donne in the home with children. There can be little doubt that with all its vicissitudes, Orbatello worked, and the question is, why.

Despite itself, the Parte is part of any answer. It placed a pillory in the courtyard "to give example ... [and] spectacle to all the ... women," and a priest in the rectory who was charged among other things with "holding the women in peace and restraining them from perpetrating bad behavior or violence either inside or outside."[51] Rules and punishment were the more likely to be heeded because the Parte captains were replaced every six months. With their own civic clientele to please, each new set of officials had good reason to "empty and disencumber" apartments so they could then exercise their pro rata right to refill them.[52] Yet a countervailing consideration worked in the women's interest. Orbatello existed to intern dependent families, and expelling them only created more public beggars, to the dishonor of the Parte. So this organization compromised with its own strict rules, and in effect allowed the women to run their asylum on a day-to-day basis. It was the matrons who governed Orbatello by manipulation of the rules.

The force of their leadership can be surmised first of all in the repeated practice of staggered matriculations, by which an individual moved in, only later to be officially followed by her child or sister or other hearth member.[53] Yet it is improbable that these later matriculants had actually been abandoned for a time by their mothers or sisters; but rather it seems that they entered surreptitiously, with the connivance of the elders, to then obtain official admission when the census allowed. Whatever the truth of this matter, such staggered admissions had the evident effect of maintaining a coherent and limited group of kin networks in the asylum. If a woman wanting to matriculate into Orbatello would do a Parte official a favor by accepting as her charge an unattached girl whose relations that official had to please, that same woman once established in the house became part of a decision-making

---

[51] *PGN*, 707, no. 104 (11 March 1558/59); 795, fol. 34r (27 March 1625).

[52] *PGR*, 13, fol. 197v. Cases *pro computo* are in *PGR*, 11, fol. 92v (13 October 1512); fol. 143v (27 May 1513); 14, fols. 12v–13r (19 August 1530).

[53] Thus the widow donna Costanzia entered 11 October 1519, her 12-year-old daughter Candida joined her 19 July 1520 (*PGR*, 12, fol. 177v; 13, fol. 37v). Donna Diamante, who on 17 August 1521 moved into 25-s with her daughter Andrea (*PGR*, 13, fol. 139v), took in her daughter Caterina on 15 April 1522 with the approval of the Parte (ibid., fol. 191r). A case of sisters is in *PGR*, 14, fols. 12v–13r.

corps who actually approved changes in Orbatello's living arrangements. Living *familiariter* in Orbatello, we find, entailed moving in with the consent of the person already inhabiting an apartment: both had to "be content" with the arrangement.[54] Women "offered" to welcome newcomers to their quarters; and in the case of one girl named Felicia, we even catch a glimpse of the *mulieres Orbatelli* described as a decision-making corporation.[55]

In 1549 the Parte discovered Felicia living in the house without license, and apparently moved to expel her. Yet it soon reconsidered; for the captains found, in their suggestive language, that Felicia had been "received by the *mulieres* of the said place" six years or more earlier.[56] These women, the Parte formulation continues, had themselves decided that the girl was "poor and seemly," and the Parte thus decided to go along with the corporate judgement to keep her. They justified their action in now giving Felicia six years' tenure in Orbatello (and thus the right to dowry aid) by noting that the girl presently lived with the widow Antonia, who, "led by mercy," had "received" her into her apartment, and who now "offered" to "retain" her in the future. The matter was settled. Over the course of six years the *mulieres Orbatelli* had individually and apparently corporately conspired to conceal Felicia's presence from the visiting captains and perhaps even from the priest. That deception did not deter the Parte from accepting their opinion and bowing to their solidarity.

The matrons of Orbatello seem to have been quite as resourceful in manipulating the moral guidelines of the asylum, aided by an often weak and indecisive Parte. Time and again that organization decreed the expulsion of women "to preserve seemliness in their houses of Orbatello," and just as regularly "drunkards and troublemakers" of every kind still lived in their apartments months and even years later.[57] No norm was more timeworn than the prohibition against foreign women and slaves, yet the Parte not uncommonly revoked or deferred its enforcement; for it was clear that some of these women were acceptable to the matrons and, indeed, that they sometimes functioned as stabilizing forces in Orbatello.[58] In March 1512, for example, the dark-skinned donna Caterina, the slave donna Apollonia, and donna Lucia daughter of Bernardina of Barbary received expulsion notices

---

[54] "Et hoc comune, que sint contente" (*PGR*, 11, fol. 76v). On "familial life," see *PGR*, 15, fol. 78v. The deal with the Parte is in *PGR*, 16, fol. 140v (6 November 1549). "Custody" of a girl by her grandmother is at *PGR*, 16, fol. 123r.

[55] For "offering," see the deal above and Felicia below.

[56] "Et quod ipsa est pauper et honesta, propter que fuit recepta a mulieribus dicti loci. Et quod hodie degit et habitat una cum domna Antonia vidua . . . , et que domna, misericordia ducta, ipsam recepit in eius habitatione, et obtulit se fuisse et esse paratam ipsam retinere etiam in futurum" (*PGR*, 16, fol. 117r [27 March 1549]) ("She is poor and decent, and because of this she has been taken in by the women of the said place. And today she lives with lady Antonia widow . . . , the which lady, led by mercy, took her into her habitation, and vouched she was and is also ready to keep her in the future").

[57] See *inter alia PGR*, 11, fols. 113r, 139r, 153r, 163r, 171r–v, 222r; 12, fol. 76r; 16, fol. 152v.

[58] One case of revocation is in *PGR*, 12, fol. 234v (18 January 1519/20).

because of their origins and conditions. Yet a year and a half later donna Lucia was not only still living in her accustomed apartment; the Parte actually assigned her the custody of the *contado* girl Camilla—in other words, made her responsible for the girl's upbringing. The Parte's, and surely the other matrons' confidence in Lucia was well placed. In 1521 they had the pleasure of seeing Camilla led into matrimony.[59]

The women seem to have been quite as unruffled by the occasional signs of prostitution in the house, from the earliest Ciompi defamation of 1378 to the 1530 evidence of a nest of ladies led by an Alberti and staffed by the likes of Lena the Grand and Caterina the Bean.[60] These and other women who sinned and stayed could not have persevered without the tolerance and protection of the establised women of the house. No judgment on the moral condition of the house is possible or desirable; but it is quite plausible that the matrons would have been more upset by the likes of donna Barbera, who set up permanent residence in Orbatello with her husband and thus prevented other women from getting their relatives admitted to the asylum,[61] than they were with the sexual torts which dot the pages of the record. In the light of all this, the protection and commiseration shown those despairing women whose sons were supposed to leave because they had reached their twelfth birthday, hardly needs mention. Boys as old as eighteen years hung on with their mothers, clearly the beneficiaries of a corporate stance of the matrons.[62]

Orbatello owed some of its evident stability to the self-administration of its matrons. As far as is known, these women left no ledgers. There is no evidence that they exercised any formal administrative duties involving record keeping. But the suggestion that the older women acted as a corporate body in accepting members; that the Parte relied on them for an assessment of the condition of the house; that they as well as the men were capable of "staging" matriculations, perhaps in part by managing available space for unlicensed sisters and their children; that the matrons controlled access to and from the cloister of Orbatello, as we shall see: all this points to a consensus system of administration of a type which received no press from the male writers of the age. Contemporaries repeated the story of Cornelia Gracchi and her Florentine counterpart Alessandra de' Bardi—those exemplary individual widows and abandoned wives who performed wonders of family administration because they were "more men than women." But these male writers had nothing good to say about women in groups. The Orbatello, however, provides some evidence that widows, while certainly profiting from their past marital experience, confronted the new and unique life experience of Orbatello with creative energy, an energy the more compelling because of the maladministration of the Parte Guelfa.

---

[59] *PGR*, 11, fols. 58r, 178v; *PGR*, 13, fol. 214v.

[60] *PGR*, 14, fol. 12r.

[61] *PGR*, 13, fol. 170r (28 January 1521/22).

[62] Cases of over-age boys staying on are in *PGR*, 11, fols. 59r, 60r, 139r, 153r, 163r; 12, fol. 112r; 13, fol. 31r; 14, fol. 12r.

Thus Luigi Passerini was surely right that the women of Orbatello helped each other in their infirmities, and the widows who took in the lame girl Caterina in 1522 and those who welcomed the widow Maria of the Leg are examples of such solidarity.[63] Yet it was a practical human administration we see at work in the asylum, and not mindless maternalism. If the women were willing to accept, they could also expel or isolate when that was advisable. The matrons must have been the ones who in 1546 told the captains that Bartolomea of Romagnola could not be left with donna Lucrezia: the latter was old and sick, while Bartolomea may have been mentally ill. Someone of such "poor judgment and [so] contentious" needed to be isolated, and the Parte moved Bartolomea into a separate residence near the gate so as to avoid the "scandal" which threatened.[64]

This female organization was predominantly familial in nature. The women of Orbatello said by their actions what the Parte never specifically stated in its statutes: Orbatello's widows preserved family solidarities. We have already sketched the biographies of some of these widows catering over the years to a series of younger relatives, many of them their own children. And I counted 39 donne with their children among the 157 donne in the records between 1511 and 1530. Ten grandmothers with their grandchildren can be discerned in the same records, several maternal and paternal aunts united with a small army of nephews and nieces, and sisters living with each other. We have seen that a few children with no relatives entered Orbatello, and one of the donnas acted as if she were a funnel for strange children, accepting first one set of siblings and then another.[65] There is no doubt that many widows lived with each other with no children, and moved from one house to another to form more perfect unions.[66] Yet when widows did not live together but rather accepted the younger generation or two generations, the chances were overwhelming that they would be their relatives.

When apartment 28-s changed hands in 1518 and 1519, the human variety of Orbatello could be seen in its microcosm. On 13 November 1518, the Parte successfully expelled two widows with all their children and *familia* "pro honestate Orbatelli."[67] Had their nefarious behavior been denounced by the *pinzochera* suora Margherita, who lived in the loft above the apartment? We

---

[63] Passerini in the introduction to T, 155; *PGR*, 13, fol. 178v; 16, fol. 26r.

[64] "Attento qualiter domna Bartolomea de Romandiola, que habitat in Orbatello et in domo segnata no. xi et una cum domna Laurenza vetula ac egrota, est persona levis et modici iuditii ac riscoza, ita quod habitando et stando in societate facile esset quod deveniri et quod deveniret ad aliquid scandalum" (*PGR*, 16, fol. 33v [22 December]) ("Considering that lady Bartolomea da Romandiola, who lives in Orbatello and in the house numbered 11 with the old and sick lady Lorenza, is an irresponsible person of such little judgment and rash, that, living in society, it could easily come to some scandal").

[65] Donna Cosa took the boy and girl of a shoemaker into her apartment 28-i in February 1521, and in the following August accepted into the same apartment two daughters of a wool beater (*PGR*, 13, fols. 88v, 141v).

[66] Single donnas entering and moving about are the most common fact in these records.

[67] *PGR*, 12, fol. 76r.

are not sure, but the good sister may have bitten off more than she could chew. Three days after the expulsion the Parte captains gave donna Domenica Valva, widow of a wool spinner, permission to move into 28-s below the saintly elder Margherita. Donna Domenica came from apartment 5-s to her new home ... with six children![68] Suora Margherita moved out less than three months later, going to apartment 1-s, perhaps to keep a pious eye on who came and went from this sometimes noisy, but rarely violent asylum.[69]

Driven by the practical need for a livable and durable environment, therefore, the women of Orbatello succeeded where the Parte itself would have failed. Yet there was another powerful motivation behind this success, and that was the productive activity within the asylum itself. The specific focus of activity in Orbatello was rearing legitimate girls for marriage, and here again, the record speaks for itself. Between 1500 and 1517, the Parte sponsored an annual average of 4.4 girls of Orbatello in marriage, 74 of the asylum's children being aided in all.[70] We have seen that their mothers provided important additions to the £50 dowry the Parte furnished the girl, and from the list of the new husbands' occupations (Table 2) as well as from their origins in city and countryside, it is clear that the mothers attracted solid working husbands for their daughters.[71] Very few of the girls became servants in nunneries and none seems to have entered the twilight zone of domestic service or the brothels.[72]

The matrons must have been pleased and gratified when, on any given Sunday or feast day, weddings were celebrated in the asylum church before them, Parte representatives, and the rector.[73] For a minimum of five years these girls had lived in Orbatello with their mother or other relative, and those elders now saw their training, financial aid, and spouse-searching pay off. The girls had entered Orbatello as legitimate offspring, and they now left *pudica et honesta* to rear another generation free, at least on the girl's side, of

---

[68] The children ranged from a girl of 17 to a boy of 3 years of age (ibid.).

[69] Apartment 1-s was at the gate (*PGR*, 12, fol. 98v).

[70] Computations based on Leoni. Parte controls over qualifications are in *PGR*, 11, fol. 171v (1513); 13, fols. 122r, 197r (1521–1522); 14, fol. 119r (1532).

[71] The distribution between in and outside the city is described above. Leoni recorded the city parishes of 55 grooms, most well removed from Orbatello. The largest contingent came from S. Lorenzo (17), from the wool workers' parishes of S. Frediano and S. Maria in Verzaia (8), followed by the nearby large parishes of S. Ambrogio (7) and Orbatello's own S. Piero Maggiore (6).

[72] Two girls became servants in nunneries, one became a nun in the convent of converted prostitutes (*PGR*, 11, fol. 238v; 15, fol. 166r; 16, fols. 75r, 123v).

[73] On the celebrations, see *PGR*, 14, fol. 3r (23 March 1529/30). The standard meal for the attending captains is recorded at *PGR*, 11, fol. 221r. None of Leoni's notarial records refers to marriages *infra missarum solemnia*, and occasionally the rector was not even present (Leoni, fols. 53v, 105v). C. Klapisch-Zuber emphasizes the meager role of priests and church at marriages: "Zacharie, ou le Père Évincé. Les Rites Nuptiaux Toscans entre Giotto et le Concile de Trente," *Annales E.S.C.* 34 (1979): 1216–1243, now in her *Women, Family, and Ritual*. The brides generally did not move out of Orbatello until the grooms had collected the entire dowry owed them; the two exceptions are in Leoni, fol. 144v.

the stain of bastardy. The matrons' labors made them part of the reproductive activities of the city at large. Orbatello was a village of hope for its inhabitants, and of honor for the Parte and commune.

The commune of Florence played the father to legions of girls who had none, providing dowries for an overwhelmingly illegitimate population of foundlings, slaves, and servant girls. Here in Orbatello the £50 went to "honorable" girls. A proven friend of the nuclear family by its dowries to bastards, the commune here protected and augmented legitimacy. In part through such support from the patronal commune, sentiment for and the sacrality of the nuclear family might grow apace in and around Orbatello, that model of a female culture whose elders provided both the caring and warmth men deemed proper to the "frivolous sex," and the "gravity" they reserved to themselves.

The Invasion of the Innocents

In the decades after 1550, a fundamental change took place in the population, life, and function of Orbatello. The change is reflected in the breakdown of notarial consistency, and it is mirrored as well in the inability of subsequent scribes to keep track of a population whose mobility within Orbatello had enormously accelerated. In 1636 one scribe thought he had devised a way of "knowing and encountering in a second in what houses the said women lived, how and when [since 1588] they had entered, so as to put an end to disorders."[74] And the scribe of the successive *Book of the Women of Orbatello*, though recognizing that "because of the necessary, continued changing of rooms, one cannot easily fix the numbers of the rooms assigned to the women who enter Orbatello one after the other," tried again.[75] Both failed. Mobility by this time was beyond control, for the house had been invaded by the girls and women of the foundling home of the Innocenti.[76]

To understand the full implications of this invasion, we must first pause to examine the larger problem of women in Florentine society, which was ultimately responsible for this mutation. The background to that problem was indicated at the beginning of this article: the property laws favoring men, the Florentine marriage pattern creating widows at an early age, the high dowries, the constant flow of female migrants driven into the city by war and famine; these and many other factors affected different women in different ways. Finally, I pointed to the demographic upswing which started around 1470. Now we must gauge these factors' impact on Florentine institutions for women. Let there be no mistake: the mass of unwanted females in the Florentine population at the end of the fifteenth and in the following century was a phe-

---

[74] *Archivio degli Innocenti, Firenze (AIF)*, XLVII, 7, fol. 1r.

[75] *AIF*, XLVII, 8, fol. 1r.

[76] Note that both of these volumes are now in the Archive of the foundling home of the Innocenti, which took over responsibility for Orbatello in the eighteenth century.

nomenal demographic and moral fact, and no want of contemporaries raged at a "scandal" for which they knew no precedent.[77]

The explosion of the Florentine nunneries was the most tangible institutional evidence of this crisis, for between 1470 and 1550 the number of religious houses for women doubled and their population grew to the point where in mid-sixteenth century, some 13 percent of the total female population of Florence lived behind their walls![78] This was the "scandal" which perhaps most outraged the good citizens of Florence, for the nuns of Florence, we remember, were recruited from the "good families" of the city. These roughly 3,000 women entered warehouses their fathers could afford, unlike the mere 250 souls who inhabited Orbatello. We must turn again to the poor females.

Founded in an age of low population, Orbatello eased the plight of one segment of this mass, the elderly widows with their children and younger relatives, a communal resource of legitimate parentage held together by familial bonds. Yet a smaller part of Orbatello's population, though at times protected by the matrons, was not welcomed by the Parte, women we may characterize as having other commitments than to Orbatello. Slaves and foreigners made up part of this group, ladies who knew only a mother if any parent. Still active women who refused to live continuously in Orbatello constituted another part—women like donna Lucia of Decomano whom the Parte allowed out for a month to "take care of her business," like donna Brigida of the same Decomano, who went to Livorno to stay with the Medici captain of that town, like donna Maria who lived in Orbatello while being an agent for a nunnery.[79]

A third order of women appeared in Orbatello at the very end of our period, and hinted at the avalanche to come. These were single women who were the daughters of communal servants. With one possible exception, neither the daughters nor wives of servants of any governmental body, including the Parte Guelfa, had come to Orbatello until suddenly, in mid-sixteenth century, the government started to find homes in Orbatello for daughters of communal familiars who could not find a husband. The daughter of a squire of the meat office entered Orbatello in 1547, followed

---

[77] See my "Prostitution," and my "Infanticide in Florence: New Sources and First Results," *History of Childhood Quarterly* 1 (1973): 98–116, and for the cultural implications my *Public Life in Renaissance Florence* (New York, 1980), chaps. 11–14.

[78] Trexler, "Célibat," 1333–47.

[79] Donna Lucia d'Antonio da Decomano entered on 22 August 1513 into apartment 13-i (*PGR*, 11, fol. 164v). On 11 October 1519 she was given permission to absent herself the following February, her room to be held for her (*PGR*, 12, fol. 177v). Brigida di Biagio "possit ire et stare Liburnum cum Bernardo Alamanni de Medicis ibidem capitano, et quod eius habitatio eidem domne preseveritur" (*PGR*, 11, fol. 194v [4 March 1513/14]) ("can go and stay in Livorno with Bernardo d'Alamanno de' Medici, its captain, with her habitation to be held for her"). The *fattoressa* Maria of the nunnery of the Murate is recorded in C.

by the daughter of an official of the Monte di Pietà.[80] The Parte also found room for the female cook of the government at this time.[81]

The significance of these straws in the wind around 1550 is that these governmental assignments became the few single girls without relatives in Orbatello—and *with* ties to the *familia* of the government. These girls' links were to the outside and not the inside, and it was that characteristic which would alter the house's population. The two different caritative family structures of the Florentine state were about to collide.

The irresistible force would come from the foundling home of the Innocenti, after the nunneries and Orbatello the third Florentine institution housing unwanted females. Opened in 1445 by the Florentine silk guild which administered it, this home for abandoned children soon found that despite promised dowries, its girls were unmarriageable. Older girls filled up both the Innocenti and another foundling home limited to such an older clientele.[82] The Italian Wars from 1494 to 1530 further stimulated the population of the Innocenti into a frightful spiral which defied the house's horrendous mortality rate.

Simultaneously the streets of Florence filled with legions of displaced and deprived women who sold sex to preserve body and soul. Prostitution had left the brothel, and spread to other areas, including a large concentration near Orbatello.[83] Who can doubt that the older girls of the Innocenti earned their pittance in these brothels? This dreary catalogue of the crises of the contemporary female seemed to peak in the masses of young children, predominantly female, who had survived infancy but were too young to sell their bodies, so begged in the streets. Duke Cosimo insisted that these victims too were human beings when he began to deal with the scourge in the 1540s. Homes for these *abbandonati,* one for males but three for females between the ages of three and ten, were established and in the census of 1562 can be found warehousing hundreds of children.[84]

Yet where would *they* go when *that* abstract age of exit was reached? The ability of the Florentines to create rational welfare institutions based on vital

---

[80] *PGR,* 16, fols. 62r, 142r. The possible exception is one donna Maria, but it seems that her husband rather than she was a "buco o quoqui dominorum," i.e., of the Signoria of Florence. She entered apartment 19-s with her four children in 1513 (*PGR,* 11, fol. 118v [26 February]).

[81] Donna Nanna "cuocha di palazzo" is mentioned in C.

[82] See my "Foundlings." A decision of 1483 to place the grown population as servants in Florentine families was abandoned, perhaps because of the sexual abuses associated with such placements; see G. Bruscoli, *Lo Spedale di S. Maria degli Innocenti di Firenze* (Florence, 1900), 16, 49.

[83] Trexler, "Prostitution." The suspicion that this brothel area was supported by "girls of Orbatello" could not be confirmed in the sources. Battara's contention that the largest concentration of licensed prostitutes in 1552 was in the Via de' Pilastri, near Orbatello, is wrong; he failed to count the population of the public brothels; see *La Popolazione di Firenze a metà del '500* (Florence, 1935), 18.

[84] In the masculine house 95, in the three female houses 346 youngsters (*ASF, Misc. Medicea,* 224, fols. 4r, 13r, 69r, 87v).

statistics was undoubted, and the festive representations of the age delighted in presenting these abstract entities: the San Giovanni festival of 1545 showed its audience 70 pairs of little boys and 70 pairs of adolescent boys, 40 pairs of girls ten years or younger and 80 pairs of girls looking for husbands.[85] Could one doubt that the republic or the principate was a loving father, and the legions of such abstractly divided human beings the sentimental favorites of the patronal state? It was not for want of mind or sentiment, but because of the clamorous demographic problems of the age that, in this unjust society, the support systems of the Florentine welfare state started to buckle. That "firm and solid column" of the Innocenti approached financial collapse, its worthy structures bulging with so many unwanted girls that they had "reached the point of becoming insupportable," in the hapless administrator's words.[86] By 1580 the sixteen hundred children, up from twelve hundred in 1552, could be held no more. The Innocenti declared bankruptcy, sent all its boys aged 12 to 16 to the galleys and forced large numbers of young women into the streets.[87] It was at this point that the women of the Innocenti, girls with no father but the state, made their first sudden appearance among the inhabitants of Orbatello.

A document of 1585 makes clear that the "women of the Innocenti" were being put in Orbatello, and creating "scandals." Young *setaioli* or silk merchants came to see their favorites, and the *Innocentine*, with no reason to be beholden to either the priest or women of Orbatello, brought them into their rooms. The Parte did what little it could. It insisted that these new arrivals were subject to the priest just like the established residents, and it set up a group of "the older and venerable women" of Orbatello to guard the en-

---

[85] Text of the description in M. Plaisance, "La Politique Culturelle de Côme Ier et les Fêtes Annuelles à Florence de 1541 à 1550," in J. Jacquot et E. Konigson, *Les Fêtes de la Renaissance* (Paris, 1975), 3:150. These groups were contingents in a representation of the Slaughter of the Innocents, and the decision to represent age and sex groups separately, rather than in the family groups proper to the Slaughter, is a stunning example of the Florentine tendency toward abstraction. Not surprisingly, the one other group in this same representation was "26 pairs of widows." Could this contingent have come from the Orbatello?

[86] Bruscoli, *Spedale*, 63.

[87] Ibid., 66. The numbers are in Battara, *Popolazione*, 28. An admittedly late document of 1642 through its breakdown of the females in this population gives an impression of the load from those of advanced age:

Milking	188	From 12 to 20	198
Below 7 years	324	From 20 to 40	177
From 7 to 12	140	Older than 40	141
		(of which 10 were 86 years old).	

According to our source, the girls, "because all were kept in the convent, little by little start to live like animals. For now the girls sleep eight to a bed, and there are only 690 of them. Think what it will be like when the 300 [at nurse] return" (*Biblioteca Nazionale, Firenze, fondo principale*, II. iv. 370, fol. 12r [31 October 1642, and undated, 1647]).

trance to the cloister; the girls would come out rather than the men going in.[88] Yet what more was to be done? The girls were subjects of the *setaioli*, the women of Orbatello responded to the Parte Guelfa; a conflict of jurisdiction was unavoidable. The girls of Innocenti were illegitimate, the women and girls of Orbatello mostly legitimate. The former had no family and were known only by their mother's name, the latter had a colleague who was a relative, and knew their dead fathers. Finally, there were so many of the new arrivals. The merest glance at the *Book of the Women of Orbatello* started in 1636 shows that perhaps one in two of the women who came to Orbatello after 1588 and was still alive in 1636 had come from the Innocenti.[89] Of course that figure must be clearly understood: since the girls of the Innocenti may have been younger when they entered than the average widow of Orbatello, more of them would still have been alive in 1636. Yet there can be no doubt that as they jammed into the houses near the gate of Orbatello, they changed that venerable institution.

From the time of its foundation in 1370 well into the eighteenth century, the Orbatello played a significant role in the total Florentine welfare effort. Though Florence had no written master plan for care of the aged, Orbatello had provided a refuge for widows and abandoned wives, and had functioned to preserve the integrity of mother-led family units. The female crisis of the sixteenth century significantly affected that function, even if widows remained a feature of Orbatello for generations to come. For a society of widows had met one of illegitimate girls, and the ultimate fate of Orbatello was to lie with the young rather than the old.

The Innocenti no less than the Orbatello was a creation of that sense of family moderns often evoke from the past without truly understanding. In two senses. It was the rational creation of a commune which conceived of itself as a father to all, but it was also a creation of the bastards' fathers, *their* "solid and firm" support. For without the Innocenti, these men's own family honor would have perished from the defamations of their lovers, forced to kill or abandon the children of these honorable fathers. Then how would these same fathers have married off their own, legitimate, daughters? The

---

[88] "Disordini causati dalle donne degl'Innocenti cavate di là, et mandate in Orbatello, quali non vogliono stare a obedienza del prete, intromettono giovani setaiuoli et altri bottegai nella clausura...." The Orbatello now seemed "Più presto luogo poco honesto, che ecclesiastico et pio...." The recommendation was that "si metta alla porta nelle stanze contigue di quelle vechie più venerande, perchè possino et debbino chiamare quelle che son volute dalli settaiuoli, o altri, presente le dette vecchie" (*PGN*, 751, fol. 70r–v [17 January]) ("Disorders caused by the ladies of the Innocenti, taken from there and sent to Orbatello. They do not want to obey the priest, introduce into the cloister young silk merchants and other merchants.... Rather an indecent place than an ecclesiastical and pious one.... Put the old and more venerable women in the rooms by the gate. In that way they can and ought to fetch those women whom the silk merchants or others want to see, in the presence of the said oldsters").

[89] Thus the third oldest living resident of Orbatello was Maria della Licia delli Innocenti, who entered in 1588, the fifth was Albiera della Ginevra delli Innocenti, who entered in 1591, the seventh was Agnola di Agnola delli Innocenti, who entered in 1592, etc. (*AIF*, XLVII, 7, at the years).

abstract welfare institutions of Florence, no less than the family-centered asylum of Orbatello, protected the family.

In the eighteenth century, Orbatello served as a forced residence for girls pregnant out of wedlock, for "women in secret labor." The contemporary Guiseppe Richa waxed pious over that latest function of the ancient house, saying without saying what block "H" of Orbatello did. It was used "... for endangered girls, being destined to save not less their honor, than the life of the creatures with whom they were pregnant."[90]

Richa meant that the girls might have killed the children if not supervised, and would have shamed their families if their pregnancy had been public knowledge.[91] Thus Orbatello continued to guard the family. Perhaps in that age, the descendants of our sixteenth-century widows played the policewoman who preserved life, or perhaps there were those elder midwives in Orbatello who eliminated the unwanted, to-be-anonymous infants.

There is pathos in the contrast between the Renaissance and the Enlightenment matron in Orbatello. In the early sixteenth century, this asylum had made the later life of many widows one of hope and contribution to future generations; it was perhaps the only island in Europe where a female community preserved family units and prepared new ones, all without being midwives. In the eighteenth century, however, the matrons of Orbatello were surely midwives, bringing new life into the world from imprisoned girls who were not Orbatello's own, but the state's. Even while birthing, the widow of this Orbatello was severed from her history. She was a technician of the Tuscan state, creating the reality and ideology of the modern nuclear family.

A Renaissance asylum where for centuries widows were communally encouraged to stay with and rear their children adds to our knowledge of preindustrial old-age dependency. It questions not only the general idea that the traditional family sufficed as a welfare institution for the elderly, but the specific one that historically, state asylums have compromised kin family solidarities. Orbatello's history suggests that we view the care of the female elderly in early modern Europe in the context of a competition for funds and attention between widow-led kin families and the "family of the state," those dependent on government as an abstract but supportive father. The female elderly were not privileged within Florence's operative if unwritten policy for this world of dependents; hence the Orbatello proved vulnerable when the internment of masses of illegitimate girls proved politically and socially more imperative than the care of the elderly and their legitimate children. Issues implicit in this eclipse of an old women's institution—the functions of the female elderly in society and their claims on municipal assistance—are not confined to early modern Florence.

---

[90] Richa, *Notizie*, 1:298, publishing this volume in 1754. Note also that in Plate 3, the upstairs of the first three houses are used for girls as well. Passerini noted the gradual decline of the widows in Orbatello and the increasing number of girls, till in 1861 it was converted into a hospital for syphilitic women and an office for the city's prostitution regulators; see introduction to T, 155f.

[91] The evasive language was typical of contemporary literature; see Trexler, "Infanticide," 98–116.

Bibliography

Archivio storico italiano (ASI).

Aretino, Pietro, *I Ragionamenti.* Edited by A. Toschini. Milan: Dall'Oglio, 1960.

Battara, P. *La popolazione di Firenze alla metà del '500.* Florence, 1935.

Battistini, M. *La confrérie de Sainte-Barbe des Flamands à Florence.* Brussels, 1931.

Beccadelli, Antonio (Il Panormita). *Hermaphroditus.* Coburg, 1824.

Beloch, J. *Bevölkerungsgeschichte Italiens.* Berlin, 1937–65.

Bernardino da Siena. *Le prediche volgari.* (Florence, 1424). Edited by C. Cannarozzi. vols. 1–2. Pistoia, 1934.

——. *Le prediche volgari.* (Florence, 1425). Edited by C. Cannarozzi, vols. 3–5. Florence, 1940.

——. *Le prediche volgari.* (Siena, 1427). Edited by P. Bargellini. Milan, 1936.

Blom, I. "The History of Widowhood: A Bibliographical Overview." *Journal of Family History* 16 (1991): 191–210.

Boccaccio, Giovanni. *Corbaccio.* In *Opere,* edited by C. Segre. Milan: U. Mursia & C., 1966.

Brucker, G. "Bureaucracy and Social Welfare in the Renaissance: a Florentine Case Study." *Journal of Modern History* 55 (1983): 1–21.

——. "The Ciompi Revolution." In *Florentine Studies,* edited by N. Rubinstein. London: Faber and Faber, 1968.

——, ed. *The Society of Renaissance Florence.* New York: Harper & Row, 1971.

Brundage, J. "Prostitution in the Medieval Canon Law." *Signs* 1 (1976): 825–45.

Bruscoli, G. *Lo spedale di Santa Maria degl'Innocenti di Firenze.* Florence, 1900.

Bullough, V. *The History of Prostitution.* New Hyde Park, N.Y.: University Books, 1964.

Cambi, Giovanni. *Istorie fiorentine.* In *Delizie,* vols. 20–23.

Cantini, L., ed. *Legislazione toscana.* Vol. 1. Florence, 1800.

Carnesecchi, C. "Un Fiorentino del secolo XV e le sue ricordanze domestiche." *ASI,* ser. 5, 4 (1889): 145–73.

Carocci, G. *Studi storici sul centro di Firenze.* Florence, 1899.

Cattaneo, E. "Istituzioni ecclesiastiche milanesi." In *Storia di Milano* (Milan: Fondazione Treccani degli Alfieri, 1953–62), vol. 9.

Chabod, I. "Widowhood and Poverty in Late Medieval Florence." *Continuity and Change* 3 (1988): 291–311.

Cohen, S. "Convertite e malmaritate: Donne e religiosi nella Firenze rinascimentale." *Memorie. Rivista di storia delle donne* 1 (1981): 46–63.

Cohn, S. *The Laboring Classes in Renaissance Florence.* New York: Academic Press, 1980.

Coleman, E. "L'infanticide dans le Haut Moyen Age." *Annales E.S.C.* 29 (1974): 315–35.

Compton, T. "Sodomy and Civic Doom." *Vector* 2, no. 2 (1975): 23–27 et seq.

Corso, R. *Patti d'amore e pegni di promessa.* Palermo: Edikronos, 1991.

——. "Gli Sponsali Popolari." *Revue des Études Ethnographiques et Sociologiques* 1 (1908): 487–99.

D'Addario, A. *Aspetti della controriforma a Firenze.* Rome: Ministero dell'Interno, 1972.

Davidsohn, R. *Geschichte von Florence.* vol. 4, part 3. Berlin, 1927.

——. *Storia di Firenze.* 8 vols. Florence: Sansoni, 1956–68.

Davis, J. *The Decline of the Venetian Nobility as a Ruling Class.* Baltimore: The Johns Hopkins Press, 1963.

Davis, N. Zemon. *Society and Culture in Early Modern France.* Stanford: Stanford Univ. Press, 1975.

de La Roncière, C. "Pauvres et Pauvreté à Florence au XIVe siècle." in *Études sur l'Histoire de la Pauvreté (Moyen Age–16e siècle),* edited by M. Mollat. Paris: C.N.R.S. [Centre Nationale de la Recerche Scientifique], 1974.

Del Migliore, Ferdinando. *Firenze città nobilissima illustrata.* Florence, 1684.

Delaruelle, E. et al. *L'Église au temps du Grand Schisme et de la crise conciliaire (1378–1449). Fliche et Martin,* 14, part 2. Paris: Bloud & Gay, 1964.

Delizie degli eruditi toscani. Edited by I. da San Luigi. 24 vols. Florence, 1770–1789.

Della Robbia, E. Viviana. *Nei monasteri fiorentini.* Florence: Sansoni, 1946.

Diario d'Anonimo Fiorentino dall'anno 1358 al 1389. In *Cronache dei Secoli XIII e XIV,* edited by A. Gherardi. Florence, 1876.

Doren, A. *Deutsche Handwerker und Handwerkerbruderschaften im Mittelalterlichen Italien.* Berlin, 1903.

Eckenstein, L. *Women under Monasticism.* New York: Russell & Russell, 1963.

Erasmus of Rotterdam. *The Colloquies of Erasmus.* Translated by C. Thompson. Chicago: Univ. of Chicago Press, 1965.

Erikson, E. *Young Man Luther.* New York: Norton, 1963.

Fontette, M. de. *Les religieuses à l'âge classique du droit canon.* Paris: J. Vrin, 1967.

Galligo, I. *Circa ad alcuni antichi e singolari documenti inediti riguardanti la prostituzione, tratti dall'archivio centrale di stato di Firenze.* Milan, 1869.

Gherardi, A. *Nuovi documenti e studi intorno a G. Savonarola.* Florence, 1887.

Gibson, M. *Prostitution and the State of Italy, 1860–1915.* New Brunswick: Rutgers Univ. Press, 1986.

Gilbert, C. "When Did a Man in the Renaissance Grow Old?" *Studies in the Renaissance* 14 (1967): 7–32.

Herlihy, D. *Medieval and Renaissance Pistoia*. New Haven: Yale Univ. Press, 1967.

——. "Vieillir à Florence au Quattrocento." *Annales E.S.C.* 24 (1969): 1338–52; and in English: "Growing Old in the Quattrocento." In Stearns, *Old Age*.

——, and C. Klapisch-Zuber. *Les toscans et leurs familles* (Paris: E.H.E.S.S., 1978), and in English: *The Tuscans and Their Families*. New Haven: Yale Univ. Press, 1985.

Hughes, D. "Earrings for Circumcision: Distinction and Purification in the Italian Renaissance City." In *Persons in Groups: Social Behavior as Identity Formation in Medieval and Renaissance Europe*, edited by R. Trexler. Binghamton, N.Y. : Medieval and Renaissance Texts and Studies, 1985.

Jacquot, J., and E. Konigson. *Les fêtes de la Renaissance*. 3 vols. Paris: C.N.R.S., 1956–75.

Johnson, P. *Equal in Monastic Profession: Religious Women in Medieval France*. Chicago: Univ. of Chicago Press, 1991.

Klapisch-Zuber, C. "Célibat et service féminins dans la Florence du XVe siècle." *Annales de Démographie Historique 1981*.

——. *Women, Family, and Ritual in Renaissance Italy*. Chicago: Univ. of Chicago Press, 1985.

Kuehn, T. *Law, Family, and Women: Toward a Legal Anthropology of Renaissance Italy*. Chicago: Univ. of Chicago Press, 1991.

Larivaille, P. *La vie quotidienne des courtisanes en Italie au temps de la Renaissance (Rome et Venise, XVᵉ et XVIᵉ siècles)*. Paris: Hachette, 1975.

Litchfield, R. Burr. "Demographic Characteristics of Florentine Patrician Families." *Journal of Economic History* 29 (1969): 191–205.

Mansi, J. -D. *Sacrorum Conciliorum nova et amplissima collectio*. Florence and Venice, 1759–98.

Marks, L. "The Financial Oligarchy in Florence under Lorenzo." In *Italian Renaissance Studies*, edited by E. F. Jacobs. London: Faber and Faber, 1960.

Martines, L. *The Social World of the Florentine Humanists*. Princeton: Princeton Univ. Press, 1963.

Mazzi, M. Serena. *Prostitute e lenoni nella Firenze del quattrocento*. Milan: Il Saggiatore, 1991.

McKenzie, K. "Antonio Pucci on Old Age." *Speculum* 15 (1940): 160–85.

Molho, A. "Tamquam vere mortue: Le professioni religiose femminili nella Firenze del tardo Medioevo." *Società e storia* 12 (1989): 1–44.

Molho, A., and J. Kirshner, "The Dowry Fund and the Marriage Market in Early *Quattrocento* Florence." *Journal of Modern History* 50 (1978): 403–38.

Mueller, R. "Charitable Institutions, the Jewish Community, and Venetian Society." *Studi Veneziani* 14 (1972): 37–81.

Orlandi, S. *Necrologio di Santa Maria Novella*. 2 vols. Florence, 1955.

Otis, L. *Prostitution in Medieval Society: the History of an Urban Institution in Languedoc*. Chicago: Univ. of Chicago Press, 1985.

Paschini, P. "I monasteri femminili in Italia nel Cinquecento." *Italia Sacra* 2 (1958): 31–60.

Passerini, L. *Gli Alberti di Firenze*. 2 vols. Florence, 1869.

——. *Storia degli stabilimenti di beneficenza e d'istruzione elementare della città di Firenze*. Florence, 1853.

Peyer, H. *Stadt und Stadtpatron im mittelalterlichen Italien*. Zürich: Europa, 1955.

Piccolomini, Aeneas Sylvius (Pope Pius II), *I commentari*. Edited and translated by G. Bernetti. 5 vols. Siena, 1972–76.

Piovano Arlotto. *Motti e facezie del Piovano Arlotto*. Edited by G. Folena. Milan and Naples: Riccardo Ricciardi, 1954.

Plaisance, M. "La politique culturelle de Côme I et les fêtes annuelles à Florence de 1541 à 1550." In Jacquot and Konigson, *Les fetes*, 3:133–52.

Power, E. *English Medieval Nunneries*. New York: Biblo and Tannen, 1964.

Pullan, B. *Rich and Poor in Renaissance Venice*. Cambridge, Mass.: Harvard Univ. Press, 1971.

Relazioni sul governo della Toscana. Edited by A. Salvestrini. Vol. 1. Florence: Leo S. Olschki, 1969.

Rezasco, G. "Segno delle meretrici." *Giornale Liguistico* 17 (1890): 161–220.

Richa, G. *Notizie istoriche delle chiese fiorentine*. 10 vols. Florence, 1754–62.

Romby, G. *Descrizioni e rappresentazioni della città di Firenze nel XV secolo*. Florence: Libreria Editrice Fiorentina, 1976.

Rossiaud, J. *Medieval Prostitution*. New York: Basil Blackwell, 1988.

——. "Prostitution, jeunesse et société dans les villes du sud-est au XVe siècle," *Annales E.S.C.* 31 (1976): 289–325.

Rothman, D. *The Discovery of the Asylum*. Boston: Little, Brown, 1971.

Rubinstein, N. *The Government of Florence under the Medici (1434 to 1494)*. Oxford: Oxford Univ. Press, 1966.

Russell, J. *British Medieval Population*. Albuquerque: Univ. of New Mexico Press, 1948.

——. "Clerical Population of Medieval England." *Traditio* 2 (1944): 177–212.

Sacchetti, Franco, *Il trecentonovelle*. Edited by V. Pernicone. Florence: Sansoni, 1946.

Singleton, C., ed. *Canti carnascialeschi del Rinascimento*. Bari, 1936.

Statuta populi et communis florentinae (1415). 3 vols. Fribourg, 1778.

Statuti dell'arte degli albergatori della città e contado di Firenze, edited by F. Sartini (Florence: Leo S. Olschki, 1953).

Stearns, P., ed. *Old Age in Preindustrial Society*. New York: Holmes and Meier, 1982.

Terroine, A. "Le Roi des Ribauds de l'Hôtel du Roi et les Prostituées Parisiennes." *Revue d'histoire de droit français et étranger* 56 (1978): 253–67.

Trexler, R. "Charity and the Defense of Urban Elites in the Italian Communes." in *The Rich, the Well-Born and the Powerful: Elites and Upper Classes in History*, edited by F. Jaher. Urbana, 1973.

——. "The Foundlings of Florence, 1395–1455." *History of Childhood Quarterly* 1 (1973): 259–84.

——. "Infanticide in Florence: New Sources and First Results." *History of Childhood Quarterly* 1 (1973): 98–116.

——. "Lorenzo de' Medici and Savonarola, Martyrs for Florence." *Renaissance Quarterly* 31 (1978): 293–308.

——. *Public Life in Renaissance Florence*. New York: Academic Press, 1980.

———. *Synodal Law, in Florence and Fiesole, 1306–1518.* Vatican City: Biblioteca apostolica vaticana, 1971.

———. "Une table florentine d'espérance de vie." *Annales E.S.C.* 26 (1971): 137–39.

Varchi, Benedetto. *Storia Fiorentina.* Florence: Salani, 1963.

Villani, Giovanni, Matteo, and Filippo, *Croniche di Giovanni, Matteo e Filippo Villani.* Trieste, 1857.

La vita del beato Ieronimo Savonarola. P. Ginori Conti, ed. (attrib.). Florence, 1937.

Volpe, G. *Toscana medievale.* Florence, 1964.

Anuman Rajadhon, Phraya

Life and ritual in old
Siam: three studies of
Thai life and customs

Phya Anuman Rajadhon

Life and Ritual in Old Siam

Three Studies of Thai Life and Customs

TRANSLATED AND EDITED BY

WILLIAM J. GEDNEY

GREENWOOD PRESS, PUBLISHERS
WESTPORT, CONNECTICUT

Library of Congress Cataloging in Publication Data

Anuman Rajadhon, Phrayā, 1888-1969.
    Life and ritual in old Siam.

    Reprint of the ed. published by HRAF Press,
New Haven.
    Includes bibliographical references.
    CONTENTS: The life of the farmer.--Popular
Buddhism in Thailand.--Customs connected with the
birth and rearing of children.
    1. Thailand--Social life and customs--Collected
works. 2. Buddhism--Thailand--Collected works.
3. Farm life--Thailand--Collected works.
I. Gedney, William J. II. Title.
[DS568.A7 1979]   959.3   78-23833
ISBN 0-313-21193-0

Reprinted with the permission of Human Relations Area
Files, Inc.

Reprinted in 1979 by Greenwood Press, Inc.
51 Riverside Avenue, Westport, CT 06880

Printed in the United States of America

10 9 8 7 6 5 4 3 2 1

Publisher's Foreword

Two of the three studies in this volume have appeared in the original Thai. "Life of the Farmer" was published in 1948 by Luang Arthaprichachanu-pakarn as an act of merit-making at the cremation of his mother, Mme. Phiw Chatinanthana, and "Customs Connected with Birth and the Rearing of Children" was published in 1949 in similar circumstances (see preface on page 101). The translations were begun in 1952 by William J. Gedney for the Human Relations Area Files and submitted to Phya Anuman for comment (his amplifying remarks have been incorporated in the footnotes). In 1955, the Yale University Southeast Asia Studies with the permission of HRAF mimeographed a limited number of copies of "Life of the Farmer" for inclusion in its translation series. "Customs Connected with Birth and the Rearing of Children" is published here for the first time in English.

The history of "Popular Buddhism in Thailand" is somewhat different in that it was written by Phya Anuman in English. The manuscript came to the attention of Robert B. Textor, Research Associate in Anthropology and Southeast Asia Studies at Yale University, who urged that it be given to Dr. Gedney for editing and published with the other two studies in this volume.

The contribution of Dr. Gedney to this volume is second only to that of the author himself. Having finished the original translations several years ago, Dr. Gedney submitted the manuscripts to a most painstaking scrutiny and re-editing. Dr. Gedney, who is presently Professor of English and Southeast Asian Languages at the University of Michigan, brings to his work as a Thai scholar a background which few Americans can equal including six and a half years residence in Thailand and a total of eighteen years devoted to the study of the Thai language.

In addition to guiding us to the manuscript of "Popular Buddhism in Thailand, " Dr. Textor offered us the use of the many photographs he had taken in the village of Bang Chan in central Thailand (see the photographic section following page 98) and gave generously of his time both to advise us on our selection and to write the captions.

The drawings of farm implements appended to "Life of the Farmer" were made for HRAF by Gary Vescelius from sketches supplied by Phya Anuman with some additional details from photographs and from consultation with persons familiar with Thai farm implements.

The photograph on the cover, of the Wat Rajabophit Monastery in Bangkok, originally appeared in Cultures of Thailand by Phya Anuman Rajadhon (Thailand Culture Series, National Culture Institute, Bangkok, 1953) and is used here by permission.

Publication of this volume was made possible in part through the financial assistance of the Asia Society, whose aid is gratefully acknowledged.

Preface

Phya Anuman Rajadhon occupies, or rather has created for himself, a position in the field of Thai letters and scholarship which is unique and paradoxical. Though he is not an academician by training, his scholarly attainments have placed all younger teachers and students at his feet and made him one of Thailand's most highly respected university professors. Though he is not a trained anthropologist, no one has made so great a contribution as he to the study of traditional Thai culture. Though he is not primarily a student of language and literature, no one can proceed very far in Thai philological or literary studies before he has to seek enlightenment from the contributions which Phya Anuman has made in these fields. Though he is not a product of Western education, hardly anyone has done more than he to introduce and popularize Western learning among the Thai. Though he is much more than a popular author, one could hardly find a professional writer in Thailand who can match the grace and wit of his prose style. Most astonishing of all, though he is not a Thai by ancestry, no student of Thai culture, history, literature, and language has displayed greater devotion to these fields.

The translator of any of Phya Anuman's prolific writings is faced with two conflicting aims. On the one hand, he wants to render the content as accurately as possible, since foreign readers are likely to be most interested in the factual material that he presents; on the other, he would like to preserve as much as possible of the delightful flavor of the author's prose style, which has all the vigor and pungency of the best conversational language. In the translations presented here it is to be feared that the latter desideratum has had to suffer at the expense of the former.

Thai terms are transcribed in the phonemic system devised by Professor Mary Haas as revised by her in Thai Reader (American Council of Learned Societies, Washington, D.C., 1954).

William J. Gedney

Ann Arbor, Michigan
May 1961

Table of Contents

Drawings (following page 58)

Water Wheels and Water Scoops
Plows and Yokes
Smaller Farm Implements
Threshing, Pounding, Milling, Winnowing, and
   Measuring Implements

Photographs (following page 98)

A Village Wedding: Informal Merrymaking on the Side
Merit-making: Never Too Young
Merit-making: Never Too Old
Procession to the Ordination
Ordination: Supreme Moment
Pilgrimage: Memorable Period in the Annual Cycle
Topknot Cutting

THE LIFE OF THE FARMER

Introduction

I will tell about farming, which everyone knows and can tell about. It seems at first glance that farming is a simple matter; everyone knows about it, just as everyone knows how to cook rice, the daily duty of the housewife. If anyone wants to know about it, he can ask questions himself; it is not necessary to explain it. Therefore no one has written a book on this subject, since no one would want it. It is true that there are books on auspices, or textbooks on modern agriculture and its superiority to old farming methods. But these do not help us to understand the life of the farmer, and so I have written a book about farmers as they were in the old times.

I feel that no story is so hard to tell as the story of farming. If one were to make comparison, it is like telling the story of oxen and buffaloes; if you make an error, even children know you are wrong. Moreover it is a simple, unexciting subject, which everyone knows. It is much better to tell about lions or nymphs, because if you make a mistake, no one knows it, for these exist only in legends and no one would dare say you were wrong. Or if you tell about camels or seals it is still better than telling about oxen and buffaloes, because these animals do not exist in our country. Even if we have never seen them, we have books written by others, and it is easy to write from them without being afraid of making a mistake. Also people prefer to listen, because it is unusual, whereas the subject of oxen and buffaloes is like "grass at the gate of the pen"; it is easy and yet it is difficult.

But let us try. We will tell the story of farming from the point of view of the observer, not from the point of view of one who knows or one who performs. Those of you who were once farmers, but have long ago abandoned farming to seek your fortune in the city, when you hear the story of farming which I, who have never been a farmer, am telling here, it may remind you of the past and refresh your memory to some extent. Also, you will undoubtedly know where my account is deficient or mistaken. I beg that you be so kind as to inform me; I will be very grateful. This is the situation. One might say that it is as if I who have never given birth to a child, and am one who will absolutely never have an opportunity to, were to be so bold as to tell women about childbirth. It feels rather odd, and so I must make my excuses in advance.

For the story of farming, Phrá Thewa Phinimmit (Chaaj Theewaaphĭnim-mĭd) has kindly noted down his memories of farming among the people of Nakhon Ratchasima. I have used these notes as data for relating the story of farming, together with the verbal accounts of many other friends who have seen farming and have been kind enough to explain farming to me. I wish to thank all of these people at this time.

Fine Arts Department
Bangkok, Thailand
11 February, 1948

Phya Anuman Rajadhon

Table of Contents

THE LIFE OF THE FARMER

The City and the Country

Not too far out from the city, one sees great vacant space as far as the
eye can reach; clumps of trees rise at irregular intervals. In the extreme
distance one sees the treetops looking as if placed in orderly rows. The sky
is clear to the distant horizon. The scene is quiet and lonely, with only the
sound of crows and the sound of the wind blowing from time to time. At
long intervals one sees a few people in the distance. The air one breathes
feels pure and fresh. This is the condition of the meadows and fields outside
of town; their characteristics are just the opposite of those of the city. In
the city there are many people; whatever places are gathering points for
people are crowded with thronging humans. There is a deafening din of people and of cars almost all the time. One cannot see anything at a distance,
for buildings and shops and houses intervene almost everywhere. The atmos-
phere is hot and oppressive and impure; one breathes with difficulty. Foul
and rotten odors assail the nose frequently. Some places are disgustingly
dirty and cluttered. Life in the city and life in the country offer sharp con-
trasts. One is close to nature; the other is remote from nature. One is the
source of food and health; the other is a place where people gather to share
their food, and disease germs. To say only this much makes it appear that
in the city there is only evil, not to be compared with the country. Actually
if one were to speak of the good points, the city has many advantages over
the country, because the center of progress is in the city. If this progress
spreads to the country in appropriate proportions, one can say that the nation,
both city and country, achieves prosperity. If the city is selfish to too great
a degree -- seeking only to accumulate wealth to provide entertainment and
comfort for itself, becoming remote from nature and never glancing toward
the country -- the progress of the city will be like a light that flares up only
for a moment and then goes out for lack of fuel, that is to say, food. The
country has the function of producing food to feed the city. Therefore the
city has to depend upon the country for sustenance. To speak of the country,
people living too close to nature will have the living conditions of nature.
Whatever life is like, it continues so, with no progress upward and forward,
because the country must depend upon the wealth, intelligence, and power
of the city for maintenance and improvement in order that the country may
advance and grow toward prosperity. World civilization and progress in the
history of various nations depend upon both city and country. Each depends
upon the other, and neither is better or worse than the other. If there are tools
but no rice, or rice but no tools, there is hardship. Therefore in Thai it is
said that nation and possessions [the expression for "possessions" is literally

"rice and things"] go hand in hand; if separated, neither nation nor possessions exist fully.

City people call people outside the city "countryfolk." When one
speaks the word "country" he thinks at once of backwardness both in wealth
and in knowledge, but if city people did not have country people to help
them, they could not live, for they would have no rice to eat, and would
have no riches or happiness. For this reason we should share our knowledge
and our wealth with the country people; thus we help the nation and help ourselves at one and the same time, for the people together form the nation.
If one divides them broadly as I do, there are only two groups, the city people and the country people. I will use the term country people [literally,
people of rural areas] instead of the term countryfolk [literally, people of
outside areas] to avoid unpleasant connotations in the story that I will tell,
namely, the story of the life of farmers and country people, who are the majority of the population of the country and who are the part of the population
that renders the country prosperous in food by farming, the oldest and most
widespread industry of mankind.

If you spread out a map of the country and look at it, cities are located
at points where they draw little circles. The big cities are big circles, and
small cities are small circles. Outside these circles is an area outside the
cities; the area is great. If you take the cities, where a great many people
live, put them together, and compare them with the area which is not city,
anyone can see at once that the area which is city is many times less than the
area which is not city. These non-city areas, aside from forests, mountains,
streams, and lakes, are orchards and gardens and farms, made by the country
people to plant crops and sustain themselves, from ancient times down to the
present. Because of the fact that the country people settle in broad areas,
since they must use much land in making a living, people live in clusters far
apart from each other, causing one to feel that the number of country people
is less than the number of city people. Actually if all country people were
assembled together, they would outnumber city people by nine or ten times.
They are the majority of the population of the country.

When we say that the country people constitute the largest part of the
population of the country or, as they say, the backbone of the country, this
is usually an end of the matter. No one is interested in knowing about country people, except to have them farm much and produce much rice, to feed
the centers of population, namely, the cities. As for the life of country people and the difference between their conditions and beliefs and amusements
and those of city people, no one seems much interested, for it is a question of
country people, who could not possibly have anything better than city people.
Whatever the country people think or believe is old-fashioned, unchanged
with the times. This is true, but the majority of country people live in small
groups, not large groups like city people, because none of them has an

opportunity to become acquainted with other people to open his ears and eyes, surrounding circumstances limiting him. Whatever country people have done and believed in the past with satisfactory results, they continue to do and believe, not changing readily. It is as if we had always used our own tools until we are handy with them; if we replace them suddenly with new tools it is like an about-face; we have not sufficient time to adapt ourselves. Such change causes confusion among the country people, for the old familiar tools are destroyed before use of the new tools has been learned; this amounts to destroying good things without providing anything better, so that the only door is broken. For this reason the country people advance slowly. Alone, they do not dare change the old for the new because they are unsure, differing from the city people who have seen things of various kinds and so advance quickly; but sometimes they misstep, because of advancing too fast. Therefore it is said, "Knowledge of the life of mankind, from the remote past down to the present, besides helping us to predict the future, shows us our duty toward the world, which each of us finally must leave more beautiful than when we first found it."[1]

Preparing the Fields

In telling about farming, I will speak first of the characteristics of the rice fields. A field is a flat piece of land with a ridge of earth all around it for holding water to nourish the rice plants. Each field so marked off by ridges is called ʔan naa, or kàbîŋ naa or tàbîŋ naa. The classifier for fields used in old books, such as Chronicles of the City of Nakhon Sithammarat (version of Village Headman Naaj Khǎaw), is tàbîŋ. Each field is usually rectangular in shape, sometimes large and sometimes small depending upon the area divided up. If the field is very big, it is necessary to work many days in plowing it. The lower end of the field is not always rectangular, because of adjoining hills, trees, marshes, or canals. This area is left over, but cannot be allowed to go to waste; a ridge is made around it according to the shape of the area. If a field has a long slender shape like a flag it is called naa sîaw. If one side is long and straight but the other side is curved, the long straight side is called wɛɛŋ and the curved side is called rúŋ, while the other two sides are called kwâaŋ as in normal fields; this sort of field is called naa rúŋ naa wɛɛŋ, but at present the word rúŋ has come to refer to the side or kwâaŋ. There are also fields with ridges of small size; these are usually sowing fields, in low places. In the wet season they are flooded for a long time, and it is not necessary to make strong water barriers, but only to divide the fields to keep separate various sorts of rice that are sown, and to serve as paths for walking. In the hot season, during the fourth and fifth lunar months, the fields are dry, and not a drop of water is to be found. In the fields one sees nothing but rice stubble everywhere, and some places are burned over in black strips, sometimes still burning. They set fire to the rice stubble in the fields to burn the rice straw and turn it to ashes to provide fertilizer for the fields again, for these fields are rainwater fields, incapable of receiving sediment from the river water which overflows its banks and provides fertilizer.

Implements used in farming are the plow and the harrow, which everyone has seen. In the farming season one sees oxen or buffaloes drawing the plow through the fields, with a person holding the plow and following along behind. You have no doubt already seen such a plow. It is a curved piece of wood waist-high. One part is called the khan jaam; the end which the plowman holds is called hǎaŋ jaam. There is another part with a hole in it to fasten it to the lower part of the khan jaam, curving forward to join the ʔèɛg nɔ́ɔj, which has two ropes tied to it. Beyond this is the ox or buffalo that draws the plow. This curved wood is called the khan of the plow, and the rope tied to the ʔèɛg nɔ́ɔj is called the khlâw rope. The bottom part of the plow appears from time to time in the water and earth; at the time of plowing lumps of earth form along the forward edge, which is a thick piece of wood about one-half meter long, the front of which curves up like a shoe and is called the "pighead." The upper part is a high projecting piece for cutting the earth, called the pighead blade. At the end of the pighead there is a piece of iron, triangular in shape and a little larger than the palm of the hand, fitted over the end of the wood, for jabbing the earth and breaking it apart so that it can be easily turned up. This iron is called the phǎan of the plow, or in some localities the pàkhǎaŋ. The plow as well as the harrow are made by the farmers for their own use, except for the phǎan iron which must be bought. These are bought from traders having oxcarts loaded with various sorts of iron, including phǎan, knives, hoes (cɔ̀ɔb), spades (sǐam), 2 etc. They come from provinces where there are people who mine iron ore and do blacksmithing for a living, such as the province of Loei. In the dry season during the third lunar month, merchants bring iron articles in oxcarts to sell among the villages, coming in groups of nine or ten carts. When they arrive at a village they stop and sell there. Whatever kind of iron implement the peasant needs, he buys at the oxcart parking lot, which is called the "oxcart dock." In every province there are regular places for this. When the traders have finished selling at one village, they move on to another. When they are sold out, if they see anything that strikes their fancy, they buy it and take it away either to sell or to use. What I have described is the story of people's trading in former times. Trading was originally like this, whether the transport was oxcart or beast of burden or carrying pole, or boats along waterways. Upon arriving in a village, a trader would stop and sell for many days, moving on to other places as the situation demanded until sold out. There was no trader serving as middleman to purchase goods wholesale for resale later as nowadays.

Farming may be said to begin at the waxing phase of the fourth lunar month, for beginning at that time the farmers prepare their farming equipment such as plows and harrows to await the auspicious day to conduct the first plowing ceremony. This is a day in the fourth lunar month, and they seem to choose even-numbered rather than odd-numbered days. They find the day in a textbook. [3] If they have no textbook, they borrow one and memorize it or copy it out, or ask those who know. This textbook is apparently obtained from monks learned in astrology and is therefore most likely to be found in monasteries. Anyone who can read and write goes and copies it out in a Thai folding book, and it is then copied again and again. It is a book in the same category as textbooks of medicines and textbooks on methods of worshiping spirits. Textbooks of this sort are found everywhere and are called household textbooks. If the villagers have a government calendar, they usually accept the first plowing day given in the calendar. As for the time, in bygone days when the textbook gave the time in hours and minutes it was not convenient, for the old-time farmers had no clocks to watch the time. Therefore they used the Indian method of telling time in stages of sunshine; that is, they measured the length of their own shadows by the number of consecutive footlengths. The number of times one had to set his foot down to equal the length of the shadow was the number of stages of sunshine. In the morning when the sun had just risen, the shadow in the open sunlight would be longer than in the late morning. They measured their own shadows with their feet, and the number of footlengths gave so many stages of sunshine.

Before the auspicious hour they built a temporary shrine to the guardian spirit of the field, called an eye-level shrine, in a place near the field appointed as the place of the first plowing. They had to prepare both objects of worship and offerings. This eye-level shrine was built only firmly enough to serve temporarily as a shrine. They used six bamboos planted as pillars, as high as eye-level, with crosspieces tied with creepers. The shrine had the form of a high rectangular platform of no very great size, only sufficient to lay the objects of worship and the offerings. The floor of the shrine was made of bamboos laid in a row, or they might be split and flattened. If it was not firm and steady they used creepers or strips of bamboo to tie it; one need not speak of nails, for they had none. What has been described was the usual method of building. If they could not find bamboo, they could use other wood; it was a question of using whatever they had, without limitations. The same was true of offerings; whatever they had to eat, they offered, as chance might afford, or as the popular phrase is, "prawn salad or fish salad." There had to be an offering of rice; this could not be omitted. They were required always to use the top rice of the pot. These offerings were arranged in a flat basket, or at the very least laid on flat banana leaves. As vessels to contain offerings they used only flat baskets or banana leaves;

even in making offerings to the gods the same was the case. This custom probably comes from India, where some groups of Indians of high caste like to eat rice from banana leaves, regarding them as cleaner and purer than other containers, which might be polluted because of having been used by others. To use a vessel that has already been used by a person of low class, such as a śudra or a caṇḍāla, is considered a sin, the stain accruing to the person using the vessel afterward; however clean one might wash the vessel, the stain is not removed, according to the belief. Banana leaves are better, both clean and convenient. After use they can be thrown away. We ourselves also like them, because they are convenient. Their only disadvantage is that we like to throw used banana leaves away everywhere, cluttering the place, disregarding the locality in a barbarous way. As to objects of worship, there were flowers, incense sticks, and candles. There was some difficulty with respect to incense sticks; in those times they did not know how to make these themselves, and it was not easy to buy them, for there was no place that sold them. The people had to depend upon monks, asking them for one or two sticks according to their needs. The candles used for worship were not hard to procure; the peasants made these themselves. Beeswax is not hard to obtain in the country; in the forests there are lots of bee's nests and beehives. Usually these are mîm bees, with small bodies; if one heats the honeycomb with fire he obtains wax. These objects of worship depended upon what one had or could procure. If one had nothing it did not matter, depending on chance. If they simply worshiped and made offerings without any marker for the place of the spirit of the land, and had a feeling of emptiness, they picked up a lump of earth and laid it on the shrine, pretending that the lump of earth was the place of the spirit. At the time of worshiping and making offerings, they would make a speech asking that their farms this year be fruitful, that their rice produce fine grain, that there be no dangers such as biting crabs or nibbling worms. When they finished worshiping and making offerings they set to work plowing a field, for which the auspicious hour had been set, to serve as a ceremony of first plowing. The work of first plowing took about one hour; when they had finished, they might return home, and need do nothing further. They left the shrine of the land spirit as it was; there would be one more ceremony of making offerings and worshiping when they began to transplant rice. In the northeast they call the spirit of the land phǐi taa hêɛg or phǐi taa rɛ̂ɛg. There is a ceremony of making an offering of a chicken and making a wish, as described elsewhere (in my work, Belief in Spirits). In some places, for example in the district of Ayutthaya, so far as it has been possible to investigate, they make four triangular flags, of white or any color, and set these up at one of the north corners of their fields. They set them up in a rectangle and then sit down and address the Rice Goddess, the Earth Goddess, and the Spirit of the Place, asking that harmful creatures such as aphis and crabs not damage the rice which they are about to sow.

In olden times people who depended upon crops as their major source
of sustenance had knowledge and experience in planting. They knew which
sorts of earth were suited to which sorts of crops, what should be done at the
time of planting to get good results, what to do to provide fertilizer for the
earth. But even if they had knowledge and experience in these matters, and
were as diligent as they could be, the people in former times were helpless
in matters of weather and crop enemies. When they thus found themselves
helpless, it was natural for them to turn to magic things for aid, with doctrines
and conduct handed down traditionally, to ensure fruitfulness for their farming. For this reason people formerly feared dangers which might befall their
farming, because nothing was such a source of disaster as failure of crops.
Because of this fear they had to have ceremonies of making offerings to spirits
and gods, and rites connected with every step of farming until their crops
were harvested and put away, before their worries were over. For the same
reason various nationalities, even those which have progressed, still have
various rites and ceremonies connected with farming which have been handed
down to the present time. These serve as evidence as to original beliefs,
behavior, and conduct. But even if the beliefs have now faded out because
famines do not occur often as formerly, and there is not much worshiping
and begging of spirits of the place as described above, nevertheless the
selection of auspicious hours has not been given up at the time of the first
plowing, because this is regarded as important. In extreme cases, some
people, even if they do not select their own auspicious hour, watch to see
when others, such as the village headman or the important man in the village,
begin the first plowing, and then begin their own. Those who are still cautious and fearful take flowers, incense sticks, and candles and lay them at
the head of the field ridge, and make vows to the shrine, speaking to it in
traditional ways. There are still people who do this; it is deep in their bones,
and they must perform one thing or another to be happy. People who believe
in auspices and who are learned make sure the first plowing is done in an
auspicious direction, avoiding inauspicious directions such as the directions
of the phǐi lǔaŋ, lǎaw lèg, thágkàthin, and yommákhǎn, which are given in
textbooks of astrology. In the first plowing they plow only three circuits to
serve as ceremony. Probably they plow three circuits because three is a number regarded as magic. In some places they have a textbook for beginning
first plowing according to the age of the farmer; for example, if he was born
in the year of the rat, he begins to plow on Sunday, and if born in the year of
the ox, he begins to plow on Wednesday, etc. [4]

When they have finished the first plowing they leave the field as it is.
When it rains and the earth is wet enough to begin plowing, they set to work
plowing the field of the first plowing before the other fields. While they are
waiting for the rain, they have to plow for sowing, that is, plow the field in
which they will raise seedlings for transplanting. In plowing for sowing, if

they are superstitious, it seems that they select an auspicious day, avoiding days when rats will bite or birds will carry off the rice; these things are told in the textbooks. Fields for sowing rice for transplanting may be made in many places, one plot for sowing "heavy rice," which is rice that forms grain slowly, taking about four months to ripen and be ready for harvesting, also called "four-month rice"; and another plot for sowing "light rice," which is rice that forms grain quickly, taking about three months to ripen and be ready for harvesting, also called "three-month rice." There are other plots for sowing black glutinous rice and white glutinous rice, etc.[5] It is also possible to sow them together in a single plot, dividing it into sections by digging ditches. For a place to sow rice for transplanting, they select a spot near enough to water that they can scoop up water to nourish the seedlings easily. The rice that they sow for seedlings is rice that they select and keep aside from the year before; they take the rice of the Rice Goddess, which they summon forth from the field at the time of the previous year's harvest and tie up in the form of a small human doll and keep in the barn, and mix this with the rice to be planted. There are only a few heads of this Rice Goddess rice which they mix in for ceremonial purposes to cause the seed rice to have life and heart (see my work on the Rice Goddess).

The method of sowing rice is to put the rice in a flat basket and soak it in water in order that the light-weight paddy grains and empty grains will float to the top; these they pick out and throw away. Then they pour the paddy into another flat basket which is lined with straw or grass, and water it constantly, not letting it get dry, until the rice germinates. This is called in the province of Nakhon Ratchasima khâaw tɛ̀ɛg càab. Then they take it and sow it in the seedling plots, which have been plowed and formed into ridges and ditches in advance. The ridges, formed of mud and made smooth and flat on top, are separated by ditches. Besides dividing the plot according to kinds of rice as described above, these ditches are also used as paths for walking while sowing, so that they need not tread on rice grains already sown; the ditches also serve as water channels. Before sowing the rice they speak a simple invocation to the Rice Goddess, informing her that they are about to plant her rice to make future crops, and asking that the rice plants flourish and be fruitful. Then they sow the rice; this is called thɔ̂ɔd klâa or tòg klâa. After sowing they must keep watch. If it rains hard during this time the seedlings are in danger, for their roots have not yet taken hold of the earth and even the distribution of the sowing will be destroyed, the seedlings being thrown together in crowded clusters; if this happens they will not grow well; the plants will be of unequal size, some small and some large.

Plowing the Fields

After sowing, if there is no rain for two or three nights, the roots of the seedlings take hold of the earth. After this even if it rains hard it does not matter, but it is necessary to watch and scoop up water, although not in excessive amounts. The farmers watch over the seedlings until they are about half a meter or more in height, when they are fit to be transplanted. If the seedlings are too long, they do not do very well when transplanted because they lose strength and the rice plants do not flourish. Rice seedlings which are oversize are called khâaw klâa kɛ̀ɛ tɛ̀ɛg khɔ̂ɔ nɔ̌ɔ kàj [literally, "old seedlings jointed like a chicken's legs"]; they turn into plants similar to those of broadcast sown fields, which are less productive than those in transplanted fields. Seedlings, if they have good earth with plenty of fertilizer and water, will grow to a size to be pulled up and transplanted in about fifty to sixty days. If they are left long for lack of opportunity to transplant them, they may grow old and produce grain, but the crop is small. The greatest enemies of rice seedlings are water birds; they like to eat rice seedlings and will come down in flocks. As soon as the rice grains burst into green leaf and are about to become plants, these birds like to descend and peck at them. In only a moment the seedlings lie flat and ruined. These wretched birds come down and eat at night, and there is no way to keep one's eyes open and watch for them; if they come to eat during the day it would be possible to give some protection. They are dreadful. The duty of watching and protecting rice seedlings includes scooping water and letting it flow onto or off the seedling plots, in order to let the young rice seedlings receive new water to nourish them constantly. This is the job of the women, because the men are busy with plowing and harrowing. You have no doubt seen rice seedlings in the fields. They are visible as patches in the fields, fresh light green in color, attractive and refreshing to the eye. When they have grown to a height of a quarter meter or more, in the fresh morning air the breeze blows in gusts and the tips of the seedlings flutter and wave back and forth in rhythm, graceful as dancers welcoming the sun at dawn. If there is also a fine shower falling, the picture is all the more refreshing and pleasing. Those of you who have been farmers but are so no longer, have you ever felt and seen this in the past? Whatever your reason for abandoning the fields and coming to live in the city, have you ever seen this sort of natural scene in the city?

During the time that the seedlings have not yet grown to the size to be transplanted, the men rise in the early morning. If the fields are distant, they must leave the house as early as 4 A.M., carrying the yokes, plows, knives, hoes, and spades on their shoulders and leading the oxen or buffaloes out to plow. If they do not carry these things themselves, they may have the oxen or buffaloes carry them instead. They set to work to plow the field where they had the first plowing before the other fields. For the plowing at this time there is no auspicious time. They do dàʔ plowing [the Thai term is retained here because no exact English equivalent is known; dàʔ is a verb meaning to plow an entire area the first time] in a circle along the boundary of the ŋaan that they have marked off in the field. If the particular field is divided into two parts, or two ŋaan, they do the plowing in two time periods. They plow one ŋaan in the morning; when it is finished, they continue to plow the second ŋaan in the afternoon. If it is a large field, they may divide it into as many as four ŋaan. They usually ask one another, "How many ŋaan (shifts) of plowing will finish this field?" The answer is, "It will probably take four ŋaan (shifts)." This shows that the field in question is very large, that it requires four shifts of plowing. At the first plowing they plow straight from the head of the field ridge in one corner to another corner. If they plow with their right side toward the field ridge, the ridge of earth plowed up falls to the left the whole length of the furrow. When they are near the end they raise the plow to help the buffaloes, and have them turn to the left along the end of the field. This is called "blaŋ hǎaŋ thǎj, lǐaw hǔa ŋaan," and means that they have finished plowing one row. Then they continue plowing till they have traversed the end of the ŋaan, and turn the plow and plow straight along the other side. Then they plow across the end and come back to the starting point. They have finished the outer margin of the ŋaan, and now plow new rows inside the first row which are gradually smaller until they reach the center. Then the ŋaan is finished and they stop to rest, and begin the second ŋaan at another time period. When both ŋaan are finished, and one field is completed, they must plow two or three more circuits around the part next to the field ridge, keeping it to the left, because when they plowed the first time they kept the field ridge to the right. The head of the plowshare which fits over the pighead turns to the left and bites more earth to the left than to the right; thus they must plow with the field ridge to the left in order to have the plow bite the earth to the left, next to the field ridge, completely. In terminology for areas, one râj is four ŋaan; this probably comes from the ŋaan or shift in the work of plowing fields. During the plowing, when the earth is broken and turned up in sheets by the plow, there are many small red earthworms turned up also. Earthworms of this kind are called field earthworms. One will see Thai mynah birds (Acridotheres siamensis) descending in flocks to eat the earthworms. These birds are tame, because people do them no harm, their flesh being unpleasant to eat and the birds being regarded as dirty; for this reason they are spared danger.

They begin to plow in the early morning. About 10 A.M. or later, that is at nɔɔŋ pheen (they have no watches to look at, and depend upon watching the sun's shadow and noticing their own hungry stomachs), they stop to rest, releasing the oxen or buffaloes from the yokes to rest and eat grass and straw. The men eat their rice; this may be called eating morning rice or, in the ancient term, eating ŋaaj, because ever since rising in the morning, when they rinsed their mouths and washed their faces, they have eaten nothing at all, except to smoke a cigarette, and, if they are betel chewers, to chew a wad of betel. They cannot be without a tobacco box, which is usually made of the inner shell of the ripe sugarpalm fruit, and a flint and iron; these are always kept on the person. If they chew betel, their wives prepare betel and areca and put them in a box for them. They wrap these in their phaa khǎaw mǎa, and tie them around the waist, or else tie on a triangular cloth bag into which they stuff betel box, tobacco box, and other things. In some places they plow in the morning and stop to eat in the late morning; then they continue plowing till pheen [11 A.M.] and stop. Thus as a rule farmers eat their morning rice or eat phraw ŋaaj in the late morning. There is therefore no midday meal; when they eat again it is the evening meal. It is the duty of those at home to prepare food and send it to the fields. Sometimes if they have the opportunity they also catch raw fish and eat them with pepper sauce. They squat and eat at the head of the field ridge or wherever convenient, selecting a big tree to furnish shade from the heat of the sun. For this reason if there are big trees they do not cut them down as in the city, where they are not tolerated because they are in the way; they usually preserve them as a place to rest and eat, sweeping the area flat and smooth for sitting and lying down. At the bases of big trees with cool shade like this, if in midday the heat of the sun is so intense as to be visible, and the wind sighs from time to time, and otherwise it is so quiet that one hears no noise at all, one feels lonely and is tempted to spread a mat and stretch out comfortably. It is precisely this which gives rise to the Thai idiom, "shade of trees, eaves of roofs," but for the farmers, even if they have endured the sun and are weary, there is no opportunity to rest comfortably like this, because there is much other work which they must do. When they have finished eating, they put the pots in the basket and hang them up on a tree branch at the head of the field. Then they go out and inspect the land. If they see grass growing thick anywhere in the fields, they cut it. If weeds have grown up obstructing the field ridges, they cut them. At points where the field ridges are broken or sunken, they plug them or raise them with earth. They keep watch to preserve and improve the land. In some places the fields are open, and it is impossible or inconvenient to find big trees nearby to provide shade for rest; they build a temporary hut for shelter, or they may build a field shed. Originally a field shed of this sort was called in Thai thǐaŋ naa, or by corruption chǐaŋ naa. Sometimes field sheds are built with elevated floors and open spaces beneath, of permanent construction. They are probably used as farming quarters throughout the season, that they are built in this way.

As for the oxen and buffaloes that are turned loose to rest and eat grass and straw, they are not turned loose to eat alone. If they are turned loose thus, to follow their noses and eat grass farther and farther away, they might easily be stolen. It is necessary to take great care with respect to oxen and

18

buffaloes, because they are the important source of power in farming, and
so there are always evildoers waiting to steal them. When they turn oxen
and buffaloes loose to eat grass, there must be a person to tend them. This
duty falls to the children. They tend them together in groups of many households; sometimes a group numbers many tens of individuals. They are called
oxherds and buffaloherds, and everyone knows full well what sort of youngsters
they are. They are hopelessly naughty, and go to extremes in their play. If
there are trees they climb and clamber up all of them. Sometimes they
play at fighting crickets, and sometimes at pitchpenny. What do they use
for pennies to pitch? They use the closing lids of large snails which occur
plentifully in the fields; these are the pennies that they pitch. Worse yet,
during the farming season when there are large snails, they roast them and
eat them. It is unnecessary to speak of quarrels and fights; they occur constantly. As for crickets, which city children have a very hard time finding
one at a time, or must buy from others for many sàtaay apiece, in the fields
in the cricket season there are plenty, and they are easily found; it is only
necessary to part the dry grass to find nine or ten at a time. Buffaloherds
being so naughty and inclined thus to play more than to keep watch, how
can they be much trusted in the matter of tending buffaloes? To trust them
is to associate with children in building houses [a Thai proverbial expression
for trusting youngsters in serious matters]. Therefore usually four or five
adults, when they have free time, go and take charge. Actually oxherds and
buffaloherds are just like monastery boys or any other group of boys, whether
of low class or high class; when they get together in a group and are turned
loose to play by themselves they are all alike, instinctively naughty, because
boys will be boys, and not adults.

When afternoon comes and the sun starts its descent, about 2 o'clock,
the boys drive the buffaloes back and plowing the second ŋaan is begun. (If
they use oxen to plow, they plow only in the morning; in the afternoon they
turn them loose and do not use them to plow, for oxen do not have endurance.)
They plow until the sun is very low, about 4 P.M., and then unhitch the
plows to give the buffaloes another period of rest. This time of day is called
bàaj khwaaj [literally, "buffalo afternoon"]. The buffaloes know well that
their work is finished for the day; they head straight for their wallows and
soak themselves happily, for they have been in the hot sun. When they come
up from the wallow they eat grass, eating and walking at the same time as
they gradually shift along. In the evening they turn their heads toward home.
They have an excellent memory for their own homes; even if they go far
astray, unless someone ties them up they know their way home. When they
arrive they enter their pens themselves; no one needs to herd them in. The
reason for turning oxen and buffaloes loose to rest like this is necessity; otherwise the animals cannot stand the work, and become chronically listless,
weak, and thin; they are no good the rest of their lives. At this time when

the buffaloes are turned loose to eat grass, there is some time left before
dark; the farmers seek fish, set fishtraps, gather vegetables, and break up
firewood, according to what they have. They carry this themselves or load
it on the backs of buffaloes to take it home. In the evening when the sun is
low, in order to rest they ride the buffaloes and let them walk idly through
the fields, trudging straight toward home. There is a breeze from time to
time, refreshing the spirit. One's weariness disappears completely, and
one's heart feels as unobstructed and clear as the vacant fields stretching to
the horizon. They ride the buffaloes along singing quietly the whole way.
The happiness and content of the farmers at no other time can equal this
evening time. This is related from the past of a man who once was a farmer.
The true life, when one forgets troubles and sorrows and worries and has
happiness and contentment for a moment, is at the time when the arduous
daily work is done and one rides a buffalo and sings quietly as described.
The meadows and fields, forests and mountains, playing a flute while riding
a buffalo, these things it is that the Chinese regard as the ideal of happiness,
peace, and contentment which mankind should seek. The farmers have too
much of this and so like to come to town, where there is naught but gaiety
and comfort, but happiness and peace are hard to find.

The first plowing as described above is called dàʔ plowing; it consists
of turning up the earth in ridges. After plowing it is left for many days in
order to let the grass rot and become fertilizer. They plow each field and
then leave it in this way, and then return to plow it again; this is called
prɛɛ [literally, "turning"] plowing, and consists of plowing the overturned
ridges back rightside up again. This is tantamount to loosening up the soil.
For both dàʔ plowing and prɛɛ plowing, it is not desired that there be too
much water in the field. If there is a great deal of water, they do not see
the furrow and may replow an old furrow or diverge from the straight line of
the first straight furrow. In this case some of the earth will be cut by the
plow blade and some not, rendering harrowing and transplanting difficult.
What has been described is what happens when they have enough time to
plow twice. If they are unable to finish in time, they simply do dàʔ plowing
and then harrow, omitting the prɛɛ or second plowing, but the transplanted
rice is not fully productive because the grass is still fresh, not having had
time to ferment and rot and become fertilizer. If the field is a sown field,
not a transplanted field, there is no previous plowing; they simply sow the
rice on the field and then plow it under, doing only the first dàʔ plowing.
But if there is much grass in the field, they must first do dàʔ plowing just the
same; they plow to pull up all the grass, and then sow and plow again to
turn the seeds under. If sown fields are plowed under only once, there are
usually grass and weeds growing up with the rice plants. These are chiefly
Triumfetta bartramia, Cyperus rotundus, and soŋ kàthiam. If these grow
among the rice to any extent it is necessary to keep watch and pull them up
often.

It is sometimes said that if we changed our plows and used iron plows like those of western countries, we would get better and quicker results than with our old plows which have been used for a long time and have never been altered or improved in any way. The explanation is given that western plows are very heavy; oxen and buffaloes can scarcely draw them, and they dig too deep into the earth. Also, they are more expensive than local plows;[6] the farmers usually do not have enough money to buy them to use. This is fact, but there is also another fact, namely, that in the case of anything that has been done in the past and has produced visible results, and has long since become custom, not normally manifesting any defects or disadvantages, it is usual among farmers not to want to change, for they do not trust new things, being uncertain that if they change they will receive the expected benefits. If their expectations are not fulfilled, they are in trouble, and so they prefer to do as they have done in the past rather than venture to change to unaccustomed things, unless someone first acts to serve as an example proving that good results are obtained, in which case they consent to change. Their ideas stopping at this point, it is impossible that there should be any thought of change or improvement to fit circumstances, unless someone acts as leader to set an example. At present it is learned that there is a new style of plow, an improvement on the old style, but this is a question of modern farming and has nothing to do with the farming of the peasants we are describing. Speaking of this reminds us of a plowing story set long ago in Burma. They say that an important European financial commissioner with intelligent ideas and good intentions desired to see the various nationalities living in the north of Burma, who are backward forest and hill people, receive the benefits of progress. He reasoned that the plowing of these people was done with backward, out-of-date plows. If they used western plows, which plow very deep, they would be richer than before. Having made his decision, with good intentions, he invested in the purchase of a modern plow and sent it to the governing committee of a local district with a detailed explanation of the method of use, requesting that they instruct the jungle people regarding the new plow. This plow that he sent for them to try out really plowed deep, so deep that it turned up the hard undersoil as well. When the jungle people saw this they were displeased, because they knew full well that it is impossible to grow anything in the hard undersoil, and so they refused to use the new plow. The welfare of the district officer depended upon his convincing the jungle people; he therefore tried in every way possible to induce the jungle people to use the modern plow. All his explanations and recommendations were useless. Finally he had to use threats, saying that if they did not consent to use the modern plow, the commissioner would be very angry, and if he ever became angry there would be dreadful consequences, because one of the eyes of the commissioner had a flaming fire to burn the stubborn to death. For this reason the commissioner had to wear a monocle to cover this eye so that it would burn no one. Even when thus threatened, the jungle people were still unwilling to use the western iron plow. Finally the commissioner learned of the matter and came himself. He reasoned with the jungle people, explaining the merits of the iron plow, and saying that he felt very sorry that these jungle people were stubborn and unwilling to act in accordance with his good intentions and his hopes for their progress and prosperity. The commissioner was absorbed in his explanation, when by chance his monocle fell out. There was an instantaneous scream, and the jungle people present fled in panic from the flaming eye, fearing that it would burn them to death. From that time on all the jungle people disappeared; searchers could not find them, for they had fled into the jungle. Thereafter they were never seen again. This is a story of breaking a knife handle with the knee or pushing an ox's horns down to force it to eat grass [Thai proverbial expressions for trying to achieve results by force]. It was an attempt to achieve sudden change, without trying to alter things gradually in order that the people may follow step by step, and so it failed.

Harrowing and Transplanting

To return to our story, after the plowing comes the harrowing. A harrow (khrâad) is an implement to comb the grass and weeds out of the earth. It is a piece of wood with teeth in a row which are called lûug khrâad, and it is drawn through the field by buffaloes. The first harrowing must be done in the plot where the ceremonial first plowing was performed. At the time of harrowing they must let water onto or off the field in order to get the proper amount; the water must cover the plowed earth slightly. They harrow back and forth until the plowed earth is broken up in mud and forms a flat smooth area. Wherever there are weeds and plants, they are pulled out and thrown away, to facilitate the transplanting of rice. When they have finished harrowing they leave the field for a night or two for the mud to settle, and then they bring the rice plants and transplant them. At the time of harrowing the youngsters catch snails, crabs, and fish in the plowed and harrowed earth in great fun. Not only the youngsters have fun; the pond herons also enjoy it, for they get a chance to catch fish, and one sees them wading through the water in white flocks.

When they have harrowed the fields and left them to stand, they begin to pull up the rice seedlings and separate them according to variety. This is the work of the women, because the men are busy with plow and harrow. The method of pulling is to stoop over and take the plants in both hands to cause the clay clinging to the roots to fall off. Then they grasp the rice plants at the base and strike them against a wooden panel, which they have prepared, in order to even up the bases of the seedlings. Then they tie the upper part of the plants together with a bamboo strip. Each bunch is called a kam, but in the province of Nakhon Ratchasima it is called a khób. The ends of the seedlings have to be cut short and even. If they are not cut, but are left as they are, when they are transplanted they are long and disorderly and the leaves will grow slowly. When they have finished they tie the bunches together in pairs, which in the province of Nakhon Ratchasima are called puŋ. They insert a bamboo which is flattened at both ends into the puŋ and use this as a carrying pole to take them to the place where they are to be planted.

Before setting to work to plant the seedlings, they again prepare offerings for the spirit of the land at the shrine which was built at the time of the first plowing. They must plant the field of the first plowing before all other fields. This field is divided into two parts. In one part heavy rice is planted and in the other light rice. The rice that is planted in this field is for use as seed rice for planting the following year, because it is regarded as rice which has been properly treated according to auspices and ceremonies in an auspicious field. Other fields are also planted in rows and sections according to varieties, without mixing. The method of planting is by stooping over, as everyone has seen. They take hold of the clump of seedlings in the left or right hand, whichever is convenient, and turn the base of the seedlings away from the body. The free left or right hand takes hold of the base of the seedlings and picks off six or seven plants, and then plunges them into the mud with the thumb. Before withdrawing the hand from the rice plant, they press the mud with two fingers to bury the base of the rice plants firmly and to smooth the mud around them. Using the thumb to press a hole in the earth, particularly if the earth is rather hard and they work at it for long hours for many days, makes the thumb very sore. For this reason in some localities they have to use a stick to poke a hole first. This method is certainly slower than usual, but if necessary it must be used. This stick is called in the province of Nakhon Pathom hŭa jôog or tàŋòog. They take a piece of bamboo as high as the knee, with a prong projecting from a node to serve as a handle, and whittle the base sharp. They jab this into the ground to make a hole as deep as desired, and then poke the rice plants in and press the mouth of the hole with the fingers. If they do not do this, but use the sore thumbs to press a hole, they cannot bury the rice plants deep, and the plants may come loose and float. Transplanters always keep their backs to the sun in order to keep the sun off the face. For this reason, in farming -- at all stages, whether plowing, harrowing, transplanting, or reaping -- it is necessary always to wear a shirt and keep the back to the sun. On the head, if they are women, they wear ŋòɔb [farm hats]; if they are men they usually take their phâa khǎaw máa, which they always have with them, off the waist and wrap it around the head. If they have betel boxes, cigarette boxes, or pocketbooks, they take them out and lay them down at the head of the field.

When they have finished transplanting and time has passed, the rice plants burst into lush green clumps. When touched by breezes or showers the tips bend gracefully with the wind, chasing each other like waves in the sea. They take up the rainwater, which gives them a fresh green appearance. This is the period between the beginning of Buddhist Lent and the tenth lunar month. When the time arrives for the rice to bloom (in the province of Ayutthaya this time is called khâaw phlôoŋ) the rice forms flowering heads, and clusters of blossoms, light green in color, appear throughout the meadows. The rice always flowers all at the same time, not at different times, because it was all planted at the same time. The farmers rise in the morning, rinse their mouths and wash their faces, and then go out to inspect the rice plants in the fields. When they see the rice plants full of blossoms you may be certain that they are happy, because the fragrance of the rice blossoms in the morning pervades everything. It is a fragrant odor like the odor of the chommánâad flower, but weaker; for this reason the chommánâad flower is called the "new rice flower." When one thinks of the morning air in the fields at the time when the rice is in bloom, one feels refreshed, for one breathes fresh air scented with the fragrance of the rice blossoms drifting down the wind. In the eastern sky one sees the sun as a great red ball just appearing and throwing its light upon the sky, yellow and brilliant as gold. It is quiet and peaceful, and one hears only the humming of the bees which hover about collecting the pollen of the rice blossoms. The farmers do not come out to the fields to admire the beautiful scene or to breathe the fresh cool air, because farmers are familiar with such natural beauty and purity. They come out rather to inspect the rice and fields. If they see that the rice in any section is bent down and about to topple over into the water, they find a bamboo to make a rail to hold it up, for if the rice plants fall into the water the tops will be completely eaten off by the Anabas testudineus and Puntius javanicus fish which abound in the fields. If weeds are growing anywhere, they pull them out. When their work is finished they either stand admiring the scene and the rice plants which are in full bloom, or return home.

When the rice begins to form fruit, short leaves appear around the heads and the stalks begin to swell, with thin leaves enclosing and covering the grain. The rice is said to be pregnant. The farmers in the province of Ayutthaya call it khâaw klàd hǎaŋ plaa thuu. At this time there is a ceremony of invoking the Rice Goddess. In the province of Ayutthaya they always select a Friday for the ceremony, probably being superstitious about the name of the day (sùg), which is homonymous with both the word for happiness and the word for ripe. They select a time for the ceremony in the afternoon, between 3 and 5 o'clock. They go out to perform the ceremony in the fields at the place where they planted flags on the day of first plowing. They prepare offerings, including one orange, one banana, and a banana-leaf cup of sliced sugarcane; the banana is a nǎmwǎa banana cut up. These things are placed together in one small wicker basket, and there are also powder, perfume, and a comb placed on a stand. They take the basket and the offering and hang them up on a flagpole, and sprinkle the powder and perfume on the rice leaves and rice plants. They make a gesture of combing the rice leaves with the comb. This is an act of dressing the Rice Goddess. The offering of an orange is said to serve as a remedy for morning sickness in pregnancy. When they have finished they pronounce an invocation, saying that at the present time the rice, or the Rice Goddess, has conceived, and so they have brought offerings to her and things to dress her; may she be happy and well and fruitful; and let no dangers disturb her. Thus the ceremony is finished. At this time they usually set up a square chǎlěew [magic pentacle figure made of two interlaced bamboo triangles], or a fish basket may be used instead. The setting up of a chǎlěew is said to be merely to provide a symbol to make it known generally that the rice in this field is "pregnant," and boat or oxen and buffaloes are not to be allowed to enter and damage the rice plants. In reality the chǎlěew is a protective device connected with spells and charms of the sort which Europeans call "magic," to keep spirits and animals out. It is the same sort of thing as the chǎlěew placed at the mouth of a medicine pot and the chǎlěew that they set up in the house when they have taken a corpse out of the house, as is done in the north and the northeast. Originally it was probably a real fence, and then no doubt it was reduced to a rǎadchǎwǎd fence and a chǎlěew, because it was seen to be rather a matter of warding off spirits or magic spells.

In the south (Chaiya District) they perform an invocation called khǒd khǎaw when the rice first starts to form fruit. For offerings they use only cakes, such as red boiled cakes, white cakes, bean cakes, sesame cakes; there are also powder and perfume. When they reach the field they select rice which seems to be forming fruit very well, and at this point they set up their offering of cakes. They light incense sticks and candles and pronounce an invocation to the Rice Goddess. Then they smear the powder and perfume on the rice leaves in the manner of anointing them. They do this to three to seven clumps. They lay the offering of cakes down in a suitable place. When they have finished they take the cakes back home, while the powder and perfume are usually put away in the barn.

The farmers in some localities of the province of Ratburi, after returning home from making merit at the monasteries at the time of the sǎad festival, take a portion of the sǎad cakes and fruit which they keep aside at the time of making merit, and put these in a small bamboo-leaf cup or funnel and lay them on a vessel which is woven in the form of a crude basket with legs. They plant this at the head of the field ridge, in a single place or in many places. This is an act of making an offering to the rice in the field and invoking the Rice Goddess to come and watch over the rice; it is called sòŋ khâaw bin. This last ceremony seems to be mixed with the Srãddha ceremonies of the Brahmans, in which they have piṇḍas of rice as offerings to the dead, and with the Sãrada or Sãrada ceremony, which is another ceremony associated with autumn; this will be treated in a separate study. The first ceremony of making offerings to the rice seems to be the same as the ceremony of making offerings to the Rice Goddess which is explained in the Old Textbook of Rice Planting (National Library edition published in 1924).

The matter of making offerings to rice and to the Rice Goddess no doubt comes from the belief that various things have life; whether a human being or an animal or a plant, everything has something abiding in it which is called the khwǎn. If the khwǎn is not constantly present, the living thing dies. Rice is regarded as having life and a khwǎn, and so the khwǎn of the rice must be treated in such a way as to cause it to remain present and not slip away, for this might cause the rice not to flourish or cause it to die (for the khwǎn see my work on khwǎn ceremonies). If the fields are near the edge of a forest, when the rice has flowered and the grains begin to form, there is usually a certain danger, namely, from forest animals such as hogs and deer. These animals like to come and eat rice; they cause great damage to the rice plants. The owner of the fields must go and sleep there in order to be on hand to drive away the animals; this is very difficult, because this is the rainy season and the ground is still wet and muddy, so that it is necessary to build a hut to serve as a shelter, or to use bamboo pounded flat and laid on the ground in a high spot, such as beside an ant hill, spread an oxhide on this, and then build a fire on either side and sleep on the oxhide. If it happens to rain there is great trouble; the oxhide used for sleeping must be taken up and used as a roof to keep off the rain, the smouldering fires go out, and there is danger from wild animals. This is the life of farmers in some localities. If they cannot endure these hardships they go hungry.

Profit and Loss

In planting rice they leave different intervals depending upon whether it is a lowland field or an upland field. If it is a lowland field they leave rather distant intervals, because the rice may form big clumps, with eighteen to twenty plants in a clump. If it is an upland field they usually plant the rice at rather close intervals, because the rice does not form very big clumps. Farming depends upon the ground. If the soil is loamy and black it is regarded as rather good, because there is sand mixed with the mud. If the soil is too clayey it is not very good; it is hard to plow and harrow, and the soil binds the clumps of rice, not allowing them to expand and flourish. But this is still better than soil which is entirely sand. If it is sandy soil it must be "duck manure sand," that is, with some admixture of earth; this is usable. If the soil is white like diatomaceous earth it is not good; although it may be possible to raise crops, the rice will not do well and produces a small crop. In fields which are newly cleared or have too much fertilizer, the rice usually grows too well; it grows so much that the plants are tall and big and the leaves are crowded thick as a kingfisher's nest, clinging together like tousled hair; the rice usually produces big grains but in small amounts and with little meat, being all hollow. Also, if the rains are not good, failing to fall when the time arrives for the rice to produce grain, the young rice grains will wither and die on the plants throughout the meadow. This is called khâaw mǎan or khâaw taaj phraaj; it is such a calamity to the farmers that they must sit hugging their knees and weeping, because the rice will come to nothing and their weary labor has been in vain. Worse still, they know they must soon reach the point of going hungry, because a crop failure is a calamity afflicting the entire community and there is no one to turn to for aid, everyone being in the same predicament. If the fields are near a river or a canal, it is possible to bring water and preserve some of the rice plants, but not enough to cause the rice to produce as good a crop as if there were rain to sprinkle the plant tops, because the young rice blossoms which are bursting open are baked all day long every day by the blazing sun, and the water below which nourishes the rice plants is also hot, combining to cause the rice to spoil. If this happens to rice seedlings they are said to taaj fǒj.

There are many other sources of damage to farms, such as floods, biting crabs, and nibbling worms. The crabs mentioned are field crabs. When they want to do harm, there is no knowing where they come from. They come in great numbers, as if they were migrating. Where they are born, where they come from, and where they go later has never been learned from research. They do not simply come; they also bite off the rice plants so that they float about everywhere. They are like beasts of fate to the farmer, because after biting off the plants they do not eat them. They simply bite them off for fun, or so it appears to one who does not know why they bite. In midday when the sun is hot they can be seen fleeing from the heated water and climbing up the rice plants; one plant has many of them, up to nine or ten. Elsewhere they may be seen wriggling and floating in rafts. Any attempt to destroy them, as by trapping, is impossible; their numbers are tremendous. The farmers are very much afraid of these wretched animals. In any year that they come, troubles are many. After investing money and labor to plow and transplant until the rice has grown, the farmer loses everything because of these dreadful creatures. Fortunately they come only at long intervals, only once in many years. It is a matter of taking a risk. You who like to eat crabs no doubt think that since field crabs are so numerous the farmers enjoy eating them. Not so, for field crabs do not have a great deal of meat like saltwater crabs. If they trap them they do not know what

to do with them, for there are too many to eat and they are not delicious.
It is possible to make a boiled coconut-cream curry of some of them, but
there are very many left over and nothing can be done with them. The only
thing is, if there is salt, to stir up live crabs with salt as they do to preserve
sàm££ crabs, to cause them to die of drinking saltwater. Then they pound
them with roasted rice and squeeze out their thick juice to use as sauce. But
if there is much of this and one eats it often, one gets tired of it.

Another kind of animal that damages the rice plants is the worm.
Worms occur in the fields at the time when the rice plants are growing well;
if one tried to estimate the numbers it would probably reach millions and
tens of millions. They float in the water in rafts so dense that one can hardly see the water, looking so green and crawling that they give one gooseflesh.
When the young shoots of the rice plants rise a little above the surface of the
water, these worms float up and eat them comfortably. They eat ravenously,
skipping nothing. They cannot resist the tops of the rice when they emerge;
as soon as they rise above the surface of the water they are all eaten off short.
The worms eat not only the rice plants; if there are grass and weeds growing
on the field ridges, they eat these as well. They eat all the leaves on a
plant, leaving only the stems and branches. The farmers are unable to com-
bat them, because there are so many of them. They can only make vows to
the shrines and invoke the spirits of the place as best they know how. The
worms descend on a field and live in it like this for about fifteen days, and
then disappear completely without leaving a trace. Worms like this appear
once in a great many years. It is necessary to take chances just as with crabs,
but they are better than crabs in that they bite only the tips of the rice plants,
whereas the crabs bite the plants off at the base; the plants are still young
and tender; the stems are flat, and not yet rounded out, and are unable to
produce new leaves to survive. A great enemy to the farmers at a time when
the rice plants have survived flood and drought are these wretched crabs and
worms. One might call them a plague descending to eat up the rice plants.
They are terrible. There is also the grasshopper, which also damages rice
plants. It is likewise a creature which comes in migrations once in many
years. They come in great numbers, flying so thick as to darken the sky.
Wherever they light, they eat the rice plants for a time, making waste a
whole area, but they are not as violent as crabs and worms. One might classify them as a secondary plague to rice. These grasshoppers are probably of
the same category as the half-grasshopper, half-cicada which in England is
called a locust, because locusts descend and eat grain plants in foreign countries in the same way.

The kind of losses we have been describing only occur once in many
years. If a natural disaster comes after the transplanting season, the farmer
is distressed to the point of tears, for it is too late to plant rice again, and he
must go hungry and poor. If this happens everywhere there is a famine,

which is a terrible calamity. There are also gains in farming, and the gains are greater than the losses. Thus in any year that there is plenty of rain, the crop is abundant beyond expectation. Rainfall that is regarded as good is heavy in the beginning of the season, moderate in mid-season, and occasional at the end of the season. If it falls according to this schedule, there is profit in farming. By rainfall that is inappropriate the farmers mean occasional showers at the beginning of the season, little or no rain in mid-season, and heavy rain at the end of the season. If it rains heavily at the end of the season, and there is too much water, or if there is moderate rain at the beginning of the season, light showers in mid-season, and drought at the end of the season, this is called "rain which deceives the farmers." When the farming is done a drought sets in and the rice dies while the grains are forming; thus the entire crop is lost. With rice that produces well it is possible to obtain fifty baskets to one basket of seed rice. It produces fine big heads, equal on all the plants, with heavy, firm grains and a minimum of empty grains, differing from the kind that has unfilled, light-weight, angular grains. If it has much meat it is good rice, with round grains without angles, the base curved and fine.

Transplanting rice is usually begun in the eighth lunar month or, if the farmers have been a little slow, in the ninth lunar month. Light rice transplanted in the eighth month begins to form heads in the waning half of the ninth lunar month. Heavy rice transplanted in the eighth month forms heads in the waning half of the tenth month. The age of rice is counted from the day of sowing the rice seedlings. When they have finished transplanting it, they keep watch over it and pull out weeds and grass and watch the water that nourishes the rice plants. When they are unoccupied, they fish and seek food. At this time the heavy work that they have done is over, and they have no worries for a time. During the farming period from the beginning of the plowing to the end of the transplanting they must leave home early in the morning; when they arrive they set to work until time to stop and rest and eat the morning meal. The working time at this period is at least four hours. The wives and children are at home; if they do not busy themselves with looking after the rice seedlings, they are not idle; they have the duty of cooking food to send out. Boys of the age of nine or ten go to tend the buffaloes. The aged who are unable to do heavy work like the others stay to watch the house and do small jobs, weaving and repairing utensils and baskets, as it is against the nature of old people to remain idle. If any family has only the husband and wife and young children, they have a very hard time; they must shut the door of the house, take up the ladder, and leave the house, carrying their infants along and hanging up a cradle for them in the hut or field shed. They do their cooking on the spot. When there is a great deal of transplanting and farming to do, it is impossible for one person to finish in time. They help each other in bees, but these are not as much fun as harvesting bees; there is only racing to see who transplants faster or slower than the rest.

Going out to farm in the early morning and stopping to rest and eat at 10 A.M. delays the time for eating until very late. They eat nothing to sustain themselves; exercising and working from early morning, they are very hungry by the time they eat. Sometimes when the time arrives they stop and wait for a long time before the people at home send food to them; they no doubt are very hungry and irritable. This sort of thing probably happens often. A story is told that a man went out to plow. When the time arrived to stop and rest, his mother had not yet brought food to him. He watched and waited, restless and irritable from hunger. When his mother brought his food, in his hunger he glanced at it and felt that there was only a little, not enough to eat. He became angry, berated and reviled his mother, and beat her. When he set to work to eat he could not finish it all. He realized his great fault in having been harsh to his mother, and felt very sorry. When this man died he was born as a tiny bird the size of a bulbul, with green body and grey head, which perches in the shrubs in the fields and cries n̂iid diaw n̂iid diaw ["only a little, only a little"]. It cries like this all day long. Wherever one goes in the fields, one always hears it crying.

Animals and Plants in the Fields

When the rice forms heads and ripens it looks bright yellow everywhere. The farmers still have to busy themselves guarding the rice, not allowing paddy birds to come down and eat it. The paddy birds come from time to time; if they are chased away they flee for a time, but if one is careless they come back to eat the rice in the fields. They come in flocks numbering thousands, flying so close together as to darken the sky. If one does not take care, they pluck off the heads of rice and carry them off, eating the grains and throwing the husks away everywhere. But the damage resulting from paddy birds, though it occurs every year, is not as violent as that from crabs that bite off the rice plants, for there is all told a great deal of rice, ripe and yellow all over the meadows. The birds eat without fear; when they descend to eat and one chases them away, they fly away to eat rice in the field of someone else. The owner of that field chases them on, and so they proceed by stages. Sometimes they disappear for many days and then return. This shows that they have been eating rice in the fields of others at a distance. It is not easy to keep watch and go out to chase them away often, and so the farmers make wooden rattles and hang them up in various places; a person sits and pulls a cord in the field shed. Sometimes they make wind-mills for the wind to turn and make a noise. The birds are afraid to alight in the fields. Sometimes the villagers make figures in the form of persons. Wherever the field is low and near to ponds or marshes, there birds of many kinds abound. It is necessary to build a hut to live in while chasing birds.

This duty falls to the women and children. If birds alight they chase them
away. One hears a cry of chasing away birds, wàa hə́əw wàa hə́əw, drifting
down the wind in the quiet midday air; it is a peculiar, lonely sound. If
birds do not come down to eat the rice, they spin cotton and silk in order not
to lose time at their work. The cotton that they spin is to be used for weaving monks' robes, in which the villagers compete in craftsmanship on the day
of presenting kàthǐn robes, which I have already written about (see my work
on the custom of presenting Kàthǐn robes). If the fields are near the forest
and there are wild animals, it is necessary to build a platform in the trees or
a tower as a place to rest while chasing away birds. When the birds come
they use a plummet made of a lump of earth with a long string to swing and
throw far out. Children like this work, enjoying the task of throwing these
at birds. If a young woman goes to chase away birds she is usually accompanied by a younger brother. This is an opportunity for the young men to
come and flirt, or if they are already sweethearts, they chase birds and eat
together; this is a story of love in the fields.

If you walk past the market, sometimes you will see them selling little
birds the size of sparrows, boiled and yellow in color, tied in bunches of
three or four. These are the paddy birds which come down and eat rice in the
fields. They make a snare out of a fishnet, with a rod to spring the snare
and cause it to fall. Sometimes there is a paddy bird tied up as a decoy
under the net. When a flock of paddy birds comes down to eat rice under
the snare, the person who is hiding and watching pulls a cord to pull the springpole loose. The fishnet which is spread falls down over the birds. They are
able to catch many tens of birds at a time; if there are a lot of paddy birds
they may catch as many as a hundred. Another kind of trap is called "tiger
sweeping its tail." It is made with a springpole which is simply a broom.
This kind of trap catches the birds dead more than alive; any bird that is
swept violently by this springpole dies, or if it does not die it is in a very bad
state [literally, "has a yellow chin," idiom for being on the point of death];
its legs are all broken. The name of the paddy bird is familiar from childhood; lying in our cradles we are told that it has a yellow head. I have had
this lullaby poured into my ears so often that I can remember it:

O yellow-headed paddy bird,
You come with two heads of rice from the city fields in your beak;
You bring them saying you are going to make a royal farm;
Your cheeks are fat.

Another kind of animal that eats rice in the fields is the guinea pig.
It digs holes and lives in the fields. If in the rainy season its hole is flooded,
it can make a nest of grass floating on the water. The amount of rice that it
eats constitutes no serious damage, because it does not bite off heads and
throw them away; it only eats the rice grains one head at a time. If there
are many of them, there is considerable loss. These animals can be eaten

by human beings. Farmers catch them and roast them like pork; they say
that they are very delicious.

Speaking of animals that occur in the fields, one is reminded of field
turtles, which are animals of two habitats; they live in marshes and ponds,
and in meadows and grass thickets. They do not like to live in fields for
they know that there is danger from people who watch to catch them and eat
them. The eleventh and twelfth lunar months are their season for laying
eggs, but nevertheless they are molested by people who seek their eggs to
take and eat. People are not as bad as the flamingo and the mongoose,
which are better than people at seeking turtle eggs to eat. In any place
where there are flamingoes and mongooses, cobras and other harmful snakes
cannot live happily; they are harmed by these two species. This is all a
matter of nature seeking a balance; if there are too many or too few of any
species, human beings are caused trouble. Look only at field crabs; because
there are too many, farmers are caused inconvenience. If there are many
cobras, one may take a false step and tread on them and be bitten; but if
there are none to eat the mice in the field, there are many mice to damage
the rice. If the flamingoes and mongooses should destroy all the snakes, it
is not known what damage these two species might then do. They say that
in some places in India tigers are very common and do harm to many hundreds
and thousands of people every year, to the point that they have to be destroyed. When they destroy all or most of the tigers, the wild pigs which are
food for tigers no longer have tigers waiting to kill and eat them, and so they
increase and there is insufficient food for all; they come and trample down
fields and eat crops that have been planted, causing not a little damage. It
takes a long time to put them down and reduce their numbers.

Speaking of animals in the fields, there is still another kind, namely,
the field waterbug [Belostoma indica], which occurs frequently in marshes,
ponds, meadows, and grass thickets. When there is rain or a storm some of
them stray into the fields. People like to eat these waterbugs. It is very
strange for they have an unpleasant odor like that of the kàthɛ́ɛ insect, but
people of every class, whether commoner or aristocrat, really like to eat
them. They tear them apart and pound them up with pepper sauce or pickle
them with fish sauce. The body of the creature has no flesh or skin. Its
only merit is its unpleasant odor, which is a fascinating smell. This is probably the same sort of thing as the odor of the human body. It appears that
not only the Thai like to eat insects and worms; other races like to eat them
as well. In the Bible of the Christian religion it is said that Saint John, who
was rather like the teacher of Jesus, was observing a fast in a lonely forest,
eating grasshoppers dipped in honey. Grasshoppers of this sort are what are
called locusts, which Africans also eat as food. If they come in great numbers, darkening the sky and covering the earth, the people catch a great
many of them and press them into bars to keep to feed to livestock. The

field waterbugs are caught in the morning, when they come up to lay eggs or are clinging to their eggs on the grasstops. People steal up and pounce on them. When the sun is hot and heats up the surface of the water, the waterbugs usually flee from the heat and climb to the tops of the grass, wriggling there, or hide in the water at the base of the grass plants. If any grass plant has waterbug eggs, it is sure that there is a waterbug nearby. If one shakes the grass with his hand, it rushes up out of the water, worried about its eggs and ready to fight to protect them. People pounce upon the waterbugs and take them away to eat. If one is not careful in catching them, they may sting one painfully with the stinger in their mouths. In Bangkok one sees people catching waterbugs at night. They are driven astray by rainstorms, and fly into big electric lights like those of the Plaza of the Equestrian Statue. Both children and adults watch to trap and catch them. When they fly low, people beat at them with cloths to knock them down. Formerly the price for which they were sold was at the cheapest five sàtaap. The upper classes in their automobiles also go to lie in wait, to trap and catch field waterbugs -- or to buy them -- showing that it is not only farmers who like to eat them; city dwellers riding in automobiles also like them.

In the farming season there is floodwater everywhere in the meadows. Wherever there are field ridges, the rice plants are in bright green leaf, attractive to the eye. When the rice heads form, some plants cannot withstand the weight of the heads, and fall over half in the water and half out. This provides bait for the fish in the fields, such as Anabas testudineus and Puntius javanicus, which eat their fill. People like to trap them for food, because they are fish with much meat and oil from having eaten their fill of rice all the time. There is an idiomatic expression, "new rice and oily fish," which probably refers to these kinds of fish. There is a kind of creature which causes annoyance to farmers, namely the leech. The water looks clear and quiet as if there were nothing in it, but if we only disturb the water and make a splash, the leeches swarm in. There are both "needle leeches" and "buffalo leeches." Wherever there are marshes or ponds, leeches abound; when the ponds overflow, they swarm out into the fields. When they are thick, the farmers who are plowing and transplanting rice are attacked by them on the legs, many at a time; it is not easy to pull them off, because they cling tightly, sucking the blood. It is necessary to prepare a cloth ball containing strong tobacco and lime and keep this tucked in the waist. When one feels that a leech has taken hold, he rubs this cloth ball against it; the leech cannot stand it, and falls off voluntarily.

In a field the water looks perfectly transparent, because it is still and the mud settles to the bottom. Fish of the sorts which like to swim near the surface are clearly visible, for example Trichopodus trichopterus and Rasbora argyrotaenia. Also one sees water-loving weeds and edible plants growing lush on the surface of the water and spreading out verdantly and attractively.

These plants include watercress (Jussiae repens), sǎaj tîŋ, Desmos crinitus, Begonia obovoidea, "turtle's liver," Ottelia alismoides, and sǎaràaj. Along the field ridges there are Centella asiatica and Ipomoea aquatica, growing down into the water. The farmers utilize these vegetables, dipping them in pepper sauce and plaa ráa. They are crisp and tasteless, not particularly delicious. Some species are rather acrid and bitter. One sees the farmers gather these vegetables and pile them up in big heaps, squatting in a circle and dipping the raw vegetables in pepper sauce and chewing them up noisily in big bites as if they enjoyed them. For food to eat with pepper sauce, they catch fish and cover them with mud and put them in the fire. When they are cooked they peel off the earth, the scales and skin coming off also; the pure white flesh of the fish is visible, very appetizing indeed. If the fish that they catch are small, they wrap them in leaves of plants such as Zingiber zerumbet and put them in the fire. If there are many bones they first chop them up fine. This kind of food is called ŋób plaa. If people who are not farmers go out to the fields in the wet season or the farming season, they cannot resist gathering the plants in the fields, for they are very lush and appetizing, and make one feel gay and amused. At this season the farmers have an abundance of fresh vegetables to eat, and do not go hungry. The best known vegetable is Ottelia alismoides. It has white flowers and floats on the water, intermittently visible like the head of a snake; the stems which are visible in the perfectly clear water are also curved back and forth like a snake, so that one has long since heard it said that when the Ottelia alismoides plant grows old it turns into a Herpeton tentaculatum snake. Actually one encounters real snakes of the group of fish snakes that watch to catch fish in the water, and so people jump to the conclusion that these are born from the Ottelia alismoides plant. Wherever the water is deep, there are lotuses in full bloom. These lotuses are pulled up and sold. They are called flexible-stemmed lotus; sometimes they are called bitter lotus, because the heads have a bitter flavor. The heads are round and large, two or three inches in diameter. The leaves are circular; the underside of the leaves is pig-blood red and hairy. The edges of the leaves are jagged like saw teeth. The flowers are white, the outer petals tinged with pink. The tips of the petals are blunt or slightly pointed. They bloom at night, and close in the afternoon of the following day. Their name in botany is Nymphaea lotus, var. pubescens. They are lotuses of the same category as the white-flowered sàdtàbùd lotus and the red-flowered sàdtàban lotus, which are domestic lotuses, not growing wild. Besides flexible-stemmed lotuses there are other lotuses which grow thick in the fields in the wet season. If you ride past on the train you will see them often. They have abundant attractive white flowers, only a quarter-inch or more in size, but it is learned that there are also big ones as large as five or six inches in diameter. These lotuses are phýan and phǎn lotuses, which in botany are called Nymphaea stellata. They have round heads about one inch in size. The leaves are oval, purple underneath but not hairy, and the edge of the leaves is smooth, not jagged, or at most the edge is wavy. The petals of the full-blown flower are long and sharp-tipped; they are entirely white, or the tips may be faintly tinged with indigo when they first bloom and then change to pink and purplish pink when they are old. These are day-blooming lotuses; in the evening they close. The species that has entirely white flowers, or faint indigo at the tips of the petals, and does not change color, is called the phу̌an lotus, while the species that changes color from indigo to pink is called the phǎn lotus. The phу̌an lotus is less fragrant than the phǎn lotus. The lotuses of which they eat the heads or roots are these lotuses, for they are not bitter. The stems can be eaten raw, for example, by dipping them in plaa ráa, but they are not boiled or made into curry like the flexible-stemmed lotus.[7]

> They looked lovable and delicate, sending forth pollen,
> The phу̌an lotuses growing lush beside the path,
> Prawn's claws [Begonia obovoidea] in overlapping layers, crowding
>   the sǎaràaj beneath the water;
> Sǎaj tŋ alternating with "turtle's liver"
> In clusters seen in rows to left and right;
> Water chestnut, water lettuce, and lotus blossoms full blown,
> Scattered white like glittering stars.
>
> Oh, if the girls come and see this
> They will descend to play in the meadows;
> Those who have little boats will float and paddle about,
> Pulling stems of phǎn lotuses and sǎntàwaa plants [Ottellia
>   alismoides].

These are lines in admiration of fields in the wet season by Sǔnthɔɔn Phûu, showing that the fields also have a distracting beauty if one has a poet's eye to see.

We have been absorbed in describing things of nature in the fields in the rainy season to the point of forgetting the frogs and bullfrogs, which come what may, there must be. At night they cry loudly, their voices very deafening, but poets hear them as "like the sound of gongs and drums resounding"; but they are certainly less deafening than the sound of motorcycles and loudspeakers. Actually things of nature, if we speak of their good points, include many lovable and attractive things occurring in the fields; they all appeal to the eye and heart. One sees:

> The rice plants in the field
> Flourish cheeringly;
> The rice is quick to form heads,
> In waving clusters.
> Their tips and leaves soar

In every meadow and field,
...
Producing dropping heads,
Most admirable.

Reaping the Rice

When the rice in the field forms heads which ripen to mature rice grains,
between the twelfth lunar month and the waxing phase of the first lunar
month, they set to work harvesting, in the first and second lunar months;
or sometimes they delay until the waxing phase of the third lunar month.
First they harvest the rice in the field of the first plowing, harvesting and
putting the rice aside in portions to be used as seed rice later. Then they
set to work harvesting the rice in the other fields. In some localities before
harvesting they first lay the rice in order to reap it easily; that is, they use
a pole held at the center by a person who walks through the field, which at
this time is getting dry but is still damp, and presses down the rice plants to
left and right with the pole, so that they lie in flat rows to be reaped easily.
If they do not do this, but leave the rice plants to fall over of themselves as
chance directs, they are tangled and difficult to reap. It is as they say, "To
have a drunkard husband is like reaping rice beaten down by pigs"; that is, it
is tangled as if pigs had gone in and trampled the rice plants. Laying the
rice is done according to the direction. It does not matter whether it is done
lengthwise or crosswise in the field. The only requirement is that it be done
correctly according to direction. For example, sections which it is desired
to harvest in the morning must have the rice laid toward the west; if it is
to be harvested in the afternoon, they must lay the rice to fall toward the
east. All this is in order to be able at the time of reaping to turn the face
away from the sun and the back toward the sun.

Whenever there are bees to help one another in harvesting rice, young
women and young men are glad to come and harvest together, for they will
have an opportunity to mingle merrily, playing while they work, reaping and
singing at the same time, and flirting gaily. At this time there are not yet
likely to be sarcastic repartee songs because it is a time for work. If such
songs are sung at this time, it is only because some young man is in love with
a woman and takes this opportunity to express his feelings by singing wooing
songs. The young woman is aware of this, knowing that if she reaps rice
near to this man she is certain to be wooed; but usually she is perfectly willing, for she will get to sing repartee songs showing off her verbal skill. If
she is not good at singing and has no confidence in herself, she invites intimate girl friends who have verbal skill to reap on either side of her. If the
man sings cuttingly, he is answered at once. The fun is in this. In reaping

rice they reap side by side in a row. When they have gathered the rice plants in the hand and cut one handful, they may tie the handful or not, as convenient. Then they carry it on the arm, or may pile it up at once. Whoever finishes reaping his row and reaches the field ridge stops to rest, waiting for the others who have not yet finished reaping their rows. When everyone has finished reaping, they go to harvest another section. Therefore whoever reaps slowly and arrives late is the victim of teasing. If it is known that someone is awkward and slow at reaping, the others reap in such a way that their own rows veer out, in order that the row of the slow reaper will be widened and he will have to lose even more time in reaping it, while those who have finished reaping their own rows go and sit waiting on the field ridge. Reaping like this is called "reaping around an island." Whoever is a victim of reaping around the island is mocked gaily by his companions, both men and women, who sit laughing at him. As the song has it, "Reach out, sister, reach out; hurry to reach the field ridge and we will be able to chat." In this merry fun the old people hardly concern themselves; they usually reap by themselves, striving only to work more than to play. Even if they play, they do not find it amusing. They let the young have their fun, for the young will be young; it is the natural order of the world, and to act otherwise is to obstruct natural laws. "If anyone complains that he is bored, don't believe him." Therefore there are some who even though old still like to let themselves go; usually these are widowers or men who leave the monkhood when they are old; they join in the fun with the others, furnishing an object of raillery for the young people.

They usually begin harvesting rice early in the morning. When the sun gets hot later in the morning they stop to rest, beginning again in the afternoon, following the same schedule as for plowing and transplanting. Whatever amount anyone reaps is piled up together in stacks. It is the duty of the owner of the rice, when the harvest is over, to tie it up in sheaves to be easily carried. For cord for tying they use bamboo strips; if they have none and it is not convenient to use these, they use rice stalks twisted into ropes for tying, called khầnèd. For tying it is also necessary to have experience and skill. If the sheaves are not tied well, or not tied tightly, they may come loose.

Let us speak of the old people who stay to watch the houses, and do not come to reap rice with the others. They do the cooking and have the children deliver the food to the fields to feed the workers in rest periods. In the evening when they have stopped reaping rice, they all play harvest singing games. At this time they play in earnest, not merely playing while they work, but playing for play's sake. This is called tên kam ram khiaw; that is, each player holds in one hand a handful (kam) of rice and in the other a sickle (khiaw). As they sing they gesture, dancing in rhythm to the melody that they sing. Please read the article on harvest songs in the book, Thai

Culture: Native Games. One suspects that playing at tên kam ram khiaw was not originally merely playing at harvest singing games for amusement as at the present time. It may be a form of playing and dancing handed down as a custom from olden times, consisting of singing and dancing in connection with harvesting rice according to certain beliefs; but later these beliefs were lost or changed and there remained only the fun, while the original purpose was forgotten. Nothing can be learned from examining the words of the harvest songs, because the words that are sung have changed with the times. There remains a bit of evidence in the name tên kam ram khiaw.

While they are playing at tên kam ram khiaw, the owner of the rice is tying up the handfuls of rice stacked up, making sheaves and assembling these in groups and stacks, while the players play on. When night falls they stop playing and everyone returns home; there is no feast of any sort. The owner of the rice and his assistants hurry to separate the sheaves of rice into groups -- seed rice, light rice, glutinous rice, etc. Then they set to work to carry it to the threshing ground at the house. If the sheaves are very big, a person who has never carried them cannot carry even two of them because they are very heavy. Once they have lifted the rice to the shoulder, they cannot set it down midway for fear that the rice grains will fall off. Carrying the rice from the fields to the threshing ground, if the distance is not great, is not very difficult, but if the distance is great and there is a large amount of rice, they haul it by sledge or oxcart, but this is the case only with people of means. Ordinary people usually carry their rice. If the fields are far from the house, it is not easy to carry it in one trip; they carry it and deposit it at a midpoint where they have a rest hut sufficient for sleeping and guarding the rice. They harvest and carry the rice in this way every day until finished.

During the period preceding the harvest, the old men who remain at home guarding the house prepare a ground for threshing the rice. (Threshing is the process of causing the rice grains to come loose from the straw.) They flatten the space to be used as a threshing ground until it is perfectly smooth and the earth is hard and firm. Then they take fresh ox and buffalo manure and dissolve it in water, mixing in wood bark that contains gum, or this may also be omitted, and smear this all over the threshing ground, covering the earth completely. If they can smear it thick, all the better. Even if a heavy rain falls the ground is not spoiled, because the water does not soak through to the soil; the water stands on the surface, and before long evaporates by itself. Rain that falls at this period is called rain that cleanses the threshing ground. Smearing the threshing ground with ox and buffalo manure is done in order to protect the rice while threshing; the rice does not get mingled with dirt and sand. When the people in the fields carry the rice up to the threshing ground, it is the duty of the old people to arrange a prism of rice on one side, keeping the varieties of rice separate. The prism is made in a shape like a triangular pillow; the size depends upon the amount of rice. They say that stacking the rice in this shape protects it from the rain. Even if it rains hard it does not matter much; only the rice on the outside is wet by the rain, and the rice inside does not get wet because the rain water runs off the surface of the triangular stack, which serves as a roof. If the threshing ground is located far from the house, they build a roof over it, and old people sleep there to guard it. There are both large threshing grounds to be used collectively by the entire village, and small threshing grounds for threshing rice belonging to one household.

When they have finished harvesting the rice and carrying it to the threshing ground, in some places they set up a flag on the stack of seed rice. This flag may be made of cloth or anything else; they generally use white or red cloth, of a single color or two colors. I have been unable to find out why they set up this flag. When they have threshed the rice and carried it up into the barn, they take this flag or a new one and set it up on the stack of seed rice in the same way. After setting it up, when the work is finished they throw it away, taking no further interest in it. Why do they set up the flag? If one were to guess, he would have to say that it is a marker to indicate that the rice in the stack is to be saved for seed; if this is stacked with other kinds of rice in one place they might forget, and a mixup might occur. The original use of flags was as markers and indicators, before they came to be used as decorative banners as well; also, flags were first used in religion, so that setting up flags has a sacred air, making them better than other things for markers. 8

After carrying the rice to the threshing ground, they go out to gather scattered fallen rice heads in the fields. There are not many. They gather them up, of whatever variety, in sufficient quantity to suffice as a gesture. This is called inviting the Rice Goddess. When they are going to gather this rice they speak the words, "O Rice Goddess, come you up into the rice barn. Do not go astray in the meadows and fields for mice to bite you and birds to take you in their beaks. Go you to the happy place, to rear your children and grandchildren in prosperity. Come you! Kŭu!" (On the word "Kŭu" they draw their voices out long.) If they do not know the invocation, they speak whatever they can think of that seems appropriate. Then they gather the rice of all kinds that has fallen and put it in a cloth wrapper or in a basket, and put it away in a suitable place in the threshing space. This rice that is gleaned is called the rice of the Rice Goddess, which is regarded as the life or the spirit (khwǎn) of the rice. When they have finished performing the ceremony of making merit at the threshing ground, they mingle straw with these heads of rice and tie them together as a figure of the Rice Goddess, which they put away in the rice barn together with the seed rice, to be used together with the seed rice for future planting, as described at the beginning.

In the province of Ayutthaya they have a ceremony of invoking the rice khwǎn to the threshing ground (according to notes made for me by Naaj Maanǐd Wanlǐphoodom). At the time of harvesting the rice and carrying it to the threshing ground, when they have carried in almost all the rice, they prepare to perform a ceremony of inviting the khwǎn of rice or the khwǎn of the Rice Goddess to the threshing ground and the house. They prepare cere- monial food, including one banana-leaf holder of red boiled cakes, one banana-leaf holder of white boiled cakes, one banana-leaf holder of "ele- phant's ear" cakes (made of glutinous rice flour moulded into a triangular shape, boiled till done, and then rolled in salt and coconut), one bunch of nǎmwǎa bananas, one boiled egg (sliced in sections), one lump of rice from the top of the pot, or this may be put in a banana-leaf funnel, and one new set of clothing, that is, one new stole and one new lower garment, which may be of either cotton or silk. For the day to perform the ceremony they choose Friday in the late afternoon. When they reach the field they unfold the garments and spread them out on the ground; or they may simply unfold them as a gesture. Then they bring out the food and make an offering. When this is finished they tie up rice stubble in the form of a small human figure and hold this up while they speak an invocation to the Rice Goddess, saying, "You have come out and borne the sun and the rain for a long time in the fields. Do you return to the cool shade of the threshing ground and the house." Then they take this figure in to the threshing ground, leaving the offerings in the field, and at that spot they must cast harvested rice, in an appropriate amount, as alms to the birds and crows. When the rice has reached the threshing ground, they must unfold the set of garments and drape them over the stack of rice sheaves which have been harvested and brought together. Then they plant the figure on the cloth, pretending that they are putting new garments on the Rice Goddess, and bring out a new set of offer- ings including the same items as those taken out and offered in the field. They offer these and make various speeches according to whatever they think auspicious for their making a livelihood. Thus the ceremony is finished.

In the province of Ratburi there is a ceremony of making an offering to the threshing ground very similar to what has been described. That is, when they have finished carrying the rice sheaves to the threshing ground, they spread a mat in the middle of the threshing ground, and sometimes spread a white cloth on top of this. They set out a meal of meat foods and sweets as an offering, and lay out farming tools such as sickles, straw hooks, hoes, spades, etc., together with a new set of garments. They light incense sticks and candles to worship and make an offering, and then take a cotton thread dyed with turmeric and tie it around the tools in a khwǎn ceremony. As for the large tools which are hard to carry in, such as harrows and plows, as well as the oxen and buffaloes, they need not be brought in; taking the thread out and tying it on them to tham khwǎn is enough. To the center pole of the threshing ground they tie one bunch of námwáa bananas and one dried coconut. When they have finished making an offering to the Rice Goddess, they put this coconut away in the rice barn together with the rice of the Rice Goddess. They simply put it away so, not doing anything with it until the time for making merit; then they bring this coconut out and use it to make offerings for the monks. As for the ripe námwáa bananas, when the ceremony is finished they are left on the center pole of the threshing ground, and are not taken away and used for anything, but they do not last long, for the children pull them off and eat them one or two at a time until they are gone. Sometimes they do not last even overnight.

In the south there is a ceremony of tham khwän when the rice is ripe and ready to be harvested, called "tying the rice." If the rice that is planted includes both light rice and heavy rice, they must perform the ceremony of "tying the rice" every time. After this there is a ceremony of tham khwän for the rice which is performed both when they are going to thresh it and when the rice has been put away in the barn; this is performed occasionally, not regularly like the ceremonies of tham khwän at other times.

This matter of gleaning fallen rice and regarding it as the rice of the Rice Goddess is strange in that various nations of Europe also have this belief, but they take the last head of rice that is harvested as the rice of the Rice Goddess. Whether harvested or picked up from the field, the important feature is the same, namely, that the last remaining rice is the life or the spirit (khwän) of the rice. If it is not brought in, the rice that is kept for seed might not grow well, because it lacks the life or the important part of the rice. (See my article on the Rice Goddess.)

The khwän ceremonies for the rice and the threshing ground are performed when all the rice is gathered in from the fields. Usually this occurs around the end of the third or the beginning of the fourth lunar month. This is only for sown fields. For transplanted fields the time is earlier, around the end of the twelfth or the beginning of the first lunar month.

Threshing the Rice

When they have finished inviting the rice of the Rice Goddess to the threshing ground, they set to work threshing. They thresh the various kinds of rice separately, always beginning with the rice harvested from the field of the first plowing. If one is going to thresh his rice at a communal threshing ground, he threshes this first rice on a special private threshing ground. There are two methods of threshing. In one method they use two pieces of wood about a meter long, tied together at the head with a rope. The rope is long enough to form a loop to go around a sheaf of rice and be caught up at the far end of the piece of wood. They raise the sheaf of rice and bring it down sharply on the floor of the threshing ground or on a mat, and the rice grains fall off the straw. This piece of wood is called a "wooden threshing pole." The method of threshing is similar to that used by westerners, who have a threshing implement called a flail. The other method, used when there is too much rice to use the first method easily, employs oxen or buffaloes to tread on the rice. They set up a pillar as high as one's head in the center of the threshing ground, called the center pole (sǎw klad); sometimes this is corrupted to sǎw cʼlad. At the top of the pole they generally tie a branch of thorns; usually this is a branch of Indian jujube. It is not reasonable that it should be for protection against birds and crows lighting. This pole also sometimes has garlands of flowers hung on it. They lay the rice sheaves in order around the center pole, placing the "heads" of the sheaves, that is, the bottoms of the sheaves, upward. The other sheaves placed next outside are laid with the rice heads up, just the opposite. Probably they desire to lay the sheaves with the rice heads up, and so they lay the sheaves nearest the center pole with the "heads" of the sheaves up to serve as a support for the rice sheaves that are laid in rows around the center pole. If there is a great deal of rice, the sheaves are laid profusely around the center pole and extend to a distance. They tie the oxen or buffaloes to the center pole, arranging them in a row extending out from the center. Then they drive the oxen or buffaloes round and round the center pole to tread on the sheaves of rice. The sheaves of rice are broken down and the rice grains fall off the rice heads and straw. Before bringing the oxen or buffaloes in and tying them up, they spread straw on the threshing ground for them to tread on. If they do not spread straw, the threshing floor, which has been properly smeared with ox and buffalo manure, might crack and break from the weight of their hoofs. They usually make baskets to put over the mouths of the oxen and buffaloes used in threshing, so that they will not eat the rice. If buffaloes are being used, they put old ones near the center pole, where the running circuit is small, because old buffaloes have less strength and walk slowly. Also, they are elderly buffaloes and not playful; they can be trusted; while other buffaloes with the strength of virile youth are not placed near the center pole because they will walk too fast, and other buffaloes in the big outer circuits will not be able to keep up. Therefore they put the young male buffaloes at the extreme outer end. If there is a mother buffalo with calf mixed with the others, the calf runs around the circle following its mother. When the buffaloes have made many circuits treading on the rice sheaves, the stacks of rice break down and the rice grains drop off the straw and fall to the bottom. At this time there are people standing in a row, usually young men and women, holding straw hooks (khɔ̌ɔ chǎaj) in their hands. These are long bamboo poles with knots in the ends, cut off short enough to serve as hooks. Straw hooks with iron hooks at the end are a modern invention. In some localities they are called mǎj dɔɔŋ hǎaj, which is the same as the term used in the old laws. The name is also corrupted to mǎj kàdɔɔŋ hǎaj. Actually chǎaj and hǎaj are the same word, meaning to make smooth (chǎaj = camhǎaj, dɔɔŋ = long pole like a carrying pole: Cambodian). When they see a rice sheaf break down, but with the straw still sticking to the sheaf, they pull it up with the straw hook and then thrust the rice sheaf toward someone else. If he does not duck in time and is struck squarely, it hurts. The one who thrusts is usually a woman, and the victim of the thrust is usually a man, but sometimes the opposite occurs. If there is going to be a game of thrusting rice sheaves it is necessary to give advance notice to be prepared. When someone makes a thrust, the other raises his straw hook and receives the thrust, like Chinese actors fighting. This can also provide fun. In some places they do not thrust the rice sheaves; they use their sickles to cut away the straw cords and bamboo strips which tie the sheaves, and then spread out the rice. This is called chĩg ʔòg. When they have spread out the straw, they have the buffaloes tread on it again, watching to pick up the straw with the straw hooks and shake it for the rice grains to drop off and fall to the bottom. In some localities this is called nɯ́ʔ. When they see the rice grains drop off and the straw come to the top, they pick up the straw and lift it outside. They do this until only rice grains remain, and then they turn the buffaloes loose and the threshing is finished.

Threshing is done beginning in the early morning. Later in the morning they stop to rest because the sun is hot, and if the straw is struck by the sun it turns brittle. There is no threshing in the afternoon for the same reason. Sometimes they thresh at night. At this time they have fun, and the young people all gather. As the verses for the buffalo khwǎn ceremony have it, "I'll tie you up to the stake, and then thread a rope through your nose and lead you around in a circle, in the presence of all the young men and young women, until the rice is leveled all over the threshing ground." If it is the dark of the moon, they build a straw fire to give light. They have refreshments, consisting chiefly of glutinous rice cooked in coconut cream with "fragrant" bananas. [The "fragrant" banana of the Thai is the familiar variety sold in the United States.] They have an uproariously gay time while they sort out the straw from the threshing floor. One can imagine that this is fun, for it is a simple sort of play mingled with work. This is work that they gladly and willingly help one another do. It is in the clear open air, with no unpleasantness to interfere. Formerly at the time for threshing rice each village usually made a big threshing ground to thresh the rice collectively, taking turns at using the threshing ground for one day or two depending upon whether the individual had much rice or little. They use what oxen and buffaloes they have for the threshing, even having ox and buffalo races; that is, they seek out oxen and buffaloes with speedy feet, and tie them at the end of the row in descending order to the number of twenty. If the animals at the end of the row are not fast enough they get dragged; if the animals

at the end of the row are very fast they can run and curve the row; for this
they are praised as good. This is all great fun. When the rice has been
trodden and some of the straw begins to float up, it is picked out. After two
or three spells they stop and rip open the sheaves and then pick out the straw
again. After two or three spells more it is finished. At this time of picking
out straw and ripping open the sheaves, the people all assemble with their
straw hooks, picking out straw and shaking it as they sing. For songs sung
while picking out straw and shaking it, they use brief, simple verses, like:

> Pick out the straw, sister, pick out the straw; brother has come
> to sit at the edge of the threshing floor and help sister pick out
> the straw.

> Shake out the straw, sister, shake out the straw; O sister with
> joined eyebrows and graceful throat, come and shake out the
> straw.

If there are good songmasters and songmistresses, they sing long repartee
songs as at the harvest. But nowadays if you go out to the country you will
have difficulty finding a big threshing ground. There are only small threshing grounds using two or three oxen or buffaloes to tread on the rice. Each
person has his own, and they do not work together well. The spirit of the
farmer has deteriorated seriously, and threshing songs have deteriorated as
well. [9]

They thresh the rice until the triangular stacks are all gone; when
every triangular stack is finished they ask everyone to help winnow the rice,
winnowing and pouring the threshed rice grains. Both men and women help.
Women who do this work must wear a crossed stole [the method is to bring a
scarf around from the back, cross it on the breast, and tie the two ends at the
back of the neck, like a modern "halter"], because they have to stoop over
constantly, and if they do not wear crossed stoles like this, they ["they" is a
euphemism for the breasts] will swing and flop unattractively, or will be half
visible and untidy looking. The winnowers stand in a long row holding wooden
shovels with which they scoop up the rice and winnow it. They pour it against
the wind, for the bran and rice dust to blow away with the wind. Even this
is not enough. There must also be people to shake the mats with their two
hands and help to blow away the dust and empty rice husks. In shaking the
mats they have dancing gestures, not simply shaking them, for they dance to
show off to the women and so must shake gracefully and in rhythm. Therefore shaking the mats becomes the duty of the young men who are strong.
They do not feel very tired, for there are people smiling nearby to cheer them.
To work like this is good in that one never gets tired. The mats that they
shake are panels woven of bamboo, in shape like big monk's fans. In the
verses for the khwǎn ceremony for threshing and winnowing rice it is said
neatly: "Oh do not take fright when you are put on the threshing and winnowing

ground for the buffaloes to tread on. We carefully sweep you up and winnow you to make you clean, and carefully scoop you up for the wind to blow you. Not even a tiny particle of straw will remain mingled with you." When they have finished winnowing every stack of rice, they scoop up the rice in triangular heaps. If there is a large quantity of rice it is slow and difficult to scoop up the rice; generally they use a board to scoop it. This board is called the "rice scooping board." Sometimes they make the rice scooping board with a rope threaded through each end to pull the board with and reduce the labor. If the heap of rice is small they use a small board with a long handle for scooping the rice. This sort of board is called thâdthaa, sometimes corrupted to krâthaa. When they have finished making the triangular stacks, they measure out the rice to be used for seed into portions, counted in basketfuls according to a "dog's tail" account. That is, they break and bend bamboo strips, and each break represents one basketful. When they have made breaks representing many basketfuls, the bamboo strip will curve up like a dog's tail, and hence the name. When they have finished measuring out and heaping up the rice according to variety, they take bran ashes and smear a streak on the heap of rice. This is called "ghost's streak" or "ghost's mark." They say the reason for doing this is to provide protection against thieves; if anyone steals they will know it, but they would probably know only that the rice was short. Perhaps they smear the rice to render it "defective," to deceive spirits into thinking that the rice is spoiled, so that they will not molest it, just as the Indians have a custom of daubing cupboards and vessels in order to show the spirits that the objects are defective. Or perhaps they smear and mark the rice to indicate that this rice is the property of spirits and gods, marked by the spirits; if anyone steals the rice he will offend the spirits. What the explanation is, is not clear, but in any case, when they put the rice away in the barn they measure it again according to the "dog's tail" account. This is a recheck for certainty. When they finish winnowing the rice, they have a traditional feast. As for the straw from which all the rice grains have dropped, they leave it piled up on the threshing ground. Later when they have time they carry it out and heap it up in a triangular stack, for feeding to the oxen and buffaloes when there is a shortage of grass. But while the straw is still stacked up on the threshing ground, they have to be rather careful, for the children are very mischievous and like to play tag and hide-and-seek in the straw. Sometimes they take wood and make a cave, cover it with straw, and crawl in to lie inside, where it is warm and comfortable, this being the cold season. Merely lying there does no harm, but if they play with fire near the straw it is as likely as not that a disaster will occur. The straw catches fire and blazes up quickly, and may roast the children to death. There have been instances of news of this sort in the pages of the newspapers.

Making Merit at the Threshing Floor

Before carrying the rice up into the barn, the time arrives for making
merit at the threshing floor. They make a pavilion and set up a place for
the Buddha image and seats for monks at the threshing ground. In the evening
of the day appointed for making merit at the threshing floor, when the time
arrives monks come and perform evening chants at the threshing ground.
The host invites relatives and close neighbors to gather and make merit, listen to the chanting, and present food to monks at the threshing ground next
morning. The pavilion is usually built of bamboo and roofed with rice straw.
Sometimes they tie rice heads on the pavilion as sprays and drooping garlands
to decorate the pavilion, and they bring the rice of the Rice Goddess, put it
in a vessel, and lay it down as one of the ceremonial items. On the threshing floor they set up parasols made of rice heads, planted on the stacks of
threshed rice in the same way that they plant parasols on sand pagodas. The
stringing of a sacred cord in the ceremony begins with the Buddha image and
goes to the begging bowl. Then it is tied around the center pole of the
threshing ground. From the center pole it goes around the area of the threshing ground and then goes back to the starting point. When the monks have
finished chanting, one part of the ceremony is completed. If they desire to
have entertainment at night, they have any sort of games they choose, enjoying themselves in the traditional manner of the peasants of the area. The
following morning they make merit by putting rice in the monks' begging
bowls and feeding monks at the threshing ground. Then they feed everyone
who has come to help. The monk who presides over the ceremony is usually
the abbot of the monastery. He sprinkles the rice of the Rice Goddess and the
rice kept aside for seed, the center pole, and the other stacks of rice with
holy water. When this is finished the monks return to the monastery. In
this matter of making merit at the threshing ground, if their farming has produced an overabundance of rice they make merit gaily and feast joyously.
If they get a great deal of rice they are very happy; it is like getting a wishing jewel, for whatever they lack, there will be people to bring it to them in
exchange for rice. If they get little rice, they are not happy, and they do
not have a big ceremony of making merit, abbreviating it to just enough to
preserve the custom. They only offer food to the monks, the crucial part of
the merit making. There is nothing strange about this because everyone is in
the same condition. In the book of collected khwăn verses there are verses
for a khwăn rite for the fields. I have been unable to learn clearly when they
perform this. It is probably a custom that is not much performed nowadays,
and so no one knows as much about it as in the case of the other khwăn rites.

When the affair described is finished, they carry the rice up into the
barn. If there are children living separately they apportion out shares for
them. If they can carry the rice up into the barn quickly it is all the better,

for the rice is stacked up on the threshing ground, and if their luck is bad there will be a heavy third lunar month threshing ground cleansing shower. They have no advance warning, and the rice may get rained on and spoiled. They must find mats and prepare to cover the rice well whenever rainclouds appear. In carrying the rice they first carry in the rice of the Rice Goddess and the rice to be kept for seed, of every variety, as a ceremonial gesture. Then they carry up all the other rice until finished. It is at this time that they recheck the rice according to the dog's tail account. The different varieties of rice can be mixed in the barn, except glutinous rice, which is kept separate in a krὲa or phɔ́ɔm. A phɔ́ɔm is a large basket, swelling at the center and with a wide mouth, but without the finished rim around the mouth found on a regular basket. For a lid, they use a flat basket of the sort used for sunning things. The rice that is kept for seed is put in a phɔ́ɔm or other receptacle and set aside in a part of the barn. Then they take some heads of the rice of the Rice Goddess, mix them with straw, and usually tie them up as a doll with legs and arms, just good enough to be recognizable as the figure of a seated person. Sometimes they dress it in clothes to show that it is a woman. The figure is not very large, usually about half a meter high. When they have finished tying it, they set it up on the stack of seed rice. While "inviting" it, they speak an invocation in the same vein as at the time of gathering the fallen rice in the fields; it is a request to the Rice Goddess to remain and guard the seed rice. In this invocation there is no offering of any kind except flowers, incense sticks, candles, scented powder, and perfumed oil. Why they tie together a figure of the Rice Goddess only when they put the rice away in the barn, unlike the European custom, which is to tie it up and bring it in from the fields when the harvest is finished, and what the purpose is, are not clearly known. There is another belief which is maintained in the province of Ratburi, namely, that once the rice is put away in the barn, they must not open the barn and take rice out often. They may open it only when they sell rice, or when there is necessity for using a great deal of rice for some purpose. When they are going to open the barn they must first light incense sticks and candles and worship the Rice Goddess. What words they speak, my informant cannot remember. No doubt they beg forgiveness of the Rice Goddess for disturbing her and taking her rice out. The reason for forbidding opening the barn frequently is probably fear that the Rice Goddess will become angry and flee away. For this reason before putting the rice away in the barn, they first apportion out enough rice to eat for a long time, so that it will not be necessary to worry about opening the barn unnecessarily.

In the province of Ayutthaya they have a ceremony of closing the barn and a ceremony of opening the barn. They perform the ceremony of closing the barn when they have finished threshing the rice and put the rice all away in the barn properly. They must leave about a bowlful of paddy on the threshing ground for use in the ceremony of closing the barn. For the day of the ceremony they likewise choose Friday. They select a woman or man born in the year of the dragon, regarding this as a zodiacal sign [so the original!] which does not harm crops, to perform the ceremony. They prepare offerings including white boiled cakes, rice from the top of the pot, and an egg, as usual. They have the person born in the year of the dragon make the offering at the threshing ground. Then they use a big spoon to pick up the paddy remaining on the threshing ground and put it in a metal bowl. As they scoop up the rice they speak, asking that the Rice Goddess cause there to be so much rice that they will never finish scooping it up and measuring it. When they have filled the bowl with rice, they take the bowl and empty it in the rice barn, like the seed rice of the Rice Goddess. When they have finished making the offering, the ceremony of closing the barn is completed.

In the south (as noted down for me by Naaj Win Chajjárád of Chaiya District) there must always be some rice left in the bottom of the barn, called the "khwǎn of the rice of the lord of the place." When the time comes to put new rice in the barn, they scoop up the remaining old rice in the bottom and place it in the center of the barn. Then they set up offerings to the khwǎn of the rice, including three heads of first ripened rice which were brought in from the khwǎn ceremony in the fields. Then they make an offering of cooked rice from the top of the pot and roasted fish. They take a little from the head and the tail and the middle of the body to serve as a ritual representation of a whole fish; they call this "fish with head and tail." This is of the same category as the offering made to spirits and gods in other regions with a whole pig, that is, the head, tail, and four feet. Besides these there is one small stone, one plate for cooked rice, one small cup for water, and one piece of iron. It is not known what the stone and iron are used for or what they mean.

The ceremony of opening the barn to sell rice out of the barn involves superstitions about days; they absolutely refuse to measure out rice to sell on a Friday. On other days they may open it to sell. (In Ratburi they add the Buddhist holy days as days when they refuse to open the barn to sell rice.) The refusal to sell rice on Friday no doubt comes from a superstition about the sound of the word Friday (sùg), fearing that they will sell their happiness [sùg]. The ceremony of opening the barn is to scoop up a bowlful of paddy with a metal bowl used for offering food to monks. At this time it is not necessary to use a big spoon to scoop. Then they speak an invocation to the Rice Goddess, telling her not to be alarmed, and asking her to abide with the home and the fields, giving them rice measuring a hundred cartloads or a thousand cartloads. When they have finished speaking the invocation, it is all right to measure out rice to sell. As for the bowlful of rice that was scooped out, they take it and grind it to white rice, and cook it to put in the begging bowl of a monk to end the matter.

In the south they have superstitions about days in which they may not take rice out of the barn, namely Buddhist holy days, the sàad days, the beginning of Lent, Sŏŋkraan day, and the last days of the year, that is, from the thirteenth day of the waning phase of the fifth lunar month to the beginning of the waxing phase of the sixth lunar month. They regard these as days when the spirit of the Rice Goddess desires to be calm or to meditate, and does not wish to move. Whoever persists in taking rice out is wicked and may be caused to become poor again. The prohibition of taking rice out on these days also applies in other regions: The reason for this is self-evident. When they take rice out to sell they must mention the name of the Rice Goddess every time, asking her pardon for daring to take away her rice. In this affair there is an offering of cooked rice from the top of the pot and fish, as usual. This duty falls to the woman who is mistress of the house.

The barns which they build for storing rice are low buildings, but in the north they elevate the floor higher than the floor of the house in which they live, probably to show respect to the Rice Goddess. There are pillars and scantlings outside the walls. The walls may be of woven bamboo or of real wood, as the builder chooses. In the main, country people hardly use boards for the walls because they are hard to obtain. Usually they make the walls of woven bamboo. In the province of Nakhon Ratchasima they weave them of a kind of grass called tàkhúʔ, which they lay on to make walls for the barn. This kind of grass has round, hard stems as big as a lead pencil and two meters or more in length. They use this kind of grass, believing that termites do not eat it. The inside of the barn walls is smeared with fresh ox or buffalo manure in order to close up any holes that may exist and prevent the rice stored in the barn from leaking out. In some places they use mud to smear. Please do not be hasty to criticize the farmers as terribly uncivilized, to use ox and buffalo manure to smear the floors and walls. If they do not use these things to smear, what will they use? These things they have already or can obtain easily; they need not spend money to buy them, and so they use them. What else can they use? It is a question of living far from modern progress and not having to spend money to buy things. They must depend upon themselves almost entirely. The good and the bad must go together. It is impossible to choose only the good; the bad must also go with it in order that we may know the good and the bad. When we speak the word barn (júŋ), the word chǎaŋ almost always follows it. A chǎaŋ is a large barn, built in a long shape as a place for storing large quantities of rice. They may be seen at railroad stations. They differ only this much. Farmers who have no barns in which to store their rice weave phɔ́ɔm for storing it, or weave big baskets, but with open bottoms, or make round baskets to cover or enclose the rice which is heaped on the ground, smearing the area with ox manure and covering it with mats. If they do not use mats, they spread straw to prevent seepage of water which might make the rice damp. Then they build a small shed covering this to keep the rain off. They merely cover the rice. The rice may burst out in the lower part, and so they twist straw into a cord and loop this around the lower part of the basket. On the inside they likewise smear fresh ox and buffalo manure. This sort of place for storing rice is called a tàlɔ̂ɔm for rice, but if they surround it with mats or weave an extension with bamboo strips, they call it a tĩam, about which there can be no doubt that it is a word borrowed from Chinese. Even if they have a barn for storing rice, if they wish to separate varieties of rice -- for example, nonglutinous rice and glutinous rice -- they may make a tĩam or tàlɔ̂ɔm as a separate storage place.

Household Tasks and Implements

The farmer's receptacle for measuring out rice is the basket (kràbuŋ), which there is no need to explain as it is well known. But the baskets which they use for measuring rice are of two sizes. The small size is called kràbuŋ lûug sàd; the large size is called kràbuŋ sìb hâa. If we compare the sizes of these two kinds of baskets in terms of units for measuring paddy, one kràbuŋ sìb hâa, when ground to white rice, amounts to about one and one-half pails of white rice. If it is a kràbuŋ lûug sàd, it amounts to about one pail of white rice. This is only an approximation; it depends on the large and small sàd measures of various individuals. Forty sàd of rice are one kwian [literally, cartload], showing that formerly the oxcarts used for transporting were used as measures of large quantities of rice. Another kind of kràbuŋ is the kràbuŋ hàab [used for carrying on a pole over the shoulder], short and squat in shape, with the bottom curved more than that of the kràbuŋ lûug sàd. These have handles for attaching cords, used for carrying paddy or other things on a shoulder pole. This kind of basket, if woven very tightly and then bathed in oil or pitch both inside and out, with a handle for carrying or for inserting the carrying pole, becomes a khrúq for carrying water. There is also the kràchəə which is another kind of basket, with flaring mouth. The flaring mouthed baskets which we always see the Chinese using to measure rice are also a kind of kràchəə. The kràchəə is used everywhere as an instrument for measuring rice, but it is not a standard measure like the kràbuŋ lûug sàd. Another kind of receptacle used for cooked rice is called the kràbaaj; in shape it is like a waterbowl. It is woven closely, and there are various sizes. If it is small in size but flat in shape it is called a kàbaan, and is used in place of dishes and plates for cooked rice. After eating rice with a kàbaan it need not be washed; they beat (khɔ̀og) it to shake off the rice still sticking to it; after shaking it clean they hang it in the sun. Perhaps it is this that is meant by the expression khɔ̀og kàbaan ["to thump the head"], that is, to knock a vessel of this kind, or really to thump the head, used in both meanings. There is still another kind of woven receptacle also similar to the kràbuŋ,. but with curved bottom, like a spittoon with bulging middle. They call this a kràthaaj, and use it to carry things about on the hip, as in the verses for the preaching of the Chuchok canto [of the Vessantara Jātaka], when they praise Lady Amitda: "The beauteous Amitda walks along with the old Brahman, holding on her hip a kràthaaj painted with appliqué figures, looking radiant and lovely." If the kràthaaj has a flat shallow shape, with very wide mouth, it becomes a kràcàad. The kràthɔɔ is the name of another kind of woven receptacle, in shape almost the same as the kràthaaj, but round like a lamp chimney, with a lid and handles for threading cords to hang it up or carry it on a pole. The kràthɔɔ is usually lacquered and gilded for holding clothing and other things which should be put aside. The kàlôo is also another kind of woven receptacle, woven closely, with round flattened squat shape like a can fruit and a wide mouth, for carrying things on the hip. I have formerly seen lady barbers carry their hair-cutting implements in these on the hip as they went to cut hair in private homes. There are two kinds of kràdôŋ: the kràdôŋ for sunning things and for use as a lid for the phɔ̌ɔm, whose shape it is not necessary to describe, since they are still used everywhere; these are mates to the tàkrɛɛŋ for sunning things, which is woven more coarsely, with large interstices. The other kind of kràdôŋ is smaller in size than the kràdôŋ for sunning things, oval in shape like an egg. This is the rice-winnowing kràdôŋ. There are wooden crosspieces for separating sizes of rice at the time of winnowing. There is still another kind, the tàkrɛɛŋ, which is shaped like a fishtrap. They use it for scooping up fish. When the word tàkrɛɛŋ is spoken alone, one does not know it, and thinks always of the shape of a tàkrɛɛŋ for sunning things.

These receptacles will soon disappear, because they have been replaced by better receptacles made of other materials, as we have seen new things substituted for old ones already. But, in any event, to speak of the past, the farmers did not buy from others, but made these things for their own use. They studied the method of weaving and making these receptacles from generation to generation. When they had free time from farming, they wove baskets. How can one accuse farmers of being lazy? They had to spend as much as eight months of the year farming, performing heavy work at least from before daylight till evening. As has been described, the remaining three months they did not remain idle. For one thing they still had to make gardens, according to their needs. Their greatest amount of free time was when they had harvested the rice and put it away in the barns, about four months, but they had other personal and traditional duties, as has been described elsewhere. The time when they were genuinely free and need do nothing at all was at the time of the Sǒŋkraan festival.

You have no doubt heard the criticism, "They pound white rice and pour it in the pot only in sufficient quantity to eat." This means that whenever the country people would cook rice, they must pound white rice right

then, pounding only a little, enough to pour into the rice pot and eat. This
seems terribly lazy; even rice, which is the daily food, they have no desire
to pound, no desire to prepare adequately in advance. If you think thus it is
because you do not know the condition of the life of farmers. The reason
for not pounding a great deal of rice in advance to eat over a long period is
that they cannot eat it fast enough and if it is kept long it does not taste
good. It is not like newly pounded rice, which is much more delicious.
They pound only enough to eat from day to day. The duty of pounding rice
goes with that of carrying water; these are minor household tasks, and fall
to the daughters and granddaughters. They usually mention the two tasks in
a single phrase. Before pounding the rice they first sun the paddy until perfectly dry. If they do not do this, when they pound it the rice husks will be
hard to break open. The first time they pound it, it becomes klɔɔŋ rice;
that is, rice that has bran still clinging to it. They must pound it again,
called sɔɔm. On the second pounding the bran slips loose, leaving only rice
grains. When they have finished pounding the rice, they winnow it for the
husks to go in one direction, and the rice grains, broken rice, and rice bran
in another. In the language of farmers this broken rice is called kɔ̀g khâaw
plaaj khâaw, to be kept and mixed with other things as food for animals.
This rice winnowing is strange: it looks easy, but when one tries to do it he
fails. He cannot separate a single grain of rice from the broken rice. He
gets angry and shakes the rice a little harder and the rice spills. If you don't
believe this, try it. As for the mortar for pounding the rice, they also make
this themselves. They cut a tree stump and whittle it into shape, and then
cut a hole in the center of a size to form an appropriate hollow. This need
not be very deep. Then they build a rice bran fire in the hole. The fire
burns down into the wood until they see that it is deep and wide enough for
use. When they use it for a long time, the rough rice husks will of themselves
polish the wood in the hole smooth. The longer it is used, the deeper the
hollow of the mortar gets, until the bottom is thin and finally cracked and
broken and unusable any longer. Then they replace it. Most mortars are for
hand pounding. There are also mortars used for pounding with a big hammer-
shaped pestle, but women do not much like them because if one is not skill-
ful the work is very heavy. Lever-pestle mortars and rice mills are later
innovations. Only some families have them, for pounding rice or milling
rice in large quantities for making merit and for feasts.

Carrying water and pounding rice are the duties of the daughters and
granddaughters. Besides carrying water and pounding rice, they must also
cook rice, spin cotton, and weave cloth. If it is a mother with small children and no one to help, she is very busy and hardly has free time. She must
apportion her time for various jobs appropriately. Any time a young unmarried woman works, no matter what the work is, there are always young
men around. This is the great drama of the world; if there is a heroine but

no hero it seems wrong. Therefore at the time of pounding rice there are young men who come to provide amusement, or even volunteer help in pounding. "When night fell I always pounded rice and waited, càgkàlan [sound imitating the lever-pestle mortar] ; brother walked down the highroad. I forgot the basket, and brother went straight to take it to his sweetheart." After the rice is pounded, next morning it is the duty of the aged women to sɔ́ɔm it again, because in the morning the young women are busy carrying water. Carrying water is done at two times, namely in the morning and in the evening. In the morning they carry water for the betel vines and other plants, while drinking water is carried in the evening. At this time they usually return home more slowly than in the morning, for young men watch for them to flirt at the landing or well or pool. It is for this reason that they say girls are always willing to carry water, for they will get to see their sweethearts. If the place where they get water is a pool in the monastery, the evening is the time when the monks bathe. If they have a sweetheart in holy orders, they thus have an opportunity to make a reverence to the reverend brother. If convenient they may remind him by asking, "When are you going to leave holy orders? How many more months or years are you going to remain a monk?" The duty of carrying water falls to the woman apparently everywhere; pictures of people carrying water in Europe and India are always of women. They always use pots carried on the head, or carry the water on the shoulder. One notices that the Chinese who draw city water along the streets are more often women than men. All this is because the work of carrying water was daily work of the household in olden times, and fell to the women everywhere, of whatever nationality, and so it has come down to the present.

Now that we have told the story of farming, it will be seen that the gaiety of farmers depends upon farming productively. It is as they say, "rice to spare and salt cheap," or "the fields are full of rice, the water full of fish." This is to be regarded as prime happiness, because there are few other needs. If one has rice he can exchange rice for all other things that he needs. There are traders who bring things to the spot to trade; it is not necessary to seek them out. If one does not have a cotton field, there are people who bring cotton to exchange for rice. When cotton is obtained, the women spin and weave it into cloth for the family's needs. The happiness that comes from not lacking food and clothing belongs not only to the countryfolk. The monks derive benefits, not lacking for food and robes. The important thing for all humans is the desire for happiness, fun, and comfort. To speak only of farmers, if they are not addicted to evil ways, such as gambling, they have not a little happiness, because they have few needs. It is happiness deriving from the surroundings, namely nature. When they have enough to eat and enough to use they are happy. We have only just recently gotten away from making things for our own use and providing our own amusement, and so we do not feel the great value of making things for our own use and providing our own amusement like the farmers. I have told the life of the farmers, which is a simple, smooth life, not adventurous, not progressive, not wealthy, and not powerful. However things are, they go on like that. It appears that farmers would seem to have extreme happiness; not so! Normally a badge on the chest has two sides. One side is beautiful and glittering. There must also be a reverse side, whether it be a big badge or a small badge; there must be a reverse side in suitable proportions.

Before closing my story I wish to ask you a riddle: "What is it that cooked in the earth can be eaten, cooked in wood is good to eat, and cooked three times becomes sweetmeats?"[10]

APPENDIX

FARMING IMPLEMENTS

Key to Drawings of Farm Implements

WATER WHEELS AND WATER SCOOPS

1. water wheel

2. bamboo tube for dipping up water

3. conduit for receiving water, sugar palm tree or bamboo conduits are chiefly used

4. drag-type water wheel made entirely of bamboo and hardwood

5. tripod-suspended dipper

6. tripod

7. handle of tripod-suspended dipper

8. dipper or water scoop

9. half-dipper, woven

PLOWS AND YOKES

10. khan of the plow

11. dâm, or handle, of the plow

12. plowshare, tip is of iron

13. "pighead"

14. ʔɛ̀ɛg nɔ́ɔj

14a. modern plow

15. yoke

16. ꩜ͅ, made of bamboo

17. hitching rope

18. khlâw rope

SMALLER FARM IMPLEMENTS

19. harrow

20. khan of the harrow

21. harrow teeth

22. iron rake, Chinese style

23. iron shovel

24. wooden shovel, old style

25. spade

26. hoe

27. sickle

28. chick-head knife

29. lĭam, a kind of big curved knife with long or short handle

30. bamboo pole for carrying rice seedlings over the shoulder

THRESHING, POUNDING, MILLING, WINNOWING, AND MEASURING
IMPLEMENTS

31. straw hook, made of bamboo, used in threshing and picking out
     straw

32. threshing "chopsticks" of hardwood and bamboo for holding rice
     sheaves and beating them

33. shovel with groove, made of lightweight hardwood, for tossing ric

57

34. mats for shaking out rice dust, woven entirely of bamboo including the border

35. board for pushing rice, of the kind having ropes which they vie in pulling ceremonially

36. thâdthaa

37. kàchəə or sàd for measuring rice, woven

38. kàbuŋ or lûug sàd

39. lever pestle, for pounding

40. lever-pestle mortar of wood, buried in the ground

41. tail of lever

42. pestle for pounding

43. pestle for sɔ́ɔm

44. hand mortar, of wood

45. big hammer-shaped pestle, for hand mortar

46. pestle for hand mortar

47. rice mill, woven

48. winnowing basket woven of bamboo bark with wooden crosspiece, for winnowing rice

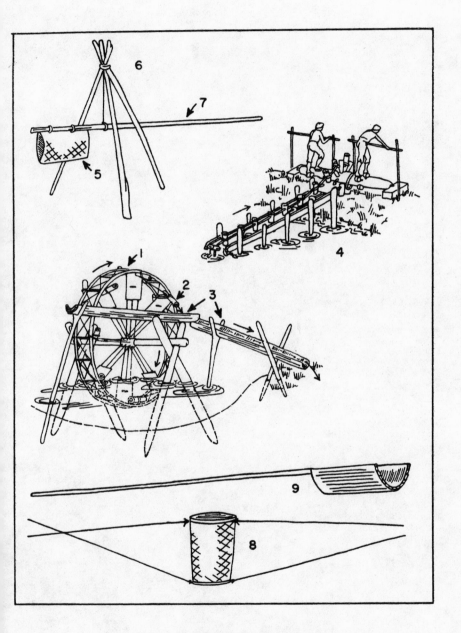

WATER WHEELS AND WATER SCOOPS

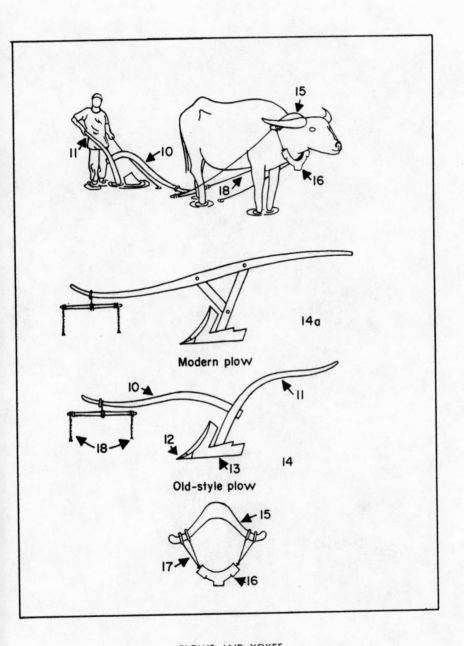

14a

Modern plow

Old-style plow

14

PLOWS AND YOKES

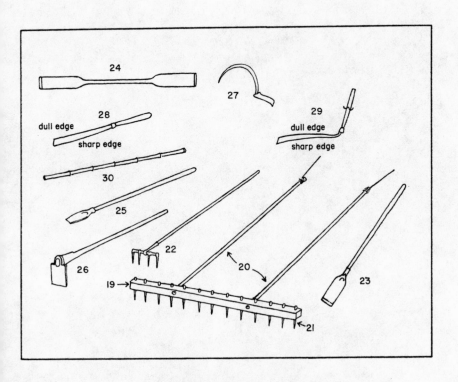

SMALLER FARM IMPLEMENTS

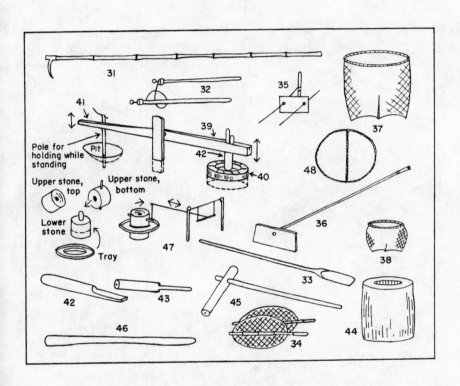

Pole for
holding while
standing

Pit

Upper stone,
top

Upper stone,
bottom

Lower
stone

Tray

THRESHING, POUNDING, MILLING, WINNOWING,

AND MEASURING IMPLEMENTS

Footnotes to The Life of the Farmer

1. Tylor, Edward B., Primitive Culture (London, John Murray, 1871). A.R.

2. The people of Nakhon Ratchasima and the northeast call a spade còɔb, and call a hoe côg. A.R.

3. See Old Textbook of Rice Planting (National Library, 1924) and "Days Forbidden for Ploughing" in Royal Ceremonies of the Twelve Months, in the section on the first plowing. A.R.

4. See Textbook of Farming According to Ancient Methods (Bangkok, Canthánáphlǐn Printing Press, 1930) by Dr. Chěŋ Cajtroŋ. A.R.

5. See "Kinds of Rice" in Manners and Customs, Part 3. A.R.

6. See the section on plows in the chapter on "Farming" in History of the Ministry of Agriculture. A.R.

7. Through the kindness of Phrájaa Wǐnǐd Wánandɔɔn (Too Kooměed).

8. See "Banners" in Encyclopaedia of Religion and Ethics, Vol. 2, p. 348. A.R.

9. See "Concerning Singing Games" by Phráʔ Phǐnǐd Wannákaan (Sěɛŋ Sǎalǐtun) in Manners and Customs, Part 25. A.R.

10. The answer is rice: it is cooked in earthenware pots, or can be cooked in bamboo tubes, or for certain kinds of sweetmeats is put through an elaborate series of processes involving three cookings.

POPULAR BUDDHISM IN THAILAND

Table of Contents

POPULAR BUDDHISM IN THAILAND

The Wat

To gain any true insight into the culture and character of the Thai of Thailand, it is necessary to learn something of their religion. Here I mean the religion, not of the educated or of scholars, but of the people in general; for religion is the mainspring of behavior as manifested by the people. The national religion of Thailand is Buddhism of the Southern School, technically known as Hinayanism. It is the religion, as generally professed, of Ceylon and the nations on the mainland of Southeast Asia (with the exception of Vietnam, which adheres to Buddhism of the Northern School or Mahayanism, as professed by China and Japan). Buddhism in essence is a religion of ethics and philosophy rather than a religion in the strict sense of the word. In Buddhism "man is as he has made himself; man will be as he makes himself"; the individual has to strive by himself to be pure of heart and deed for his own salvation without the intervention of God or any other divine being. This is the gist of Buddhism. But the Buddhism of the people, as a result of almost inseparable accretions through long popular practice, is otherwise.

In Thailand, as in the other Buddhist nations of Southeast Asia, the countryside is dotted with Buddhist temples and monasteries popularly called wat (wád) in Thai. The wat is divided into two sections: the first comprises the temple with its chapel, called bòod in Thai, where the monks assemble for their religious duties, together with the wíhǎan (vihǎra in Sanskrit) where Buddha images are housed; the second consists of the monastery building where the monks live. This is the usual arrangement of the wat in its bare outline. Most wats also include a number of stupas or pagodas of various sizes, called phrâʔ ceedii in Thai. They are roughly pyramidal in form, tapering to a plain or decorated tip and supported by a round or square base; bigger ones may rise from a terrace added for circumambulatory purposes. Originally a phrâʔ ceedii was a tumulus containing relics of the Buddha, but the smaller ones in many instances have been built to contain the cremated bones of some deceased persons. It is the Buddhist Thai custom that a corpse be cremated and the incinerated bones and ashes deposited in a phrâʔ ceedii or elsewhere within the precinct of the wat. This is equivalent to the Christian custom of burial beneath a cross in consecrated earth.

In every wat there is also an open hall called a sǎalaa where the congregation meets to hear sermons or to make merit, as occasion demands. The sǎalaa may be utilized as a rest house for wayfarers; or, in a bigger wat, it may be used as a place of religious instruction. In such a case it is called in Thai a sǎalaa kaan pàrian or the hall of learning. A wat also contains a bell tower and sometimes a drum tower as well. If there is no tower for the purpose, the drum is hung somewhere in the monastery. The bell or drum is used to summon the monks or the congregation to their religious devotions, or to assemble them for other purposes. Some of the bigger wats have a library to house the Tripitaka or Buddhist scriptures. Occasionally the library building is built in the middle of a pond to prevent insects, especially white ants, from getting access to the library.

As to the monastery where the monks live, it is divided into groups of houses, if the monastery is a bigger one. In each group there is usually an open hall surrounded on all four sides by the monks' cells, each separated by narrow open spaces. This hall is used as the dining place by the monks occupying the cells around it, as the recitation hall where monks chant their evening devotions, and sometimes also as a schoolroom where a monk-preceptor teaches boys of the monastery a rudimentary knowledge of reading and writing. A monks' kitchen is attached to each group of cells. For the purpose of saying something about Thai life in connection with the wat, I am going into great detail in describing a typical wat, though certain features are omitted in the larger wats, especially those in Bangkok.

Wherever there is a village of reasonable size, there is always at least one wat. The village folk regard the building of a wat as their first duty, unless one exists already. The act of building a wat is regarded as highly meritorious and as a praiseworthy sacrifice of time, labor, and wealth; so it was if we go back to the old days, when communal activities and the attractions of life were centered in the wat. Religious and social gatherings as well as most artistic and educational activities were to be found nowhere except in the precincts of the wat. The Thai rite de passage of life from birth to death has been inseparable from the wat. It was the desire of every Thai, from the king down to the common people, according to his means to build a wat, either individually or cooperatively, in order to gain the great merit accruing from such an undertaking and to gain the approval of his compatriots. A wat is also sometimes built to commemorate some great achievement or success in life. A victorious general on his return from a war must, if possible, build a wat to commemorate his achievement and no doubt also to atone for having deprived a number of human beings of life, which is deemed a great sin in Buddhism. One may wonder why there are a number of wats left in ruins -- why, instead of repairing them, people have continued to build new wats. Before King Vajiravudh's time, every king had built a number of wats. King Vajiravudh himself did not build a royal wat, giving as his reason that there were already a more than sufficient number and that making repairs to certain old deserted wats that were in ruins would surely bring as great religious merit as the building of a new one. But the popular belief persisted that merit for the repair of a wat would accrue to the original owner, so that the only way to gain merit for oneself was to build a new wat of one's own. Although the selfishness of this reasoning might seem all but to preclude the repairing of wats, there have been many cases where an old site has been restored and renamed as a new wat. Today there is seldom a newly built wat in Bangkok (with the exception of Wat Sri Maha Dhat near the Bangkok Aerodome which was built nearly two decades ago) but in the provinces the building of a new wat by an individual, or by a group in cooperation, is controlled and sanctioned by a faculty from the Buddhist Council of Elders.

A person desirous of making merit on behalf of deceased relatives may assign some of his immovable property to a wat. Such property may be a piece of land, a rice field or an orchard garden, or a piece of vacant land with or without buildings. In the old days such assigned lands were worked by a class of people called "wat slaves" under the supervision of a wat supervisor who ministered to the wants of the monks. Wat slaves, or in other words pagoda slaves, were household slaves or prisoners of war whose owner, as an act of merit, had transferred them to the wat as a religious offering. The status of wat slaves was in no way different from that of household slaves, but perhaps they fared better in some cases than the latter in their manner of living, for they were treated tolerantly and not as outcasts. The institution of wat slaves was based on traditional custom; and though slavery was abolished by King Chulalongkorn nearly a century ago, the institution survived implicitly by the consent of the people in certain parts of the country. It came to an end automatically in 1932 with the commencement of the present regime.

When a wat has been built and consecrated, monks from another wat or perhaps several wats are invited to take up their abode in it as a nucleus for the new wat. The monk who is going to be the abbot of the wat is usually selected by the villagers but in some cases will be sent by the church. The abbot-designate is usually a monk with at least ten years' standing in the monkhood who has thus earned the right to be called "thera" or elder. He is a man of learning in religious matters and if possible a man of sanctity with a knowledge of traditional lore such as is needed in a typical small community. A monk who has some knowledge of the healing art, or exorcizing and incantations, is always in demand by the villagers. Here I speak of the situation in the past, though it still exists in the present in some outlying localities. In certain instances when a monk who is desired by the villagers as the abbot of their wat is not able to place himself permanently in such a position, he may be asked to grace the wat for at least a few days as the first abbot of the wat and as a good omen for its prosperity. The coming of the abbot-designate is fixed beforehand on a certain auspicious day and at a time calculated according to the knowledge of astrology, which is to the present day a determining factor in many decisions. There may be a procession and other signs of rejoicing at the approach and arrival of the abbot-designate.

In his old age the village elder may become a monk and later be made the abbot of the village wat. In common language, particularly in central Thailand, an old monk is called as a sign of respect lǔaŋ puu, lǔaŋ taa, or lŭaŋ phɔ̂ɔ, meaning respectively, "great (paternal) grandfather, " "great (maternal) grandfather, " and "great father. " Other monks who are unlikely to attain such a status are addressed as lŭaŋ luŋ, lŭaŋ ʔaa, lŭaŋ náa, or lŭaŋ phîi, that is, "great uncle" or "great elder brother. " (In Thai an uncle is luŋ if he is an elder brother of the father or mother; a younger brother of the father is called ʔaa, and a younger brother of the mother is called náa). The custom of addressing monks with such words as an expression of relationship and intimacy points to a time in the old days when the monks in the village were no strangers but kinsmen.

It may be said that traditionally a male Thai whose parents are Bud-dhists ought if possible, on reaching a full twenty years of age, to become a monk for a while. Many of the monks have in their younger days been mon-astery boys learning elementary reading and writing at the monastery or wat, and some of them have been novices observing the rudimentary rules of the order. This gives them some experience of the religious life, thus smoothing the way to becoming a monk in later years. It is a popular belief that by be-coming either a novice or a monk one gains great merit and so also the per-son or persons who sponsor the undertaking. A childless person desiring re-ligious merit will sometimes sponsor someone, not his own kith and kin, as a candidate for ordination. He will sometimes even go so far as to relieve the man of his financial debts; or, in the old days, if the candidate was a slave, the sponsor might redeem him from the state of slavery, as otherwise he could not be ordained. For a person to become a monk he must be free from both pecuniary debt and other obligations. For instance, a government official is traditionally a king's man and must receive the royal sanction be-fore he can be ordained. Also a candidate must be a normal and healthy per-son free from leprosy.

A son who becomes a novice or a monk is in popular belief a mysterious agent for helping save his parents from hell when they die. A novice will be able to help his mother from such an unhappy state in the next life, and a monk will do so for his father. Thus parents are desirous of having at least one of their sons become a novice, or better still a monk. If possible, the son-candidate ought to be an unmarried man; if he has been married, all the merit thus gained will go to the wife instead of to the parents, and more-over his thoughts are likely to be more on his young wife than on religion. With rare exceptions, the Order of the Church will not allow a married candi-date to be ordained without the implicit consent of the wife. If it is desired to gain religious merit for a person when he dies, his son or, if he was child-less, anyone else, may on the day of the cremation become a novice, if he is a boy, or a monk, if he is a man. By so doing he expresses his gratitude to the deceased, and shows that he holds his memory sacred. Such an act is deemed highly meritorious to the deceased person, even if it is done only for one day. When King Chulalongkorn died, a certain high official became a

monk expressly as an act of devotion and gratitude to his late majesty, thus
transferring to his king all the reward of good deeds or merit accruing to him.
Similarly, when King Vajiravudh died, one high official became a monk in
sacred memory of his majesty: this person is still in the monkhood (1957).

A man who has not passed through the monkhood is regarded as a "raw"
or "immature" man. The people will have an unfavorable opinion of him as
an uneducated and imperfect man who is not "a son of the Tathagata, " that
is to say, a monk. It will be difficult for him to find a wife, for decent folk
will look at him askance wondering whether he is a proper and suitable man
to be a husband or a son-in-law. Here I speak of the good old days but the
custom lingers to the present time, especially among the country folk. A
man who has passed through the monkhood and again become a layman is
called dĭd, an abbreviated form of the Pali word familiar in Anglo-Indian as
pandit, which means a scholar or a wise man. The word dĭd has now in certain instances degenerated in meaning, to imply that there is something in
the man of a clumsy person who is a tyro in the ways of worldly life. An ex-
monk who has graduated from some school of Buddhist religious instruction is
called máhăa, which means "great" in Pali. The word may be used as an
honorary prefix to his name, but sometimes a man may be annoyed or object
implicitly to being addressed by such a prefix, for no other reason than that he
will not seem up-to-date in the eyes of his modern-minded compatriots.

All I am discussing here pertains to a time in premodern days, when
the culture-pattern of the people, especially in central Thailand, was more
or less identical. It is still the culture-pattern of the personality of the Thai,
despite the fact that there are some radical changes in behavior and thinking
among present-day people, mostly in modern towns or cities through contact
with modern civilization. In the old days when schooling was practically
limited to the wat, it was no wonder that the people were desirous of having
their male relatives become at least temporary novices or monks. When a
man becomes old he sometimes as a devotional act becomes a monk for life,
or if for various reasons he is not able to do so, he will frequently on Buddhist
holy days repair to the wat and observe certain religious precepts and hear
sermons. Many retired officials in Bangkok still observe such a practice. In
the next section I will speak of life in a wat.

The Ordination

The ordination of monks can be performed by a council of Buddhist
elders at any time. But in practice there is a certain time of the year when
ordinations usually take place: this is in the month before Buddhist Lent during which the monks make a religious retreat lasting throughout the three
rainy months from the full moon of the eighth lunar month to the full moon
of the eleventh lunar month (roughly from August to October).

A young man who has reached the full age of twenty years or more can become a monk. If he desires to do so either on his own initiative or, usually, through that of his parents, the first step is to prepare a salver containing one or more wax tapers, incense sticks, and fresh flowers, which he carries to his senior relatives or to his superiors, to pay formal respect and inform them of his intention of becoming a monk. He hands the salver of offerings with both hands to the appropriate person, who ceremonially receives and places it in front of him. The young man, assuming a demeanor of worship, prostrates himself thrice before this person, first placing his palms together and then bending his head until his forehead touches the floor between his hands now outspread palms down on the floor. Then sitting on his heels with hands raised and placed palm to palm, he solemnly addresses the person in formal language thus: "May any act or acts of mine, whether of thought or word or deed, which have trespassed against you, be kindly forgiven as an act of cancellation." The person thus addressed, while his right hand touches the salver, will say a few words congratulating the young man on the occasion of his entering the monkhood followed by a short exhortation and blessing. The young man then makes another triple prostration to the person and takes leave bringing back with him the salver, which may be similarly offered to other appropriate persons.

Now if the young man has a fiancée, he ought to inform her too of his intention of entering the monkhood. His fiancée will, as a matter of fact, make no objection, knowing very well that it is a tradition for a good young man to enter the monkhood before he marries. Of course, the girl will show mild surprise when hearing the first news and there may be some questions and answers between the two. For instance, the girl will ask how long he will stay in the monkhood. Why should she ask such a question, since she knows full well that the normal period a man spends in the monkhood is not more than three months, during the lent term only? But who knows for certain that the man will be in the monkhood for such a brief period? There have been instances when a young man, in the course of his novitiate, has become attracted and inspired by the noble teaching of the Dharma or Law of Buddha, and continued to stay on after the prescribed time. In such a case a decent girl is in a difficult position. She, by custom, cannot marry anyone else for fear of public opinion, and no other young man dares to marry her when it is known among the villagers that she is the betrothed of such and such a monk. Such has been the custom of the people but it is now weakening. Sometimes if the young man has remained a monk for a longer period of years with no decision that he will again become a layman, he will in conformity with custom and in justice to his betrothed inform her that probably he will continue to lead the life of a monk for how long he cannot say, and express a wish that she marry someone else if she wishes. Thus the girl is relieved of her moral obligation, and becomes free to marry anyone, for she is a "chaste woman" in the eyes of the villagers. In rare cases if the girl is determined she will reply to her man, the monk, thus: "If you do not intend to leave the monkhood then I will wait and marry no one at all. "

There is a well-known folktale prevalent in central Thailand of a certain powerful giant who was killed by Phrá? Raam (or Rama, the famous god-hero of the Indian epic, Ramayana) with his magic arrow made from a sedge stem. The giant died lying flat on his back and became a huge mountain with a sedge arrow still sticking in his breast. This mountain is said to be at Lopburi, a town some 154 kilometers to the north of Bangkok. In the course of time the sedge arrow, which pierced deep into the heart of the giant, will little by little withdraw from the wound, and in a thousand years it will loosen and fall out; then the giant will come to life again and devour all the people. Phrá? Raam, therefore, created a magic cock which he stationed at a place near the stone giant. If the sedge arrow becomes loosened the cock will give a crow as a signal. On hearing such a sound, Hanuman, the monkey king and an ally of Phrá? Raam, will proceed through the air to the stone giant; and with a mallet he will strike at the sedge arrow until it penetrates to its former place. It is believed that if a quantity of vinegar is poured on the wound of the stone giant, the sedge arrow will by its effect be withdrawn from the wound and the giant will revive from his death and devour people.

Now this giant has a daughter, who up to now has lived in a mountain cave a few miles north of Lopburi town. She is the betrothed of Phrá? Sĭi Ann (Sri Arya Mettraya in Sanskrit), the embryo Buddha (Bodhisatva in Sanskrit), who will attain Buddhahood in succession to the present Buddha whose Dharma or Law will come to an end after the lapse of five thousand years after his death. Half of this number is now begun in either 1956 or 1957 A. D. as computed by the Buddhists in Thailand or in other countries. His betrothed, the giant's daughter, is still waiting for him, and she comes day by day weaving a piece of cloth made of the filaments of lotus stalks. She intends to present this piece of cloth as a robe to him when he becomes the Buddha. Such a story may inspire a betrothed girl to take it as an example of being faithful to the end to her lover who is still in the monkhood. The story bears traces of Mahayana Tantric Buddhism, and has also a resemblance to an episode in the Raamákian, the Thai version of Indian epic, Ramayana which contains no such story. However we will leave the study of this tale to the folklorist.

In village life where each man is a law unto himself, every man carries a weapon for self-defense if he goes beyond the village. A young man on his rounds to pay his respects to someone in connection with his expected ordination as a monk will go accompanied by defensive weapons as a safeguard. Why does he have to do so? If an enemy of his knows that he will become a monk, there will be no way for that enemy to square up the feud or avenge an injury, as is his right. The yellow robe of the monk will act in most cases as a protection, for no one will dare to injure a monk with his yellow robe, a

symbol of sanctity. The last and only chance for an enemy to take revenge
is the little time left before the young man becomes a monk. Hence the
carrying of weapons, and traveling in company, are necessities for the young
man. In some cases and localities when the young man goes round on such
an occasion, a gong is beaten at intervals along the way. This is to inform
the villagers that the young man is going to become a monk. A person on
hearing such a sound and seeing the young man pass by, will raise his hand in
a worshiping attitude as an expression of rejoicing and approval. This is the
pattern of custom in general among religion-minded persons. When one is informed that a friend or any other person is doing some meritorious act, or
one sees a procession in connection with the making of merit go by, one raises
the hands automatically in such a worshiping attitude to express one's approval. One usage among the folk when doing a meritorious act, or when one
has achieved such an act is to announce it by beating a gong and by word of
mouth. This was the way of making a public announcement in the old days.
It is called in Thai idiom tii khɔ́ɔŋ rɔ́ɔŋ pàw or "to strike a bell and proclaim
in loud voice. " If you ask someone for a share or a subscription for any meritorious project you say bɔ̀ɔg bun which literally means "inform (to make)
merit. "

On the eve of ordination, there is a great stir in the house of the sponsor. Neighbors will bring presents either in money or things to the sponsor "to
help in making merit" as we say in Thai. Some of them will give a hand in
cooking or doing other things as may be required. The stir continues throughout the night, and there is fun and flirtation among the young people while
they are working. Here in Bangkok when one is invited to any social function
such as a wedding ceremony or a funeral ceremony we sometimes say paj
chûaj ŋaan; this means literally "to go (and) help a function" which reflects
the old spirit of the people in which there has been always cooperation and a
helping hand in such social functions among neighbors whose social status is
more or less on the same scale.

Now we have to speak of the young man who is going to receive ordination as a monk. For a month or two, and sometimes three months, the young
man, if he can, will reside as a layman in the monastery training himself in
matters relating to the ordination of a monk. He learns how to make re -
sponses in Pali to questions which will be put to him also in Pali by the offi-
ciating elders, to worship in the prescribed way, and to commit to memory
certain Pali verses in the devotional service. On the eve of the day of ordination in a village, or on the actual day in Bangkok, the young man has his
head, eyebrows, and moustache shaved and is dressed in white, a symbol of
purity. His attire will consist of a lower garment gathered in pleats in front
like that of a Thai female dancer and a robe similar to that of a monk.

On the afternoon before the day of ordination the candidate makes a
progression in procession through the neighboring villages. The candidate

walks with someone holding an umbrella over him; a wealthy one may ride a pony or an elephant. The procession moves from one village to another. Passing the open fields and villages on a hot afternoon, sometimes the procession has to stop for a rest under a shady tree where the fun and amusement of the folk continues; the procession starts again in progression when the sun has passed its highest point after two o'clock in the afternoon. The procession returns home sometime after dusk, when there is an entertainment with food and drink. After that there is a ceremony of tham khwăn which means strengthening or confirmation of the khwăn.

Khwăn is a Thai word identical in sound and meaning with the Chinese word for "soul." Owing to the adoption of a Pali word for "soul" in Thai, the word khwăn has lost its original meaning. Its present-day meaning is vague and denotes something definite but invisible in a man. It gives health, prosperity, and happiness when it resides in him, but if, on the contrary, its fickle nature causes it to leave the man and fly away, then if it does not come back in time, that man will die. Khwăn is translated in English as "vital spirit." At every formal turning point in a man's life and on other appropriate occasions, the ceremony of tham khwăn is performed. As for the ceremony in connection with ordination it is called tham khwăn nâag. The word nâag is nāga in Sanskrit and Pali, a generic name for a class of mythological snakes. A candidate for monkhood is called nâag. Why should he be called by such a name? A folk story supplies the explanation that during the Lord Buddha's time, a certain nāga or mythological snake, by its magical power turned itself into a man and became by ordination a monk. One day the nāga monk during a deep sleep turned back into a nāga and was seen by brother monks. The matter was reported to the Lord Buddha, and the nāga monk had to relinquish his monkhood, for no kind of creature except a human being may be ordained as a monk. The nāga asked a favor of the Lord Buddha that his name as a nāga might be given as a namesake to a candidate for monkhood in memory of the fact that it was once a monk. The Buddha consented, and so the word nāga is given as a name to all candidates for the monkhood. The above story bears a trace of a snake cult in far-off days. To come back to the word khwăn, in the Thai language khwăn is a word that enters into not a few Thai idioms which reflect how the building of words and expressions was done in the old days. To describe the ceremony of tham khwăn further here is to interrupt the thread of the story; for treatment of the khwăn requires a monograph of its own.

The time for ordination may be any time of the day by arrangement with the wat. Usually when the ordination takes place in the morning, there is a morning feast for the monks beforehand, which means some time after eight o'clock in the morning. If the ordination takes place in the afternoon, there is a forenoon feast, the last meal that monks may partake of on that day. A feast for monks may be presented by an individual or by a body of people when there is more than one candidate. I speak here of life in a village, while in Bangkok such a presentation of food to monks on the occasion is sometimes omitted.

The candidate proceeds from the house to the wat in procession. He is usually dressed, whether in a village or in Bangkok, as a conventional celestial being with a white conical hat studded with tinsel, a brocade lower garment, and a long thin embroidered robe worn over a shirt or singlet (a university gown of Chulalongkorn University is one of this kind). He may walk, ride on a pony, or sit in a palanquin or in a car, and he has to hold a wax taper, an incense stick, and a flower (usually a lotus) between his palms in an attitude of worship. He is shaded by a kind of umbrella with a long handle. Included in the procession are the eight requisites of a monk: an alms bowl; the customary lower garment, a mantle, and a shoulder scarf all dyed yellow; a girdle, a razor, a needle, and a water strainer. There are also robes and other things appropriate for presentation to the monk who will be the future spiritual teacher of the candidate and to other elders in the council who participate in the rite. We will leave out the details of such a procession, which of course includes music and other entertainment. In some cases, as in Bangkok, the candidate and his party proceed to the wat in the ordinary way without the attraction of a procession.

On reaching the wat, the procession enters the precinct of the bŏod, or the wat chapel, and makes a circumambulation thrice round the chapel in a clockwise direction. The candidate, who has already dismounted before entering the precincts of the bŏod, walks directly to one of the boundary stones in front of the bŏod where he makes an obeisance to it and says a formula in Pali. He rises after paying respect to the boundary stone and walks into the bŏod. But before doing so, he sometimes stands by the portico of the bŏod and throws handfuls of cash to the crowd below as alms.

Why does the candidate worship a boundary stone? In one of the two sects of official Buddhism in Thailand such an act is deemed unnecessary. Perhaps the worship of the boundary stone of the bŏod is a survival of animistic belief that at the boundary stone either of a city or some sacred places, there is a guardian spirit which requires a propitiation before any important undertaking. Beyond the boundary stones of a bŏod one steps actually on sacred ground. Here everybody who wears shoes takes them off and places them somewhere. In old days the people wore no real shoes. They went barefoot or in slippers, and if one wore anything on his feet he had to take off his footwear when entering a house. There was a water jar or water container at the foot of the stairway at every house. A person washed his feet at the water jar before entering a house, where the floor was kept clean. Instead of sitting on a chair, which was not a necessity, he sat in a squatting position right on the floor or on a mat, or in later times on a carpet. The typical Thai house is raised on piles, unlike the western-style house, with a ground floor which in the old days was actually on the ground; hence the necessity in the West for evolving a chair. Accustomed to the traditional way of life, a Thai, even if he wears western-style dress, will in most cases take his shoes off before entering a sitting room, because although he may sit on a chair he feels he may bring mud and dirt into the room on his shoes. With the introduction of chairs in the European style, there is of course no necessity to take shoes off when entering a house, except for those who do not ride in a car who might bring in mud from the muddy roads. Now in a bòod, which is a consecrated place, if there are no chairs provided and one squats on the floor, if he does not take off the shoes, apart from soiling his own wearing apparel, he may be the agent of soiling other peoples' apparel. One will also notice when entering a bòod or other places where a religious ceremony takes place, that there is usually a raised platform expressly provided for the monks. Sometimes this platform is raised relatively higher, while chairs are provided below for the laity, for monks must not be allowed to take a lower position than a man.

When entering the ordination room in the bòod the candidate or nâag is led by the hand by his parents or his sponsor and followed by a number of his relatives and others who desire the merit which will accrue from their participation. Everyone walks in line, touching or holding lightly a piece of string made of unspun cotton yarn which is attached to the candidate. The string acts, so to speak, as a conductor of merit, so that all the participants may have an equal share. One will notice also that the persons who lead the candidate by the hand are usually the parents of the young man. The one who carries a monk's alms bowl on his shoulder by a sling and holds a monk's conventional long-handled fan made of palm leaf is the father, and the one who carries the yellow robe is the mother. The rest of the monk's requisites and presents for monks are carried by other persons.

Once they are inside the ordination hall, after all the articles mentioned have been put in their proper places in front and every one has sat down, the candidate lights a wax taper in adoration of the Lord Buddha, whose sacred image rests on a high dais in front of him. Below the image sits an assemblage of elders. The candidate fixes the lighted taper at the place provided and performs the usual act of worship. The fixing of a lighted taper is popularly deemed a prognostication of the candidate's monkhood. If he fixes the taper in an upright position he will be in the monkhood serving the religion a long time; if there is an inclination of the taper, he will not be very long in the monkhood; relatively the more inclined the taper from its upright position the shorter will be the time in the monkhood.

The yellow robe, a set of three pieces, is handed to the candidate, whose head by now is shaved. His gown was removed before he entered the ordination hall, as he advanced toward the assembly. He sits on his heels before the assembly with the robe in his hands in the respectful position, that is holding it with both hands. He then asks the assembly in a loud voice in Pali words for his ordination as a novice. When consent is given, he goes out to robe himself. Here someone with experience will help him robe. He comes back to make his vows and accept from an older monk who performs the ceremony the ten Buddhist commandments for a novice. He is now a Buddhist novice. Next he asks the assembly if he may join the brotherhood. He presents the alms bowl to the president of the assembly, who hangs it on his shoulder by a sling. Someone may have secretly put amulets and talismans in the alms bowl as there is a popular belief that such articles will obtain an increase of miraculous power. The novice is now directed to a place at a short distance from the assembly where two elder monks will ask in Pali the prescribed questions concerning his status as a free and healthy human being. He will reply in Pali with yes or no. It is hard for a man to understand the questions in a language he does not know. The only thing he can do is to repeat the yes's and no's in the order of the series of questions which he has committed to memory. Sometimes in his apprehension he may reverse his yes or no: for instance, when asked whether he is a human being, he says no, and whether he suffers from leprosy he says yes. Then the formula has to be repeated. The questioners go back to give a report to the assembly while the candidate stands waiting. Then a pronouncement is made and the assembly ordains him with formal words and manners as a member of brotherhood. He now becomes a full monk. The actual time of his ordination as a monk is noted, as there may be a number of monks ordained; monks must go by seniority of ordination in their religious functions rather than by seniority in age. In old days when there were no timepieces, the noting of time was by the sun where a shadow of man was measured by the man himself in so many footspans. There is a superstition that when the assembly makes the actual pronouncement of ordination no pregnant woman may be present. Unless she leaves before the pronouncement is made, she will have to suffer a hard labor. Presentation of articles to the elders by the new monk begins and he in turn receives articles from friends and relatives who have been invited to the ceremony.

Life of a Monk

The young man has now become a monk and a changed man as far as his manner is concerned. He is meek and mild in strict observance of the exacting rules of the Buddhist brotherhood. A lay person who is very humble or shy in manner is compared in the Thai idiomatic expression to a newly ordained monk. A monk after ordination may reside in the wat where he has received his ordination, or he may select the wat of his choice as his residence. Usually he resides in his village wat for obvious reasons; for he has to rely on the support of his own people for his subsistence during the term of

his monkhood of three rainy months, and at the same time serve as a means
for his folk to "make merit. " The old folk, especially the women, are always glad and happy to "make merit" through the newly ordained monk who
is their own kinsman. Usually the wat where the young monk resides has an
abbot or a monk who is an elder relative of his; so much the better. He will
not feel a stranger in his new way of life. In fact the young man may have
been a novice or a "monastery boy" during his boyhood days, in which case
he is no stranger at all and will not feel lonely in his new mode of life.

During the first few days after his ordination, the new monk is busy
adapting himself to his new life and receiving visitors who come to present
him with the articles necessary for monks. These are the individuals who
have been unable to attend the ceremony on the day of the young man's ordination. Perhaps his fiancée will pay her visit too. Customarily there is a
celebration of rejoicing by the parents of the new monk at his old home. In
such a case the new monk will, of course, have to be present and receive the
customary alms from the people. A monk usually goes out for his morning
alms; for it is his duty to do so. Such an act by a monk is called in Thai
prood sàd, which means literally "to show mercy toward creatures. " It is
through monks that there is an opportunity for a "creature" to make merit,
for the monk in such an instance acts indirectly as a priest ministering a
merit to the donor of alms. It is thus logically the donor of food to the monks
who has to express thanks to the receiver, that is the monk, instead of the
monk having to express thanks to the donor of food.

Now we come to the daily life of a monk. Every morning at dawn,
about four o'clock, a bell in the bell tower of the wat is sounded at intervals.
This is to arouse monks from their sleep and also to awake villagers to prepare food for the monks on their morning visit for alms. The main food of
the Thai is rice, and it requires boiling for at least half an hour before it can
be taken as food. No rice left over from the last meal is suitable to present
to monks as an act of merit. The young monk after rising out of bed robes
himself in the customary way. Within a wat compound monks will robe themselves with their right shoulder bare, but with both shoulders covered when
they leave the wat. The young monk will recite such appropriate portions of
the Buddhist scriptures as he at that time has been able to commit to memory.
This is how a monk learns by heart gradually a fair portion of the sacred text,
by practicing every morning. Such a recitation as chanted by a chapter of
monks in ritual and ceremony is not prayer in a strict sense of the word.
Logically there is no prayer in Buddhism, but in popular practice, there is,
of course, a prayer to the Lord Buddha or to unseen beings. The young monk,
after a short recitation of the text, goes out on his morning round of alms
gathering. In the village, monks of the same wat go for alms in single file
with the abbot at the head and the most recently ordained monk at the end of
the line. In Bangkok or in large towns such a practice is now inconvenient,

because of traffic; therefore each monk goes by himself, although when receiving alms monks line up in queue. If a monk, owing to sickness or other adverse circumstances, is unable to go out for his usual morning alms, he is allowed by custom to send his "monastery boy" to represent him.

During the act of putting food into the monks' alms bowls, a person who is wearing slippers or other footwear that leave the heels uncovered must take them off as a sign of respect. A monk may not "show mercy toward a creature" who by an impudent manner pays no respect to the religion. After putting food into the alms bowl, the donor will raise his hands in worship. By etiquette no one must stand with his head above that of a monk. One ought to bend one's head low or stoop down a little as a sign of respect before a monk, just as one might show a respectful attitude by bowing before a superior. This practice is observed also toward a superior or an elder layman. If such a person is sitting on a chair, one ought to stoop a little as a sign of respect while going near or passing by. If the person is squatting on the floor, one has either to crawl or sit down. To speak to a person squatting on the floor while one is himself in a standing position above that person is a sign of disrespect, for one must not overshadow a person's head. The average Thai deems his head a tabooed part belonging to his personality. His fortune or prosperity will be weakened if perchance anything undesirable touches his head, and he deems it a grave insult if anyone dare to do so without his permission.

After presenting alms to a monk, the donor will perform a libation by pouring water from a basin or other utensil with a continuous running down of water without interruption into a clean place. This is a ritual act of allowing one's merit to accrue not only to one's own deceased relatives but generously to all other sentient beings as well.

Here we have to say something of the "monastery boy." In Thai he is called lûug sìd, which means a pupil or a disciple. But actually a lûug sìd or a "monastery boy" is a boy who serves a monk by doing his chores. In return the boy receives religious instruction and knowledge of reading and writing. In premodern days there were no schools in the modern sense. It was only at the wat that teaching was carried on by some of the monks voluntarily during their spare time as requested by the abbot. The knowledge of reading and writing thus gained by a monastery boy was relatively rudimentary or higher in level according to the monk-teacher's knowledge. Parents desiring their boy to know something of religion, reading, and writing sent him to a certain monk in a wat to be trained. If the monk who would be a guardian of the boy was the parents' elder relative or an acquaintance, so much the better. The boy might be a young child some eight or nine years of age, or already a grown-up boy. If the boy was a young child the monk-guardian would look after him as a father looks upon his son. Thus an old monk was called by the boy lǔaŋ phɔ̀ɔ or lǔaŋ puu, that is, great father or

great grandfather. In some cases the monk-guardian was himself the actual
grandfather of the boy. People at present call an old highly respectable
monk lŭaŋ phɔ̂ɔ or great father as an honorific prefix to the monk's name.
The boy stayed either in the wat with his great father, or he might return
home every evening if his home was near by. The boy, if he was not too
young, would serve the monk with whom he stayed after his school hours by
arranging the monk's food, clearing the plates, sweeping and cleaning the
monk's quarters, and so on. The boy might be ordained as a novice if his
parents desired. The life of the boy in the wat was interrupted every now and
then during the year. His parents might require him to do some light work as
a helping hand in getting their livelihood, which, in central Thailand, was
by rice growing; and this required more help at certain stages of its growth.

Monks of the Hinayana or Southern School of Buddhism can take their
daily meals only in forenoon. There are two meals a day, one in the morning and the other, the last meal, at eleven o'clock in the morning; and he
has to finish this last meal before the sun has passed the meridian. Before
the introduction of the mechanical clock the time was measured by the sun's
shadow. A drum hung in the wat is sounded at eleven o'clock in the forenoon
for the monks to partake of their final meal of the day. It is the duty of
monastery boys to arrange the place and to present food in the customary way
to monks. Monks usually take their meal in groups in a particular dining
hall. There are rules and manners for the partaking of food by monks as laid
down in the Buddhist Code of Discipline, which we need not go into. The
monastery boys take their food after the monks and then clear the place.
What about an evening meal for the monastery boys? They eat the food that
is left after their last meal if there has been any; or after a few days of
getting accustomed to the life in the wat they do not take any evening meal.
As for a young boy, if his home is near, he will go back home to take his
evening meal and return later to the wat.

The newly ordained monk, after partaking of his forenoon meal, will
proceed to the abbot's quarters to receive instructions and training in religious
matters. It will take him many afternoons or sometimes a month or two to
finish the course of instruction and training for newly ordained monks. He is
to learn by heart certain formulas and texts in Pali as required of monks.
This is relatively easy for a literate monk, for he can learn by heart from a
book, but not so with an illiterate monk. In the old days most of the monks,
not only of the village folk but also of the people in towns, were illiterate.
In such a case the monk had to learn the text and formulas by heart orally
either from the abbot or from his deputy.

As to a monk who has been in the monkhood for a number of years, or
in the Pali idiom for a number of "vassa" or rains, he has time at his own
disposal for he no longer attends instructions from the abbot. He may take
an afternoon nap to compensate for his early rising. In a village wat all is

comparatively silent in the afternoon. A layman will hardly pay a visit to any monk unnecessarily in the first hours of afternoon, for he is aware that probably the monk is taking his siesta. In Thailand there is a certain set of common words in the vocabulary as used in connection with monks. For instance, to sleep for monks is not nɔɔn, the ordinary term in the language, but cam wád; to partake of food is not kin but chǎn; to take a bath is not ʔàab náam but sǒŋ náam. A monk, if he does not have his afternoon nap, may choose to pursue his own studies or go out on certain personal business c follow a special course of study elsewhere not available in his wat.

If he is a teacher to the monastery boys, the first thing he does, after partaking of the forenoon meal, is to turn the dining hall into a schoolroom. The boys will sit around the monk-teacher with their wooden slates and pencils. Both articles in the old days were home-made. The slate was made c soft wood cut to a required length and width and blackened on one side with soot. The pencil was made from a certain kind of hard subsoil clay. The boys squatted on the floor in a sideways sitting position with legs bent backward and soles upturned. One will often see people sitting on a carpet or a mat in this position, for it is deemed graceful or good-mannered to do so. No one will dare to sit cross-legged in a sacred place or before a superior where there are no chairs provided. To sit cross-legged is done only among intimates or by a person assuming an air of superiority. A Thai woman will seldom sit cross-legged, or sit with legs wide apart, for it is deemed indeco rous for a woman to do so. The only conventional way of sitting for a wom on the floor is to sit sideways as mentioned. A person unaccustomed to such a conventional sitting position will not be able to continue long in it; indee one has to change from one side to the other every now and then to relieve the discomfort.

Learning to read and write by the boys in the wat is in outline like thi A tray containing a wax candle, an incense stick, a bunch of flowers, and a handful of jâa phrɛ̂ɛg (Bermuda or dub grass) is offered by the boy with both hands to the monk who is going to be his teacher. The boy makes an obeisance by thrice prostrating himself before an image of Buddha and then to th monk, his intended teacher. This is the customary way of offering oneself as a pupil or as a protégé. The monk accepts the tray and places the articl in it on an altar or shelf before the Buddha image. The boy is now a pupil of the monk. The ceremony of offering oneself as a pupil either to a monk or to a layman is always done on Thursday, which in Thai is called wan khruu or "teacher day." The teacher in this instance is the Hindu divine tu' of the gods, whose name, Brihasapati, is honored in Thai as both the name for Thursday and the name for the planet Jupiter.

The ceremony itself is called wâaj khruu or the ceremony of paying r spect to a teacher. It is traditionally carried on by schools and colleges rig up to modern times. The ceremony takes place on a Thursday after the opening of the first term of the year. The flowers used by a pupil, as prevalent in central Thailand, are flowers from a shrub of the "Ixora" family and "Solanum" family. The former bears flowers in florets, which, when not yet in bloom, resemble needles. It is called dɔ̀ɔg khěm in Thai or "needle flower." The latter, called dɔɔg mákhy̌a or mákhy̌a flower, bears purplish white flowers in clusters. Its edible fruit contains numerous seeds. A person invoking a blessing on a pupil cites these two kinds of flowers figuratively thus: "May your intellect be as sharp as the needle flower, and may it develop and grow profusely like seeds of mákhy̌a flower and the dub grass, and (in addition) salty like salt." "To be salty" is an idiomatic expression for cleverness.

A boy student, if he is a beginner, will begin by memorizing the first series of the letters of the Thai alphabet which his monk-teacher writes for him on his slate. He will learn them by rote, repeating them in a loud voice, and also trace each letter with a small piece of wood as his first act of learning to write. A test of his learning will be made by the monk-teacher later in the day. The monk-teacher will test his boy pupil by erasing certain letters in the series, or by rewriting new ones by shifting their places. The boy will write the right letter in its place or read the letters in their jumbled positions. This goes on from day to day until the boy has a command of all subsequent series of the alphabet both by reading and writing. He now learns to read and write in syllables and words, as laid down in the Thai system. Such a process will take him some time, the period varying according to his intelligence and effort. When he has mastered all these he can now read and write fairly well.

But the average "monastery boy, " if he comes from a village, does not stay long in the wat. He has to go back home every now and then to help his parents in their livelihood and finally leave the wat before he has completed his learning. How much he has learned is, therefore, dependent on the individual. Here we speak of the learning to read and write of the average people as conditioned by time and social surroundings.

The school hour of the wat in the first part of afternoon will take only half an hour or so by the monk-teacher if there are only a few students under his charge, which is usually the case. The monk-teacher leaves the rest of the time to the boys themselves. The boys will read aloud what has been given to them as lessons, while the monk-teacher retires to his cell for an afternoon nap or does other things. Here it must not be taken for granted that the boys will always adhere to their studies for the time prescribed by the teacher. At first they will read aloud the lessons, but will stop reading them if they think their teacher is by that time sound asleep. After a few minutes silence to assure them that their teacher is not awake, they will play pranks and get into mischief as monastery boys will always do if left to themselves. "As mischievous as a monastery boy" is a saying in Thai.

The monk-teacher wakes up from his siesta about three o'clock. He tests the boys as to how much of their lessons each one has committed to memory. There may be, of course, some whippings for lazy boys. After this the monk will take his afternoon bath, usually about four o'clock. Monks who have nothing to do in the afternoon will sweep the ground of the wat or give a helping hand in any work as required by the wat.

During Buddhist Lent the number of monks in a wat will be more than usual; for most of the young men ordained as monks stay in the monkhood for a period of three months during the rainy season only. Some of them for various reasons will stay longer, or for life, which is a matter for the individual concerned. A monk may further his studies by becoming a preacher, a doctor, an astrologer, an artist, an artisan, or so on. In the old days such callings for certain monks in a village wat were a necessity. The average villagers, unlike the monks, had no time for such studies because most of their time was occupied in the arduous work of rice growing. Monks with ample time at their disposal would take some course of study as a hobby or a vocation. A monk with such knowledge, especially a doctor or an astrologer or one well versed in magic, was in demand by the people. The specialized service was given free by the monk, and in return the villagers would present to him an offering of all the necessary things befitting a monk's use. Where would a monk acquire such knowledge? Usually in some of the wats there were monks who specialized in such knowledge. If a monk required some knowledge, say of astrology, and there was not a monk-astrologer in the wat where he was staying, he would retire to another wat where there was such a monk-astrologer. He would present an offering to the monk-astrologer of tapers, incense stick, and flowers, in the same manner as a boy student to his monk-teacher, and ask for initiation as a pupil. The monk then would attend the study at his monk-teacher's residence regularly every afternoon. He might have a layman for his tutor if he could not find a suitable monk-teacher. There was no teacher-fee in the modern sense. The teaching was given free to accepted students. When a monk-student had completed his course of learning he might become an astrologer himself and give his services free to the people of his village. Every year at a certain period of time and always on Thursday he held a wâaj khruu or "worshiping of the teacher." Those who had received help from him would come to the annual wâaj khruu commemoration to pay respect and present him with necessary things. Such a practice has been observed traditionally up to the present day. A doctor of the old school, whether he is a monk or a layman, will give his professional aid free of charge, save small expenses as incurred. He will tacitly collect his full professional fee from his clients on the day of wâaj khruu. Such a practice survives, though weakening, to the present day.

An abbot of the village wat, if he is a man of age, full of lore and wisdom, is a highly respected person in the village. He is called lǔaŋ phɔ̂ɔ or "great father" by the villagers. His counsel is eagerly sought in case of difficulties and differences. The villagers seek his advice and decision even in a serious case rather than refer the case, if they can, to the official authority for decision. A decision by the authority or the legal court will take days, and also a certain amount of money has to be paid out in fees and other expenses. But not so with the venerable abbot, their spiritual father. The abbot in his spare time will make a round of afternoon visits to the villagers, giving advice or distributing his home-made medicine or other things as needed.

Some monks, after having been a number of years in the monkhood, leave the brotherhood to lead a layman's life. Whatever knowledge a monk has gained during his monkhood will be turned into useful occupation. If, for instance, he has learned something of a certain craft, he will turn to it as a profession if the village he resides in is a big one where there is a demand for such craft. If he is a successful and recognized artisan or artist, there will be one or two young men apprenticed to him. A young man in apprenticeship, if he comes from another village, will stay with the master-artist, with free board and lodging, as one of the members of the family. He learns his art and trade while at the same time serving his master in all domestic matters. If he has attained sufficient skill in his art, the master-artist will put him to some easy and odd jobs ordered by someone. Any fee received will be apportioned to the young pupil as his share. After staying for some time as an apprentice and intimate of the family, he may marry a daughter of his master or one of the master's female relatives. He now becomes one of the members of the family. After he has finished his apprenticeship, he may carry on his professional calling independently but live in a combined house and workshop of his own in the vicinity. Seldom will a young artist, whether he marries into the family of his master or not, live and follow his profession far from the master's house or in another village unless he is a recognized skilled artist. No one will hire him for a job, for most jobs come usually through his master. As time passed there would arise in that vicinity a village of artists most of whose inhabitants have a connection somehow or other by blood or marriage with the master artist. Such a village usually bears traces of the name of the inhabitants' profession -- for instance, as in names of districts in Bangkok, Bâan Mɔ́ɔ or the Potter's Village, Bâan Lɔ́ɔ or the Image Caster Village. The latter still exists as a place where the casting of bronze Buddha images is carried on as a profession by many families in the district.

The Sacred Recitation

Among the Buddhist Thai, important events in a person's life (birth, coming of age, birthdays, marriage, death) as well as all feasts, festivals, or other special occasions (New Year's Day, the erection of a new house or building) are marked by a tham bun or "merit working" ceremony. A tham bun in the usual form consists simply of the presentation of food to the monks on their morning round of visits for alms, but in an extended form the tham bun will consist of inviting monks to one's house or to some particular place to recite certain texts from the Buddhist scriptures. An extended tham bun will ordinarily consist of a recitation in the afternoon followed by a feast for the invited monks the next morning. Nowadays, especially in Bangkok or other urban areas, such a ceremony is often shortened to one day, the sacred recitation being given in the morning, followed immediately by a feast for the monks. In addition, the recitation itself will be shortened to half an hour instead of the hour or so customary in former days. This abbreviation of the ceremony has been made necessary by the changed conditions of economic life among urban populations where free time is not always at one's disposal. But to devout people in a rural district, the shorter recitation is regarded as less spiritually satisfying. In rural areas where there is more time, the people want to hear more of the sacred recitation in order to gain more merit, for the recitation represents something mystically inspired. Of course there was no mysticism originally in Buddhism. The recitation itself, if one knows either Pali or a translation of the texts recited, is a selection of certain incidents in the life of the Lord Buddha containing words of wisdom appropriate to the occasion. To hear a recitation by monks as mentioned one has to sit in a solemn and respectful manner with one's hands raised in a worshiping attitude.

In all religious ceremonies in connection with auspicious occasions, a certain kind of mystically consecrated cord made of unspun threads is essential This cord is bound thrice in a clockwise direction round the pedestal of the image of Buddha on the altar. The image of the Buddha is usually placed facing east or north. The cord is then passed out of the house through a window or other opening from the place where the ceremony is going to take place. It encircles the perimeter of the house also in a clockwise direction and returns to the altar where it is bound thrice in the same manner to an alms bowl and other vessels filled with water which are placed nearby. The remainder of the cord is rolled into a ball and placed on a tray near the altar.

The chapter of monks invited to the ceremony must number more than four, so as to form a monks' quorum. Although four is a quorum at a monks' council, the number is exclusively used for the recitation of certain formulas in connection with funeral or memorial ceremonies and therefore it is tacitly accepted that it should never be used for an auspicious one. The monks sit in a row according to seniority in age and rank in the brotherhood. A special place has been prepared for them, arranged so that their right shoulders face the altar where a Buddha image is installed. When the time for the recitation arrives the host or the honored person in the congregation will light the candles and incense sticks placed before the flower-decked altar and perform a triple prostration before the image of the Buddha. Whoever is acting as master of ceremonies on the occasion will pronounce in Pali a formula denoting an act of faith in "the Three Gems, " i. e., the Buddha, the Law, and the Brother-hood of Monks. The head monk who sits first in the row will hold a monk's conventional fan (an adaptation of the ancient palm-leaf type) before his face and pronounce thrice in Pali the three "refuge" formulas of the Buddha, i. e., "I take refuge in the Buddha, I take refuge in his Law, and I take refuge in his Brotherhood of Monks. " The congregation repeats these word by word. The head monk then pronounces in Pali the code of five precepts of the Bud-dhist religion beginning with the first one: "I undertake to abstain from kill-ing, I undertake to abstain from stealing, I undertake to abstain from com-mitting adultery, I undertake to abstain from lying, I undertake to abstain from alcoholic drinking. " The congregation will repeat the formula word by word as a declaration of intention to observe this fivefold commandment. Such a ritual is necessary as a preliminary to any Buddhist ceremony. The head monk then removes his fan and places it nearby. Next the master of ceremonies must make a formal request, also in Pali, to the monks' council for a recitation of the sacred texts for the welfare of the congregation, in-tended to disperse ills and calamities. Thereupon the head monk will take the roll of sacred cord placed in a tray, unroll it a little and hold it in his hand, then pass the remaining ball to the next monk, who does likewise and again passes it over. Now the monks begin to recite the ceremony of the rec-itation of sacred texts. Before we go on with the ceremony, there are some things to be described incidentally in order to have a better understanding of the subject.

One may ask the meaning of the sacred cord tied in the elaborate man-ner described above. The popular belief is that the sacred cord acts in a mystical way like an electric wire, carrying the sacred words as recited by the monks at one and the same time to every place and corner where the sa-cred cord reaches. It is a realistic and a practical device, for at one stroke everything within the orbit of the sacred cord is consecrated and receives the mystic words of the sacred texts which give it a protection and blessing. Even the water in the monk's alms bowl and other vessels, or other ceremo-nial paraphernalia that are used in some cases becomes hallowed and fit for lustration. The binding of the sacred cord to the pedestal of the image of the Buddha is evidently to render the mystic influence of the Lord Buddha as real-istic as one can imagine. It gives a psychological feeling of satisfaction to a devout person similar to what a Christian feels for his cross.

The sacred thread made of unspun threads is a traditional one. In the old days most of the Thai households in rural districts wove their own clothing. Unspun threads or yarns were to be found in every home; when a cord or a long string was required, and nothing else of this kind that was suitable could be found, it was logical to utilize the unspun threads. A single thread was too thin and easily snapped; hence either three or its square nine, the mystic number derived from *the Three Gems" or Buddhist Trinity, are made into one strand with ritualistic elaborations of process due to later development. Unspun threads thus made into a single strand might be used also for various purposes other than religious ceremonies but, with the introduction of better things, are seldom seen nowadays. The sacred cord is commonly called săaj sĭn; the last word is from the Pali word sĩncana which means "to sprinkle." No doubt it has something to do with the water in the alms bowls and other vessels which turn into consecrated water after the ritual recitation and which is sprinkled on the congregation and also used for lustration. The Cambodians call this sacred cord a "boundary line," which points to the fact that it is used as a mystic protection for everything within the radius of the sacred cord.

The ceremony of the recitation of sacred texts originated in Ceylon and was undoubtedly brought to this country in the latter part of the thirteenth century during the time of Ram Kamhaeng the Great of the Sukhothai Dynasty when the Thai had adopted the Ceylonese sect of Hinayana or the Southern School of Buddhism. The Thai, like all peoples of primitive times, were animists. They probably adopted Mahayana or the Northern School of Buddhism before they came to Thailand; this was more or less true of the ruling classes as in the Thai kingdom of Nan Chao in southern China. When they came to Thailand they adopted Hinayana Buddhism, no doubt from the Mon of Dvaravadi, and later mixed this with Mahayana Buddhism as imported from the Srivijaya Empire in the middle of the tenth century through the conquest of a king of that empire. To add more to the melting pot of religion, Hinduism was apparently also an element in the beliefs of the Thai, especially the ruling class, through the influence of the Cambodians, at certain periods of history. In looking therefore at the Buddhism of the Thai on its ritualistic and popular side one must bear in mind the above facts. To analyze the component parts which came to be integrated as a whole into Thai Buddhism requires laborious work and an unprejudiced mind.

The conventional monk's fan which forms a part of a monk's equipment in religious ceremonies is peculiar, as far as is known, to Thailand and Cambodia. The fans used by the Ceylonese and Burmese monks are natural ones made of the big rounded leaves of the toddy palm. They are utilized as monks' sunshades only. In Thai Buddhism the monk's fan is made also of a toddy palm leaf but is artificially shaped in an ovate form with a long handle made of wood with a pointed tip. This is used by an ordinary monk. Another kind of monk's fan is made wholly of silk, wool, or brocade and is either

embroidered with artistic figures or letters or is plain. The long handle is
made either of wood tipped at both ends with ivory, or made wholly of ivory.
No precious metals such as silver or gold can be used for monks, as by the
rules of discipline he cannot touch them, though gold and silver are sometimes tolerated in a veiled form, for instance, as part of the brocade. One
sometimes sees such fans with beautiful artistic designs worthy of a work of
art. Monk's fans presented by the king to a prelate or to a monk with official
status are different from the unofficial ones. Fans of this group have various
shapes or forms, colors, and decorations as befit the rank of the monks. One
may be able to recognize, provided one has some knowledge, a monk's rank
in the hierarchy if he carries his fan with him. Such a fan is used exclusively
in a royal ceremony when the king or his deputy is present. A Buddhist prelate wears no uniform to distinguish him from other monks. Hence the difficulty in recognizing a monk's hierarchical rank unless one knows him per-
sonally. Perhaps a king in the old days instituted such a gradation of monk's
fans and these have become a tradition. Later, in King Vajiravudh's reign,
a special kind of monk's fan bearing a royal cipher with many grades was instituted and presented by the King to monks as a royal personal favor. In
short, these fans, both the official and the royal cipher ones, are used on occasions in the same manner as one wears a uniform with decorations and med-
als. Perhaps as an extension of the above practices, people have also made
fans of their own to present to monks on occasions of making merit, replacing
gradually the primitive fans made of palm leaves, which are now seldom
seen. A monk with many unofficial fans in his possession may use any one of
them on suitable occasions.

A monk's fan may be used on five special occasions only: when he pronounces the three "refuge" formulas and the five precepts; when a recitation
begins; when he expresses formal thanks; when a monk is in the act of drawing to himself a robe laid on a coffin during a religious service; and when a
quartet of monks chant certain sacred formulas before and during cremation.
The drawing to himself of a robe laid on a coffin is called pamsukula in Pali
which literally means a "dust heap." In ancient days monks collected dis-
carded robes and rags from dust heaps and washed, dyed, and used them as
robes. This act of the monks has developed into what is described above.
Why a monk's fan may be used only on such five occasions, or when, where,
and why it originated is for me impossible to say.

The stories and substance of the recitations that are ceremonially
chanted by monks are too long to be included here, even in their shortened
form. We will therefore omit them and continue with the ceremony.

After the monks have continued with their recitation for some quarter of
an hour, the head monk will light a wax taper attached to the rim of the alms
bowl. After a while, when the recitation reaches a certain point appropriate
for the occasion, he takes the lighted taper in his hand and begins to drop

molten wax from the taper here and there into the water in the alms bowl.
When the recitation reaches a certain text the head monk dips a lighted taper
into the water, stirring it for a while; and the recitation continues on until
the end. The sacred thread is re-rolled into a ball and replaced in the tray.
The ceremony then comes to an end. The monks sit for a while drinking tea
or chatting with members of the congregation and then take leave.

An enquiry into the ritual dipping of a lighted taper into the water in the
alms bowl in the northern and northeastern areas of the country elicits an
identical ceremony but one that sometimes varies in certain details. In
northern Thailand three tapers are used for dipping. This is the same number of candles as is used by a Roman Catholic priest in consecrating water for
baptism. No doubt the dipping of a lighted taper into the water is a ritual
act to purify the water for sacred purposes. In the Roman Catholic ritual suc
consecrated water has a little mixture of saliva (see W. J. Wilkins, Paganism
in the Papal Church, pp. 93-94). It finds a parallel also among the Thai bu
in an indirect form. In certain cases a monk famed for his mystical power is
asked to blow out from his mouth consecrated water or medicinal solution in
a spray on a person who is sick or possessed by a malignant phĭi or evil spirit.

The next morning the same group of monks who gave the recitation on
the previous afternoon arrive at the appointed time, either in the earlier part
of the morning or at a time a little before 11 A.M. to partake of the food
provided by the owner of the house. If the appointed time is the earlier one,
the monks have to bring their own alms bowls too. This is a necessity for
monks. If they partake of their earlier meal at the house, there will be no
food for them when they return to the wat to take their final meal of the day
The alms bowls they bring with them will therefore be handed over to the
people to present food for their final meal after returning to their wat.

Before partaking of their feast, the monks will recite a eulogy describing the Buddha's Eight Victories over certain heretical beings, as found in the
episodes of the traditional story of the life of the Buddha. This may be com
pared to saying grace before a meal. A special tray filled with various foods
in small quantities is placed in a formal way on a white cloth before the
image of the Buddha at the altar. After placing the tray, the person will
kneel with hands upraised in a worshiping attitude before the image of Buddh
and pronounce thrice the usual Buddhist opening formula invoking the name
of the Buddha, and then recite a certain word in Pali presenting the food to
the Buddha. After the presentation the monks may begin their feast.

By Buddhist rules a monk cannot handle food or other gifts unless they
are presented or offered by someone. The presentation is done by approaching him in a respectful manner. The food or other gifts are held with both
hands, or a small thing may be held with one's right hand only but with the
left hand raised a little. The gift is raised and then lowered directly into the
monk's hand. If the presenter is a woman, the thing presented to a monk

cannot be put directly into the monk's hand in this way, but is to be placed on a piece of cloth laid before the monk where he can take it after it has been offered. It is sinful for a monk in his celibate life to touch the body of a woman whether willingly or unwillingly. The practice extends also to other creatures of female kind.

During the meal, music is played if any is available. In strict discipline a monk cannot enjoy music, which is an enemy to celibate life. In popular practice music is permissible if played during a feast. The people want their monks to enjoy the feast, and they are delighted if monks take more food as it is offered. The more food taken by monks the more merit it is believed will accrue to a person who offers it to them. On the other hand, by discipline a monk must not take more food than is necessary for the sustenance of life. Music plays a subsidiary part in Thai ritualistic Buddhism. It is played to mark stages in the ceremony. There is music in the ceremony when the monks arrive, when a preaching or a recitation comes to an end, when the monks depart, and so on. There is a particular tune appropriate to the occasion, and a person familiar with the tune will know when he hears it what stage in the ceremony has now begun.

Among the people in central Thailand a person serving monks at their feast or taking part as master of ceremonies usually wears a piece of cloth on his left shoulder with both ends hanging down across the torso in something like a loop or a sash, or better in the manner of a Scot wearing his tartan. A cloth, called phâa khǎawmáa or "khǎawmáa cloth, " worn in this way is a symbol of respect before a superior or sacred thing. The phâa khǎawmáa is a piece of fabric woven in a distinctive checkered pattern of different stripes and colors which may be utilized in many ways. In a hot country, the unsophisticated wear shirts only when they work in the field, to protect themselves from the intolerably hot sun. On other occasions they usually leave the upper part of the body bare if they can. The only piece of cloth they have with them is the phâa khǎawmáa which they put to various uses. It is used as a shawl, a turban, a sash, a bathing cloth, a bag, a binding or for such other practical uses as one can devise. The people take their bath in the open, therefore a bathroom is not a necessity. But a phâa khǎawmáa is necessary. Accustomed to such a behavior pattern a Thai, and not only the villager, wears a phâa khǎawmáa when taking a bath even in a bathroom. Only the sophisticated ones take a bath in the western style. The women wear their sarong-like lower garment when bathing. In his traditional way of life, a person usually has a phâa khǎawmáa hanging on his left shoulder; if the air is hot he may wet his phâa khǎawmáa to relieve the heat. A dandy will drape his costly phâa khǎawmáa across his shoulders in a showy and careless manner. Hence when he comes before a superior or a sacred thing, or into a wat, he will take his phâa khǎawmáa off or wrap it around the upper part of his body as already mentioned. As to a woman, she wears a piece of cloth wrapped around her breast and another piece of cloth used as a shoulder shawl. She will take off her shawl and arrange it in the same manner as a phâa khǎawmáa when entering a wat or meeting the monks.

When a householder is feasting monks, he does not forget the house spirit or tutelary guardian of the house, whose shrine is a miniature house perched on a single pillar found at most Thai houses. The spirit also receives a share of the feast, but he takes his portion after the monks. He is only a lay spirit whose status is below that of a monk; similarly the monk does not partake of the feast until after a special meal has been offered to the image of the Buddha. The tradition is obviously a popular animistic survival from primitive days.

The monks after partaking of the feast will return to the seats where the recitation took place on the previous afternoon. They will then recite a formula of gratitude and blessing to the donor of the feast. During this recitation the donor will pour water from a vessel in the same manner as already described as a libation to departed relatives and to other creatures and beings as well. Libation as defined in the dictionary is a pouring of a liquid, usually wine, in honor of some deity. It develops into the drinking of wine in honor of some person or, as we say, drinking a health to such and such person. In Hinduism after a feast is given to a body of Brahmans, a pouring of water called tarpana is performed to transmit to departed souls the merit gained through feasting Brahmans. Evidently the feasting of monks and the pouring of water for the benefit of departed persons, the tarpana of the Hindus, and the drinking of wine in honor of some person developed from the same primitive source as the libation in honor of some gods as performed by the ancient Greeks.

After a recitation of thanks and blessing by the monks, the ceremony comes to an end. Certain articles befitting a monk's use are now presented. If there is a present of money to monks on the occasion, the money is given in his name to a reliable monastery boy or to any other person acting as an agent or a banker for the monk or monks. A slip of paper written in a formal wording informs the monk that a certain sum of money is made over to such and such agent of the monk. If he wishes to acquire certain articles as befit a monk's use, he may call on that person who will buy them for him. In theory a monk cannot touch money.

Before the monks depart to their wat the head monk will bless the congregation by sprinkling consecrated water from the alms bowl. He sometimes sprinkles sand along the boundary of the house also as a protection against the unseen evils that may lurk in the vicinity. The traditional instrument for sprinkling consecrated water is a bunch of lalang grass, which is used as a thatch grass of the villagers, or a bunch of májom branches (star gooseberry). There is some reason for the use of these two things, though a superstitious one. The former has to do with a story of popular Hinduism. A semidivine being, half-man, half-bird, named Garuda stole the water of immortality from the gods, and a few drops of this elixir fell on lalang grass, hence its sacredness. The latter, the star gooseberry, bears the name in Thai májom, the last syllable being identical in sound to jom in Thai or yama in Sanskrit and Pali, the King of Death of whom evil spirits are in fear. The sprinkler made of májom branches is tantamount to Yama's rod with which he chastises evil spirits.

Buddhist Feasts and Festivals

Feasts and festivals observed by the Thai Buddhists are mainly religious and are related to the changing seasons. Here we have to say something of the Thai traditional calendar, for most of the feasts and festivals are based on it.

The Thai traditional calendar, like all the calendars of this part of Southeast Asia, is a lunar one, consisting of twelve moons or lunar months of twenty-nine days and thirty days alternately. The former are called odd-number months, the latter even-number months. There is an intercalated month between the eighth and ninth months every third year. The Thai name their lunar months in numerical order; the first month begins at nearly the same time as December, except in northern Thailand where the first month answers nearly to October, two months earlier than in other parts of the country. Evidently this first month, as its name shows, marked the first Thai New Year's Day in former times. The old Thai word for their first month of the year was ciaŋ or ceŋ month, a word no different from the name of the Chinese first month. Nevertheless the Thai traditional New Year's Day is now otherwise.

A month, called dyan in Thai, which means "moon," is divided into two parts, the waxing moon from the first to the fifteenth or full moon of the month, and the waning moon beginning with the sixteenth which, however, is counted as the first of the waning moon; the waning moon ends on the fourteenth or the fifteenth according to whether the month is an odd or an even one. Hence there are two numerical series of days in a month. The days, like the months, have their odd and even numbers also. No marriage ceremony is performed in an odd-number month, with the exception of the extra month added in an intercalary year. This month is the beginning of the Buddhist lenten season when no marriage ceremony is traditionally performed. No cremation takes place on an even-number day of the waxing moon or on an odd-number day of the waning moon, for its first day is regarded as the sixteenth day of the month considered as a whole, and sixteen is an even number. Everything in number that pertains to a marriage ceremony is in pairs, and everything that pertains to a cremation is in odd numbers. Logically a

marriage ceremony requires a pair of man and woman to consummate the ritua
and a cremation is confined to a dead man alone. Any odd or even number
of either month or day is viewed superstitiously and with apprehension with
the notion that "like produces like. " A marriage ceremony performed in an
odd-number month will result in one of the wedded couple not surviving long
in married life. So also the cremation performed on an even day to a superstitious mind requires another living man to follow the dead one to complete
such a number. The superstition is now weakening in urban areas, especially
in Bangkok perhaps because of the reckoning of days and months by the solar
system.

The Thai New Year's Day traditionally takes place on the first day of
the waning moon of the fifth month, roughly in the latter part of March.
Nothing in the nature of feasts or festivals is observed, except the usual presentation of food to monks on their morning round for alms. Until a decade or
so ago there was an official ceremony called "the cutting of the year" with a
ritual driving away from the city evil of spirits lurking behind from the old
year. Evidently the ceremony was introduced from Buddhist Ceylon with in-
digenous animistic beliefs added. However, the New Year was actually celebrated with feasts and holidays from the thirteenth to fifteenth of April, the
so-called Sŏŋkraan, better-known as the Water Throwing Festival, of which
we will speak later. In 1888 King Chulalongkorn instituted a calendar on a
solar basis beginning on the first of April. The first of April became an official New Year's Day but the popular one was the Sŏŋkraan Day. The months
of the newly instituted solar year are named from the twelve zodiacal signs
with a suffix of aakhom for a thirty-one-day month and aajon for a thirty-
day month. February, with twenty-eight or twenty-nine days, has aaphan as
a suffix peculiar to its name. In 1951 the official New Year's Day was change
from the first of April to January 1 and this remains in force to this day. The
celebration of this official New Year's Day is like that of Sŏŋkraan. In fact
it is a replica of the latter, but the people at large still observe the Sŏŋkraan
celebration.

Now we will begin a description of the seasonal feasts and festivals beginning with Sŏŋkraan. As this festival has been described and analyzed by
me in detail elsewhere (see my story of Sŏŋkraan in Thai Culture Series No. 6
and The Journal of the Siam Society, Vol. XLII, part 1, July 1954) we will
give it only in its bare outline. Sŏŋkraan is a Thai word derived from
Sankrānta, of Sanskrit origin, which means the entry of the sun into the sign
of Aries, the Ram. It begins on the thirteenth of April and ends either on the
fifteenth or the sixteenth in accordance with the actual time when the sun
enters the Aries. It is therefore a fixable feast on a solar basis. In fact,
Sŏŋkraan is the celebration of the vernal equinox. Though Thailand has no
spring season, the month when the Sŏŋkraan occurred coincided splendidly
with an opportune time of the year, when the mass of people of Thailand are
unoccupied with their agricultural work.

Early in the morning of the first day of Sŏŋkraan, the thirteenth of April, the people in their new clothes repair to the wat of their village to offer food to monks. A long bench, either temporary or permanent, is erected in the compound of the wat where monks' alms bowls stand in a row on either side of the bench. There is a special alms bowl bigger than the rest placed at the head of the row. This is meant as the alms bowl peculiar to the Buddha. Into the alms bowls, first into the so-called Buddha's alms bowl and then into the others, the gathering crowd in pious mood queues up to put boiled rice, and into the covers of the alms bowls lying upturned other food, fruits, and sweetmeats. Paradoxically there is more food than a monk can take in a day even though a monk by discipline cannot take food offered to him if any is left after his last day's meal. Economically it is really a waste, but it was not so in the old days when food, especially rice and fish, were in abundance and money to a people with simple needs was not a necessity. The people attached the highest value to their religion; and this is the only way for them to express their faith.

In the afternoon and on the next days there is a ceremonial bathing of the Buddha image and also of the abbot of the wat, followed by the well-known "water throwing festival" which in the old days was considered a magic means to cause abundance of water or rain but which has degenerated into a form of amusement pure and simple. On this day and also on the succeeding days there is a ceremonial bathing of elder relatives and respected persons carried out by the younger generation. A memorial service to the departed ones and the releasing of live fish and birds are also performed as deeds of merit. During the three days of Sŏŋkraan young people of both sexes amuse themselves by throwing water at one or another, playing games, dancing, singing, or other such pastimes as they can devise.

The month of April is the hottest month in Thailand, and about the middle of May comes the beginning of the southwest monsoon rain when the people are busying themselves with their ploughing. There are no feasts and festivals this time of the year until the Buddhist Lent begins in mid-July. The only exception is Visakha (Wísǎakhǎa) Day, the anniversary of the Birth, Enlightenment, and the final entering into Nirvana (death) of the Buddha, which coincides with the full moon in the sixth month (May). The observance in commemoration of this great triple event in the life of the Buddha is mainly among the monks, but the people also participate. In rural areas the commemoration is observed for three days, commencing on the fourteenth of the waxing moon, and ending on the first of the waning moon (or the sixteenth of the month). On the first day there is an evening recitation of the sacred texts at the wat followed by sermons on the life of the Buddha. At dark the ceremony comes to an end for the first day. Next morning, that is, on the day of the full moon, there is an offering of food to the monks. There is also a circumambulation round the chapel three times in a clockwise direction with lighted tapers. In some places such a circumambulation is performed on the previous day also. Sermons as a continuation from the previous day are preached from morning until evening and further continued to the third and last day.

In Bangkok Visakha (Wísăakhăa) Day is a one-day observance in the evening of the full moon. There is a circumambulation, after which there are sermons preached by monks in succession and continuing throughout the whole night. In some of the bigger wats there are huge crowds of people circumambulating the chapel. In the Royal Chapel of the Emerald Buddha the king and queen, followed by the royal family and officials, honor the Buddha by thrice circumambulating the sacred building with lighted tapers in the evening. Hung around the royal chapel are decorated candles and lights with which the royal family and officials honor the Buddha on this important occasion. These candles and lights are mostly decorated with fresh flowers in many beautiful designs. In some wats there may be exhibits along the corridor of the chapel of altars decorated with rare and beautiful pieces of brass or porcelain ware.

After Visakha (Wísăakhăa) Day there may be a ceremony of presenting milled rice and other unprepared food to the monks. It is called the ceremony of "placing milled rice in alms bowls." Actually it is usually done in the afternoon. Milled rice and unprepared food contributed by the people are placed in a common heap, then divided proportionately among monks in the wat. Each monk receives his share, which is carried to each particular kitchen of the monks by the monastery boys or other persons. Such a ceremony shows forethought on the part of the villagers. They are too busy with their ploughing and their planting of rice, which is a race against the time of the coming rain. Most of the villagers go out to the fields very early in the morning, before dawn if the fields are some distance from home. In many cases the whole family leaves the house together, carrying with them their young children if there is no one left to look after them. To leave one's house unoccupied does not mean that a thief or thieves will steal something in it as there are of course no valuable things worth stealing. What about the monks in the wat? They will have an insufficient amount of food for their daily needs in their morning round for alms. Few people will be in the village to present them with food. The milled rice and unprepared food presented in this ceremony therefore will keep them supplied with their daily wants for the time being until the time of Buddhist Lent when there are more people making merit.

The ceremony of placing milled rice in alms bowls is shifted in time in urban areas to the period during the three months of the Buddhist Lent, when there are unusually more monks in the wats because newly ordained monks swell the number. These monks, owing to their increase in number during the lenten season, will sometimes have insufficient food in their morning alms if they have to depend on the usual number of donors of food. The ceremony further develops into a means for raising funds indirectly for the wats at any time of the year. The milled rice presented by some wealthy persons will be in big bags, and these are sold to bidders. The money realized from the sale will go into a fund to be used as needed by the wat. People will part willingly with anything if it is done in the name of religion.

There is another Buddhist ceremony called "food tickets" in which food belonging to a group of monks in a wat is distributed to the monks by tickets. This is done at any time when occasion arises. In Thailand it is usually performed by the people when any kind of fruit is in season. A group of families each contributes food to a monk with such seasonal fruits forming the predominant part of the offering. The food with sweetmeats and the fruits are placed in a tray or trays which are again placed in two baskets suspended from the two ends of a shoulder-carry (the Thai never carry things on their heads). In rural districts the carrying pole made of bamboo with beautiful curved ends is a thing treasured by a village girl. On festive occasions, such as this instance, the carrying of food to the wat is done by a girl in her best dress. Each girl in the file proceeding to the wat will vie with the others in carrying her pole on the shoulder. If the pole is gracefully curved, giving a beautiful rhythmic movement, it is greatly admired. At the wat the food is distributed to the monks by ticket. The ceremony in this instance is to provide monks with special fruits of the season, which monks seldom have from their usual morning alms.

On the first day of the waning moon of the eighth lunar month (roughly in July) comes the beginning of Buddhist Lent when monks make their retreat for the three rainy months. It ends on the full moon of the eleventh month (roughly October). During this period of time the ploughing and planting of rice have begun. The farmers have comparatively little to do but to wait until the rice ripens, in December or January at the latest. Before the lenten days begin the people cast a big candle of molten beeswax. The ceremony may take place at a village or, as is usually the case at the present time, in the compound of a wat. This candle, called the lenten candle, is lighted and kept burning continuously throughout the three months of the lenten period. If the lenten candle is cast in the village, it is borne in a decorated cart or other conveyance with a procession to a wat, where there is a celebration. People also present articles to the monks as befits the occasion. These things are decorated with artificial flowers and leaves of varied colors and designs. There are more persons than usual presenting food to monks on their morning alms. Devout and elder people go to the wat every day to hear sermons. A Buddhist sermon preached by a monk always begins with the triple "refuge" of the religion, i.e., the Buddha, the Law, and the Brotherhood, followed by the five precepts for ordinary days or the ten precepts for the Buddhist holy days for observance by the layman. In the old days all theatrical or other

amusements were voluntarily suspended during the lenten period; even a ha-
bitual drinker of spiritous liquors will sacrifice his delight and turn into a sober
man, at least during the three months, as an offering to religion.

During the interval there is an autumnal feast called Sàat in Thai which
occurs on the last day of the tenth lunar month (early October). Sàat is a
Thai form of the Sanskrit word śārada, which means "autumn." In central
Thailand there is a certain kind of special sweetmeat made of pounded-flat
glutinous rice, groundnuts, teelseeds, popped rice, and green peas mixed
with molasses and formed into a sticky mass of brownish color. This is presented to monks with a certain kind of ripe bananas to neutralize the great
sweetness of the sweetmeats. There are variations in the details of the Sàat
feast and dates of performance in other areas of the country -- in fact, the
feast is called by various names and in some places no such sweetmeat is
known. But the feasts, though different, betray themselves as an autumnal
feast in connection with the "first fruits" as an oblation to departed ancestors.
The Sàat feast forms a subject of its own on which I have written elsewhere.

The full moon of the eleventh month, usually in the latter part of October, marks the last day of the three months of Buddhist Lent. On this day the
people make special merit by offering food to monks and listening to special
sermons preached by the monks at the wat. The next and succeeding days
until the full moon of the twelfth month (November) make up the well known
Kàthĭn or the period of presentation of robes to monks, which subject was
treated at some length in my article, "The End of Buddhist Lent" (The Journal
of the Siam Society, Vol. XLII, part 2, January 1955). On the last day of
Buddhist Lent there is the ceremony of Lɔɔj Kràthoŋ or the floating of lights in
leaf cups which has nothing to do directly with Buddhist festivals. After this
date there is a lull in feasts and festivals. The people, especially the farmers,
are busy harvesting their rice. On the full moon of the third and fourth month
(February and March) there is the festival of pilgrimage to Phrá? Bàad or the
footprint of the Buddha. During these times the people have in most cases
finished harvesting rice, and there is the usual ceremony of recitations of Buddhist texts and a morning feast for the monks. The people have a time of
comparative leisure to make the pilgrimage to the famous footprint and enjoy
their vacation, though it is of a semireligious nature. There are pilgrimages
to other sacred shrines, which are to be found in many parts of the country,
and fairs and amusements for the people to make their vacation enjoyable.
Some shrines in urban areas such as the Golden Mount in Bangkok and the big
pagoda of Phrá? Pàthŏm have their festivals during the full moon of the twelfth
month (December) when the rains come to an end.

On the full moon of the third month (February) comes the Buddhist
Maakhá Buuchaa or Buddhist Saints' Day. It was on this same day during Bud-
dha's time that 1,250 arahantas or Buddhist saints met coincidentally at
Veluvan Monastery in Rajagriha, then capital of the Magadhan Empire in

India. Because the 1,250 arahantas assembled at the place, and all of them
had been ordained as monks by the Buddha himself, and they had come by
themselves without any previous notice, and it was the full-moon night when
the moon entered the sign of the Maakhá asterism, it is commemorated as
one of the Buddhist festivals. The observance of the Maakhá Buuchaa is a
one-night festival, and the performance is done in the same spirit and manner
as the Wísáakhãa Buuchaa, the anniversary of Buddha's birth, enlightenment,
and entering the final Nirvana, save that the sermons preached in the chapel
have as their subject the Buddhist Code of Discipline for monks. It was on
this day that this Code of Discipline or the Vinaya was promulgated or preached
by the Lord. No decorated candles and lights are hung on this occasion as is
done during the Wísáakhãa Day.

To complete the cycle of feasts and festivals of the Thai people it is
necessary to include the "Festival of Thêet Máhãa Chãad" which means the
festival of a recitative sermon of the Great Birth in connection with the Buddha's last but one life on earth in his transmigrations of births before he per-
fected himself and became the Enlightened Buddha. The festival is usually
performed during the Sàat or mid-year autumnal feast in October, or on any
special occasions such as the raising of funds for the wat. The recitation is
done in the preaching hall within the precincts of a wat. The recitations begin early in the morning and continue sometimes to late midnight. It is a
traditional belief of the people that whoever hears this recitation of the "Great
Life" in its complete story will gain great merit. The recitation is in Pali
verses, and a free translation in the form of a Thai prose poem forms the best
literary work in the Thai literature. The story of this Great Birth is a very
well-known one in Thailand and influences immensely the life of the mass of
the people. The story serves as an inspiration to Thai poets and artists, for
the story contains noble sentiments, humor, pathos, and beautiful descriptive
scenes which give play to their power of imagination and artistic expression.
The story is very popular not only in central Thailand, but also and not less
in the northern and northeastern areas of the country. There are many versions
of the story both in the standard Thai language and in other Thai dialects.
The oldest version, dating back some four hundred years, is used as a subject
of literary study in Chulalongkorn University. I have written a detailed descriptive story of this festival as a separate subject.

I now have described the customs of the Thai people in connection with
their religion and traditional way of life. As one will see, the wat or monastery played a significant role in shaping the life of the Thai. In former
days, and to a large extent in the present, the wat was and has been the place
of education in arts and crafts and for the social gatherings of the people.
One will wonder why there are so many feasts and festivals in the year. The
answer is not difficult to discover if we imagine ourselves back in the old days
among the unsophisticated folk who formed the great mass of the population.

Unlike their brothers in the cities, they had few attractions other than in the wat. The wat provided, and still provides in the villages, everything for them in what we call arts, literature, morality, and philosophy. Theatrical performances, music, fireworks, and exhibits of artistic works are to be seen frequently at the wat during certain festivals and ceremonies. Poets, artists, and craftsmen generally originate from the wat. If one wishes to witness a fashion show, if I am permitted to use the word, it may be found in a social gathering at the wat during festive occasions. We have a saying in Thai that "such and such a girl may go to the wat" meaning that she is an attractive girl. The wat is also a sanctuary for animals both wild and tame. People will never dare to shoot birds or to fish in the compound of the wat. Even fish in a river in front of a wat find a sanctuary there. If any person disobeys this traditional custom he, if caught red-handed, will receive his punishment by being beaten by the monks in the wat. An arbitrary punishment given to a person is called idiomatically in Thai "to punish in a wat manner." A fowl, if the owner deems it to be unlucky, is not killed but released in the compound of the wat. Such a fowl is shorn of its tail before release in order that people may recognize it as a fowl belonging to a wat. A delinquent son expelled from home is said metaphorically "to be shorn of his tail and released in the wat." If all the highly valued things are to be found in the wat, so also there are things to the contrary. Everything has a reverse side. Animals found in the wat, especially pigs and dogs, are parasites of their kind, and to say that a man is a "wat dog" is an insult to the person in Thai idiomatic expression. To say a man's knowledge of reading and writing is of the wat's kind is to mean that the knowledge is only elementary. It reflects, therefore, the fact that the teaching of such knowledge in the wat was carried in former days no further than the elementary stage, unless one stayed longer in the wat and learned Pali. But such literary language in a village was incompatible with their way of life. Leaving this minor drawback out one is justified in saying that the wat was a great civilizing influence in the past in rural districts, and it is still a living force which, as a Thai, one cannot ignore without harming one's own foundation of culture, unless one builds a new one on that of the old.

A Village Wedding: Informal Merrymaking on the Side

A wedding in Bang Chan, as anywhere, is an occasion for good fellow-
ship. The bride and groom receive the blessings of their elders and
make merit through their first joint offering to the monks. Family
and friends celebrate the event with festive hilarity.

MERIT-MAKING: NEVER TOO YOUNG

Children learn ritual merit-making from a very early age. Here a child places his merit offering onto an alms receptacle. In the pulpit a monk recites a sermon from a palm-leaf manuscript while the adult audience listens reverently.

MERIT-MAKING: NEVER TOO OLD

As a person enters middle age his or her thoughts will turn more and more to earning merit for the next life and lives. The merit-maker places a little rice in each of the alms bowls, one for each monk in the temple plus one for the Lord Buddha.

PROCESSION TO THE ORDINATION

Above we see candidates for the monkhood parading from home to the Bang Chan temple. Ornate umbrellas, a regal symbol, shade the candidates and the ceremonial receptacles containing the orange robes that the candidates will soon be wearing.

ORDINATION: SUPREME MOMENT

The elderly bishop in the center of the picture receives the new monk
into the order of the Sangha. The newcomer is resplendent in his
bright orange robes with alms bowl suspended from his right shoulder.

PILGRIMAGE: MEMORABLE PERIOD IN THE ANNUAL CYCLE

After the holy season, during the coolest months of the year, many monks leave the temple, in small groups or alone, on pilgrimages to holy places. A monk is sometimes gone for weeks and may travel a distance of hundreds of miles, much of it on foot. The monk in the picture, equipped for his pilgrimage, carries an alms bowl over his left shoulder, a portable tent and an all-purpose travel bag over his right shoulder, and, in his left hand, a teapot.

TOPKNOT CUTTING

The raising of a child's topknot is a Brahmanical tradition now on the wane in Bang Chan. When the boy or girl is seven, nine, eleven, or thirteen years of age—odd numbers are considered auspicious—the topknot is ritually cut.

CUSTOMS CONNECTED WITH BIRTH
AND THE REARING OF CHILDREN

Publisher's Preface

Colonel Lŭaŋ Te-chásĕ-na·, in preparing to conduct the funeral of
Mme. Te·chá·sĕ·na· (Can Te·chásĕ·n), his wife, at Wat Mákừd
Kàsàdừlja·ra·m on 8 December 1949 requested permission of the Fine Arts
Department to publish the book Customs Connected with Birth and the Rearing
of Children, by Phya Anuman Rajadhon, for distribution at the ceremony.
The Fine Arts Department feels this to be appropriate, because the deceased
was a close relative of the writer of this book, and so has granted permission
to publish as desired.

[Two paragraphs concerning publication omitted.]

Fine Arts Department
24 November 1949

[Three-page dedication by publisher omitted.]

Author's Preface

Customs are always undergoing changes, because they are easy to imitate; when people like others' customs, they adopt them. Old local customs
gradually disappear, and new customs move in to take their place; or the old
customs are retained but altered to fit new living conditions. Customs therefore consist of complicated and overlapping layers. It is difficult to trace the
reasons for practicing them, or why they are performed in one way or another,
and to what nationality or what locality they belong, and when they originated. When one asks people about customs, he usually does not get detailed
information. People who are old enough to have witnessed old customs, when
asked, are unable to give very much information, because they did not observe and remember; they are able only to tell about things they have seen.
Persons who can give complete information are therefore very few. It is necessary to ask a great many people, learning a little from one person and a
little from that one, and noting down and putting together whatever one gets.
This procedure enables one to get better information, but it takes a long time;
if one is not interested he cannot do it, for one receives no reward except
knowledge and personal satisfaction.

Originally I never thought of collecting old customs, because I had no
interest in learning about them. Later when I had read books on customs
written by foreigners, I came to see from those books that customs are an

important feature of a society; they are like a mirror reflecting the life and minds of the majority of the people of the nation, showing the stages of progress they have passed through, and this information helps us not a little to understand our conditions of life at present and in the future. If we regard old customs with a generous spirit, we know that customs originate for a reason or because of necessities relating to surrounding conditions or the spirit of the times. When they are performed continuously over a long period, the reasons and necessities for some customs disappear; some are given up but some remain. They follow the general rule that if the people still regard them as good, they still observe them and do not give them up; if they regard them as bad, and acquire others in their place which they regard as better, then the old customs must be abandoned. But do not forget that the people who make up a nation are complicated, forming classes having thoughts, knowledge, and mentalities not all of the same level. It is possible to make them uniform only in larger matters; smaller matters that are characteristic of particular localities and agree with surrounding conditions always exist. It is impossible to force all of these things into a uniform mold. One need look only at the Thai people. The majority have Thai facial features, manners, and speech, but if one looks at the minor characteristics he sees that no two Thai are exactly alike in facial features, manners, and speech; at best, they are merely similar. If my wife were exactly like me in every way, cast in the same mold, then she could certainly not live with me.

I feel regretful that when I became interested in learning about old customs of the Thai, not so very long ago, and thought of asking this person or that, in some cases it was already too late, because many of those who had known about these old customs were already dead. Some customs must be investigated in localities where they are understood to be still extant, but I had no opportunity to go there because I was busy with my work. I have therefore been able to investigate only as much as I had opportunity for, and have arranged the results according to categories, like the old things in a museum. Doing only this much is still better than doing nothing at all, because if there is further delay it will perhaps be impossible to obtain anything, since customs will have vanished.

I have divided my books on Old Customs of the Thai into five parts, namely:

1. Customs Connected with Birth, the Rearing of Children, and Education.
2. Customs Connected with Marriage.
3. Customs Connected with House-Building.
4. Customs Connected with the Life of the Thai, such as Merit-Making, Amusements, and Occupations.
5. Customs Connected with Death.

Of these books on customs, I have already published Part 3, "Customs Connected with House-Building," and Part 5, "Customs Connected with Death." The books have not been published in numerical order, because I work on them according to whim; when I am satisfied with any part I publish it as opportunity affords. Part 4, "Customs Connected with the Life of the Thai," has had various sections published separately, because it is a big subject. Parts already published are "Life of Monastery-Dwellers," which at that time I called "I Shall Take Holy Orders," and "Life of the Farmer." Besides these there are certain short sections which have been published in the Journal of the Fine Arts Department as opportunity afforded. "Customs Connected with Birth," that is to say Part 1, is here published for the first time, but it is not here printed in full, because it still lacks the last part concerning education, which I am not yet ready to publish. "Customs Connected with Marriage," that is to say Part 2, has not yet been published because I am not yet satisfied with certain details, for these are customs which differ in almost every locality and every case, depending upon individual models or individual textbooks; besides there is always a mixture of the old and the new, as well as influence of Chinese, Vietnamese, and western customs.

To speak in particular of the customs connected with birth described in this volume, I am fortunate in having acquired most of my information from my own wife. According to western custom, when anyone has compiled something and has acquired information from any book or has received help from any person, he states this and renders thanks in his book; even if it is his own wife that has helped, he thanks her. I approve of this custom, and so will follow it here, and take the opportunity to thank my wife for giving me information of many kinds on the subject of birth, I thank her even though I know that I can thank her without having to announce it to other people in print; the western custom is like this, and I approve of it and so follow it, feeling that it does no harm. I must also render thanks with the deepest respect to my elders who have been kind to me, and there are also many others who have given me help on this subject whom I am unable to remember and note down, having obtained a little from this person and a little from that person. I have also obtained information from a great many books, and so I render thanks here collectively. . . .

Sàthǐan Ko·sè·d
[Pen name of Phya Anuman]
22 February 1949

Table of Contents

CUSTOMS CONNECTED WITH BIRTH AND THE REARING OF CHILDREN

Preliminary Matters

Birth and death are things that go together. Birth is the beginning and death is the end of the life of every person. Birth and death are therefore closely connected. Humans regard both these events as important, because they are the beginning and the end of life; they must be attended by traditional ceremonies for the purpose of seeking happiness in this world and the next world. To speak only of birth, even though there are fewer required traditional customs than at death, there are many small matters which today are regarded less seriously than formerly and so are gradually disappearing. People are changing over to modern opinions and beliefs in accordance with medical knowledge and progress.

Beliefs of people of former times which have been handed down traditionally, if considered from the point of view of modern opinions, may perhaps be regarded as foolish and unreasonable. This is because we are using the new as a yardstick to measure the old, or using our own measuring basket to measure other people's rice. How can they be the same? Beliefs of people of any given age or any given locality are always suited to the life and needs of that period or that locality, for customs which arise must always have a reason, so that they are regarded as beneficial or useful to the majority according to the opinions and beliefs of people of that period or that locality. When later on the opinions of the people in the group undergo changes according to the progress of the times, any custom which is appropriate to one age but perhaps is not appropriate to later ages declines and disappears, or is altered to make it appropriate. Gradual alterations and additions occur cumulatively and steadily through many generations, until national customs arise. Every nation thus has its own independent set of customs.

As a rule if anything is handed down traditionally as a custom, it survives for a long time. If there is no forcing circumstance, people dare not change; even though the usefulness or necessity is gone, people still believe in it stubbornly, for if they change from what they have been familiar with, they usually have a vacant and uncomfortable feeling. It is as if after one has eaten his meal he is accustomed to eating dessert; if he has none he feels strangely unsatisfied. Customs which have been handed down and still survive to the present are usually of the sort which have successfully passed the test of collective opinion of the group. Nations which have advanced therefore preserve their original customs; even though they no longer serve a useful purpose, they are stubbornly observed, for customs are national symbols, causing members of the nation to feel that they belong to one and the same nation and have for long generations. There is an exception only in the case of customs that are harmful or that obstruct or delay progress, being no longer appropriate to the times. These must be dropped or cast aside, or else changed and improved to render them more convenient. In such cases they are not maintained stupidly; people do not cling stubbornly to one way without change or alteration; nor, if they are not stubborn, do they cast aside everything old because they regard it as out of date, and seize upon new things which are not suited to the mentality or lives of all the people of the nation as a whole. Both of these methods result in damage.

Customs are an important branch of knowledge, because they give evidence regarding the life and opinions of people in former times which cannot be obtained from any other source. When we study history or any other subject whatsoever, we desire to learn about its development and expansion in order to know how to apply this information to the work of adapting new things appropriately and smoothly to our conditions and mentality. The same principle applies to the study of customs.

Books that deal with our customs connected with birth are hard to find, because these are regarded as matters that everyone knows and has seen. We therefore do not have old manuals on this subject like the Gṛhyasūtra and the Yajurveda of India, which contain much material concerning birth. We have only the textbook called Pàthŏmcindaa, which says that Phráʔ Máhǎathĕen Tamjee was the author. Whether Phráʔ Máhǎathĕen Tamjee was an Indian or of some other nationality, what he has written in this book is in accordance with the beliefs of those times. His intentions toward his fellow human beings were good, and he should receive some credit, but his name is instead an object of scorn, because it happens to coincide in sound with the name of a kind of plant which has an irritating poison all around the edges of the leaves. [1] Moreover, we call the person who delivers babies a tamjɛɛ doctor; but nowadays it is necessary to change this, because tamjɛɛ is regarded as an impolite word, and midwives[2] are regarded as skilled in magic spells and enchantments, which are ancient knowledge now out of date. Indeed for the most part this is true, and it is the misfortune of Máhǎathĕen Tamjee that his name ought to be an object of praise but instead has become a low name which no one likes to pronounce.

If one were to classify beliefs and ceremonies connected with birth, he might classify them according to the reasons that give rise to them, which may be grouped under three headings:

(1) For prevention of dangers which might befall a pregnant woman, because formerly it was believed that a period when one is liable to danger is the period when one is about to be a mother.

(2) For facilitating delivery and preventing dangers resulting in death; the period of giving birth to a baby was regarded as so important that pregnancy was compared to a woman going forth into battle or, as they say, like setting out in a little boat to cross the sea, one foot in the water and the other on the gunwale of the boat.

(3) For protection and care of the newborn child, at a time when its body is frail and weak and it may easily die, in order that it may survive to grow up later.

All three of these reasons were originally for the most part matters connected with protection from and driving away evil spirits which, it was believed, would come to molest and harm the child and mother. This was the belief of people in former times, when it was thought that anything not known and understood was to be assigned to the effects of spirits and gods as the agents which caused them. Later when there had been some advancement, even though the belief in spirits as cause faded out, the fear remained, because this belief lies deep in the bones. It is hard to eradicate; it varies only to a degree according to the time and locality. If anyone stubbornly refuses to follow the customs in which others believe, he offends the spirits and traditions to the point that he may cause suffering to the majority or to members of the group. It is therefore necessary to act alike in order not to go against tradition.

The customs connected with birth which I am about to describe have been compiled from old stories insofar as I have been able to seek them out. There are some that are still observed in certain localities, and some that have been given up. Even in the same locality there are practices and beliefs which are not uniform; there are certain omissions, additions, or alterations, depending upon the ability, beliefs, nationality, class, and knowledge of the people. I will not, however, speak of things which I regard as modern methods, which have nothing to do with research into old things, the purpose of this series of books.

Conception

It appears that formerly there was a belief that at the time of conception, the pregnant woman usually had a strange dream which was a token to inform her in advance whether the child in her womb would be a boy or a girl, whether it had good or bad characteristics, and what sort of person it would be in future when it grew up, as in the story of Khǔn Cháaŋ Khǔn Phěɛn, at the birth of Khǔn Cháaŋ, where it says:

Lady Thêebphathɔɔŋ lay asleep. She rolled and tossed, spoke in her sleep, and dreamed that a male elephant died and rolled down a steep bank; it bloated up and its head rotted and sent forth a foul odor.

There was a bald-headed pelican that came flying aimlessly from the great forest. It took the elephant in its beak and laid it down, entering the central house where she slept.

In the dream she called the bird, "Come here, you old bald-
headed fellow." She took hold of the bald-headed creature and lay
embracing the bird and the elephant happily.

When she awoke she straightway awakened her husband. She
vomited and trembled, unable to restrain herself. The foul odor
of the elephant and the bird clung to her. She retched and cried,
"O husband, I beg you, thump on my neck."

Khun Sǐi Wǐchaj was much alarmed. He started up, his eyes
bulging, and stroked and massaged her neck with his hand till she
recovered from her nausea, and then she told her dream.

Khun Sǐi Wǐchaj interpreted the dream: "You will be with child;
nothing is wrong. Our child will be a boy, according to the prediction, like the big pelican that came carrying an elephant in its
beak.

"He will be wealthy and prosperous, my love, but this child of
ours will disgrace us. Bald-headed from birth, he will be rich,
possessing more than five cartloads of money."

When one has dreamed of anything, he must relate the dream to someone who knows how to interpret it. Interpreting dreams is a good thing, because if the dreamer has a dream that seems bad to him, it causes him worry
and uneasiness; one who relates his dream and has it interpreted feels relieved. This applies only to people who still believe that dreams are signs of
good or evil; if one does not believe in them that is the end of the matter.

As a rule persons who conceive are not at first aware that they have
conceived, and it is a waste of time to speak of dreams. They occur often
only in stage plays; when a woman has conceived she has a dream, and then
someone interprets the dream. This appears to be a convention of literary
composition, not a convention of ordinary people. If one writes a book,
when someone conceives she must dream that she eats something inedible.
Perhaps the woman who conceives has heard many stories of this sort; she
happens to dream about it and so it comes to be regarded as a convention that
when one has dreamed she must tell the dream and have the dream interpreted.
However, this is a question of individuals, not a convention that is held
everywhere.

The period from conception to delivery is regarded as a time when there
are dangers all around one. The pregnant woman must risk various dangers
until the period is passed, and this makes her uneasy and unhappy. It is therefore necessary to find methods of protecting and defending her by various devices, for example:

They find a phǐdsàmɔ̌n talisman to tie on the wrist or hang diagonally
over the shoulder for protection. A phǐdsàmɔ̌n is a sheet of palm leaf on
which a magic formula is written, called loŋ khun phráʔ. Then it is folded
into a small square, and is usually strung on a cord or cotton thread. It is

tied or hung around the neck for a long time, many months. As time passes perspiration turns it black, for it is a cord that is worn constantly until the child is born and the mother leaves the fire; then she takes it off and keeps it in a jar containing turmeric and delivery articles. It is odd that this phɨ́dsàmɔ̌ɔn talisman is similar in name and characteristics to the talismans for tying around the neck to ward off dangers used by people who hold the Moslem religion, which have magic formulas praising Allah and are called Bismallaha. The phɨ́dsàmɔ̌ɔn [Siamese] talisman is tied on to ward off evil spirits which might cause harm to the pregnant woman. In the times when beliefs of this sort were general, anything harmful that might occur was ascribed to spirits, and especially in the case of a pregnant woman, because both mother and child might die if careful precautions were not taken. No doubt people had heard of such cases. As regards the death of a mother and child at this period, if they die before delivery, they are said to die thǎŋ klom. The word klom is said to be Cambodian, meaning "completely," that is to say, both mother and child die. If they die after delivery they are said to die phraaj, and usually become fierce phraaj spirits waiting and watching to harm pregnant women because of a feeling of disappointment and envy. This causes people to be all the more fearful and uneasy, and so they use whatever devices they have as protection.

Also, pregnant women are usually inclined to feel very thoughtful; they like to think of various things, and usually think more of unpleasant things than of pleasant ones. If they have magic objects that they firmly believe can be used for protection, their fear is somewhat relieved. It is not only we who have these notions; other nationalities have them as well. For example according to Indian belief, spirits like to molest and harm children and women because they are weak, whereas spirits do not dare molest men with strong hearts, just as dogs like to bite children and women. At the time of pregnancy and the time of delivery there are likewise many methods of protection against spirits that might come to do harm. I will relate these here in order.

Pregnant women may not go to a cremation, and may not go to visit persons seriously ill. This is probably protection against thinking too much, which might cause fear and loss of confidence. They are also forbidden to go and see other women give birth, because it will make delivery impossible, the children in the womb being embarrassed by one another and so refusing to be born. If one were to guess at the reason for this prohibition, it is probably that the person who goes might lose confidence when she sees the intense pain of delivery, and so she might be made uneasy. When monks conduct the sǎŋkhǎkam ceremony and chant the jádtɨ́, it is forbidden for pregnant women to enter the precincts of the ceremony; it is believed that they will have a hard time giving birth. Probably they regard the sound of the word jádtɨ́ as similar to the sound of the word jád [meaning "to stuff in, cram in"] and so they forbid it. Actually it may also be a question of the ceremony, in which purity is desired, for according to Indian custom when a ceremony is held, I understand that they forbid pregnant women and strangers to enter, regarding this as a defilement of the ceremony. Besides these things, it is also forbidden to fish, to kill animals, to tell lies, to drive nails or tacks, or to sew up the end of a pillow or mattress which has been stuffed with kapok but is not yet sewn up, for this will have an effect upon delivery, causing accidental closing of the passage in the same way. It is forbidden to sit, lie down, or stand in a doorway. When ascending or descending stairs, one must ascend or descend at once; it is forbidden to stop midway on the stairs. The reason for these prohibitions is easy to understand, and they are very widely observed. When sleeping, one must lie on the side; it is forbidden to lie on the back because it is believed that the child will bulge out and cause the belly to break open. I have asked women who have been pregnant and they say that if they sleep on their backs they feel uncomfortable.

When there is a solar or lunar eclipse, they are to fasten a sewing needle in the waistband of the lower garment, believing that this prevents the unborn child from having squinting eyes or a deformed body or facial features, such as a misshapen mouth resembling the eclipsed sun or moon. This belief is similar to a belief of Indians who hold the Moslem religion; they believe that a lunar eclipse is caused by evil spirits which eat the moon. They forbid pregnant women and their relatives from eating anything at this time; neither may they smoke cigarettes, for it is a time when spirits have come out and are roaming about. Moreover, if one chews betel at that time, the child to be born will have folded ears like betel leaf. (When Indians chew betel leaf they fold it rather than pleat it as we do.) It is also forbidden to twist or cut anything, for this will cause the child to be born with deformed fingers or swollen lips. [3] I do not understand why they fasten a needle in the waistband, believing that this will prevent squinting eyes. Perhaps it is a protection against spirits, which the Indians believe to be roaming about at that time. There is nothing that spirits fear so much as a sharp piece of iron; this is a belief held by many nationalities, as I have related elsewhere. [4] Concerning prevention of deformities in the child to be born, we also forbid deformed or ugly people from walking behind a pregnant woman, fearing that the child in the womb will be affected in the same way.

It is forbidden for pregnant women to "rub themselves" at night, because it is believed that at the time of delivery they will be pained by excessive liquid or will give birth to "water twins." If it is necessary to bathe, they should disrobe completely to bathe and then there is no danger. Women formerly did not bathe often; at best they "rubbed themselves" instead. "Rubbing oneself" here does not mean actually rubbing oneself; it is a method of bathing by pouring water on the upper part of the body without wetting the lower part of the body, which is covered by the lower garment. When they are going to "rub themselves," they must tuck up the lower garment as high as possible, bend over low, and then pour water from the vessel onto the middle of the back. If they do not bend over low, or if they do not pour the water exactly in the middle of the back, the water may run down and wet the lower garment. "Rubbing oneself" instead of bathing all over is not much seen now; this is different from former times, when it was still popular. The custom arose from not wishing to change the lower garment frequently, or from not having a lower garment to change to. The original source may have been shortage of water; it was necessary to economize on water because there were not enough vessels such as jars and jugs. If one were to bathe, it was necessary to go down to the landing in the dark when it was impossible to see and one might fall or be harmed by wild animals, and so bathing at night was forbidden. This is a supposition based on conditions of life in the country where things were formerly like this.

The prohibition on pregnant women bathing or "rubbing themselves" at night is not a belief confined to us. Other nationalities, so far as I have ascertained, also forbid it. For example, according to Vietnamese belief it is forbidden to bathe at night, because it is thought that it will cause a chill to the body of the pregnant woman, and at the time of delivery she will not give birth easily. According to Indian belief, besides forbidding bathing, they also forbid combing out the hair. When asleep it is forbidden to place the head on a high pillow, and it is also forbidden to sleep with the head low. On this subject of forbidding bathing, I have been told that the peasants in some localities in Thailand -- I am sorry that I cannot remember what localities -- believe that on the last day of the month pregnant women should seek an opportunity to take off all their clothing and bathe at night, but they must take care to allow no one to see them; what will happen if they are seen, my informant did not say, but he said that if they can do this they will be able to give birth easily. This belief concerning nakedness is strange. It is believed that spirits are very much afraid of it; no doubt these are spirits with culture! For example, if one is going out to collect herbs to treat illness, he must go naked, and must not allow his shadow to touch the medicinal plant. If there is a spirit in a tree acting as if it were going to haunt one, one must take off his clothes and tie the garments and some illuk grass to the tree, holding one's breath while tying them. After these things are tied, the spirit will not be able to come down from the tree and haunt one again.

Pregnant women must find work in order to exercise, such as carrying water or pounding rice, which are normal duties and tasks of women in the country. This is in order to keep the womb loose, and to prevent the child in the womb from becoming so fat and big that delivery will be difficult. This agrees with the belief of the Vietnamese, who likewise recommend heavy work.

Besides this they forbid reaching the arms out to full length, believing that the child in the womb will have trouble sucking the umbilical cord, because the cord of the afterbirth will contract and rise up high. They also forbid driving nails just as we do, but their prohibition is broader; even other people in the same house are forbidden, because it will cause the child in the womb to have a deformed body.

Concerning our prohibition against pregnant women fishing, killing animals, and telling lies, probably it is desired that they should be pure in heart. This is similar to the Indian custom of having one speak only auspicious words and perform sacrificial rites. This is all good; they say that it causes pregnant women to have beautiful clear complexions and happy dispositions. As it says in one place in the story of Khǔn Cháaŋ Khǔn Phěɛn:

I will tell of Thɔɔŋ Pràsǐi, who was heavy with child. She was truly lovely, her hair becoming to her face. Her complexion was as if burnished with gold, and her face like the orb of the moon on the night when it is full.

Her two cheeks were like golden fruits, and her two breasts were full and firm. Her skin was soft and beautiful to see, and her countenance radiant and fair.

She observed the precepts and said her prayers regularly, humbling her heart and raising her folded hands above her head. She made religious offerings with lotus blossoms, and had no fear of danger.

The quotation that I have cited here shows the beliefs of people in former times as to how pregnant women should behave. Besides this, the lotus blossoms which they had offered were boiled and eaten in the advanced stages of pregnancy, because they were regarded as a medicine beneficial to the fetus, making the child strong in body, and preventing the mother from vomiting with morning sickness. Sometimes they took the lotus blossoms and had monks say magic spells over them; this is still believed and practiced today. It is associated with strong belief in the efficacy of the Buddha, fostering religious faith and cheerfulness. This is also very helpful. If one desires really good results, she should wrap the stamens of giant lotus blossoms with black candle seed (Abroma augusta sterculiaceae) in a cloth as a massaging pack, boiling it in the milk of a young coconut. This is a specific medicine for the fetus. Coconut milk has certain properties which help the fetus. People in former times used it and saw the benefits, and so they handed it down as a prescribed treatment. People of this day and age may not agree, but their disagreement is not the result of chemical analysis of the constituents of coconut milk to see what elements it contains. So long as they have not really tested it scientifically, they cannot pronounce any definite opinion. Recently I read in an Occidental newspaper that coconut milk contains certain substances which are good for unborn children.

There is another belief connected with pregnancy. If she would like to rear her child easily, a pregnant woman must seek an opportunity to walk under the belly of an elephant, but it is necessary to choose an elephant with a kind disposition. If she has passed under the belly of an elephant, the child that is born will be easy to rear. The reason for this is not clear, but it is strange that many nationalities have beliefs similar to this. For example, Arabs and Iranians believe that if a pregnant woman has passed under the belly of a camel she will give birth easily. Peasants in Sweden, if they desire to give birth easily, must pass through a tunnel formed by shrubs and trees; sometimes they pass through a tunnel beneath stones, or pass through an iron barrel hoop. It is even believed that if children who are ill pass under an animals's belly or through a tunnel three times, they will recover.

Besides the miscellaneous beliefs already described, there is another matter that must be taken care of. One must entrust one's unborn child to a midwife, paying an amount of money as a sort of deposit, customarily one-half tamlyŋ or one tamlyŋ, that is two bàad (tical) or four bàad, or it may be more or less than this according to cases, depending upon the status of the patient and the locality. After this agreement is made, if anything occurs in connection with the pregnancy, one can summon the midwife to help, no matter what the time. Usually it is a matter of raising the womb, by lifting the womb with the hand, in order not to allow the fetus to drop down low, for this will make it difficult for the pregnant woman to walk because the fetus has fallen low.

Pregnant women usually have a desire to eat strange things. Usually these are things which human beings do not normally eat. This condition is called phɛ́ɛ thɔ́ɔŋ, and is the result of changes in the nervous system. It is a matter of psychology, causing a temporary desire to eat very sour things, very salty things, or strange and unusual things. There is also nausea and frequent vomiting. This is the opinion of modern doctors; you can make your own inquiries. This condition sometimes causes one to feel almost gluttonously hungry; I do not know whether this is because the woman deliberately says that she is hungry or because she is really hungry, for it is very difficult to judge the hearts of women. I will quote an instance of this pregnancy sickness from the story of Khŭn Cháaŋ Khŭn Phɛ̆ɛn, as follows:

I will tell of Lady Thêebpháthɔɔn. Her belly was huge and protuberant. She rose and sat with difficulty, and so she shuffled about, and trembled with hunger for liquor and meat.

Her saliva drooled like that of kàsŷy spirit, and she wept and moaned, imploring her husband. It was as if she were possessed by a ghost. The more one gave her to eat, the more she craved.

Eels, chickens, frogs, turtles, lizards, caterpillars, bullfrogs, all were insufficient to her guts. She snatched up huge bites and gobbled them down. In a moment the liquor jug was empty; it was impossible to buy it fast enough.

Strange things that pregnant women like to eat include pitch from
torches, hard chalk, diatomaceous earth, uncooked white rice, and burnt
earth (mud baked in sheets in the sun and then burnt). Formerly one saw hard
chalk stacked up for sale in shops (I have seen it at the Big Swing; more recently I have seen it for sale at Sàphaan Hǎn). At present one does not notice
it; probably the fashion for eating it has gone out. This hard chalk is not in
long thin sticks like the pencils which school children use for writing on slates;
it is a kind of diatomaceous earth of a soft yellow color and friable, for use in
writing on blackboards and black paper books like chalk. The good variety
is called "widow chalk" because it writes easily and need not be touched up
with saliva frequently to make it soft and possible to write with. Some wom-
en when they are pregnant feel nauseated and feel that their own husbands
are malodorous. The husband cannot come near, but must sleep in a different place, or sleep at a distance from her; if he comes near and she smells
him, she feels nauseated. This is very strange.

In the textbook <u>Phromcindaa</u> the symptoms of pregnancy sickness are
described as follows:

If the mother desires to eat meat and fish and raw things, they
say that a creature of hell has come to be born.

If she desires to eat honey, cane sugar, and palm sugar, they say
someone has come down from heaven to be born.

If she desires to eat fruit, they say an animal has come to be
born.

If she desires to eat earth, they say that Brahma has come down
to be born (because Brahma came down to eat delicious earth).

If she desires to eat hot, spicy things, they say that a human
being has come down to be born.

It is probably because of the belief that they like to eat earth because
Brahma has come down to be born, that women formerly liked to eat hard
chalk and burnt earth, so that Brahma would come down to be born as their
child. Also, during pregnancy it is necessary to be careful for the child in
the womb. Even if the woman desires to eat hot, spicy food, which is something she likes, she must refrain from eating it. When she sits or lies down
or moves about she must be careful of her body, not to fall down or jar herself too much. This is to prevent the child in the womb from being hurt or
damaged in any way.

When pregnancy approaches the seventh and eighth months, the flesh
of the belly around the navel stretches and protrudes, closing the navel. If
it protrudes above (the navel), the navel is said to be supine; if it protrudes
below (the navel), the navel is said to be prone. If any woman's navel turns
up, they say that the child in her womb will be a boy. If the navel turns
down, they say it will be a girl. This prediction is probably based upon the
characteristics of being turned down or turned up. At this time when

pregnancy is far advanced, the belly is very large and protuberant. The skin
of the abdomen is very taut, making it necessary to have medicine to smear
on the belly to prevent cracking. They say this is because the child in the
womb has grown very large, stretching the skin of the abdomen to the point
of cracking. For this medicine they use the rind of the bael fruit dried in
the sun and ground up with clear lime-water in an earthenware potlid. Some
women have white streaks on the belly; this is said to be the result of the
belly cracking at childbirth. Besides applying medicine, they also tread on
the front of the legs, saying that this relaxes the tendon. in the groin and
facilitates delivery. It is also necessary to take medicine to nurture the fetus
as already related.

When pregnancy is far advanced, the man who is the husband must go
and cut firewood in advance, for the wife to lie near the fire after the birth of
the child. It is forbidden for other people to cut it for her. He is to select
the wood of Combretum quadrangulare or tamarind wood, and the pieces
must be large. The reason for selecting these two kinds of wood is that in
some localities they grow in open woods and are easy to find, and it is said
that when these two kinds of wood burn to charcoal they leave only a little
ashes, not causing much annoyance or inconvenience. If it is another locality which does not have these two sorts of wood, they may use other woods,
depending upon their traditional practice. When they have cut the wood and
brought it in, they cut it up in sections. Then they must stack it up vertically in a suitable place. In some localities they have a belief that the cutting
of the firewood for lying near the fire should be done very near the time of delivery, that is, in about the eighth month after conception. Also, in the
matter of the kinds of firewood, besides Combretum quadrangulare and
tamarind, there should also be wood of Erythrina lithosperma. But the wood
of Erythrina lithosperma is said to give off a great deal of smoke; probably
they put only enough into the fire to observe the custom. The use of
Erythrina lithosperma wood when lying near the fire is said to prevent pains in
the womb and to cure bad blood. But if it is a first child, they are to use
wood of the "five species," [5] because this is supposed to accustom the woman to lying near the fire made from woods of various kinds when she has her
later children. There are omens observed in cutting firewood. If the firewood is cut in long pieces, the child to be born will be a boy. If it is cut in
small pieces, the child will be a girl. This is a matter of predicting from
the characteristics of shortness or longness, similar to the question of the
turned-up navel or turned-down navel. Similarly when the firewood is assembled in a stack: if the stack of firewood is observed to be high in the
center, the child will be a boy. If the center is not high, but flat and normal,
the child will be a girl. This is a matter of omens of the same sort.

According to the beliefs of the Mons (as recorded by R. Halliday in
The Talaings, Government Press, Rangoon, 1917, p. 55), the firewood for

lying near the fire must be cut in the seventh or eighth month. Halliday goes on to say:

> If, however, one stick is cut in the seventh month the rule is considered to have been observed and the remainder may be cut at any time. It is usually green wood, smoke evidently being desirable as well as heat. [But the Thais use slightly moist wood, not too fresh and not too dry, because it is desired that the wood not burn quickly and that it form coals; it is not desired that it produce much smoke. Phya Anuman Rajadhon.] In cutting the wood (young saplings) the first tree must fall clear to the ground. Should it fall and lie against another tree it is rejected. [Because it is stuck halfway, this will affect the delivery of the child. Phya Anuman Rajadhon.]

The belief restricting the cutting of the firewood to the husband is probably handed down from olden times when there was yet no hiring for wages and no purchasing. Also, it is a small matter not requiring the calling in of neighbors to help. Thus every family must do its own work and depend upon itself. Later on, even if it were convenient to hire someone to go and cut or purchase the firewood, there were those who believed firmly in the original custom and still observed it. This is to be regarded as a good thing; it is an act that shows the feelings of man and wife toward one another; no doubt the pregnant wife is made happy. But in localities where firewood is hard to find, or in times of progress and advancement, there are probably few people who still stubbornly observe this custom, because its usefulness and necessity are gone and it is out of date. Persistent observance of it causes hardship, and it is not progressive or appropriate to the times.

On the stack of firewood that is piled up vertically they must lay Indian jujube thorns (the Mon use bamboo thorns), believing that they ward off spirits. At the time of cutting these, they are to speak the following formula: namo buddhatassa.[6] When they reach the syllable hat they are to cut[7] at once with a knife. (This formula makes use of syllables of similar sound, that is, námoo = năam, thorn, and phúd [tàd] sá^ = phúdsaa, Indian jujube.) In any case, the spreading of thorns on the pile of firewood is a good thing. Besides warding off spirits, it also keeps away animals and naughty children who would get up and walk on the stack of firewood and knock it down. Why is it necessary to use Indian jujube thorns? Cannot other kinds of thorns be used? The answer is that they probably can, but Indian jujube thorns are easy to find, since they grow in forests and deserted places, and so it is stated flatly that the name is auspicious as explained above.

The central meaning of the spreading of thorns is protection against spirits. If these are kràs̆yy spirits, they fear thorns more than spirits of other kinds, for kràs̆yy spirits are said to be people like ourselves. Usually they are old women. At night in the dark of the moon when it is very late and everyone is asleep, the woman who is a kràs̆yy spirit goes out in search of food, taking along only her head and entrails from her body. Wherever she goes she can be seen as a flickering greenish light forming a big orb. The things that a kràsỹy spirit likes to eat are raw meat and excrement. She is especially fond of women who have just given birth and have tiny pink babies. She usually seeks an opportunity to enter the belly of the woman and devour the delicious entrails of the woman and baby with enjoyment. For this reason persons who are thin and dry with only skin covering their bones, and fruits such as small flat bananas without much flesh, are called "people sucked by a kràsỹy" or "bananas sucked by a kràsỹy." In the matter of spreading thorns to ward them off, it is necessary to spread them also under the house where there are cracks and holes, because wherever a kràsỹy spirit goes she drags her entrails along with her. If she tries to pass through the thorns, her entrails catch on the thorns. She is therefore very much afraid of thorns. When a kràsỹy spirit has finished eating the thing she normally likes, namely excrement, her mouth is smeared. If she sees anyone's clothing hung out at night outside the house, she will usually wipe her mouth with it. If in the morning one sees clothing that has been hung out faintly marked with round brown spots, one knows that a kràsỹy spirit has wiped her mouth with it. If one wishes to know who the kràsỹy spirit is, one is to boil the soiled cloth. The woman who is a kràsỹy spirit will be unbearably hot at the mouth and will have to come and ask to buy the cloth. Clothing that is soiled in spots because a kràsỹy spirit has wiped her mouth with it is usually seen in the rainy season. The cause is that the clothing is moist and gets no sun and so becomes mouldy; if it is hung in the sun for a long time the spots disappear of themselves. The saying that kràsỹy wipe their mouths with it is a good thing; people take care not to leave their clothing out in the dew till it becomes mouldy and is damaged.

Persons who are kràsỹy spirits are said to die very hard. When they are to die they must suffer very much. Thus they do not die easily, until some child or grandchild[8] accepts the heritage of being a kràsỹy spirit by receiving the saliva of the kràsỹy spirit, who spits it out on her. Then the kràsỹy spirit can die. This matter of saliva is strange. It is usually regarded as something peculiarly magic or the like. In the Northeast it is believed that if a person who is a pɔɔb spirit spits on anyone, that person must be a pɔɔb spirit, [which is a spirit of the] same category as kràsỹy spirits in that area. When I was a child I lived in a locality where kràsỹy spirits abounded. It was an area where there were many people of Mon and Tavoy descent. I have often heard stories of kràsỹy spirits. Next to my home there was an old lady who lay ill for a long time. The neighbors said that she was a kràsỹy spirit and died hard because she had no children or grandchildren to receive her saliva and carry on as a kràsỹy spirit. I was so frightened that I did not dare trespass into her yard to play. Later she died; I don't know whether it was because someone consented to be her heir or not, but I remember the story

well and so have related it here. By coincidence recently an old lady who
had lived at my home ever since girlhood came to visit me, and so I took
the opportunity to ask her about this story. She said that the old kràsy̆y spirit
had no children or grandchildren to accept the heritage of being a kràsy̆y
spirit, and so she had to have a cat accept it instead; that is, she smeared
her saliva on the cat, and so she could die. This is very amusing.

An elderly person once spoke to me about kràsy̆y spirits as follows:
"This name kràsy̆y is peculiar. The world regards only bright lights as kràsy̆y,
for example kràsy̆y worms[9] and kràsy̆y lamps.[10] But because it is known that
there are only female kràsy̆y, a male was invented and called kàhăaŋ, but
what they speak of is a mere concoction, said to be made with flat baskets
for wings and a rice-pounding pestle for a tail. The thing as described would
seem to be half man and half bird, but when one draws a picture which is
half man and half bird, it is rather called 'àràhăn.[11] This name is strange.
Why they should take the name of an enlightened person with divine wisdom
and apply it to a filthy figure like that, I don't know."

In the north they do not trust mere spreading of thorns. They also
make a fence around the area under the house directly beneath the delivery
room, and then put thorns all around the fence. Around the delivery room
upstairs they make a circle with a magic cord, hang up cloths on which
magic figures are drawn in all directions, and then stretch a net across the
ceiling with a peak in the center. These strong defenses they say are to ward
off phooŋ spirits (probably from phlooŋ, that is, they have a shining [phlooŋ]
light like kràsy̆y spirits). They usually make holes in the floor (probably
floors made of flattened bamboo strips) and come up to suck the blood of the
mother where she lies. They like to drink the blood at the tip of the heart
of the mother and child who are lying near the fire, and they are capable
of transforming themselves into cats, pigs, birds, or whatever they please.
It is therefore necessary to take strict precautions.

Labor Pains

When the time of labor pains arrives and the child is to be born, the
people in the house must hurry to knock down the firewood that has been
piled up, and then pull out two or three sticks of it, and go and light a fire
to boil water in preparation for the time of delivery. They use a piece of
wood from this fire to start the fire that the mother will lie near later.

They must open the doors and windows and unlock all bolts and locks
of cupboards, drawers, and anything else that is locked up. Also pieces of
wood and other things that are fastened or stuck under the beams or roof must
be removed. In the northeast amulets which are "closing-the-portal" charms
must be taken away elsewhere; only after the birth can they be brought back
and put away in their original places.

It is forbidden to sit or stand in a door or midway on the stairs, or to speak the words "stuck," "fastened," "hung up," "stuck midway," "difficult delivery," or other words of similar meaning; none of these can be spoken, because it is believed that they might come true.

It is forbidden for pregnant women to come in and visit, because the children in the womb will be embarrassed and refuse to be born.

These prohibitions are superstitions to prevent obstruction and facilitate delivery. They are ideas remaining from olden times and are common to all nations. Among the Arunta in the middle of the continent of Australia, the husband must take off all personal ornaments; whatever he has in bags or pouches must all be poured out; anything tied up in a coil or knot must be undone. The matter of opening doors and windows, unlocking cupboards and drawers, and untying knots and coils at the time of labor pains before delivery, are beliefs held by many nationalities, both Occidental and Moslem. It is even believed that corks in bottles and spigots must be taken out. Domestic animals in pens, coops, or sheds -- such as horses, oxen, ducks, and chickens -- or those that are chained up -- such as dogs -- must be set free temporarily. Hair that is coiled up must be unfastened and let down. Jackknives that are closed must be opened. In sum, no matter what it is, if it is fastened, or stuck, or closed, or tied, or locked up, it must be released, freed, or undone.

At the time of delivery the direction must be selected. Usually it is good if the face can be turned toward the east, or the head may be pointed toward the north; the child will be able to move down easily.[12] In some cases they have a master of magic select the direction for them. Some select the direction according to a hen which is laying an egg; in whatever direction the chicken turns its head, the face should be turned in that direction in order that the mother may bear the child as easily as the hen lays its egg. In some cases they have the woman in labor turn her head toward a door, which is a "way out."

When the labor pains become frequent, they are to light candles and incense sticks and worship the spirit of the plot of land as an act of begging forgiveness and in order to inform him, for they have taken the liberty of coming and giving birth on his land. Probably they regard giving birth to a child as a blemish. This is a belief held by many nationalities. They do not say outright that it is a blemish, but one can tell from various prohibitions of theirs that they so regard it. I will save these and relate them in the section discussing reasons for lying near the fire. Besides this, if one wishes to make vows to any other spirits or gods, it is up to one's beliefs. In the book, Khŭn Chăaŋ Khŭn Phɛ̌ɛn, in the section, "Birth of Khŭn Chăaŋ," it is said:

> Some spoke charms and sprinkled white rice, their lips mumbling incoherently.

In another place, in the section, "Birth of Naaŋ Phim," it is said:

Some took cowries and stuck them on the wall, making vows and mumbling incoherently.

Speaking charms and sprinkling white rice are still popular with some people, because this period is one of emergency, and whatever knowledge or beliefs one has, he puts them into action. The Palaung, who are a hill people living in the north of Burma, sprinkle sacred water all around the room to ward off spirits; this is the same sort of thing as our sprinkling of white rice. In the north of Thailand they make holy water and float the unripe pods of Acacia concinna in it; then they tie leaves of the camphor plant, which spirits fear, in bunches, dip them in the holy water, and sprinkle it all over the delivery room, as well as in every corner and cranny of the house in case a spirit is hiding somewhere; when touched by the holy water the spirit cannot endure it, but must flee away. But the custom of sticking a great many cowries in the roof or fastening cowries on the wall and making vows, as in the story of Khǔn Chǎaŋ Khǔn Phέεn, is a belief which at present no one seems to observe or to have seen. And why was it necessary to use cowries? I have found evidence that rural people in some areas, at the time of labor pains before delivery of a child, take fŷan or sàlŷn coins and fasten them with beeswax to a cotton thread, and then hang them up at the head of the woman in labor. Or they may hang them up at the spirit shelf in the house. When they hang them up there are also betel and areca, flowers, incense sticks, and candles as offerings. When the incense sticks and candles have been lighted they are taken down and set upright below. This is a way of making a vow and asking for an easy delivery. After the child is born, they take the money and buy things to put in a monk's begging bowl or offer to a monk. If one considers this he will see that the cowries are simply money offerings, because in former times cowries were used as small money. Even at present, sàtaaŋ coins or banknotes may also be used instead. In those days if one wished to insert a silver bàad coin in the wall or roof to make a vow, he could do so, but this was a very large amount, and if it disappeared the owner might be ruined, for a silver tical in those days was not a small sum, even to royalty. For example, it is known that His Majesty the Second King of the Third Reign received from the king only ten catties of silver per year, or eight hundred bàad. This was regarded as a fabulously great amount, sufficient to maintain the honor of the palace of the Second King. His Majesty King Chulalongkorn once told a story that country girls said to their mothers as they paddled their boat past the King's palace, "No doubt the King has a whole catty of silver, and eats glutinous rice with coconut cream every day." Little did they realize the accuracy of their remarks. When the King ascended the throne he had one catty, or eighty bàad, of personal money left.

There is an important requirement connected with the time when the delivery is about to take place; they must go after the midwife to whom the womb was entrusted. When the midwife has come, they are to arrange a bowl filled with an appropriate amount of white rice, with three areca nuts (some people say five nuts or seven nuts, or in some cases slices; this is indefinite), three bunches of betel leaves (some people say five or seven betel leaves), one bunch of bananas, three incense sticks, and three candles. There is silver fastened to the candles according to custom; this may be one tamlyŋ, two tamlyŋ, or three tamlyŋ (four bàad, eight bàad, twelve bàad, depending upon the fee in the locality. There may be other things added to the bowl; this is not restricted. All of this is called "setting up the rice bowl"; that is they take the bowl filled with rice, money, and various things mentioned above, and set it up in a suitable place as an offering to show their gratitude to the midwife for coming to assist in the delivery. When the midwife has performed the delivery and has for three full days come to help make other arrangements in connection with the delivery, the duties of the midwife are finished. Then they turn the rice bowl over to her; this is called "presenting the rice bowl." In some cases they present the rice bowl when the mother has left the fire; some people leave it set up for a longer time than this, for what reason I do not know. The rice bowl of the Mon has no rice; it has only areca, betel, and silver, with a cotton thread for tying the navel of the child when the umbilical cord is cut. The midwife takes a chew of areca and betel and then sets the bowl down in its original place. I do not know what sort of bowl they call it, but they undoubtedly do not call it a rice bowl for there is no rice in it. In the south, according to notes kindly furnished me by a friend, they call it the rice bowl only in the case of physicians who treat diseases. If it is a rice bowl for a midwife they call it râad. They prepare a skein of raw cotton thread, one unit of beeswax, one mountain-shaped pile of areca and betel, one unit of white rice, and one unit of cowries or silver coins. These things may vary in amount, depending upon how they are arranged on the stand or in the bowl to look nice. The amount of silver may be six sàlyŋ (one and a half bàad), one-half tamlyŋ (two bàad), one tamlyŋ (four bàad), or at the most one and a half tamlyŋ (six bàad). The money demanded is usually more than for children born later. The mountain-shaped pile of areca is made by smearing lime on betel leaves and forming them into a conical pile like an inverted funnel in the center of the bowl or stand. There is no prescribed number of leaves. The areca nuts are placed inside the funnel, while the other articles are arranged on the stand, except the raw cotton, which they tie around the mountain-shaped pile of betel. This râad bowl is laid at the head of the bed. When the mother leaves the fire, the midwife comes and dismantles the râad bowl and takes the things away. Normally the thread and wax are offered to monks to make candles for worshipping Buddha images.

The things in the rice bowl are all things that can normally be eaten or used, but why do they chiefly use the number three? If one tries to explain this along the lines of a religious catechism, as people are accustomed

to do categorically in matters having to do with funerals, one will say that
three is the number of the Buddhist Trinity. But why do they not use three
bunches of bananas? Probably it is because it is too much to put into the bowl.
If one were to use only three bananas it would be too little and make a very
poor showing, and so it is preferable to use a whole bunch. Bananas seem to
be a usual article of food, because they are grown easily and occur at every
house; therefore they use bananas along with the white rice and the areca and
betel, which are articles used for food and for chewing every day. As for the
bowl, it is used as a vessel for washing the face. Incense sticks and candles
are included as articles of worship, but the inclusion of silver seems to be
something that arose at a later stage when it was necessary to use silver, but
it was nevertheless an amount which, if compared proportionally with the
present day, is only a little. No doubt it was sufficient for purchasing needs
in those days, which were a period of exchanging labor, and not yet a period
when everyone had to do his own hiring.

At the time of labor pains, when the child is almost to be born, there
must be someone to support the back; that is, a person is used like a chair
back for the woman in labor to lean against. In some cases the person supporting the back sits in turn upon a water jar; this is probably to make it
easier for the woman to lean back. Besides this, the person supporting the
back also has the duty of being assistant to the midwife. If the midwife says
to push, she must press both sides of the belly of the mother with her two
hands; this is said to prevent the child in the womb from squirming away in
this or that direction. If the midwife says to press down, she presses the upper part of the belly of the mother with her hands in order to cause the child
to move downward. If the woman in labor faints, she must pound up lemon
grass for her to use as an aromatic medicine. If they have other aromatic
medicines they need not use lemon grass.

If trouble arises in the delivery and the child is slow to be born, they
must use various devices. One that is much used is exorcising water sprinkled
and rubbed on the body of the woman in labor, and also given to her to drink.
This exorcising water is made in many ways, for example, by soaking a
charmed amulet in water and using this water as exorcising water, or by pouring water over the great toe of the husband and then catching it and using it
as exorcising water, or by throwing water up on the roof and then catching it
until they have done this three times, and then enchanting the water that is
caught the last time with a Buddhist formula pronounced backwards, and
using this as exorcising water. Sometimes the exorcising water is enchanted
with a spell that is humorous and obscene; it is the sort that I cannot cite as
an example here. This spell must be pronounced loudly so that the woman in
labor will hear it; this probably gives her some comfort and no doubt makes
her laugh at the words of the spell, and so the exorcising water is effective,
the woman in labor being relieved of her pain and strengthened in her efforts

to expel the child. In the north they use magic formulas, covering the head of the pregnant woman with the hands and pronouncing the spell; this is called "pressing down." Another method is to enchant water and sprinkle the head of the mother with it or have her drink it. This is nothing else but exorcising water, but I don't know whether they have spells for their exorcising water that have obscene wording like our spells or not. According to Indian custom, if the delivery is difficult they likewise drink exorcising water; they write cabalistic figures, soak them in water, and have the mother drink it, or else have them drink water in which the feet of the husband, or the husband's mother, or a virgin girl, have been washed.

Some nationalities have strange methods of facilitating delivery, for example the Arunta on the continent of Australia, as has been described. They take the cloth with which the husband binds his head and wrap it around the upper abdomen of the wife, in order to keep the infant in the womb from moving upward. This is the same sort of thing as our method of pressing downward on the abdomen. If they see that the child still can't be delivered, the husband must remove his clothing and walk past his wife, at a distance, assuming mannerisms and posturing as if to invite the child to come out and follow him. (No doubt this is because the child in the womb will regard a naked person as similar to itself, and so will come out and follow him.) Among the people of some of the islands in the Philippines, when the wife is in labor and about to give birth, her husband must remove his clothing and stand boldly in the doorway of the house, or go up and exhibit himself upon the roof, one hand brandishing a sword back and forth continually; this is to threaten the evil spirits and prevent them from coming and interfering with the delivery. The Ching-paw or Kachin people, who are mountain dwellers living in the north of Burma, when a woman is in labor, must worship and make vows to the spirit of the places; this is the same sort of thing as with us. Then they perform a rite of expelling forest spirits and ghosts of women who have died in labor. If they would perform the rite in the very best way, they must have young men assume obscene postures in front of the woman in labor; when the spirits see this they will be embarrassed and flee. (No doubt these are female spirits and shy.) The Maltese use a flower of the kind called in English "rose of Jericho." It is kept in water in the room. Whenever the flower blooms, this is a signal that the child is about to be born.

As regards devices to facilitate delivery, every nationality whether occidental or eastern or any nationality whatsoever that has people of the peasant class has various methods. Many examples can be found in western books on the subject of birth customs, and so it is not necessary to cite them here. The sum and substance of the matter is that at the time when knowledge had not yet achieved its present level of progress, human beings of every nation have regarded childbirth as an important event. It is a matter of life and death for a woman. When there is difficulty and the child is not delivered with normal ease, she is liable to die easily, and so people view childbirth with great apprehension, and various methods must be devised in accordance with the people's beliefs to prevent danger to the woman who is to give birth. Even at the present time, when people know that childbirth is a natural event not different from the reproduction of animals, there is still feeling about it, and people still hold to the traditional beliefs that any interference with the birth of the child is due to the work of spirits. People who are rural farmers are still frightened about it, and so they seek ways to assist matters by preventing evil spirits from coming and causing trouble. Although such beliefs as these are gradually disappearing as knowledge advances, it will probably be a long time before they disappear altogether.

When the child is almost to be born, that is, the head of the child has passed the portal bones but still remains in the vagina, they are to take fairly large lumps of salt, choosing those with sharp edges, and scratch the "stitches" till they part.[13] At the same time they are to press downward on the abdomen in order to cause the child to slip out. In some cases they use the fingernails to cut the "stitches," but this is probably not so good as salt because the latter is salty and may have fewer disease germs on it than unclean fingernails. This is spoken from the point of view of modern feelings; in former days they had no such feelings because they knew nothing of germs. If anything happened which was due to disease germs, they simply blamed it on spirits. At the present time it is not necessary for the "stitches" of the woman giving birth to be damaged to the point of severance, because maternity doctors have ways of assisting. They wash their hands clean so that there are no disease germs and then gently assist the head of the child to emerge. They have knowledge which they regard as superior, and so they do not consent to call themselves midwives. In the north midwives are called mɛ̂ɛ hâb.[14] Probably they regard her function as that of "receiving" the child as it emerges. The wounds arising from delivery are to be washed with liquor, and then they pound Zingiber casumunar with salt and apply it; it is necessary to endure the smarting caused by this until the flesh feels no pain. Wealthy city people generally apply processed opium, because it is not necessary to endure as much smarting as with Zingiber casumunar and salt. If the wounds occurring as a result of delivery are long because the child that is born is large in size, no matter how much Zingiber casumunar and salt are applied, even though they heal, they do not close as before. When one walks or does heavy work, this causes the womb to move downward into the vagina. This is called dàag ʔɔ̀ɔg[15] (different from the dàag ʔɔ̀ɔg in the rectum).[16] This ailment was formerly very common, because they did not know how to make stitches like modern doctors. In the old times they regarded wombs as of two kinds, namely, lotus-leaf wombs and stone wombs. Women with the former kind of womb were not usually liable to prolapsis uteri. If they had the latter kind of womb they were usually liable to this, because it is round and not flattened like the former kind, and so can slip down easily. Some peasants believe that prolapsis uteri is a dropping of the diaphragm. Diaphragm here is the "pelvic diaphragm," not the diaphragm which is in the center of the body. Also, during the first three days after delivery the mother usually does not urinate. They say that this is because she is shy and so does not urinate. Actually she probably wants to urinate, but no doubt she is afraid of smarting and so she restrains herself as long as possible. In such cases they put warm water in a basin and have her soak herself in order that the flesh, which is to say the nerves, will become adjusted. Then she can urinate into the basin and there is little pain. But in the real old days they probably did not do this; they probably left the matter to take care of itself, but no one was dissuaded from giving birth to children. In these times if there is reluctance to urinate they insert a tube to cause the urine to come out.

Birth

When the child is born and slips out onto the floor they call it "falling to the bamboo floor." Originally the child really fell onto the bamboo floor. An old midwife has told me that at this time of birth it is necessary to spread a cloth to receive the child. When the child slips out, they must first cover it with the "tail" of the lower garment of the mother to keep it from the wind. I think that this is correct, because if a newborn child is touched by the outside air before it has time to adjust it may have convulsions. This old midwife has another special practice of her own which she boasted much of and asked me to put down just as she described it; I ask that it be regarded simply as an old belief. She said that when the child slips out, if it is seen to be a girl, one must first grasp the "golden turtle";[17] if a boy, one must first take hold of "that thing";[18] then one lets go. She said that if one does this, when the child grows up it will have no deformities, but will have very beautiful characteristics, because it was "adjusted" from the very first.

They usually take note of this time of "falling to the bamboo floor" and remember it. If they can read and write they note down the time, day, month, and year in order to have an astrologer make note of the planets' positions and write out the horoscope. If they cannot write they may ask a monk to write it for them. I have seen horoscopes in the north; they were written on palm leaves and then rolled up round and put away. If they have no clock to note the time of birth, they estimate it from the shadows of the sun in daytime and from the cock's crow during the night.

When the child has been born, the person supporting the mother's back must press the abdomen of the woman in labor firmly, in order to prevent the afterbirth from "flying up," that is to say, they fear that the afterbirth will not emerge. They are usually very much afraid in this matter of the afterbirth "flying," because there have been many cases of harm caused by failure of the afterbirth to come out. Nowadays if it does not come out it can be pulled out.

At the same time, the midwife holds the child in her arms, face down, and then puts her finger into the mouth of the child in order to extract mucus or blood in the mouth. If this mucus is not removed at once the child will have trouble breathing; this is called "choking on filthy water." The "filthy water" is the mucus on which the child was nurtured in the womb and which spurts out at the time of delivery. It is like lubricating oil to facilitate birth of the child. If at the time of birth it is observed that there is little of this mucus for lubrication, they put in coconut oil to help. Nowadays they probably use vaseline, or I do not know what oil. When the mucus has been removed from the child's mouth, if the child does not cry they must beat its bottom hard enough to make it cry. If it still does not cry, they must wait for the afterbirth to emerge, and then put a spade or any piece of iron in the fire and heat it red hot, and press it against the afterbirth. The heat will pass along the umbilical cord to the body of the child. When the child feels hot it will cry. If even after doing this the child does not cry, this shows that it will not survive. They say that failure to cry may be caused by a lump of blood stuck in the throat which they failed to notice and remove.

When the child has cried out, they wrap it in a cloth and leave it for the time being. If they do not hurry to wrap it in a cloth, the child may have convulsions and turn blue in the face and die, because the air is too cold. In some cases at this point they take honey and gold leaf which they have prepared in advance and swab the base of the child's tongue. They say that this is a way of preventing pharyngitis. This procedure of swabbing with honey and gold leaf is found only among certain peasants who know it; they generally use honey of the fifth lunar month, which is regarded as good honey. In the north they believe that if they do not remove all the blood from the mouth and do not swab with honey and gold, the child may have pharyngitis which will develop into asthma. According to Indian custom the midwife must clean out the child's nostrils (probably by sucking and then spitting), in order to open the passages and facilitate breathing, and she must clean out the anus in order to get rid of obstructions that may remain there. If the new-born child is a boy they perform a ceremony called játakarma and give the child honey and clarified butter to eat.

When the child has been put aside, they must see to getting the after-birth out, because this stage is a matter of life and death to the mother, more important than the child. If the afterbirth does not emerge within a proper interval after the birth of the child, that is within about five minutes, they have the mother rise to a squatting position and have someone pound her back with a pillow. Sometimes they lower a rolled-up betel leaf or some

other article down the throat or nostrils in order to cause squirming or cough-
ing and sneezing, so that the afterbirth will come out. (In India, if the afterbirth has not come out then everyone present must be perfectly silent; if not,
the afterbirth will flee upward.) When the afterbirth has come out, they
have the mother take medicine at once. This medicine is a dish of moist
tamarind fruit and salt put together (this is nothing more nor less than a pur-
gative). They believe that this washes and cleanses the blood which remains.
Later she takes medicine "to prevent action of the blood"; they explain that
if the blood rises and floods the heart it will cause a feeling of oppression and
difficulty in breathing. It is necessary to take medicine to drive out the bad
blood. (In southern India they likewise take moist tamarind fruit.) When
she has taken the water of moist tamarind fruit, the mother must lie still for
a time, until they have arranged the fireplace for her to lie near the fire.
At this point the midwife returns to take care of the matter of cutting the
child's umbilical cord.

Duties Relating to the Newborn Child

Cutting the Umbilical Cord. The people take cord or raw cotton thread
(sometimes also dyeing it with indigo), and tie two knots in the umbilical
cord, drawing them tight, leaving an interval between them at the part which
is to be cut. Sometimes they break the thread and tie three rabbit-neck
knots[19] and pronounce Buddhist incantations over all three knots. The reason
for tying the knots tight is to stop the flow of blood and air. The child will
feel numb, and they believe that when the umbilical cord is cut the child
will feel little pain. They leave a part of the umbilical cord attached to
the child's navel reaching down to the child's knees. They use the outer
bark of Thrysostachys siamensis[20] to cut. It is forbidden to cut with an iron
blade. (Almost all nationalities in the Indochinese peninsula, so far as I have
read in books, use the outer bark of bamboo to cut the umbilical cord.) The
reason for leaving a long section of umbilical cord attached to the child's
navel is that if they leave too short a length, much blood will flow when the
cord has been cut. If this happens they must make haste to untie the cord or
thread which has been tied, and retie it closer, tightly enough to stop the
flow of blood. Otherwise if the flow of blood does not stop the child will be
in danger. They must grind or pound fresh turmeric and apply it. If after
applying this the flow of blood does not stop, there is no hope of saving it;
the child must certainly die.

The method of cutting is to use a lump of dirt placed under the umbilical cord in place of a cutting board; some people use a ginger tuber instead
of a lump of dirt. Then they cut it with the outer bark of Thrysostachys
siamensis, sawing the umbilical cord at a point between the places that have

been tied until it parts. According to northeastern custom they tie the umbilical cord with black cotton thread, lay it on a lump of charcoal, and cut
it with a sharp mollusk shell. These methods of cutting the umbilical cord
may be regarded as bits of antiquarian information. An elder has kindly informed me that in the case of a prince or princess who is of the rank of phrá?
ǫoŋ câaw, [21] they use a golden wedge as the cutting board. This is no doubt
a custom which arose later when people had become wealthy.

Also, the umbilical cord has black lines inside it, called "charcoal
lines." If the charcoal lines are close together, they believe that the mother
who bore this child will later have children in close succession. If the charcoal lines are far apart, she will have children at long intervals.

Bathing the Child. When the umbilical cord of the child has been cut, they
bathe the child in warm water. If there is much grease or mucus sticking to
the body of the child, they must first rub the child's body with coconut oil
and then rub the grease off with a cloth. They then bathe it clean in water.
To bathe it, the bather sits with both legs stretched out straight in front and
lays the child down in the hollow between the shins, with its head toward the
feet, in order to wash the head and face of the child easily. The bathing is
not a mere matter of cleansing. There must also be flexing of the child's
arms and legs in order to make the child's arms flexible and its legs straight.
If they would "adjust" other parts to make them beautiful as the old midwife
did at the time of birth, it can be done. They proceed in this way every
time they bathe the child. This method of bathing upon the shins is perhaps
a traditional survival from ancient times when there were still no vessels such
as basins for laying a child down to bathe it. This is likewise a bit of antiquarian information that has survived.

Bathing a child upon the shins is called "bathing," and bathing a child
in a basin is called "soaking." If they are wealthy people, they arrange silver and gold valuables such as rings and necklaces in the basin, if they use
"soaking," in order to cause the child when it grows up to be a person of
wealth and property. This is a custom which arose after there were silver
and gold. According to northeastern custom, when the child has been bathed,
a relative takes the child together with its cushion up in the arms and goes
down from the house to the ground, to a distance from the house stairs of
about two meters or more. Then the person carrying the child bends down
low and touches the right foot of the child to the earth three times. They
say that they perform this rite in order not to have the child tread incorrectly
on the earth, and to make the child as steadfast as the earth. (This is similar
to the children's rite of treading the earth in the south and the royal ceremony of touching the earth, which will be described later in the section dealing with rearing children.) When the rite of treading the earth is finished
and they have reascended to the house, elderly relatives such as the

grandparents tie auspicious white cotton threads around the neck and wrist of child and mother. Then they let the child lie in a flat basket, with a net covering the basket. Sometimes the mother also goes to lie inside the net. They regard the net as an effective protection against evil spirits, because when the spirits see that the net has many eyes they are afraid.

When the bathing is finished, they take a square piece of cloth of adequate size and rip a long hole in the center. Then they slip this over the umbilical cord and lay the cloth around the navel, bringing the umbilical cord up through the hole so that it lies on the cloth. They bend the umbilical cord in a circle on the cloth, and sprinkle turmeric powder mixed with diatomaceous earth on it, or they may apply moist pounded turmeric, in order to dry the umbilical cord so that it will slip loose from the navel quickly. Then they bind the abdomen of the child with cloth, to prevent the curved umbilical cord from moving.

Children Dying at Birth. If after a child is born, none of the methods to make it cry as already described is successful, this shows that the child will not survive. If a child dies at this period, they usually smear the corpse of the child with soot or red lime, on the face or the arm or the buttocks or any part they choose. This is a marker so that when the child reenters the womb and is born again it will be recognized as the same person, for the child that is reborn will have a birthmark on its body at the place where the marker was smeared. If the child born later has a black birthmark, it means that the corpse was marked with soot; if it has a red birthmark, it means that it was marked with red lime. The corpse of the child is to be covered temporarily with a net; this is understood to be a prevention against the dead child's becoming an evil spirit which will do harm to the mother. Then they invite a witchdoctor to come and "do up" the corpse of the child; that is, he places the corpse of the child in a large earthenware pot, makes a cabalistic design at the bottom of the pot, and then covers the mouth of the pot with a square white cloth of adequate size, tying it with a magic cord. Then he sinks the pot in water or buries it, whichever is appropriate.

They are very much afraid of a child that dies at birth, because it may take its mother with it, that is, cause her to die as well. They must therefore protect the mother of the child by tying a magic thread around her wrist; this is a way of summoning her guardian spirit. Soon, when the mother lies near the fire, her breasts will be very taut because there is no child to suck them. The milk must be pressed out into a little bowl and set out at a triple crossroads (see the subject of triple crossroads in my book on death customs) for the spirit of the child to eat. They do this for three to seven days and then tie up Jussiae repens plants in a bundle and beat this against the breasts frequently. They do this for about three days to dry the breasts and reduce the swelling. This is a matter of mingled love and concern and fear.

The matter of covering the corpse of the child with a net is strange.
It is also used in the exact reverse of death. For example, in the Vessantara
Jātaka, when Jāli was born, they used a golden net to receive him, so that
he acquired the name of Jāli, meaning "net." It is said in the book,
Pathamasambodhi, that when the Lord Buddha was born, Indra and Brahma received him in a golden net in order not to hurt his person. Sir James Frazer
says in the book The Golden Bough that nets are characteristically full of
knots, and many nationalities have beliefs that knots are firm and fast and
cannot be untied, so that they are efficacious as protection against spirits or
against harmful magic spells employed by people. For example, in Russia
the peasants in some places have the custom of using a net to cover the bride
at a wedding to protect her from the magic spells of enemies, while the bride-
groom and his assistants have a net tied at the waist. A cord tied in square
knots at intervals is used by Russian peasants as an amulet. According to our
custom, when we tie the guardian spirit or tie the wrists, we tie a square
knot. In the north they must make three or five knots in the cord before tying it on, and when they tie it on they pronounce a magic spell of exorcism.
If these matters are compared with the practice of covering a child's corpse
with a net, as has been described, the meanings are similar; that is, the net
has knots which serve to prevent the spirit of the child from coming out and
doing harm to its mother, or, in the contrary case in matters of birth, a net
is used to cover the child and protect it against spirits that might come in to
do it harm.

Concerning the Afterbirth. When the umbilical cord of the child has been
cut, they are to take the afterbirth and the part of the cut umbilical cord
which is attached to the afterbirth and wash them clean in water. They say
that this prevents skin diseases which might appear later on the body of the
child. Then they take the washed afterbirth and umbilical cord and place
them in any vessel of earthenware which may be procured easily in the locality, such as a sugar pot. Then they cover them with salt to prevent decay.
It is forbidden to throw the afterbirth away. They must bury it, but not until
three days after the birth. I do not know the reason for this. In the textbook,
Pàthŏmcindaa, it says, "Evil spirits will be attracted by the odor and come
to eat. When they have eaten, they will proceed to come after the mother,
causing various dangers." For this reason it is required to bury it. Besides
this there are many other requirements connected with the afterbirth. I will
save these and describe them later. At this time they are to set the pot containing the afterbirth down beside the place of lying near the fire, in order
to cause the umbilical cord of the child to dry rapidly. Also, they must set
the pot containing the umbilical cord up straight; otherwise they believe that
the child will have a crooked mouth.

Bouncing on a Basket. After bathing the child and taking care of the umbilical cord, they carry the child in the arms and put it down upon a flat basket.
They use the bottom rather than the top of the basket, because the bottom is
convex and resilient, and can be bounced like a spring. They need not fear
that the child will roll off, because it is still young and has no stength to
squirm about. Nevertheless, sometimes at this point if they have not finished
preparing the cushion and diapers (why they do not make them in advance I
will explain later), they use other cloths such as blankets to lay the child on
temporarily. On the basket in which the child lies, if it is a boy, they are
to place a book and pencil; if a girl, they are to place a needle and sewing
thread instead; this is in order that when the child grows up it will know how
to read and write or know how to do needlework, depending upon whether it
is a boy or girl. But this is done among the wealthy and aristocratic people,
for these arts are regarded as knowledge befitting the children of aristocrats.
The ordinary peasants hardly do these things. Sometimes these things are
not done at this point but are done at the time of the rite of placing in the
cradle. Besides these, they are to take the outer bark of Thrysostachys
siamensis which was used to cut the umbilical cord of the child, and the
lump of earth which was used in place of a cutting board for cutting the umbilical cord, and tuck them under the cloth in the basket also.

When this is finished the midwife lifts up the basket and bounces it
lightly, enough to serve as a gesture. Then she drops the basket, but lightly
also, in order to cause the child to be frightened and cry. They say that
they do this in order to accustom the child, so that it will not be startled
later on. The midwife does this three times, saying the while, "Three days
a spirit child, four days a human child! Whose child is this? Take it!"
Some person among those sitting there, one who is a woman who has reared
children successfully and is a kind and well-behaved person as well, will
answer, "It's my child." The midwife passes the basket and the child to
that person. The receiver in this rite is called mɛ̂ɛ jóg.[22] She will give
money to the midwife, usually in former times an ʔàd, equal to one and one-
half sàtaaŋ at present, to serve as a gesture of buying. Then she takes the
basket and lays it down in the circle surrounded by a magic thread, near to
the child's mother. She must lay the child down gently in order not to
frighten it. They usually place the basket on supports resting in water, to
prevent ants from coming up and biting the child. In the north they call a
midwife "receiving woman",[23] if we compare this with the "lifting mother,"
the meanings are very close. After this, they take a cloth and form it into
a tent covering the basket in place of a mosquito net, in order to prevent
much wind from entering which would destroy the warmth and cause convulsions. But these tents are usually made of thick cloth such as blankets,
and the space inside is so small and confined that air does not enter easily.
This may destroy the strength of the child. Therefore they sometimes use

bent rattans to stretch the tent out wide in order to allow a good deal of air for the child to breathe. That part of the subject of bouncing on the basket which relates to the spirit of the purchasing mother involves many matters which must be described and discussed as to reasons, and so I will leave it for the section concerning the purchasing mother.

Children which are newly born are not yet allowed to eat anything. They have them eat only burned cockroach excrement mixed with a little salt and then dissolved in honey in a small cup. They hang a small bit of cloth down in the cup, letting the other end hang over the edge of the cup for the child to suck. They say that this medicine containing cockroach droppings is a laxative to expel the child's first faeces. The first faeces are the child's faeces which are in its abdomen when it is born. They are hard and black. It is believed that if they are left and not expelled they will cause the child to be ill. They have the child eat this for three days and then they let it suck its mother's milk. They cannot let the child suck its mother's milk from the beginning, because the mother does not yet have milk which is pure enough to feed the child. Even if she has, they cannot let the child take it until it is sufficiently strong. If they persist in letting it eat, the child may be in danger because its stomach has not yet expanded.

According to Indian custom they have a newborn child eat clarified butter and honey. They likewise use a container similar to a flat basket to hold the child, but they place cowdung, ashes, turmeric, and two or three silver coins in the basket with the child, and they sprinkle holy water on it. If the child is a boy they lay a brass tray there, believing that it drives away spirits. If it is a girl this is not necessary, because the sex of the girl is a protection in itself, and spirits cannot come to bother her.

Lying Near the Fire

I will drop the subject of arrangements for the child temporarily, and return to the subject of the child's mother at the time she lay still after having given birth, when the midwife was busy with the child, as described above. I will speak of the husband and other people; they help one another arrange a fireplace for lying near the fire. It is forbidden to prepare this fireplace in advance. They may only prepare the framework of the fireplace. Similarly they are forbidden to make the cushions and prepare the diapers in advance. If they do not prepare them in advance, when the emergency arrives they will not be able to do it in time. They are therefore allowed to sew the cushions and stuff them with kapok beforehand, but they are forbidden to sew up the mouths of the pillows, as has been described, because they fear that if they sew up the mouths the child will not come out to receive the diapers and pillows which have been prepared. Also, children often die at birth. If they prepare these things in advance and the child dies, the effort is in vain and the diapers and pillows are wasted. In olden times these things were not easily procured.

When they have laid the framework, they cut sections of banana tree trunks, split them in two, and lay them parallel in the frame. They scatter dirt over these and then light the fire. They call this "laying out the fire-place," and if they are superstitious they must seek a good day for it. If they cannot make the fireplace in time, they have the mother who has given birth lie beside an old-fashioned stove at first. (This old-fashioned stove is a port-able stove made of baked earth, in shape similar to a horse saddle.) They use three sticks of firewood per day and have her remain for three days. Then they perform the rite of lying near the big fireplace. Banana trees may be used for many purposes and are easy to grow. They grow in every village. Bananas therefore enter into various ceremonies at many points, even though in some ceremonies the necessity for them is no longer present; for example, decorating crematoria with banana tree trunks, or setting up banana trees at the ritual fences in ceremonies such as the preaching of the Vessantara Jātaka. They still survive, however, as customs until the present time. As for the use of banana tree trunks under the fire, it can be seen easily that it is de-sired that the fire not spread downward to the floor of the house. Nothing can be used so readily as banana tree trunks, because they are more easily procured than other things.

In connection with lying near a fire there are many rites which must be performed. For example, they must perform a ceremony of quenching the poison of the fire, make a circle with a magic cord, and fix cabalistic de-signs in eight directions around the place for lying near a fire. Sometimes they use as many as ten cabalistic designs; that is, they add the directions up and down as well. For the direction down they place a cabalistic design under the bed. Then they must scatter thorns. Usually these are thorns of Indian jujube, thorns of Manila tamarind, or bamboo thorns, because they are easily found. They scatter these around the pit under the room used for lying near the fire. Wherever there is a crevice or hole in the floor they like-wise scatter thorns, to keep off spirits which would come to do harm, es-pecially krasy̌y spirits, because the crevices and holes in the floor are general-ly used for pouring out filthy things onto the ground below; krasy̌y spirits will be attracted by the odor of the filth and slip up through the crevices and holes. Sometimes even these precautions are regarded as inadequate, and so they also weave mat-like panels and curl them around to form pipes lead-ing down from the pits and holes in the floor of the house where things are poured out. Besides warding off spirits, probably this prevents domestic ani-mals from coming in and making the place filthy as well. As for upstairs in the house, besides cabalistic designs and the magic thread, they also fasten leaves of the camphor plant at the door to the room. Leaves of the camphor plant have an unpleasant odor; when spirits smell them they are afraid and dare not enter.[24] In some cases they also stretch a net over the place for lying near the fire, to prevent spirits from approaching from above. This protection is like that used by the Thai Lue people.[25]

Planting Magic Pentacles of Bamboo. In the northeast they make magic pentacles of bamboo, equal in size to the lid of a monk's begging bowl. They wind black, red, and white cotton threads around the angles of the pentacle, but alternating the colors, and then tie the pentacle to the end of a piece of bamboo and plant it to the right of the foot of the stairs of the house. They leave it planted there until the mother emerges from the fire, and then they pull it up and throw it away. The purpose of planting the pentacle is to serve as a symbol to tell visitors to be careful of their speech. At the time of lying near the fire it is absolutely forbidden for anyone to speak the words "warm" or "hot," because it is feared that the person lying near the fire will have prickly heat or rashes and blisters, called "fire spots." These bamboo pentacles may also be used in other affairs; they are not limited to lying near the fire. Thus they are planted at the edge of pools, wells, or fishponds to inform everyone that it is forbidden to go down and dip up water or catch fish in that place. In funeral ceremonies in the north they also plant pentacles in the area of the house at the time when they remove the corpse from the house. This is no doubt to prevent the spirit from returning.[26]

According to Vietnamese custom, they scatter thorns of Indian jujube and pineapple leaves outside the room. Inside the room they plug up all cracks and holes with cloth; in the room it is therefore dark and close, for the air cannot pass in and out easily. They must keep the fire in the room burning all the time, both day and night. Then there are cabalistic designs hanging in the four corners of the room. These things which are done are self-explanatory as being protection against spirits. The lying near the fire of the Vietnamese is more violent than the lying near the fire of the Thai, because besides lying beside a charcoal stove, under the bed on which the woman lies there are three more charcoal stoves burning. This is tantamount to broiling, and is the same sort of thing as Yogis practicing austerities and burning their passions to a crisp. As for the Thai method of lying near the fire, at first they kindle a fire to produce only a little heat, enough to boil water for drinking. Later on when the flesh and skin of the person lying near the fire are accustomed, they increase the heat of the fire gradually. Otherwise they say that "fresh boils" and "fire spots" will occur. (These are bumps with pussy heads similar to those of smallpox but smaller in size.) These are poisonous and cause one to feel sore and hot. In lying near the fire there must be someone to keep watch. If the fire is seen to be too strong and is spreading to too much of the fuel, there is a cloth wrapped around the end of a piece of wood and a pot of water kept in readiness to dip the cloth in the water in the pot and extinguish the fire.

When someone is going to lie near the fire, there is first a quenching of the poison of the fire. They must find a person who knows to come and enchant white rice and salt with a Pali stanza as follows: "Buddho lokanātho maggallāno aggīsayāyam mama." (What this means is not clear; we know only that it has to do with fire.) The reference to Maggallāna is probably due to the story that this chief disciple once went to relieve the creatures in hell. When he arrived the fires of hell all went out. This spell should be called "Maggallāna extinguishing the fires of hell." When he has pronounced this spell, he chews up the white rice and salt and spits it out onto the belly of the woman lying near the fire three times, onto her back three times, and into the fireplace three times. Then he sprinkles thɔɔrāniisǎan holy water on the fireplace. [27] They obtain exploded rice, flowers, incense sticks, and candles, together with a banana-leaf cup of offerings including prawn and fish salad; these are an offering to the supporting columns of the fireplace and an act of begging forgiveness of the god of fire. Generally they use four incense sticks and four candles, setting them up at the four corners of the stove.

Before the mother lies down upon the fire board, it is necessary first to perform the "fitting the rafters." [28] This is done by lying on the side and having the midwife tread on the hips. They believe that this makes the "rafter bones," which spread apart because of childbirth, reenter their proper position. Then she can lie down on the fire board. Before lying down she must prostrate herself and implore forgiveness of the fireplace, because it is believed that the fireplace is a magic thing inhabited by a guardian spirit. (This belief is similar to that of the Chinese in a lord of the stove, that of India in the grhyāgni fire, and that of the Romans in the penates.) This is to ask for protection in order to live happily, and she is to think of the goodness of the god of fire, the god of wind, the earth goddess, and the goddess of water, asking to regard these gods of the four elements as her refuge. Besides this the midwife enchants turmeric and red lime and smears these on her belly, and pounds up Zingiber casumunar with salt and applies it to the wounds in the vulva to prevent infection and facilitate rapid healing. If they have liquor, they wash the wounds first with liquor. What has been described seems like a terribly arduous affair. One would think they would never want to have children again. But they must endure it and act according to the customs of olden times, which are beliefs surviving from the worship of spirits in ancient times. Such customs as these, when the beliefs of the owners of the customs have changed, will normally of necessity disappear of themselves, because they conflict with or hinder progress in living. It is not necessary to force the people to drop them.

During the time of lying near the fire, neighbors who know of it come to visit. In visiting they do not come empty-handed. If they have nothing else, they bring anything that comes to hand and offer it in a friendly spirit,

such as turmeric, diatomaceous earth,[29] dried fish, or bananas, usually the
kind of bananas called broken-faceted bananas. These are all things which
are used and which can be eaten, not being harmful foods. This custom is
now fading out because of the pressure of modern progress. Formerly no matter what sort of affair it was, whether a wedding or a funeral, those who went
to assist in the affair always carried something along to help. Nowadays social conditions have undergone a great change, and it is too much to do this
always, except in places where social conditions have not changed greatly.
When one speaks of the necessity in going to visit of carrying something along,
one is reminded of the Indian proverb which says, "Persons who go to attend
upon the king, or visit children, or visit pregnant women, or visit teachers,
and those who go to worship an idol in a temple -- these visitors should not
go empty-handed." Our proverb has it: "When one goes to attend upon the
king, when one goes to see a religious preceptor, when one goes to see a
judge, when one goes to see a young woman, when one goes to see an old
woman who has a daughter that one loves and covets, the ancients forbid
going empty-handed." I should like to add another group in order to make it
fit present times, but I do not dare add it.

Persons who go to visit a woman lying near the fire are forbidden to speak
of heat or cold, of prickly heat or boils, of illness or fever or death or anything of that sort; these subjects are regarded as inauspicious because it is
feared that the woman lying near the fire will lose morale, and what is spoken
of will come true. (Some people believe that after three days it is not forbidden, observing the rule of three-day and seven-day prohibitions.) In this
matter of forbidding people to speak of things which should not be spoken of,
peasants are rather strict. In visiting the sick they also have this sort of belief. I have asked many persons who have formerly lain near the fire, and
they all answer that what is spoken will come true. Probably it is because
they believe it, and are already on the watch for this sort of thing, so that
when what is spoken of happens to come true they become excited. Besides
this, in lying near the fire it is forbidden to kindle another fire from the fire
in the fireplace, or to use this fire to roast meat or fish. Fires that are forbidden in this way are of three kinds, namely a fire for lying near, a fire for
cremating corpses, and the fire of incense sticks and candles which are lighted
for worship. The reasons for these prohibitions are self-evident.

The person lying near the fire must wear a loincloth, and has turmeric
and red lime mixed with liquor into which she constantly dips cotton to close
the navel and swab the abdomen and the back. They say that they do this
in order to quench the poison of the heat and care for the body. Besides this
there is also medicine to sprinkle upon the coals of the fire in order to steam
the eyes, to prevent infected or sore eyes. There is also a jar or jug of water
placed beside the fireplace. When the fire in the fireplace blazes up ex-
cessively or becomes hotter than is desired, they can take a long dipper (or a

stick with the end wrapped with cloth, if they have no dipper), and reach out and dip up water in the jar in order to splash it on the fire and put it out; or if it is desired to dip water out into a vessel to boil for drinking, it will be near at hand.

As for food of the person lying near the fire, normally she eats rice with dried fish or rice with salt for many days before she has some curry. They say that eating mild curries causes production of much milk. Besides this, for water they usually drink hot water placed in a coconut shell or a thick dish which can be held without being hot in the hands. For washing and cleaning various impurities they mostly use coconut half-shells, because after use they can be thrown away. In the north they likewise have women lying near the fire eat rice with salt, but they have a special item in that they require that the husband be the person who prepares it for her to eat. For the most part they make rice balls for the women to eat. Rice balls are cooked glutinous rice formed into balls, impaled on a stick, and toasted in the fire; they are eaten with salt. They eat these for ten to fifteen days, before they are allowed to eat rice with salty fish. Persons lying near the fire, besides eating rice with salt, must also take special medicine for the blood. They must take this morning and evening every day until they leave the fire. According to Vietnamese custom, during the first seven days that they lie near the fire they eat rice with salt and pepper. Some say that they eat mild curries also. Later on they eat Vietnamese-style boiled salt pork; this is really salty, with no sweetness in flavor.

Doors and windows, if any, in the room for lying near the fire must always be kept closed, because it is feared that if the wind enters and touches the body of the person lying near the fire she may contract a fever. The susceptibility to fever is said to be due to the fact that the person lying near the fire is still weak. Perhaps they also fear that spirits will slip in through the windows and doors. According to Indian custom they must also close the doors and windows, but they must keep a light burning both night and day because not much light can enter, and they do not lie near the fire; the room is therefore dark and close, and a light must be kept burning. But the excuse they give is that if they keep a light burning spirits will be afraid to enter. This is clever reasoning, because fire and light are enemies to spirits (to say nothing of spirits, thieves also dislike them). They believe that the god of fire stands guard against evil spirits and is the destroyer of evil for the gods, because fire can be used as a cleansing agent. They say that ladies are his attendants, and the menses of women are his person. Probably the meaning of this is that blood is red, which is a symbol of the god of fire and of fire. Various nations therefore regard the color red as powerful, feared by spirits, and auspicious. [30] European peasants, for example those of some parts of England, Germany, and Sweden, keep lamps or candles burning all around the child, believing that this keeps spirits from coming to carry off the child. Our custom of closing doors and windows of the room for lying near the fire to make it dark and close is said to be because of the desire for warmth and the dislike of cool air. They also use hot medicines, believing that if coldness is encountered the womb may swell and be poisoned. I believe that this is a later opinion; originally it was more likely a matter of warding off spirits, for when spirits enter we do not see them, but know that they have entered because a gust of cold air touches the body, and so fever is contracted.

Concerning the making of a circle with a magic thread and the hanging up of cabalistic designs, this is because cabalistic designs are magic objects, having letters of the alphabet and designs drawn in mysterious fashion and containing magic spells; thus they have power to ward off danger or are capable of retaining things which it is not desired to have lost or disappear. The cabalistic design which is popular as a preventative of danger particularly in the matter of lying near the fire is called trinisimhe. [31]

The magic thread which is laid all round the place for lying near the fire is the raw cotton thread used in chanting the paritta stanzas. [32] They wind it around the pot of holy water, and then carry it to the monks who take part in the chanting ceremony, and they hold onto it. Everybody has seen this often; it is not necessary to give a great deal of explanation. This thread is regarded as a magic article, because it leads from the pot of holy water, and so they use it as a protection in auspicious ceremonies. The technical name for it is parittasūtra, that is, the cord of the paritta chants. Siñcana[33] means to sprinkle or scatter with water. If we were to interpret from this translation, we are tempted to understand that originally it was a cord for sprinkling holy water, and so it is believed that the magic thread in a sense contains holy water in itself. When it is used to make a circle around a place, it is as if that place had been sprinkled with holy water, and there is a general prohibition against the husband's trespassing inside the circle formed by the magic thread; they believe that if he has any magic spells they will lose their efficacy. This prohibition is good; why it is good, please judge for yourselves. The magic thread, besides being used to encircle the place, is also used to cut in short lengths to tie around the wrist for protection against danger. Used in this way, it is probably similar to the "protective thread" worn by the Brahmans (rakṣabandhana). It is related in the Viṣṇupurana that when Kṛṣṇa was a child he was tormented by spirits as he slept, and so his father Vasudeva had to tie a protective thread around the wrists of the boy Kṛṣṇa.

While still in the house of fire, if the weather is cold or it rains they say that the child will have convulsions (that is, it is affected by the weather). It has blue, pale hands and feet, trembles like a young bird, and has a stiff chin; it may die. They have a method of prevention, to wit: they burn the shell of a horseshoe crab or duck and chicken feathers, the shells of sea-crab claws, camphor leaves, onion, garlic, buffalo horn, or leaves of the "rank smell of vultures and crows" plant; what other things there are I do not know. They may select any one or another of these things to burn, depending upon which they can procure. When it is burnt the odor is all-pervading and unbearable, reaching to eight or nine houses. [34] No doubt readers have experienced this odor and know how bad it is; if not, try burning some and you will know. If a child has pharyngitis they likewise burn things for the child to inhale, such as the bones of a black dog, the horns of an albino buffalo, cat hair, and many other things, all of which are things which when burned give off an unbearably bad odor. I do not think these are things which can cure disease. I suspect that the burning of them is connected with the driving out of spirits also, which is a belief surviving from olden times; when the spirits smell the odor they flee. Diseases of children and infants, as will be related in the chapter on the purchasing mother, are said to originate from the action of spirits. I will cite an example given in the invocation of the purchasing mother called säaradèed wíthii jàj:

> Hail! O great one, I salute you. I fold my hands in reverence and
> raise them above my head, and prostrate my body to you. May the
> pure precepts, and goodness and virtue, in which power inhere, be
> bestowed upon me. Come and destroy the hosts of evil spirits, the
> ghostly ambassadors of wickedness who harass the three worlds, who
> destroy by means of invisible diseases, diseases that are visited
> upon us, of which the one called cholera is the most prominent.
> There are both bird-spirits and convulsions. Heat rashes are caused
> by the demon Rahu. Foreign ailments come in countless numbers,
> all of them evil spirits, ghosts, giants, powerful in various ways.
>> Some diseases transform themselves
>> Into various shapes.
>> Some have a crow's head and a dog's body.
>> Some have a giant's head and a horse's body.
>> Some have a dog's head and elephant's feet.
>> Some have a deer's head and a crow's body.
>> Some have an ass's head and a tiger's body.
>> Some have a stag's head and a lion's body.
>> Some have a monkey's head and a human body.
>> They command a powerful army.
>> Diseases of the forest, of dry land and water,
>> Diseases in caves and marshes,
>> Diseases that fly through the air,
>> Come to the fire,
>> I will burn you all up with fire.

Phrá̱ Theewaa Phínimmíd (Chǎaj Theewaaphínimmíd) has kindly noted down the texts for exorcising convulsions and children's diseases for me, and so I print them here, for purposes of research, as follows.

Various Spells. Before reciting any spell, one must first pronounce the following, which is called "Invitation to the Teacher to Enter Me":

Behold the Blessed One! I will raise all ten fingers of my hands in reverence. I invoke the blessing of the Lord Shiva to come to my left shoulder. I invite the Lord Vishnu to come to my right shoulder. I invite the God of the Wind to come and be my breath. I invite the Lord of Serpents to be for me a belt. I invite the Goddess Kali to be my heart. In whatsoever I may do, let no spirits come to interfere or cause annoyance. I invite my revered teacher, who is most exalted, to come from his dwelling. Bestow upon me your blessing. Reverend lord, bring me success. Let my enemies be destroyed.

Spell for Exorcising Convulsions. Prostrate yourself three times, saying: Hail, O Lords of the three worlds! O Sariputta, O Lord Buddha! Let me drive out all kinds of convulsions, the one whose body is a buffalo and whose head is a human head, with evil feet and hands, a bad convulsion; the one whose head is a snake's head, terrifying in form, with the body of a stag; the butterfly convulsion with yellow head, red chin, and flashing eyes, with the head of a lion; the one with an evil mouth and the head of a dog, carrying a stick; and demons and all enemies of every kind. The purchasing mother shows her teeth and makes gestures; she gazes at the roof and cries 'Ah, ah,' curling up her fingers and toes, and moaning; she hides in the heart. Bring the spirit of this child; bring back the spirit of this child. Bring it back at once, and don't come yourself. The Lord Shiva has sent me to drive out all convulsions. Don't you recognize me? My name is the great king Sǔ̌i Kan. My mother's name is the Earth Goddess. My father's name is the God Kuvera, who is a master of all the hosts of spirits. If you don't go out I will cut off your heads. O Lord Buddha and the Three Gems! I will flog you with rattans. Hail to the Buddha! Hail to the Law! Hail to the Order!

Another Spell.

Hail! Convulsions of the rocks, convulsions of the cliffs, convulsions of cloth, convulsions of the pillow, convulsions of the bed and of the head of the stairs -- all these convulsions I know. I know your birth and your death. Your father was named ꞁàꞁ ꞁaaj. and he died in the middle of the forest. Your aunt had a ghostly name and she died a violent death; she fell out of a tree and they stabbed her. Your mother was named ꞁii phɛɛŋ. You make children cry every day. I will spray magic herbs on you. I will put a heap of iron upon you. Hail!

(To be pronounced while spraying water with the mouth, in the evening or when the child is sick.)

Spell for Exorcising Children's Diseases.

> Behold the Blessed One! I will make obeisance to the Sage who planted medicinal herbs all around Mount Sumeru, the stems in the land of demons and the twigs in the land of gods. I have counted nine hundred thousand twigs of medicinal plants. I will exorcise the disease of spots in the tongue and in the eye. I will exorcise the disease of wicked spirits. Let the disease of gourds come out beyond the skies. I will exorcise yellow diseases and fiery diseases, the wicked ones; I will slash you and knock you together. I will spray water to extinguish the poison and effect a cure. Buddha, cure him! Law, cure him! Order, cure him!

(To be pronounced while spraying water with the mouth, in the morning before sunrise.)

The subject matter in the invocation of the purchasing mother as quoted above shows that convulsions originate from the action of spirits, and so it is necessary to burn things which create a foul odor in order to drive away the spirits. But because the burning of things makes the air in the room closer, this affords some help to the child which has been affected by the weather and has convulsions. If it recovers from the illness they assume that the spirits fear the foul odor and flee. The rightness or wrongness of this opinion is up to you to consider, but it is strange that many nationalities agree in having the practice of burning things to create a foul odor in order to drive away spirits. Probably they believe that even humans regard these odors as unbearable, and it is unnecessary to mention that spirits will be similarly repelled. According to Vietnamese custom they burn duck and chicken feathers, ox and buffalo bones and horns, and other things which when burned have a strong unpleasant smell; this is a way of driving out spirits. According to Indian custom, when a child is ill, they burn rice bran, dry chilis, lettuce seeds, salt, or other things which when burned give off an unpleasant pungent odor, and carry them round and round the child. They say that if they do this the spirits cannot bear the foul odor and flee. The matter of carrying things round and round the child is similar to our carrying offerings or the rice of the purchasing mother round and round a child when it is ill. This procedure in Indian is called ārati (ārātarika). The circling candles rite may perhaps be a form of ārati. I will leave this to discuss under the subject of khwăn rites.

After she has lain near the fire for three days, there are many ways of caring for and performing superstitious rites for the woman lying near the fire and for the child. I will speak first of matters concerning the woman lying near the fire.

Methods of Producing Milk. Normally a woman who has borne a child has milk to feed the child, which when it has passed three days of age is counted as having escaped "the beaks of hawks and crows," which is to say, it has passed one stage without dying. When the child is first born, its mother does not yet have genuine milk. There is only yellowish milk, not white like ordinary milk. This is called yellowish milk and is regarded as poor milk. They have the mother eat boiled leaves of Cardiospermum halicacabum and Ipomsea aquatica, in order first to expel the yellowish milk. When it has all been expelled, the mother's breasts will be firm and will produce milk. If the child does not suck it, the mother will feel pains; sometimes she may even have fever. If the pains continue like this for many days, a boil may arise on the breasts because the milk goes into the wrong tubes. The midwife must roll and press the nipples in order to cause the pimple-heads which plug up the milk tubes to come out, and then take many hairs together and poke with them to make a hole; then the milk can come out easily. If after this the milk still does not flow out easily, they must use cupping. An easy method is to burn paper and throw it into a pickled garlic jug or into another bottle or vessel which is hollow and plugged at one end, depending on what can be procured easily, in order to create a vacuum inside. The mother bends over and thrusts the breast into this jug or vessel, and there is suction as in cupping blood. At first the breast hurts very much, but it is necessary to endure the pain. If the cupping method is not used, they can suck with a bamboo tube. Finally, in later times there have been instances of sucking with a lamp chimney. If it is the breast of the mother of a first child of the sort called a "blind breast," that is, without a projecting nipple, usually only one of the breasts is "blind," the other having a nipple, called "monkey breast." If the child sucks only one breast, that is, the breast having a nipple, this will cause only the breast that is sucked to grow large. The other breast which is "blind" will not grow large. This is of the sort called "Lady Monthoo with only one developed breast."[35] This is not beautiful because it is not symmetrical. It is necessary to seek a trick to make the child suck the "blind breast" also. They have a method of correcting this so that the breasts are equally large: they roll the "blind breast" with warm water and then pull the nipple out so that it projects; then they fasten it with a clamp made of bamboo like the clamps for broiling fish but small in size, in order not to allow the nipple to shrink back again. When the child sucks, the clamp is removed; when the child has finished sucking, the clamp is applied as before. If this is done for two or three days, the nipple will continue to project, and the child can suck it in the normal way.

The Womb Enters Its Cradle. In from three to seven days after the child is born, the midwife comes and "restores the belly" every day; that is, she presses on the pubic mound with her hand in order to lift the womb back into its "cradle." I suppose the place where the womb lies is a hollow, and so it is called this. When it has been restored, she presses and rolls the pubic mound. This is called "soothing the womb," to make the mouth of the womb shrink and return to its original position. At this time of "soothing the womb," water with a fishy odor spurts out, making the mother feel comfortable.

Women lying near the fire must enter a tent and have hot applications, and bathe with a salt pot and sit over coals.

Entering the Tent. Before the mother enters the tent, they grind or pound the "golden lady" plant, pressing out only the juice and mixing it with liquor and camphor. This is smeared all over the body of the woman lying near the fire; when she has been smeared, she enters the tent. This tent has a frame made of bamboo like the frame of a mosquito net, or other things which it is easy to lay hands upon, such as a large basket, may be used. This is covered completely with cloth and set up on the porch or other high place. Underneath the place where the tent is set up they set a stove to boil a medicine pot with a sealed lid. Into this they insert a bamboo pipe, leading up into the tent, in order to make the steam from the medicine in the pot which is boiling violently rise through the pipe into the tent. The person entering the tent will receive the vapor from the medicine. In doing this it is necessary to have someone stand watch and see that the proper amount of steam is sent up; or if this is not convenient, they may take up the medicine pot which is boiling violently and put it into the tent. The woman in the tent opens the lid a little at a time and bends her face down to the mouth of the pot, so that the steam may whirl up and bathe her face. The medicine that is boiled includes pomelo rind, leaves of Acacia concinna, sweet flag, lemon grass, Ipomaea aquatica, a kaffir lime cut into four sections, and one pinch of salt. Some of these may be omitted, or others added, depending upon what can be found.

Entering the tent is supposed to improve the complexion and prevent blemishes on the face, prevent the lymph from going bad, and remedy many other conditions. The woman steams herself for about half an hour, or if longer than this then all the better, but usually she is unable to remain long because it is unbearably hot and confined. She is flooded with perspiration as if bathing in water; then she can emerge from the tent. Entering this sort of tent is called "entering a medicine tent." If they are poor people, unable to procure anything easily, they use bricks heated red-hot in a fire. These are taken into the tent in place of the medicine pot. Then they pour salt water over the bricks; there is a sizzling sound and steam swirls up bathing the face and body. This is called "entering a brick tent." Entering the tent is usually done in the morning.

Guesses as to Reasons for Lying near the Fire. This matter of entering a tent
as described the Occidentals call "bathing in sweat" (sweat bath). [36] It is
said that the natives of North America everywhere like to enter tents, saying
that it cleanses them of impurities and perspiration in the body; it is a
method of cleansing them of impurities ceremonially as well. [37] One need
not doubt that our practice of entering the tent is not merely to improve the
complexion and prevent blemishes on the face. It is no doubt a matter of
cleansing impurities arising out of childbirth also, for various nationalities
regard childbirth as an impurity. If anyone approaches and merely smells
the odors of childbirth, he is rendered impure, and if he possesses any magic
spells they will lose their efficacy. For example, among the Palaung in the
north of Burma, at the time of childbirth a man cannot come within the area
for fear that if he has charms tattooed on his body or possesses magic objects,
these will lose their efficacy. Therefore they must keep a child posted in
front of the house to inform those who do not know, so that they do not wander
into the area of childbirth. If anyone happens to enter the area, he must
leave at once, and go and bathe in order to wash off the impurities. [38]
Some Kha tribes in the Banthat Mountains on the left bank of the Mekhong
River, at the time of childbirth, take pieces of bamboo or rattan and fit them
together to form a sort of large pentacle, planting this at the head of the path
in order to inform all of the prohibition, so that they will not trespass. The
practice of the northern and northeastern Thai in calling childbirth jùu kam [39]
(I believe the spelling jù- kam[40] would be more correct, because kam means
"to hold, to believe") and planting magic pentacles is the same sort of
superstition. In India they close off the woman who gives birth, not allowing
her to remain in the same room or house, or under the same roof with other
people, until she has been ceremonially cleansed completely of impurities;
then she may return to the association of other people. This is like our old
custom that women who come pregnant from elsewhere, or are pregnant outside the marriage ceremony, may not come and give birth in the house;
they must go and give birth elsewhere. At best, if the situation must be
accepted, they build a shed or hut for her to give birth at a distance. If it is
necessary to give birth in the house, they must perform a ceremony of purification according to their beliefs. Palace custom, according to M.R.W.
Pèèd Theewaathîrâad Maalaakun, has it that if anyone gives birth to a child
in the palace, a purification ceremony must be performed. [41]

If one considers the practices and beliefs relating to childbirth that
have been described, he feels that both entering the tent and lying near the
fire are matters of cleansing the impurities that arise from childbirth more
than matters of care and treatment; for the bearing of children occurs in the
natural way, and does not require special medicines as in treating diseases.
Rather, the original purpose has been forgotten, and so it is assumed that it is
a medical treatment. In childbirth there is discharge of blood and filthy

matter; this is regarded as impure, and for removing impurities there are
two methods, namely cleansing with water or with fire. Lying near the fire
is cleansing with fire, in order to dry up the things which are impure. If
water were used to wash and cleanse ordinarily they would not all be removed,
and so they must wash with heat. When the mother emerges from the fire
they must still sprinkle thɔɔrániisǎan holy water also. Thus they cleanse
with both fire and water. Lying near the fire is a procedure connected with
childbirth belonging to various nationalities in the Indochinese peninsula and
in the Indonesian archipelago. In India they use a brass stove with a charcoal
fire placed under the bed for ten days.[42] This is as much as I have found
given in books. It is impossible to know what nationality was the first to lie
near the fire, other nationalities following their example, because these were
nationalities that originally all believed in spirits and gods and the magic
efficacy of various objects. It was not difficult to imitate one another.
This is the sort of phenomenon that westerners call diffusion of cultures. Perhaps the practice of lying near the fire had its origin among the people of the
Indonesian archipelago, but it is impossible to know. This opinion is a guess
based on what has been related. It all depends upon what the individual pre-
fers to believe.

Hot Applications. These consist in taking the liquid medicine remaining
from entering the tent and pouring it out of the boiling pot, mixing it with
cold water, and then making a ball for massaging. They use Zingiber
casumunar, the "golden lady" plant, Curcuma zedoaria, tamarind leaves,
leaves of Acacia concinna, pounding them and then mixing them with salt;
they wrap them in a cloth and tie them tightly, forming a ball for massaging.
They dip this in the liquid that has been mixed and rub it over the face and
body. In the case of a young mother who has had her first child, they must
use three balls, one for sitting upon and the others for massaging. They
massage the breasts and roll the nipples with the ball also, in order to relieve
the tension and facilitate the flow of milk, because at this time the breasts
contain hard lumps which hurt and cannot bear to be touched; after the
lumps have been massaged with a ball, the pain gradually lessens. Sometimes it takes as long as seven days before they are normal and the pain
disappears. After massaging with the ball, they bathe in the liquid medicine
that remains, and then wash this off with plain warm water. They do this
every day until they emerge from the fire.

Pressing with a Salt Pot. Pressing with a salt pot consists in putting salt into
a sugar pot covered with a lid and putting this onto the fire until it is very
hot. The salt in the pot pops and crackles, but does not jump out because
the lid is closed. They take up the salt pot and lay it down on leaves of the
castor-oil plant or leaves of Crinum asiaticum, depending upon which kind

of leaf is easy to find, and then wrap up the sugar pot, together with the castor-oil or <u>Crinum asiaticum</u> leaves on which it rests, in a large square cloth, leaving enough of the ends of the cloth to gather together in a bunch for carrying. They take this and rub it all over the body, especially rolling it over the pubic mound, saying that this causes the womb to shrink and return to its original position in its "cradle." Usually they apply the salt pot once in the afternoon and once again in the very early morning. This is done every day, if they have the diligence to do it, until they emerge from the fire. Midwives of Indian nationality use sifted ashes, putting them in a bag and placing them over a fire till warm for sitting upon, instead of pressing with a salt pot. After using the bag of ashes and bathing in water, they use a sheet of raw cotton cloth as long as four to five yards to wrap the abdomen and below. They do this for three to four days and then stop. Those who have done this say that it is quite comfortable.

<u>Sitting on Coals.</u> They use the rind of a kaffir lime dried in the sun, sweet flag, "golden lady" plant, <u>Zingiber</u> casumunar, <u>Curcuma</u> zedoaria, a quid of betel from which all the juice has been chewed out, the plant chârûud, powdered turmeric, and camphor leaves. These things are chopped fine and put in the sun to dry in readiness beforehand. These are sprinkled a handful at a time into a small stove, so that the smoke swirls up toward the buttocks of the sitter. They say this has to do with the healing of the wounds arising from childbirth.

The procedures that have been described are methods of medicinal treatment. I have included them in order to show what methods of care and treatment of mothers were used in olden times. It will be seen from this that the medicines frequently used, such as turmeric, lime, betel leaves, salt, lemon-grass bulbs, and kaffir limes, are all medicines which are easy to procure; almost all of them are regular household articles or can be found easily. Even quids of betel from which all the juice has been chewed out can be used as medicine. If they really have nothing and can obtain nothing, they use methods of enchanting, such as enchanted lime or enchanted <u>Zingiber casumunar</u>, and this is regarded as efficacious because it has to do with psychological beliefs. The addition of certain strange medicines to the group that can be procured easily is no doubt a later modification, when these other things became easy to obtain. As for vessels employed, the basic items are pots and lids. For lids, they use "widowed" lids, that is, lids whose pots have been broken. If it is not a "widowed" lid, use is forbidden. The reason for this prohibition is obvious; if they used a lid which has a pot and then used it to cover the pot when it contained rice or curry, it might cause the fire or curry in the pot to have an unpleasant odor, or might cause uncleanness in cooking. In the south they roast fish on "widowed" lids, forbidding roasting on the lids of good pots. These utensils show that we common people

formerly were terribly poor, and lacked the convenient equipment that we
have nowadays. There were also no modern doctors to be found; there were
only village doctors, and even these were not easy to find. For the most
part people had to depend upon themselves. They used whatever traditional
methods of treatment had always been used. Even though our ancestors had
hardships and lacked conveniences to this degree, they were yet able to keep
us alive and see us through, according to the intelligence and ability that
they had in those days, with the result that today we have progressed and expanded. This is to be regarded as another item of antiquarian information
worth knowing; one should not simply judge the knowledge and opinions of
those times by the standards of these times. If you had been born in those
times you would necessarily have had the knowledge and opinions of those
times; it would be intrinsically impossible to think like these times. We
think our fathers are stupid and ignorant, and our children have the same
opinion of us: this is the thought of a stanza of poetry by an English poet
named Pope.

Prescribed Number of Days for Lying Near the Fire. These are 7, 9, 11, 13,
15, 17, and 21 days, or sometimes at most 29 days. All of these prescribed
numbers of days for lying near the fire are odd numbers, because there is a
belief that in lying near the fire "an even number of days, children in close
succession; an odd number of days, children at long intervals."[43] I do not
know the reason for this. It is of the same category as the saying about the
number of steps in a flight of stairs: "Even-numbered, a spirit's stairway,
odd-numbered, a stairway for human beings."[44] The belief, however, is
the opposite of that which is held at the time of bouncing on a basket, "Three
days the spirits' child, four days a human child," and in the oath, "May I
die in three days or seven days," which are odd numbers. The number of
days a woman lies near the fire, chosen from the list of prescribed numbers
above, is up to her. The longer she can remain, the better. They say that
if she can remain a long time, when she emerges from the fire her complexion will be clear and lovely. If she is a young woman who has had her
first child, they usually have her remain many days.

When the prescribed number of days for lying near the fire is up, at the
time of emerging from the fire they make an offering of the sort colloquially
called "prawn and fish salad"; that is, whatever small items of food they
have, they put in a small banana-leaf container to offer to the female spirit
of the fireplace. The mother prostrates herself and talks to it, taking her
leave respectfully, and then puts out the fire and bathes in thɔɔrániisăan holy
water as an act of warding off evil. Thus the lying near the fire is ended, but
in some cases one day before emerging from the fire they have the woman
lie near a chaff fire; that is, they use chaff instead of firewood, laying sea-
holly leaves over the chaff to make it smolder. When she has passed one

night lying near this sort of fire, they sprinkle the fire and the child with thɔɔrấniisăan holy water, and the mother takes her leave of the fireplace, comes out and bathes in holy water, and so has emerged from the fire, She is forbidden to lift chaff baskets and kapok baskets for about a month. Why she is forbidden, I do not know. It would not seem to be for fear of prolapsis uteri resulting from excessive strain, because chaff baskets and kapok baskets are not so heavy to lift as other things on which there does not appear to be any prohibition.

Furthermore, after emerging from the fire and throughout a period of three months, the woman was forbidden in olden times to sleep with her husband. Sometimes the woman's mother might come and sleep with her to protect her in this matter. The prohibition was due to a belief that if it were disregarded the woman would have children in close succession, her womb not yet being completely dry. How many modern people have feelings about this sort of thing?

Concerning the Child

The Umbilical Cord. During a period of from three days upward after the birth of the child, the portion of the umbilical cord which was tied and bound as described above will come loose from the child's navel. When it has dropped off it is put away in a little box, cup, or any other sort of vessel, and is sprinkled with turmeric. Why it is kept I do not know; they simply do it as a tradition. When it has been kept for a long time it gets tossed about, no one taking any interest in it, and finally it simply disappears; when it disappears no one complains. I have run across information about beliefs of westerners and various other nationalities which allow of some comparisons. They believe that a child's umbilical cord that drops off is an object having magic power, and later on when the child to whom the umbilical cord belongs falls ill he can suck on it to ward off danger. Among people in the city of Berlin, Germany, the midwife gives this dry umbilical cord to the child's father to preserve with care. So long as he preserves it, the child will grow and be free of sickness. Among the English over a century ago there were often advertisements asking to buy dried umbilical cords. They believed that these were magically powerful to prevent shipwreck and to bring good luck to the owners. If one had one of these objects on his person and fell into the water, he would not drown even if he did not know how to swim. The Burmese believe that if one carries this object with him it will cause everyone to be kindly disposed. Hindus of some localities mix the ground umbilical cord with egg for the child to eat, believing that it causes intelligence. If they sew it onto the clothing of the child, he will be very brave. The Palaung people take good care of the umbilical cord, believing that if it is rubbed on an aching tooth the ache will vanish immediately. The people of Ceram Island and other islands in the South Seas, including Australia, tie the dried umbilical cord around the child's neck as a talisman, believing that it prevents children's diseases, or if the child falls ill they use the umbilical cord as medicine. In addition, the umbilical cord will cause the child to grow fast and learn easily, and it will serve as a talisman to ward off danger when traveling or when going to war.

Consideration of the beliefs of various nationalities as described above leads to the conclusion that the umbilical cord is an important part of the child, because the child lives in the womb by depending upon the umbilical cord as its means of sustenance; it is therefore fitting that it be regarded and preserved as an object of magic efficacy. Having this thought in mind, I made inquiries among some elderly people and obtained the information that the Thai preserve the dried umbilical cord to use with other medicines. When anyone is seriously ill and nothing that is taken relieves him, they grind the dried umbilical cord and mingle it with other medicine, as a magic remedy. Besides this they also use the dried umbilical cord ground up with lime juice to smear on insect stings.

Also, if the umbilical cord is about to drop off but there are still fibers holding it to the navel preventing it from coming completely loose, in the very early morning when the mother of the child awakens, before washing her face and rinsing her mouth she is to spit out her saliva and allow it to drop on the child's navel. This kind of saliva is called "rotten saliva." This name is correct, for it has a rotten odor. This procedure is probably due to a desire that the germs of decay cause the remaining fibers to decay also, so that the umbilical cord will drop off. They dare not use anything to cut it loose. This saliva before rinsing the mouth is regarded as an efficacious substance. For example, when a boil has first appeared they usually touch the finger to this sort of saliva under the tongue and rub it on the boil, which will then go down. Westerners say that the Romans, when they were going to speak well of themselves, had to spit on their own chests, believing that this kept the gods from despising them. When they were going to perform a religious ceremony they had to spit, because saliva was magic and drove away spirits. (To say nothing of spirits fearing it, human beings are afraid of it too, and run away from it.)

When the umbilical cord has come loose, the mother of the child takes three betel leaves and heats them in the smoke of a torch or the smoke of charcoal till they are moderately hot, touching them with the hand to see how hot they are. Then she applies these to the abdomen of the child. The use of three betel leaves is said to be in order to heat them alternately over the fire, and perhaps the number three is also regarded as magic. When the betel leaves have been applied, they heat a kaffir lime in the smoke of a torch, and roll it about on the abdomen in the area surrounding the navel.

This is said to make the belly thick like the rind of the kaffir lime, so that the child will not have stomach ache. Then they take three roasted pepper-corns, roasted diatomaceous earth, and crystals of Pagostemon cablin, and grind these things together to sprinkle on the child's navel to knit the wound. If after sprinkling this medicine it still does not heal, they are to scrape out the skin from the inside of a coconut shell, grind it together with crystals of Pagostemon cablin, and sprinkle this on the navel. Then they put ground assafetida and sweet flag mixed with kaffir lime juice into a potlid and heat this over a fire to apply to the area surrounding the navel. This is likewise a medicine to apply to the belly of a child to make it thick. In applying it they must not allow it to touch the navel, because the child will feel smart-ing pain. When this is finished they roll assafetida into long bars of small size, wrap them in thin white cloth, and tie them to both wrists of the child in the manner of bracelets. When the child happens to raise his arms they will touch his nose and he will inhale the odor of assafetida; he will thus not be subject to fainting.

Medicine for Swabbing the Child's Throat. Besides these there are also medi-cines for swabbing the throats of children when they are ill. They use the bulbs of lemon grass, grinding them on the bottom of a curry pot that has been used, because there is soot adhering to it. When a child is already sucking the breast, they sometimes grind Strychnos roborans, roots of holy basil, and Vitex glabrata bark to swab. In some localities they use the piece of bamboo which has been used to hold open the mouth of a fish-condiment jug, burning it and grinding it to powder and then dissolving this in honey and applying it to the child's tongue.

Hot Applications for Children. If the child is a boy, they heat betel leaves in the smoke of a cajeput torch and apply them to the scrotum, pressing upward, so that when the child is older he will not have scrotal hernia. For girls there are also applications to give her organ a proper shape. Then they rub the breasts, squeezing out the milk, because this is regarded as milk existing from birth; it is transparent milk like lymph, and not good. If it is not squeezed out it may cause boils to form, because it is in lumps. Besides these things they pull the nose in order to make it arched and beautiful, because we do not usually have arched noses.

Infant Menstruation. During the period three to seven days after the day of birth, some girl babies menstruate. This sort of menstrual discharge is re-garded as a good thing.[45] They usually wipe it off with cotton and keep it, believing that if they have it on the person when they go to gamble they will not lose. The reason that the menstrual discharge of infants is regarded as a "good thing" is perhaps that they regard the menstrual discharge as a symbol of birth, having special power to destroy the efficacy of spells and charms or the power of spirits and gods, or perhaps they have the same belief as the Indians, that a woman's menstrual discharge is pure because it is a symbol of the god Agni.

Capturing a Cold. Young babies are liable to become ill easily, because their bodies are still delicate. For example, they may take cold and have blocked noses so that they cannot breathe easily. If a child has these symptoms they must make a medicinal poultice to apply to the top of its head. They use onions or bulbs of sweet prɔɑ[46] pounded and mixed with turmeric, red lime, and liquor. They dip cotton into this medicine and form it into a flat, round, thin plaster with a hole in the center, and apply this to the child's head. The juice of the pounded onions remaining from making the poultice for the head is used to apply to the bridge of the nose and to the body. This method of applying a poultice to the head and smearing the body of the child until it appears red and blotched all over is called "capturing a cold."

Coated Tongue. About fifteen days after birth, the child's tongue may develop a white coat called "fine powder." If it is left it will become thicker and thicker and turn into pharyngitis, making the tongue stiff so that the child cannot suck the breast. It is necessary to take a diaper which is moist with the child's urine and wipe the white coat off the tongue. Sometimes they use the "gum" of raw bananas to wipe; if they can get the "gum" of "water bananas," then all the better. They cut the raw banana in two and wipe out the "gum" onto a cloth.

Heat Rashes and Hiccups. Sometimes children have heat rashes; that is, they have rashes on the face and body consisting of fairly large transparent white pimples. If these pustules burst, the pus will spread and be messy and malodorous. They are to sprinkle diatomaceous earth and crystals of Pogostemon cablin. If a child has hiccups, they must tear off a corner of a diaper and apply it to the top of the head or the forehead of the child. While applying it they must hold the breath. If they fear that the cloth that is applied might drop off, they are to moisten it with saliva. This is a terribly simple procedure.

The things that have been described are not exhaustive, because small children are given to having a great many diseases. Those which have been mentioned are only the ones which are treated by the methods of the folk, without having to go to the extremities of calling a doctor to treat them. It can be seen that most of the medical remedies are things that can be found easily, just like the medicines that have been described earlier.

Diapers. Also in the matter of diapers there are special rules that must be followed; for example when washing them it is forbidden to wring them out. They are merely to squeeze them enough to make the water run out, believing that if they wring the diapers the child will feel twisted. This is the sort of thing which in English is called homoeopathetic magic, according to the principle that things which are similar produce similar results, or can be contracted one from another (Law of Similarity and Law of Contract or Contagion). [47] When washing diapers it is necessary to be careful not to throw away or discard any; they say that the child will cry without ever stopping. When a child cries incessantly and no reason can be found for its crying, they usually count the diapers to see if any are missing. If it is found that some are missing, someone or other is inevitably scolded with such words as "Do you see? The old saying is not wrong. People disregard it, taking up the beliefs of westerners, and so things have come to this pass!" In the afternoon when the sun sinks low, diapers that have been hung out must be gathered in. If they persist in leaving them out until dark, the cloth will be covered with dew and the child will catch cold, in the manner of a contagious disease. When diapers are soiled they must hurry to wash them; they must not leave them in a heap. This is a good thing. If it is the rainy season sometimes it rains hard all day long, and there is no sunshine to dry the diapers fast enough for use. They build a bonfire on the ground, cover it with a chicken coop, [48] and then lay the diapers on this, in order to dry the wet diapers. When touched by the steam and heat they dry more rapidly. Later on when there were charcoal stoves to use, they used charcoal stoves, but if care is not taken the fire may become very hot and burn the basket and the diapers. This is a question of using new and more convenient things without making suitable adjustments; people think they are like the old things and so this sort of damage results.

Piercing the Ears. When the child has passed three days in age, if it is a girl the midwife usually pierces the ears as part of her job. The method of piercing is to prepare a needle threaded with cotton thread dyed black with Diospyros mollis. [49] At the time of piercing she must roll the outer ear until it is numb and examine the ear so as not to pierce it at a nerve. [50] Then she takes a betel-leaf stem, dips it in lime, and touches it to both sides of the ear to serve as a marker. A tiny slice of the rhizome of Zingiber casumunar or turmeric is placed under the ear as a support, and then the ear is pierced, allowing the thread to remain. After piercing, they apply coconut oil and turmeric to knit the wound, and pull the thread back and forth constantly, continually dropping coconut oil to prevent dryness; or if they can use household oil which is applied to infant's sores and pimples, then all the better. They take shell from the bottom of the coconut, leaves of the neem tree, jasmine leaves, and gummy turmeric, pound these together and then squeeze out the juice. Then they sprinkle salt on this and place it in the sun until it dries and turns to oil, and then it can be used. Another method of piercing causes the child little pain but is slow and time-consuming: they take an angular piece of lead with both ends bent to form a ring and clamp this to the ear, gradually pressing it in a little at a time until the ear is perforated. I have heard complaints that this method is not good, and cannot compare with the more rapid method of piercing with a needle, but I suspect that the method of piercing with a needle is a recent method. After the ear is pierced, it is desired to make the hole large; that is, when the wound heals and the thread has been pulled out, they enlarge the hole with the stem of a head of dried garlic or young grass, or use the wood of Sesbania roxburghii or roots of Sonneratia caseolaris, which expand when touched with water. The hole can be made as large as is desired; for example, in some localities they gradually replace this wood that is inserted by pieces of larger and larger size. This procedure of piercing the ears is done only to ordinary people. It is known that women of the old upper classes, such as royalty, did not pierce their ears, because they regarded it as a low thing. The reason that it is necessary to pierce the ears while the child is still very small is that at this time the child is not yet very sensitive to pain, because the flesh is still immature, and also the child does not yet know how to pull and tug at the thread so that it comes out.

Burying the Afterbirth

I beg to drop the subject of the child for the time being and return to the subject of the afterbirth, which was placed in a sugarpot and set beside the place for lying near the fire. When a period of seven days after the birth is past, they may perform the ceremony of burying the afterbirth. Sometimes they wait a whole month or even three months before taking it out and burying it. Sometimes they bring the pot containing the afterbirth and enter it into the khwǎn and shaving of the fire hair ceremony when the child reaches the age of one month. When they take the pot containing the afterbirth out to bury it they have a superstitious way of carrying it, to wit: they shift it alternately from left hand to right, saying that when the child grows up it will be ambidextrous. If they carry the pot containing the afterbirth in only one hand, the child will be handy with only that one hand. When they return from burying the afterbirth, if the afterbirth is that of a boy, the people who took it out must sing a song or chant in the cadence of preaching. This shows that this sort of thing was popular in olden days. If it is a girl, when they return from burying the afterbirth they are to gather edible plants and firewood; when the child grows up she will be diligent and be a good housewife.

For burying the afterbirth there are many procedures laid down in text-books. In the textbook, Phrommácháad, it says: "If the child is born in the fourth, fifth, or sixth lunar month, the afterbirth must be buried to the north," and so on.

In the textbook, Pàthŏmcindaa, it says: "When you are going to bury an afterbirth, you are to take fragant powder, perfumed oil, exploded rice and flowers, powdered aloewood and sandal, incense sticks and candles, and offer them to the gods of the air, and worship the gods of the trees and the gods of the earth, and then you may bury it." Besides this it is specified that the afterbirth in the fourth, fifth, or sixth lunar month is to be buried to the southwest, contradicting what is said in the textbook, Phrommácháad, which says north, saying that the child will be easy to raise. If it is buried to the south, the child will be in danger and will be many other bad things. "If the cord of the afterbirth was wound around the child at the time of birth, you are to roast it over a fire until crisp, and then grind it up in rice and give it to the child to eat." It will never whine or cry at all. It will have good fortune and many other good things. "If the afterbirth is wound around the neck, put the afterbirth in a pot of one thousand (one thousand what, I do not know), and then spear it in the middle with an iron and roast it dry over a fire. Grind it up for the child to eat, and the child will have a beautiful figure," and so on. (Much like the story of European children sucking the dried umbilical cord as already described.)

Another procedure: "If the child was born on Sunday, the purchasing mother is on an anthill. The afterbirth must be buried in an anthill." If it was born on some other day there are also rules about various other places for burial, and so on.

Before burying the afterbirth, they are to place the desired articles with it in the pot, and then take it and bury it in the prescribed direction. It is said that the child will be expert in the three Vedas, will behave like its father and mother, and other things. (See the details in the above-named textbooks.)

According to northeastern custom, they place the afterbirth in a new pot with a lid. If there is no lid, they cover it with cloth and seal the mouth. They take it and bury it under the stairs in front of the house. Then they bring a section of log and light it at the edge of the grave, keeping it burning brightly both day and night until the period of lying near the fire is up, and then they stop. The reasons for this I do not know.

Concerning burying the afterbirth, to judge from the above textbooks, it is necessary to perform many ceremonies, as if the afterbirth were a thing of importance. But so far as I have been able to observe the usual procedure of the peasants, they do not do a great deal, except to take it and bury it at the base of a big tree. Burying it is proper; there does not seem to be any purpose in keeping it. Burying it at the base of a big tree is said to be a superstition that it is in a cool and shady place, and the child whose afterbirth it is will live "in coolness and happiness"[51] and will have a long life like a big tree. Sometimes they do not bury it beneath a big tree, but bury it under the stairway of the house. According to Indian custom they put a one-pie coin, turmeric, an areca nut, and a little salt in the pot with the afterbirth, and then bury the pot underneath the bed for lying near the fire. In some places they throw it away.

Regarding customs of the south of Siam it has been ascertained that they have ceremonies requiring the selection of a good direction, a good day, and a good place, such as an anthill, which is, for example, regarded as good. They are superstitious about throwing the afterbirth into water; the child whose afterbirth it is usually comes to harm by falling into water and drowning. Only this much has been learned.

In burying the afterbirth there is a belief that they must employ a right-handed person to dig the hole; otherwise the child will be left-handed. Sometimes after the burial they are to plant a coconut tree. Probably it is desired that it serve as a marker. In some places there is not only burial of the afterbirth and planting of a coconut tree, but also sprinkling of the pot containing the afterbirth and the coconut in advance as well. This is said to be to cause the "silver and gold coconut" to flourish, and the child to have happiness and prosperity. It is learned that the "silver and gold coconut" is an ordinary dried coconut, but it is covered with silver and gold papers which are supposed to be real silver and gold. This is the same category of thing as the silver and golden bricks laid down in auspicious moments.

For burying the afterbirth it is necessary to seek persons named "Steadfast Merit," "Enduring Merit," "Abiding Merit," and "Having Merit" to do the burying.[52] If they cannot find people with these names, they may let it pass; they may have other people with other names do the burying, but they must do the burying correctly with respect to direction as determined for them by the astrologer. These are all matters of superstition. No doubt they are beliefs of astrologers, and ordinary people probably do not perform them.

Why do they plant only coconut trees? May they not plant other trees? Or is this a belief belonging to some other place where they are fond of planting coconuts, and we acquired the belief? Or has the original conception been modified, and not only coconut trees but other trees may be planted as well? Perhaps this is connected with the matter of titulary trees of children, for there is a belief that every person born has a personal tree. Thus in the textbook, Phrommáchâad, it says that the guardian spirit abides in banana trees and coconut trees. The Semang, a Negrito people in the Malay peninsula, believe that a person is born with a titulary tree. The father selects this titulary tree beforehand; it is a tree near the place where the child is to be born. When he has made his choice, he cuts blaze marks in it as a sign;

these marks extend from the base to breast height. This tree is the place where the afterbirth is buried, and it is absolutely forbidden to cut it down. When the child is grown, he is forbidden to damage any tree of the same species, or even to eat the fruit of it. [53]

The textbook, Pàthŏmcindaa, says: "If a child is born in the year of the rat, it is attended by a god and the coconut tree. If born in the year of the ox, it is attended by a male human and the sugar palm." For other years there are other trees; for example, year of the tiger, a male butterfly and the tree Pentacme siamensis. If it is held that the afterbirth must be buried and trees planted as laid down here, there are certain difficulties. In some years, for example in the case of persons born in the year of the tiger, it must be a Pentacme siamensis tree. This would seem to be no easy matter, if it is a locality where Pentacme siamensis does not occur or where it is hard to grow it, as in Bangkok, where it can hardly be made to grow because it is lowland. What is to be done? The answer is that if it cannot be found, then stick a branch of some other tree in the ground instead and pretend that it is Pentacme siamensis, or else write the Thai name for Pentacme siamensis on the tree, in the same way that the name of a dead person is written in the funeral ceremony, or a name is written and cremated in place of a corpse. Perhaps this is what has happened. It would seem likely that it would be possible simply to alter the customs in this way. Some textbooks say that if a Pentacme siamensis tree cannot be found, a breadfruit tree may be used. I do not know why Pentacme siamensis and breadfruit trees may substitute for each other. Furthermore, the breadfruit is easy to find in the south, but is rare or nonexistent in the northeast. The Pentacme siamensis tree is easy to find in the northeast, but rare in the south. No further convenience than this is allowed by the regulations. I should therefore like to guess that the belief has been modified to permit the planting of coconuts, because it is easy to find them to plant and they are more useful than Pentacme siamensis trees. Combined with this the coconut is a tree used in divination; if it grows straight upward it is regarded as a good thing.

According to tradition the coconut is a symbol of fertility and plenty. The people of India call the coconut śrĭphala, that is, the tree of Srĭ, the goddess of grace and fortune. In various ceremonies of the Indians the coconut cannot be omitted. They offer it to the gods and use it in various auspicious rites. An offering of coconuts is auspicious. In making an offering to the goddess Lakshmi, a coconut may be used as a substitute if they have no image of the goddess. Beliefs about coconuts seem to be Indian, and have been diffused to us. For example, in khwăn ceremonies there must be coconuts, and in offerings there are also coconuts. In Malaya when a child has reached the age to speak but is slow to talk, they perform a ceremony to open its mouth. They split open a young coconut and feed its milk and meat to the child. The person doing the feeding must count from one to seven, and when she reaches seven she gives the child a bite. The Fijians in the South Seas, when they bury a child's umbilical cord, must plant a coconut or breadfruit tree. They believe that this tree that is planted has a connection with the child to whom the umbilical cord belonged. Whether the child encounters difficulty or good luck in the future depends upon the tree. If the tree grows and flourishes, the child will do well; if the opposite, then so also with the child.

Why are there so many beliefs about what must be done in burying the afterbirth? So far as one can see from what usually happens, once it is buried no one seems to take any interest in where his own afterbirth is. It is buried, and that is the end of the matter. Even in the case of the afterbirth of royalty, so far as has been ascertained, there is no ceremony performed, and there is no special royal term in the textbooks for the afterbirth of princes and princesses, except to call it phrâ̰q tràkuun, [54] which, however, is a word not generally known. Thus it may be seen that the afterbirth is not a thing of any importance, differing from the prescription as set down in the textbooks, that it is necessary to select the direction for burying. Or perhaps the original conception has long since been modified, for reading of works on the subject of the afterbirth of various nations, as set down in western books, shows that nationalities which are still at a low stage of development believe that the afterbirth is a part of the soul.

For example, people of the continent of Australia believe that people have many souls, and one soul resides in the afterbirth (similar to our belief in the khwǎn; our entering the pot containing the afterbirth in the khwǎn and shaving the fire-hair ceremony bears some resemblance to this). When they bury the afterbirth, Australians plant many sticks in the ground and gather their tops together to form a cone to mark the place of burial. This is probably comparable with our planting coconuts; originally it was probably planted as a marker of the place where the afterbirth was buried.

The Purchasing Mother

If a child is ill -- for example, its body is hot and it sleeps restlessly -- they believe that the purchasing mother is punishing and haunting it. It is necessary to perform a ceremony of throwing rice to the purchasing mother. They are to take cooked rice from the top of the pot (probably it is easy to scoop up, and it is hot rice and still pure, no one yet having scooped it up to eat, and it is easier to mould into balls than rice which has cooled; it is part of the category of first fruits;[55] (see my work on the Sarda festival) and form it into four balls of four colors, namely, white (which it is already), yellow (mixed with turmeric), red (mixed with red lime), and black (mixed with soot). They lay these four balls of rice in a potlid, a dish, or a banana-leaf container, and then raise them one at a time and carry them three times around the child. Then they speak words to ward off evil:

> Purchasing mother of the city below, purchasing mother of the city above, purchasing mother who treads the air, purchasing mother under the bed, come and accept your child's rice. Let all disease and illness go away!

There are also words to ward off evil which differ from the above, for example:

> Purchasing mother of the city below, purchasing mother of the city above, purchasing mother who treads the air, purchasing mother at the head of the stairs, purchasing mother under the bed, do you come and accept the balls of white, yellow, red, black rice (changing the color of the ball of rice as the words are spoken) of your child. Do not let the rice that it eats be bitter; do not let it vomit the milk it sucks; do not let it start in its sleep. Let it recover from illness.

Another version is:

> Purchasing mother of the city below, purchasing mother of the city above, purchasing mother under the bed, do you come and accept the balls of white rice, red rice, yellow rice, black rice.

Another version is:

> O purchasing mother, O lady! Your child is our child. Do not come pinching or scratching it; do not trouble and torment it; do not cause it distress and illness. We will rear it in happiness and contentment, to live with us until old age.

These versions were obtained from the memory of a number of persons who could remember them, and so they vary from one another.

When they have spoken these words to avert evil, they take the white, yellow, and red balls of rice and throw them over the roof of the house. Any ball may be thrown first; there is no rule. As for the black ball of rice, it is to be thrown under the house or thrown onto the ground anywhere. Then they take water and wash the potlid or dish in which the rice was laid, and toss this water after the riceballs. When they throw the rice they are to shout out "woo" in unison. Some people say that the ceremony of throwing the purchasing mother's rice is to be performed at twilight. There are also instances of using white rice, black rice, and yellow rice, without red rice, a total of three balls, and throwing them over the roof. Some people say they must be thrown from the east toward the west. In some instances they throw across the roof from the front of the house to the back of the house. This is as much on the subject of ceremonies that are performed as I have been able to learn.

This rice of the purchasing mother dyed various colors has the same characteristics as the balls of black rice and red rice put in a ceremonial

container of some sort in some regions; and it can be seen that we use things
for dyeing which are easily found at home, just as in the case of obtaining
medicines as already described.

Who is the purchasing mother? I will first quote the Invocation of the
Purchasing Mother for you to read, in order to facilitate discussion of the
subject.

Invocation of the Purchasing Mother (inscribed on the walls of a pavilion in the grounds of Wád Phrá? Chêedtùphon):

Hail to the gracious and auspicious powers! I prostrate myself.
I will recite an invocation inviting all the great gods. I invite the
great god Vishnu, and also the god Shiva of majestic power, who
is the lord of Mount Krailasa. I bow down and do homage to you.
Also the goddess Uma, whose grace sustains the world. May you
conquer diseases. I invite the god of the wind and the god of fire,
the blazing god Kala and the god Brahma. Also Yama and the
guardian of the four quarters, the god of the sun and the god of the
moon. Also the Lord Indra who is monarch of the world of the gods
-- twelve great deities in all. I fold my hands in reverence and
raise them over my head. I invite you to come and take up your
positions over my head. I offer you incense, candles, and lamps,
and white rice and flowers and perfumes; also a ceremonial fence
with flags of victory. I beg you to bestow your blessing, endowed
with magic power. Grant wisdom to me. I will invoke the figure
instead of the human being. Purchasing mother of the city above,
and purchasing mother of the city below, seven beings of seven
different kinds, the purchasing mother in the middle of the path,
bold and harsh, the strong purchasing mothers of the particular days
having traditional names, to wit: the purchasing mother of Sunday's
child is named Wíchdtrànaawan; the purchasing mother for Monday
is named Wádthánaanoŋkhraan; the purchasing mother for Tuesday
is named the pure giantess (yág bɔɔrísùd); the purchasing mother
for Wednesday is named Lady Sãamáláthád; the purchasing mother
for Thursday is named Lady Koolaathúg; the purchasing mother for
Friday is named the lovely giantess (yág noŋjaw); the purchasing
mother for Saturday is named the Lady Eekaalaj. If you hear your
name, make haste, and bring with you all ghosts and spirits. I
will reward you to your heart's content. When you have eaten then
go, do not stay, as I command you.

Hail to the gracious and auspicious powers! I invite you, O purchasing mothers. My teacher taught me how to recognize you, the
purchasing mother of the city above, the purchasing mother in the
middle of the path, the purchasing mother of the city below, each
one causing a different kind of harm.

Some purchasing mothers inhabit the entrails, and cause the child
to cry and moan. Some purchasing mothers lie athwart the navel,
causing wind and diarrhea and making the child sob and squirm.
Some purchasing mothers inhabit the head and cause vomiting and
dry voice. Some purchasing mothers hide in the flesh, making the
child toss in its sleep and scream and have nosebleed and turn pale.
Some purchasing mothers inhabit the top of the head, making the
child cry out with fright and causing its feet, hands, and calves to
be chilled. Some purchasing mothers inhabit the veins, making the
child cry and twist its body and its four limbs, and scream till it is
blue in the face. Come, all you purchasing mothers, and abide
here, all twenty-eight of you who are the authors of harm. Do not
be angry; restrain your tempers. Come and partake of meat, fish,
and liquor, and of the cups of water and rice, and of the ornaments.
Crowds of people are gathered all around. We invite you to accept
our offering. Eat your fill, you and all your kinspeople. Come
and admire the figure instead of the child. Be auspicious. Do not
think of harming the little child who has been born among humans.
He is not of your kind, living in the great trees that grow in the
forest, or in caves or among cliffs and marshes, or in woods and
thickets beside streams and caverns and mountains, or on rocky
shores, or in forests and meadows or among tall trees, or beside the
paths that humans walk, or beside monasteries and pavilions. When
you have eaten, go where you like. Be not slow. Do not tease
and fondle and play with the child that has been born. Let the
child flourish. We invite you to be kind to the child, to protect it.
We offer you rice, water, crab, and fish. May the child support
and maintain religion and not be idle. If it is a boy let him become a monk; if it is a girl let her become a nun. Let the child
obey the precepts and be gentle in heart. Let the child dedicate
half its merit to its mother for having reared it. We beg to purchase
this child for a price of thirty-three cowries. For three days it is
the spirits' child; after the fourth day it is a human child. It is
not your child; do not yearn after it. We give you a figure in its
place. Take the figure in this vessel away and admire it. We have
paid you with these offerings. Do not linger here. When the child
grows we will send merit to you to assist you to escape grief and
attain Nirvana. Make haste. Be enamored of our offering that we
make to you. Make a promise, as if it were a sealed contract,
that you will not after this day cause harm to the child. We ask
to keep the child and care for it. We will grind turmeric and mix
it with chalk to make golden powder like moon-rain to anoint the
child, and also rice made golden with turmeric. We will blend

these together and enchant them and put them on the forehead of
the child to guard and protect it. Do not tarry to admire the child.
Hurry and begone, and take with you all illness and disease, coated
tongue and bloated stomach and sore throat; let none of these remain behind. Purchasing mothers of all seven days, make all these
things vanish, leaving the four elements and the three sources in
full measure. Let none of these vanish or be in danger. Let the
child be easy to raise, so that it may support and foster the religion
of the Buddhas -- of Kukkusandha, and Dasabalakonagamana, of
Gotama, of Kassapa, and of Ariyamaitri, all five of the Buddhas,
to whom we dedicate a share of the merit in all that has been said.

This invocation is called the Small Sarateja rite for driving out the
evil caused by the purchasing mothers. Three days after a child has
been born from the womb of its mother, let a doctor do all the fore-
going. This must be done after three days, and then the child will
flourish. This concludes it.

Discussion of the Subject of the Purchasing Mother

When one has read the material quoted above he learns that the purchasing mothers are spirits which come to molest and abide in the body of
newborn children. There are seven purchasing mothers assigned to the birthday of the child. Besides these there are the purchasing mother of the city
above (that is, the city of the sky), the purchasing mother in the middle of
the "path" ("path" means "way"; it probably lies in the middle of the air?),
and the purchasing mother of the city below (that is, upon the earth). Then
there are purchasing mothers inhabiting the entrails, the navel, the flesh,
the top of the head, and other places in the child's body, making a total of
twenty-eight. But in this invocation there is no mention of the purchasing
mother under the bed; probably she is included in the twenty-eight.

The purchasing mothers usually trouble children and cause them various
illnesses. Probably they want to carry the children off because they love
them, and so it is said, "tease and fondle and play with the child," and so it
is necessary to play a trick and ask to buy the child from the purchasing
mother; that is, haunt the ghost in turn. The price is thirty-three cowries.
Three days after a child's birth, they are to make an offering and mould a
figure of the child for the purchasing mothers to carry off and admire in place
of the child. The child will remain here and have comfort and happiness,
when the purchasing mother has eaten the offerings, which are like a bribe or
reward. "When you have eaten then go, do not stay, as I command you."
This is an act of chasing away the purchasing-mother spirit, like the Chinese
making offerings to spirits and then lighting firecrackers to drive them away.

It has been related at the point where the child was born that when the umbilical cord has been cut and the child placed on the basket, the midwife bounces the basket and says, "Three days the spirits' child, four days a human child." This is probably derived from this matter of asking to purchase the child from the purchasing mother. Probably the midwife is assumed to represent the purchasing mother, but the ceremony that we perform does not coincide too well with the original ceremony set forth in the Invocation of the Purchasing Mother. Our performance has lost the part requiring thirty-three cowries, and the bouncing must be done after three days have elapsed, not on the day of birth. Also, in the bouncing ceremony it is necessary to make an offering, moulding a figure of the child and placing it with the food offerings; this has also been lost from our performance. If one examines the subject as set forth in the textbooks on medicine, in the part dealing with characteristics of purchasing-mother illnesses, it appears that they make an offering and mould a figure of the child and put it in every time that they perform anything relating to the purchasing mother. For example:

"Siddhikāriya. I will describe the purchasing-mother illnesses of children born on Sunday. If it is born in the waxing phase of the moon, the illness is localized above the navel; if in the waning phase, it is localized below the navel. The purchasing mother named Wîc'ldtrānaawan abides in the cradle. If the child falls ill it will have various symptoms; it will feel pain in its body, and will not be able to take rice or milk. Let doctors know the following:

"If you would cure it, take earth from the two banks of a river and mould it into a figure of a mother holding a child in her arms. Then make offerings to it with white flowers, five incense sticks and five candles, and all sorts of fragrant things. Then exorcize the illness with the following mantra three times:

"'Om namo bhagavampati danikāmukkham dharanikhibalimapakādabalā buñcayyah savāha om rddhi. Begone! Savāhah.'

(Many mantras used in Tibet end "Savāhah. Begone!" Probably there is a common origin in the Tantric Buddhism of India.) "When the mantra has been recited, place the figure in a begging bowl and place it toward the east. If this is done for three days the child should recover. If it does not recover, make up the following prescription for an inhalant to drive out the poison:

"For the medicine use the seeds of chard plants, gum from sŏŋ fruit, hairs from a cat, hairs from a human, sàdaw leaves, and beef tallow, in equal parts. Heat this as an inhalant for the child; it is very good." (This agrees with the Indian belief that if you want to drive spirits out of a child's body you must use medicines that are swallowed, inhaled, and applied externally.)

This matter of taking earth from the two banks of a river and moulding it into a figure of a mother holding a child in her arms is strange. An elderly person told me, "This is startling, for I have seen enameled dolls in the form of a mother holding a child in her arms as described here. There are some at the enamel kilns of the city of Sukhothai, and some at the museum in the island of Bali in Java. I do not know whether they were used as dolls in rites or not."

Why must we perform a ceremony of bouncing a baby and asking to purchase it, saying, "Three days the spirits' child, four days a human child?" This is probably derived from the belief that when human beings are born spirits form them to be born. "Spirit" [phǐi] is here an old Thai word, referring to those having power over human beings, invisible to human beings unless they cause themselves to be seen. Later on we called aristocratic spirits "gods" [using Sanskrit-Pali devatā, "divinity"], and called bad spirits "evil spirits" or simply "spirits." When spirits are going to form human beings they take earth and model a figure, as is related in the verses teaching children to read words ending in -d in Muunlábòd Banphǎkìd:[56] "The spirits who mould children straightway affixed the nose and eyes," or in the story of Khǔn Chǎaŋ Khǔn Phἔεn:

> I will sing verses on the birth of all the characters. When they first entered the womb, it is said, a most evil spirit on a treetop in the nighttime moulded a figure, giggling and pinching and squeezing it shapelessly. He moulded and moulded, snickering all the while, taking a little of this a little of that and squeezing and adding them until complete.

> One night the spirit was moulding on the treetop. There was a creature in hell, enduring severest sufferings. When he had expiated his demerits he was freed from torment and was delivered from the status of creature of hell. He scurried about running in search of happiness. He could not go to heaven, for he had not yet escaped sorrow. The spirit moulded him and tucked him into the womb.

So we humans are born because spirits or gods create or mould us. What business is it of gods or spirits that they should constantly create human beings? Because spirits want to carry human beings off. If a child that is born has an attractive figure, the spirits like it and would like to take it and rear it, or, to speak frankly, cause it to die. This coincides with the belief of westerners that "those whom the gods love die young." If the spirits don't like the child, they leave it for human beings to rear. Because of this belief, it is necessary to find various methods of protection against spirits, for example, by asking to purchase the child. It is forbidden to admire a child directly with the word "lovable." They must speak the reverse, saying that the child is "detestable." When the spirit hears this he will believe that it is true and will not take the child away. Sometimes they even give children the names Pig, Dog, Frog, Treetoad. This is to deceive spirits, because spirits are usually more stupid than people.

The belief that it is the spirits that shape human beings that are born is also held by the Australians. They believe that spirits form earth into the shape of a human being, and then take the soul which inhabits the buried afterbirth and put it into the human figure. Then they put it into a woman's womb. The custom of admiring children but having to speak the reverse also exists among many peoples. Among some nationalities, for example Europeans and the people of Uganda in Africa, they even spit on the children. [57] The ancient belief of various nationalities that spirits will come and carry off newborn children is due to the fact that newborn babies are very delicate and may easily die in three days or seven days. (We swear with the words, "May I die in three days or seven days." This comes from this matter of children.) In those times medical care of children was not sufficiently advanced, and whatever happened to children was all blamed on spirits. If a child cried a great deal, they said that the purchasing mother teased it. If it had a stomach ache, they said that the purchasing mother had entered and was disturbing its intestines. Or if its umbilical wound hurt, they said that the purchasing mother was lying athwart the navel. Therefore it is probable that in olden times children often died in the first three days after birth, and hence the saying, "Three days the spirits' child." When the three-day limit was past they were somewhat relieved, and hence the saying, "Four days a human child." The Indians believe that a newborn child may die very easily because the spirits will carry it off, and the child is called for the first three to seven days not a human being but a creature, because they do not have confidence that it will survive. Europeans also believe that spirits may carry off a newborn child, and so a protective ceremony must be performed to cleanse it of sin. In English a small child is referred to as "it," showing that at this time it is not fully human.

This assumption that the midwife represents the purchasing mother is also strange. It looks as if the midwife were a spirit, and the word "witch" which is used together with the word "doctor" also would seem to be a matter of spirit doctors. [58] Moreover, nowadays the word "witch" is also used in connection with spirit possession; this suggests that medical treatment in former times was a matter connected with spirits. The Shans call the midwife mɛ̂ɛ kɛ̀b [literally, "gathering mother" or "collecting mother"] and call other children which one brings in and rears lûug kɛ̀b [literally, "gathered child" or "collected child"]. The word kɛ̀b here perhaps means that the midwife gathers or collects children that are born, and so they must be purchased. The Vietnamese call both midwives and spirits that come to disturb children bâa mùu or mâa mùu; apparently one is to understand that the midwife and the purchasing mother are the same person. Perhaps it is also because of this notion that people detest the word "midwife."

There is a matter that I still do not understand. Why is the word "purchasing mother" reversed in meaning? The midwife who bounces the child should be the "selling mother"; she is the person who sells the child for other people to purchase and take away for a price of thirty-three cowries. Or perhaps the word "purchase" [Thai, sýy] was not originally the same word as the ordinary Thai word, sýy, meaning to purchase. But the things that are done include purchasing, and so it is difficult to try to interpret it in some other way.

In the Invocation of the Purchasing Mother the names of all seven purchasing mothers assigned to the days are mentioned, but the other twenty-eight have no names. The names of the seven purchasing mothers assigned to the days are strange; each rhymes with the name of the day immediately following, as follows:

Sunday [Thai, ʔaathíd], name wícídtrànaawan, rhymes with
Monday [Thai, can], name wannánoŋkhraan, rhymes with
Tuesday [Thai, ʔaŋkhaan], name jâg bɔɔrìsùd, rhymes with
Wednesday [Thai, phúd], name sǎamonláthâd, rhymes with
Thursday [Thai, phárýhàdsàbɔɔdii], name kaaloothúg, rhymes with
Friday [Thai, sùg], name yâg noŋjaw, rhymes with
Saturday [Thai, sǎw], name ʔeekaalaj, rhymes with
Sunday, see above.

These names were probably not obtained from India, because some of the names are not words from Indic languages. Phra Theewaa Phínímíd (Chaaj Theewaaphínímíd) has kindly noted down the names of the seven purchasing mothers for me, together with the shape of the purchasing mothers and the weapons that they carry. Some of the names that he gives differ from the above.

1. Sunday, name Lady cídtraawan; head and face of a lion, vermillion in color; left hand carries a bow, right hand carries a fan.

2. Monday, name Lady (man)thánaa noŋkhraan; head and face of a horse, white in color; right hand carries a sword, left hand carries a fan.

3. Tuesday, name Lady jâg bɔɔrìsùd; head and face of an albino buffalo; right hand carries a sword, left hand carries a fan.

4. Wednesday, name Lady sàmùdtháchâad; head and face of an elephant, orange in color; right hand carries a sword, left hand carries a fan.

5. Thursday, name Lady lòogkàwágkháthùg; head and face of a deer, light yellow in color; right hand carries a spear, left hand carries a fan.

6. Friday, name Lady jâg noŋjaw; head and face of an ox, yellow in color; left hand carries a bow, right hand carries a fan.

7. Saturday, name Lady ʔèegkhàmaalaj; head and face of a tiger, black in color; right hand carries a long-handled trident, left hand carries a fan.

If one considers the forms of the purchasing mothers he will see that their bodies are those of women, but the heads change according to the animals which the gods of the seven planets ride. I am puzzled as to why each one carries a fan, for it is precisely because each one carries a fan that the purchasing mothers are called mɛ̂ɛ wâaj mɛ̂ɛ wii [wii is an old Thai word for "fan"]. On the back of the sheet of cloth with the figure of the god thǎaw

wĕedsàwan that is hung over the cradle they draw a figure of the purchasing
mother having the body of a woman and the face of a horse. This would
logically mean that the child lying in the cradle was born on Monday, but
the artists who copy old pictures make it always a horse's head. No matter
what day the child was born, they draw a horse's head, not changing the face
according to the animals which the gods of the seven planets ride. From
this it can be seen that astrologers have invented something new; it is not
the original thing. As to what the faces of the other twenty-eight purchasing
mothers are like, I have found no mention. The figure of a woman and face
of a horse are strange. I have tried investigating the figures of gods and
spirits of various nationalities and have found many that have human bodies
and horse's heads, but they are all male gods and male spirits, not agreeing
with the matter of the purchasing mother with a horse's face. There is a
similarity to the graha spirits of India, whom they worship and ask to protect
children, but their faces are rather those of goats.

In the Yajurveda of India it is said that the spirits which come to molest children are collectively called graha (which probably means "to drag
off"; it is the name of evil spirits which cause children to be ill and die).
It says that there are nine, four males and five females, which have a special
name pūtanā (the name of a giantess, daughter of King Balī). In one text
it says that there are twelve spirits attending upon a child, all of them female spirits, called mātṛkā. These spirits usually come and pounce upon
children, or cause children to be ill. There is yet another spirit which the
Hindus reverence a great deal, called Saṣṭhī (meaning "the sixth"). Six days
after a child's birth they must perform a ceremony of worshiping Saṣṭhī,
which is a god or spirit attending the child's person. (In the Brahmavaivarta-
purāṇa it says that Saṣṭhī is the favorite wife of Khandhakumāra.) The ceremony that is performed consists of taking four lumps of rice, one lump white,
one lump mixed with turmeric to make it yellow, one lump mixed with red
lime to make it red, and one lump mixed with ashes of chaff to make it
black. (Indians do not use earthenware pots, regarding them as unclean.
They must use metal pots for cooking and must polish them clean. Therefore they must use ashes of chaff instead of soot from the bottom of an earthenware pot.) These four lumps of rice are laid in a vessel and the ceremony
of worshiping is performed. During the worshiping they tell stories about
Saṣṭhī, and then call the child to come and eat. [59]

The matter of the purchasing mother's rice and the story of Saṣṭhī seem
to be similar to something found in a western book, that children six days old
often die of lockjaw (which has the symptoms of a stiff chin and twitching
muscles, similar to the disease called in Thai làq, which is caused by poison
from the navel when the umbilical cord is not cut properly and disease germs
arise). The people of India are very much afraid of this sixth day. They believe that Saṣṭhī will change herself into a black cat (the cat is the mount of

Sasthī) or into a chicken or a dog and come to chew up the skull and heart of the child. They must stand watch and keep lights burning all night on this sixth day, to prevent cats or other animals from coming near. The Orāon people (a Dravidian group) are afraid of black cats. They believe that black cats are the spirits of women who died in childbirth; they will transform themselves and come to do harm to a woman who has given birth or to the newborn child, and so they must stand guard all night. [60] It is perfectly proper that they should be afraid of cats that might come to do harm to a newborn child, but it is stretching it a little too far to think that if a cat crosses a corpse the corpse will rise up.

To summarize what has been said, the purchasing mothers are evil spirits. It is fitting that their bodies and faces be made detestable and frightful, for example, like those of giants (jắg), but the astrologers have gone astray in decreeing that their faces are those of the animals ridden by the gods of the seven planets. There is another strange point, that the spirits of children's illnesses and of epidemics are all female spirits.

Why must they mould four lumps of rice, of four colors, as in our throwing of the purchasing mother's rice? I have inquired of Hindus and obtained no information. The Tamil have a ceremony called dṛṣṭiparihāra which employs lumps of rice of various colors. Brahman P.S. Sastri has related to me the following: "I have seen this performed only once at a wedding ceremony. I recall that there were lumps of black, red, white, and yellow rice. A woman performed the ceremony, and she let no one know what she spoke when she performed the ceremony, or where she threw away the lumps of rice. In the case of a child they perform the dṛṣṭiparihāra ceremony only in abbreviated form: they use rice of only one color; it is usually a lump of rice floating in water in which turmeric and white lime are dissolved. If they use lumps of white rice, they hold them in both hands and encircle the child three times, the right hand circling to the right and the left hand circling to the left. Then I believe they throw the rice over the roof. I have never heard Tamil people speak of purchasing mothers." What is described here seems to be the same as the throwing of the rice of the purchasing mother.

The Vietnamese also have a custom of moulding lumps of colored rice. When the child has reached the age of one month, they shave the fire hair, which they perform as a ceremony with glutinous rice moulded into three lumps, one lump dyed red and one lump dyed yellow, and there is also a cup of pulse boiled with sugar, to offer to the bâa mùu, that is, the spirit connected with children. This matter is very close to the throwing of the purchasing mother's rice. As regards the colors, according to Indian belief yellow, red, and black are detested by spirits. The color red is good to use in chasing away spirits for it is the color of fire and of the god of flames. [61]

The Palaung people have a belief that when they build a new house it is very bad if a dove flies into it; they must perform a ceremony to remedy matters. They make five balls of rice and color them green, red, black, yellow, and white. Then they cut up paper of various colors and make flags which they fix in the balls of rice so that the colors match. A little curry and tobacco is mixed with the rice. They find a bowl of water, and then place all of these things at the door or window. They recite a magic spell and then throw out the balls of rice, following them with the water. If a dog eats this rice that is thrown out, it is regarded as a good omen. [62]

This is a ceremony similar to our throwing the rice of the purchasing mother. According to northeastern custom, when they perform the ceremony of averting evil they also throw white, black, red, and yellow rice.

Why are four lumps of purchasing mother's rice used? Perhaps this means that they are for the purchasing mother of the city above, the purchasing mother who treads the path, the purchasing mother of the city below, and the purchasing mother under the bed, for the number is just right, and also only three lumps are thrown, the other lump, black, being tossed under the house. Probably this refers to the purchasing mother under the bed. Or the throwing of four lumps of rice may be an offering to the spirits of the four directions, like offerings to spirits in other ceremonies in which offerings are placed on banana leaves and laid out in the four directions. But in this case they do not throw them in various directions, so I do not know the reason for doing it.

The encircling of the child with rice is comparable to the ārati ceremony of India, already described. It would seem that the encircling of the child is due to a desire that the disease or spirit come out, as with the people of some settlements in the western part of the island of Borneo. If anyone is suddenly and violently ill, they believe that a spirit has possessed him. The doctors are mostly old women. The doctor takes a stick of wood and whittles it into the shape of a human being. She touches this seven times to the head of the patient, saying, "O disease, this figure will substitute for the patient. Enter this figure!" Then she puts white rice, salt, and tobacco into a small basket together with the figure, and lays this down in a place that is believed to have been the dwelling-place of the spirit. She sets the figure upright and then says, "O spirit, this is the figure that substitutes for the patient. Release the soul of the patient and then enter into this figure, for it is truly more beautiful and fine than the patient." This is a matter of using figures and food to entice the spirit or disease out. In the Invocation of the Purchasing Mother it says, "Do you go and admire the figure in the offering," and our ceremony of propitiation would seem similar in the purpose for which it is performed. Therefore the lumps of rice of the purchasing mother are perhaps food to entice the purchasing mother to come out. Why do spirits like to eat rice, and not fresh, raw things as is generally understood? Probably we acquired the idea of rice offerings from India, but their rice offerings are made to the spirits of deceased ancestors, and are a symbol that the dead ancestors still come and share the meals with the family and are not cut off. Or perhaps the performance has been modified from the offerings to the purchasing mother mentioned in the Invocation of the Purchasing Mother, which we know are still sometimes made.

Perhaps the throwing of the rice of the purchasing mother is like the Chinese throwing of liquor to offer to spirits because they do not know how to send it to the spirits except by throwing it out. In India there is a custom of taking balls of rice and small offerings and throwing them up into the air behind the house. In the Laws of Manu it is said in two places (chapter 3, sections 83 and 90) that when one has finished making an offering he is to toss the sacrificial rice in four directions, beginning with the east and circling to the right, i.e., to the east, south, west, and north, in order to dedicate it to the gods Indra, Yama, Varuna, and Soma together with their attendants. Perhaps we acquired the rite of throwing rice from this ceremony.

The Khwăn and Shaving of the Fire-Hair Ceremonies

Three days after the child's birth it is regarded as having passed one stage of danger of being a spirit child. The parents are glad of this and arrange a khwăn ceremony. [63] This khwăn ceremony is not done showily; they probably perform only an abbreviated ceremony among the family, not informing many people. The reason for doing it quietly is probably that they have not yet lost their fear that the spirits will come and carry the child away. Only when the child is a full month old do they perform the big fire-hair-shaving and khwăn ceremonies. They have probably lost their fear and believe that the child will survive, and therefore the big khwăn ceremony is performed when the child is a full month old.

In the third-day khwăn ceremony they arrange a baaj sĭi in a dish and offerings to sacrifice to the spirit of the place, including an Ophicephalus fish made into soup, a young coconut, a bunch of water bananas, boiled red pudding and boiled white pudding and other sweets as may be appropriate, and flowers, incense sticks, and candles. The equipment used in the khwăn ceremony includes scented powder, scented oil, or perfumed flour to anoint the white rice placed in the metal bowl in which three candleholders are set. [64] Then they bring the magic thread of cotton and enchant it, tying it to both wrists of the child; this is called "tying" the khwăn. Then they bestow blessings in the customary way. At this point they may transfer the child from the flat basket to its cloth cradle, but in some cases they have it continue to sleep in the basket.

Also, on the third day parents whose children usually do not survive or are as they say hard to raise customarily invite a person who raises children successfully to come and tie the khwăn for the child. In the days when there were f$\acute{y}$aη and s$\grave{a}$l$\breve{y}\eta$ coins, the object that was tied was one of these coins which they were to purchase from a widow or they made the purchased coin into a "spirit-fetter" bracelet, that is, a smooth bracelet which could be adjusted in size. The person invited to come and perform the khw$\breve{a}$n ceremony was usually the person who purchased the f$\acute{y}$aη or s$\grave{a}$l$\breve{y}\eta$ coin from a widow or the person who made it into a bracelet. The parents of the child must pay the person tying the khw$\breve{a}$n an amount of money equal to the price of the silver tied on. In tying the khw$\breve{a}$n they used raw cotton thread tied on the wrists; it must be tied with a square knot. Sometimes a small lock was also strung on it, with the idea of having tied the khw$\breve{a}$n and locked it. This lock was a little odd in that it was made from the wood from a support under the monks' water closet, cutting off only a little and carving it into the form of a Thai lock. An elderly person has told me that this Thai lock was a brass lock like a Chinese lock, except that in the center there was a sharp projection like a girl's cache-sexe, in which a hole was bored for inserting the key to unlock it. The key was like that of a European lock; after turning it they squeezed the lock, causing the bolt to slide to the side. But it may be that this kind of lock is Malayan, and we received it from them.

If they do not tie on a lock, they may substitute the bone of a frog's leg, which is like a Chinese lock in shape, or may tie on a vulture's bone made into a cylindrical talisman. This is probably the oldest of all. Sometimes they tie on little bells. Things that are tied on in place of a lock are understandable as meaning that the khw$\breve{a}$n is tied on to remain with the body, but why are little bells tied on? It might be said that it is good to tie them so that when the child wanders off we will know from the sound of the bells, but that would be for bigger children who can come and go, whereas in what is described the child is still small, and there is no need for knowing where the child has gone from the sound of the bell. I have obtained a clue from the beliefs of the people of the part of Africa called the Slave Coast, that when a child is ill and thin it is believed that it is inhabited by a spirit. They must tie iron hoops and little bells to the child's ankles, and place a great many iron hoops around its neck. They say that the sound of the iron and bells knocking together will frighten the spirit away.

Customs concerning tying the khw$\breve{a}$n for children resemble other customs concerning birth; the methods depend upon the locality and the time and the popular beliefs thereof. In times and places that are not yet advanced, they do these things simply. Later their practices may change and become more elaborate, but a clue as to their origins remain. You can see this in my critique on khw$\breve{a}$n ceremonies, which have been already treated in detail separately.

Shaving the Fire-Hair. When a child reaches the age of one month and one day (probably they wish to make sure that it is a full month, and so they add

another day), it is past danger from illnesses which are understood to be in-
flicted by spirits. They arrange a big fire-hair-shaving and khwăn ceremony.
Sometimes they also name the child at this time; this is a matter of receiving the newborn child into the register of membership in the family.

In shaving the fire hair they must make an offering for the spirit of the
place according to custom. When they shave the hair they leave a clump at
the top of the head, saying that it protects the top of the head which is still
thin. The hair that is shaved off is placed in a banana-leaf container with a
Caladium or lotus leaf laid in the bottom; sometimes flowers are mixed in.
In cases where things are done well, the whole is placed in turn on a stand.
Then it is taken and floated on the water at low water, or is thrown away,
whichever is convenient. The person who takes it and floats it must say,
"We ask for a life of coolness and happiness like the sacred Ganges," or some -
thing else of this sort. In the Gṛhyasūtra text of India it is prescribed that the
hair that is cut or shaved is to be hidden in a cowshed or in a pool or in a
place near water. Our floating the hair on the water is probably derived from
this last Indian custom; it was probably inconvenient for us to put the hair in
a cowshed as in the first custom. Then the relatives perform a ceremony of
tying the khwăn cotton thread around the child's wrists and ankles, and give
a blessing according to custom; or if things are done well there are also gifts
for the child. What has been described is the ceremony which ordinary people may perform. In the case of wealthy or prominent people the ceremony
may be as large as their resources, ability, and birth permit. That is, they
must have an astrologer name the auspicious day for the khwăn ceremony;
there must be Brahman and astrologer's ceremonial things (the astrologer goes
and speaks in a low tone beside the eye-level shrine on which offerings are
laid; what he says I do not know, but if you ask an astrologer he can no
doubt tell you); there are various offerings;[65] there must be a baaj sĭi;[66]
there is a person to perform the khwăn ceremony, called the child's purchasing mother; there is encircling with candles; and there are monks to give
Buddhist chants in this ceremony. Sometimes the pot containing the afterbirth which has been saved is also entered in this ceremony, together with
the silver and gold coconuts for planting when the afterbirth is buried. What
has been described briefly is not always performed exactly like this. There
are sometimes additions or deletions. It is rather a matter which depends on
one's teacher.

In the evening the monks recite their Buddhist chants. Next morning
the holy water that they have blessed by their chants is placed in a big metal
bowl and set in the ceremonial circle. The child is placed with its face
turned in the direction prescribed by the astrologer. When the auspicious
moment arrives the elderly person who is presiding is invited to pour holy
water from a conch shell over the head of the child, and then he cuts the
hair with scissors. At that moment the monks give the victory chant. If

there are Brahmans they blow conch shells and rattle their ceremonial drums, and the astrologer worships the auspices. The orchestra plays a piece of victory and blessing. When the ceremony is finished, the child is turned over to others to shave the fire hair. They put the shaved hair in a banana-leaf container with a <u>Caladium</u> or lotus leaf, set this in turn on a stand, and then take the banana-leaf container and float it on the water. This is a brief account of the fire-hair-shaving ceremony according to mingled Buddhism and Hinduism. This is chiefly an affair of wealthy city dwellers. There are a great many ceremonial details, too many to relate; even if I were to describe them there might be omissions or misunderstandings, for my knowledge is not sufficient for me to give a detailed description. I have asked persons who have this sort of knowledge, but they usually guard their textbooks closely, not allowing one to borrow or examine them. It is impossible to criticize them, for this is their way of making a living; if they alone know, no one can say whether they perform correctly or incorrectly. I speak in this way because it applies to myself. On second thought, I wonder if it is possible that there are no written textbooks, and so they say simply that they cannot lend them, for in olden times in Thailand there were few writers of textbooks; what there were, were only on things that could not be remembered, such as medical books. Even if the owner of a textbook died he could not take the textbook with him; the textbooks would have had to survive for us to see.

The leaving of a clump of hair in the middle of the top of the head in shaving the fire hair, and then leaving this hair to grow long, is in order to leave a topknot and perform a topknot-shaving ceremony when the child grows up and is almost to reach the period of young manhood or young womanhood. I have seen Chinese children with a clump of hair on the top of the head and the rest shaved smooth. Sometimes there is a patch of hair toward the side, or sometimes two such patches. This makes one wonder, if it is to protect the thin top of the head, why patches are left on the side also. Sometimes a clump of hair is left forward, beyond the center of the head. Sometimes the clump is precisely at the whorl in the hair. One is reminded of some groups of people in Java and Malaya who, when they shave a child's head, leave a clump of hair. They believe that this is to provide a dwelling place for the <u>khwăn</u>, and that if no hair is left the <u>khwăn</u> will have no place to stay and so will flee elsewhere, causing the child to fall ill or even to die. Even if there are head lice and it is necessary to shave off the hair, they refuse to shave it all off; they must leave a clump so that the <u>khwăn</u> will have a place to stay.

Leaving hair in the center of the head is probably the same sort of belief, because the top of a child's head is thin and can be seen to pulsate, as if the <u>khwăn</u> or life were right there. In India they call this thin spot at the top of the skull the <u>brahmarandhara</u> because they believe that the soul of a

person enters and leaves at that point. When a Yogi dies they usually break
the skull at that point to assist the soul to leave the body easily. This is the
same sort of belief. Later they substituted a dried coconut shell, which we
also took over; that is, we break a coconut before cremating a corpse.

Ceremony of Entering the Cradle. When the khwăn and shaving-the-fire-
hair ceremony is finished, they perform a ceremony of placing the child in
the cradle. They are to procure a white gourd (washing it clean and then
smearing it with flour), a medicine-pounding mortar and pestle, and a tomcat. They must tidy up the cat first. Besides these things there are small
cloth bags, one filled with paddy, one with pulse, one with sesame, and
one with cottonseed; there may also be other things depending on cases.
(These are like the things prepared for the ceremony of making a bridal bed
and the ceremony of entering a new house.) These things are laid in the
cradle. If the child to enter the cradle is a boy, there are to be a notebook
and pencil; if it is a girl, there are to be a thread and needle laid in the
cradle also (if this was not already done at the time of bouncing on a basket,
already described). Besides these there may also be a baaj sǐi in a dish and
encircling with candles. In some places they also make an offering to the
cradle. When the objects named above have been placed in the cradle they
begin at once to swing it because the cat does not like this and if there is any
delay it will jump out of the cradle. When they have swung it three times
they take the cat out of the cradle and carry the child in the arms and put it
in the cradle in place of the cat. They swing it three times in the same way,
pronouncing a blessing upon the child according to custom, as they swing it.
Thus the ceremony is finished. If the child is also to be named at this time,
some teachers write the child's name on a paper and lay it in the cradle also.

Of the various things, including the cat, that are placed in the cradle,
the rice and vegetable products probably refer to prosperity and fertility,
while the gourd, pestle, and cat probably refer to the proverbial blessing,
"May you be cool as a gourd and heavy as a pumpkin; may you stay at home
like the stones of the fireplace, and guard the house like a tomcat." This is
a blessing given by old people not only to children; when they bless a bridal
couple they use the same words. It is probably a very old blessing, for the
words are simple and ordinary, unlike the blessings that are pronounced today,
which contain terribly few old Thai words. The "pestle" in the blessing is
"stones of a fireplace." Probably the stones of the fireplace were earlier,
and were changed to a medicine pestle later. The change is a good thing,
for stones of a fireplace are terribly dirty and unpleasant. As for the tomcat
it is a large male cat, an adult cat with whiskers. If compared to a human
being, it is like a person who has attained legal age, and so it is a cat that
does not abandon its home. Its superstitious use can be understood. Tidying
up the cat before putting it in the cradle is a good thing, as protection against
dirt resulting from its fondness for sleeping on the stove.

Rearing Children

When a child is about three months old and has become stronger, it can roll over on its belly. The first time that it rolls over on its belly, they usually lay a metal bowl of cold water on its back. They explain that they do this because when a child turns over on its belly its face will drop down; it does not yet know how to bend its head backward, and might turn on its belly, stick its face in the pillow, and be unable to breathe, which might be dangerous. They place the bowl of water on the child's back and it no doubt feels that there is something heavy and cold, and so it is automatically startled and throws back its head. Later if it turns over on its belly it may be able to raise its head of itself because of the experience. If an adult helps to hold the child's head up when it turns over on its belly, no one has ever seen it. The child might not learn to help itself, even though it has the physical ability. It is probably for this reason that in olden times they forbade helping a child directly when it practiced turning over on its belly or walking; they preferred to have the child learn to help itself. This means that they knew the correct methods of teaching.

At the age of three months, the child may be allowed to eat some rice mashed up with nâm wáa bananas; that is, mix cooked rice with a little salt and pound it up with the bananas till a paste is formed, or the bananas may be first cooked. Only the flesh of the bananas is to be used; the hard core is not used, because it is said to be hard to digest. For bananas to feed to children, select the kind that have white or light yellow cores. Bananas with pink cores are not popular because they are sour and not good to eat. These bananas with pink cores are called by a special name, kàlíi ʔɔɔŋ bananas, sometimes distorted to máalíi. For a utensil to mash up the rice and bananas use a coconut-shell spoon; that is, cut and scrape a coconut-shell to make it the shape of a spoon, and then rub and polish it till it is smooth and lovely. Take this coconut-shell spoon and mash up the rice and bananas in a vessel such as a bowl until they are seen to be fine and well mixed. Then take up the mashed rice with the hands and form it into small lumps of appropriate size and feed these to the child. If it ate rice alone this might stick in its throat, and so water must be dropped as well. Dip all five fingers into a vessel containing cold water and then draw the fingers together to hold a little bit of water, and let this drip into the mouth of the child in order to moisten its mouth and facilitate swallowing. In some cases this mashed rice is put in a vessel and set on the fire to cook the rice, unless the bananas have already been cooked.

From what has been described it may be seen how short of things our ancestors were; for vessels they had only coconut shells, which are natural products. We call thick, poor quality, enameled dishes "coconut-shell" dishes. This is probably a name surviving from the times when coconut-shell

dishes were used instead of china dishes. There are still vessels made of coconut shell, including water dippers, ladles, curry spoons, and rice-measuring
vessels. A coconut-shell water bowl can also be used instead of a mirror;
there is still a saying surviving to this day, when one would criticize a person for not having taken a good look at himself: "You did not dip up water
and put it in a coconut-shell bowl and bend over to look at your reflection."
Today we have progressed and can have better, more beautiful, and more
convenient utensils, but in some rural localities they still like to use vessels
made of coconut-shell, because they are convenient and easily found, not
requiring unnecessary expense to buy these things. Actually coconut shells
are produced on an elevated place, but we usually turn them into various
kinds of vessels for low use, for example for washing the feet or buttocks.
This has given the coconut shell a low status. Even if it is polished and
smoothed beautifully, we never get away from the notion that it is a low and
poor thing. The use of the fingers to dip up water and drip it into the child's
mouth is also more due to the lack of small-sized spoons to use than anything
else. What has been said applies only to poor people. Even wealthy people
sometimes do the same, following easy and effortless methods. Some people
use spoons made of clamshells, called clamshell spoons, for dipping up water
to drip into the child's mouth instead of using the fingers. Nowadays we also call china spoons "clamshell spoons." People who still use coconut-shell
spoons to mash rice for children to eat, not using better spoons even though
they have them, explain that they deceive spirits that the child that they are
feeding is a child of no consequence, and so they use a poor coconut-shell
spoon to feed it. Some people say that if they use vessels made of china the
china may break and chip into the rice. This is probably a question of always having done one thing and so continuing to do it. Even though it is
seen to be inappropriate, they still do it, and so must find various rationali-
zations, for customs are slow to die.

There is another method of feeding rice to children. They chew the
rice up fine, sometimes with banana also, and then take it out of the mouth
and feed it to the child, at the same time dipping the fingers in water and
dripping it into the child's mouth. The Shans call this sort of rice khâaw
màm. Feeding rice to children in this way is certainly not good. It is probably a custom surviving from very long ago. No doubt many nationalities
did this when they were still at a low stage of advancement. Perhaps it is believed that the saliva of the chewer also helps to digest the rice for the child.
Formerly I frequently saw khâaw màm. Usually those seen to do this were
low-class Chinese women. It is a practice of uneducated people, not a general thing.

I forgot to describe the ceremony of opening the mother's breasts,
which is performed the first time they let the child suck the breast. The
ceremony of opening the breasts is more frequently performed among

aristocrats than among common people. They invite a woman who raises children successfully -- if it is an aristocratic woman of prominence, all the better -- to come and suck the breasts as an auspicious first event. They believe that if they do this the child will grow big and not be ill.

When the child reaches the age of seven months, it will be able to rise up and assume a squatting position, or in some cases will be able actually to sit up. When another month has passed, it is able to crawl. Some do not crawl; they inch or shove themselves along on the buttocks. Next, at an age of approximately nine months, the period is reached for the teeth to appear, called "flowers arising." They forbid referring to these as "teeth"; for what reason, I do not know; or perhaps they believe that such words as "tooth" [which is homonymous with a verb meaning "to slash, cut"] are not auspicious words. (In old people whose teeth are all lost, if new teeth appear they call them faaŋ, not "teeth" (fan); actually fan and faaŋ are probably the same word.) Next the child will practice standing, called "setting up an egg"; then it practices walking. The time periods that have been mentioned are only approximations, because there are also some children who are faster or slower to learn than this. The Chinese texts fix these periods as follows: "Seven sit, eight crawl, nine teeth arise." The Thai have it: "Three lift (probably meaning to lift the head), six sit."

During the period that the child is learning to sit and crawl, its teeth appear, and it practices standing, the child usually has symptoms of fever, choking, and diarrhea at each stage; some children have none of these, and some have some of the symptoms at some of the stages. This is all probably due to changes and growth of the organs, causing abnormal symptoms at every stage. These symptoms are regarded as an ordinary thing; they say that if they are disregarded for three or four days they disappear of themselves. It is merely forbidden to speak of them. It is believed that if [these symptoms] are mentioned, the child will have diarrhea as many times as one speaks. If it is observed that three or four days have passed and the child has not yet recovered, this is suspicious, and they summon a doctor. They set up a metal bowl filled with rice, which in former times contained money for the fee for treatment in the amount of one and one half bàat. If the child has fever they usually perform a rite of throwing the purchasing mother's rice. In some cases they swab the throat, using lemongrass bulbs and a little salt, ground up on the bottom of a pot or in the lid, as medicine for swabbing. The medicine that is left over from swabbing the child's throat they smear on its forehead; this is the same sort of thing as anointing. They believe that it prevents recognition by the spirits, for the illness of the child shows that spirits would come and take it away. This is the way they treat the child; if it still does not recover they go and see a doctor.

At the time when the "flowers arise," in some places they take gold, which may be a ring or anything which is gold, and rub the child's teeth gently, believing that the child will have a mouth of silver and gold. Or there may also be other reasons; I have not been able to ascertain clearly. Probably this is the sort of thing which in English is called "sympathetic magic." In some cases at this stage they mash up rice mixed with gold and have the child eat it, believing this will cause its voice to be euphonious and its complexion to be like gold. [67]

When the child is able to stand up for the first time they call it "setting up the egg," because it still cannot stand up straight for a long time; it is like an egg placed on end, and so it is called thus. At this time the child will try to take steps. The ancients forbade helping the child walk, because this would keep the child from learning to help itself. They therefore have a method of teaching walking: they have the child stand against the wall, with its back and arms braced against the wall. Then it tries to take a step. An adult stands in front of the child at a short distance, making a gesture with the arms of receiving the child. The child will stagger forward toward the adult. The first time it will be able to take only one or two steps before falling. The adult in front of the child must take care to catch it, not allowing it to fall. Then it tries to take a step again. At the time when the child can hardly hold itself up straight, the adult sings out, "Set up an egg; if the egg falls, boil it and eat it. If the egg falls to the ground, I'll eat it up." [68] This singing is to amuse and distract the child, so that it will learn to stand up and take steps. After a child has sufficient skill in taking steps, some people make a circle of wood for the child to cling to and walk and turn itself around, to make it stronger and more agile.

When a child is able to prattle, but not yet in language, it is called "playing with saliva." Soon afterward it will practice speaking. If it speaks early it is called "light-mouthed." If it speaks late, perhaps only after one year, it is called "heavy-mouthed." If the child is heavy-mouthed to an abnormal degree, it may be a mute. One should observe by clapping one's hands to call the child behind its back; if the child turns to look, the child is not a mute, because mute children are usually deaf also. When one carries the child in one's arms and it points and cries "ʔûu ʔáa," it can be observed that it is not a mute, but merely heavy-mouthed. If one calls or jests with the child behind its back and it does not hear, or if when it is carried it merely points and opens its mouth and cries "ʔěɛ," and acts like this every time, the child is certainly a mute.

For children of wealthy aristocrats they have a mouth-opening ceremony. They invite a woman of good lineage who raises children successfully to come and speak auspicious words, teaching the child to speak politely and nicely. Sometimes they also give the name at this time. They usually seek out someone with knowledge of astrology to give the name, selecting the name according to the rules laid down in textbooks of astrology. (There are already books on the subject of giving names. They are not very hard to find;

it is therefore unnecessary to speak of this.) Some people have the mouth-opening ceremony on the next day after birth, but I regard this as inconvenient; one should not perform it at this stage.

On the subject of naming the child, probably no invariable time can be set down. In some cases, when they have shaved the fire hair they give the name at the same time. In some cases they wait until the child is big; when they go to turn it over to a monk to be his disciple, the monk who is its teacher names it. If one notices the names which were given in former times, they are seen to be Thai words, but at present names which are Thai words are very few indeed. Now names are mostly Pali and Sanskrit words. Probably people imitate the aristocracy, in order to avoid the names of ordinary peasants. In ancient times the giving of the name was probably a temporary matter. They called children according to sex and relative order, for example, ʾâaj, ĵii, sǎam, and sǐi. This sort of naming is also found among the Shans and among the Indonesians, that is, Javanese and Malays. Perhaps it also occurs among other nationalities. This sort of name is changed when the child goes to the monastery to study, or else when it reaches the age of three or four years; then a name is given in accordance with the rules that they believe in. If the child is often ill, or they think that the original name was not auspicious, they may rename the child, in order to make the spirits think it is a different person; they will not molest it and cause it to be ill often, this being a sign that the spirits would carry it off. Old-time names, such as Pig, Dog, Frog, Tree-toad, Worm, are probably names given to deceive the spirits that these are not people, but only pigs and dogs; the spirits will be convinced and will not carry them off. This is a phenomenon which in English is called "cacophemism," which occurs in old customs of all nations. Some names, such as Tiger and Elephant, are given according to dreams or events that occur. There are also names given according to the figure, face, and other characteristics of the child, such as Fat, Pudgy, Squat, Little, Topknot, Pigtails. These are probably names that people call the child, not real names that are given to it, and these names stick to the child and are not changed. Sometimes names are also given according to color, such as White, Red, Purple. There are also names given which are names of things of value, such as Silver, Gold, Jewel, Ring; or characteristics of wealth and prosperity, such as Much, Wealthy, Possessor. There are also names implying admirability; names of this sort are very numerous, such as Refreshing, Cheering, Graceful, Admirable. There are also many names of plants, such as Cinnamon, Sandal, Pinflower, Pandanus. There are also names which have no meaning, for example sěem, cɔɔn, cûj, lǎm. Probably some of this last group are shortened forms of words of many syllables, and probably some are distorted forms of words from other languages.

When a child is learning to sit, if it is often ill, besides renaming it, they usually also let patches of its hair grow. This is probably derived from the belief in the khwăn; they fear that the khwăn will flee, and so they leave locks of hair for the khwăn to reside in, as has already been described. Also if a child is fat, it is forbidden to speak of this or admire it as fat or lovable; one must speak the opposite, that it is detestable. This is a trick to deceive the spirits into not carrying the child away.

If a child's mother becomes pregnant again before it is weaned, the child usually is not strong; it is inclined to be ill and fretful. This is called "losing out to the younger sibling," for the mother's milk for feeding the child has less value than before she became pregnant; it is impure milk, and insufficient to give the child normal nourishment. The child must eat other things to help, some of which are difficult for a child to digest, and it eats irregularly, not at fixed times. Finally its digestion goes bad and its body gradually weakens. This may turn into the disease of bloated belly. If a child has symptoms of "losing out to the younger sibling," they employ the method of having the child's mother, when she bathes, take the child between her legs, her thighs holding the child so that its head projects and comes even with the upper edge of the lower garment. When she dips up water and bathes, part of the water flows off the edge of the cloth and falls directly onto the head of the child. This is done only enough to serve as a matter of form, until the child's head is wet, and then they stop. I do not know why they do this. I cannot think how this might cure the disease of "losing out to the younger sibling."

There are miscellaneous rites relating to the rearing of children which are performed by some people in some localities. For example, when they are going to take a child out of the house to spend the night elsewhere for the first time, they must first smear the child's face with soot, and then it may be taken out of the house. This is probably a matter of deceiving the spirits, as usual. Another one: if the parents have necessary business requiring them to go away overnight, they are to rip a cloth or cloth remnant which is part of the parents' clothing and tie or wind it around the child, saying, "Do not cry out for father and mother." When one considers this custom, it is moving, for it is a matter of love and concern for the child. They have nothing to fasten it with, so they use instead a part of their own clothing to tie it, for the garments are regarded as like oneself, as has been described in my book on the khwăn ceremony. According to a belief of the Palaungs, when a child is frequently sick they must smear its face with soot in order to make it unattractive to the spirits so that they will not carry it off. This is comparable to the practice of smearing with soot described above.

In the south they have a ceremony of the child treading on the ground. It is performed at the time when the mother of the child has emerged from the fire. They are to carry the child in the arms, holding a parasol over it, and arrange a stand on which are laid the clothing of the child, which a person carries after the child. The person carrying the child takes it down out

of the house to the ground, and then touches the child's foot to the ground;
or they may merely make a gesture, the foot of the child not actually touching the ground. This ceremony is similar to the earth-treading ceremony in
the northeast, but there they perform it on the day of birth, when the cord of
the afterbirth has been cut. In the ancient royal ceremonies such a rite also
occurs, called the royal ceremony celebrating the touching of the earth by
the king's children. This royal ceremony has long been abolished.[69]

When the child reaches the age of one year, if it is a boy there is usually something tied to its waist, such as a phallic talisman, a clamshell, or
cowries strung on a cord and called "paying-the-vow cowries." They tie
these on if the child is often ill; sometimes they tie them on [even] if it is
not ill. Sometimes they tie them at the neck, saying that they protect the
teeth. Sometimes they make silver and gold into the shapes of peppers or
other shapes; this belongs to the period when people had become wealthy.
Besides these, I cannot remember whether there are other things that they tie
on. If it is a girl, they usually tie a cache-sexe and figures of turtles around
the waist. I have read an account of customs of Ceylon concerning the tying
on of the cache-sexe, written by a westerner. He explains that it is not to
hide shame, but is to ward off spirits and protect [the child] from what westerners call the "evil eye." This is striking, for little children have no reason
to be ashamed or to hide anything; they are still in the age of innocence.
The belief that the cache-sexe is tied on to hide shame is perhaps an opinion
which arose later. The cache-sexe (càbpîŋ) is also sometimes called càpîŋ
and tàpîŋ; it is a word derived from a Portuguese word referring to a metal
plate of small size for covering various holes and openings, as keyholes or in
boats. Then it came to be used with children. We probably got this custom
from the Malays, because formerly Malay girls also wore these cache-sexe
and called them by the same name. To speak only of our own country, the
cache-sexe most often seen in use is of silver. If it is better than that, it is
a cache-sexe of a copper-gold alloy. There are also cache-sexe of gold,
not merely of gold but also inlaid with green and red jewels. They say that
these golden cache-sexe are worn also even by some persons who are not children, but I have never seen this and so I can say nothing. If it is true, then
considered from the modern point of view it is terribly stupid. Poor people
sometimes make the cache-sexe out of coconut shell, and I have sometimes
seen these edged with silver. In later times the cache-sexe that has been
described came to take the form of a silver or golden mesh, like the cord
around the waist and a piece hanging down in front in ancient India, which
was called a girdle. Today these are no longer used because children have
to wear lower garments, lest the westerners criticize them as savages, and so
the cache-sexe is gone. The feeling of embarrassment of the child increases
because of wearing a lower garment. There is a matter I forgot to relate:
formerly girls wore anklets made of silver, copper-gold alloy, or gold,

depending upon the station. They wore them until puberty or later, if they had not yet established a household of their own, showing that formerly one could tell by looking at the ankles; if a girl wore anklets she was still unmarried and had no home of her own. Today anklets are worn only on the stage. Nevertheless they sometimes change from gold anklets to anklets made of cloth embroidered with gold.

Also, in the case of a child that is frequently ill and hardly likely to survive, if it is a boy, the parents usually take the child to "cast cloth in the forest,"[70] that is, to offer it to a monk. The monk who receives it takes cotton thread and ties it around the child's wrists. If it is a girl, the monk gives the cotton thread to them, for them to tie it themselves at home. The reason that the child is often ill is that spirits deliberately cause it to be ill; spirits hate adults, and can do nothing to adults, and so they work on children. If the child is not ours, but belongs to a monk, the spirits will not dare to continue to afflict it, for spirits fear monks. (Whether true or not, I do not know.) So the child recovers from illness. If a child falls accidentally and then afterward has symptoms of fever, the adults usually take a metal bowl with rice covered with a cloth and carry it together with a big spoon to the point where the child had the fall. They call out to the khwǎn, which they understand was left deserted from the moment of alarm. Then they dip up air as if dipping up the khwǎn, put it in the metal bowl, and return home. Then they have a khwǎn rite for the child that had the fall.[71]

While the child is lying in the cradle, besides singing lullabies and swinging it to sleep, there is also a fish or a waterskipper for the child to look at, hanging over the cradle toward the head, but not too high, for the child will roll its eyes upward to look at it. When a child rolls its eyes upward like this, they believe that this is a time when the purchasing mother comes to molest it. These fish are tied and woven of nipa palm leaves in the form of a fish of fairly large size, and painted green, red, and yellow. Then there are many small fish which are supposed to be its young, hanging from it. Even now these are sometimes seen for sale. As for the waterskipper, originally it was made of bamboo woven in the form of a waterskipper of the kind that has the body of a spider and swims on the top of the water. Later when there had been progress they took various remnants of colored or figured cloth and sewed them together, stuffing them with kapok like a square cushion with bulging center. At the corners were small triangular cushions, supposed to be its young, hanging down in a row, seven to each corner, arranged in descending sizes, but these young were not called waterskippers; they were given another name, that of "water chestnuts," because they were triangular in shape, resembling water chestnuts that are eaten. The sound of lullabies sung to children which one used to hear, a melancholy, tranquil, rhythmic sound, is not often heard now in Bangkok, because it has been replaced by the sound of cars, the sound of automobile horns, and other sounds.

The sound of lullabies can be heard only at a distance from crowded centers, and it is more frequent in huts and old houses than in brick buildings or modern houses. This is a matter of changing tastes. Formerly there were many lullabies; today so few can remember them all the way through that the melodies are becoming shorter and shorter. Finally they will probably become antiques existing only in the museum. There is also the matter of amusing children, as by spreading out the hand and turning it back and forth in front of the child's face while crying, "They are bringing Granny in a procession; when they reach the pavilion they set Granny down." These may also disappear in the same way. (Fortunately H.R.H. Prince Damrong Rajanubhab ordered the Royal Institute to collect these verses in all localities, lullabies, teasing verses, and children's playing verses. If they vanish from memory, they will then survive only in the National Library.)

There remains another matter, namely, the dolls and toys of children. One that I have seen ever since childhood is the Brahman doll. A good kind is the palace-dweller doll, modeled of clay and then fired and painted. It is a small figure of a palace lady, wearing a figured lower garment and a diagonally draped stole, in a sitting position resting on an arm. This is a girl's doll. If it is for a boy, there are tumbling dolls made of straw paper and then painted, hollow inside, usually in the form of a child with a topknot. At the buttocks there is a clay weight to make it heavy. When it is pushed over, it automatically rights itself. Then there are also figures of very fat children painted bright yellow, likewise made of paper and hollow inside. There are also masks and other sorts of things which I cannot remember. I recall only small leather drums and small cymbals, which are Chinese things, not Thai. Drums which children make themselves for fun are sugarpot drums. They stretch rags over the mouth of a sugarpot, and then fasten them tight at the sides with clay, beating the sides of the sugarpot with a stick to make the cloth tight. Then they mix mud with water and smear it on the cloth, and beat it with a stick to make a noise that deafens the neighbors. However great their strength, they put it all into the beating, until the sugarpot drum can stand no more and breaks to pieces, and then they make a new one. Besides these, they model oxen and buffaloes of clay. I have never seen them model elephants and horses, probably because they are harder to model. Then they also model cups with the thinnest possible bottoms, to cast face down with full force on the ground, to make a loud explosion which breaks the thin bottom of the cup open into a large or small hole, depending upon the case. The other children in the game must pay up an amount of clay equal to that lost in the explosion. They take turns playing in this way until they are bored, and then they stop. I believe that games involving modeling of clay probably existed before others. As the period of progress was reached and better dolls and children's toys were imported from abroad, the old things vanished. Wherever progress is retarded, some of these old things still remain.

The change is gradual, following in the wake of national progress. It makes one feel he would like to get an old-fashioned doll to have to look at, to serve as a memento of the days when one was a child. But no one makes them for sale as they did so generally in the old days, because if they made them no one would buy them. There is nothing beautiful about them; why make them? There are still some, only of the hollow paper doll kind. These are figures of elephants and horses and actors which they make to offer to spirits and to the guardian spirit of the land. Even so, the figures of actors are cut out of paper rather than modeled of clay. This means people are more clever, but this is cleverness mixed with cheating. They assume that the spirits do not object, and so they make them worse, and the spirits can do nothing. There are also Brahman dolls offered. These are probably offered for the spirit to take and use as servants. There are still corpses of more than ten Brahman dolls at a spirit house right here in Phuttan Gardens.

Footnotes to <u>Customs Connected with Birth and the Rearing of Children</u>

1. Tamjɛɛ, "nettle."

2. "Tamjɛɛ doctors."

3. Crooke, William, <u>Religion</u> <u>and</u> <u>Folklore</u> <u>of</u> <u>Northern</u> <u>India</u> (London, A. Constable, 1896), p. 203. <u>A.R.</u>

4. See my <u>Customs</u> <u>Connected</u> <u>with</u> <u>Death.</u> <u>A.R.</u>

5. Meaning "assorted or miscellaneous." We call all wood, with the exception of teak and a few other kinds, "five species." <u>A.R.</u>

6. Pronounced in Thai, <u>nǎmoo phǔdthǎtàdsàʔ.</u>

7. "Cut" in Thai is <u>tàd.</u>

8. The word for grandchild in Thai also includes nephews and nieces.

9. Glowworms.

10. Bull's-eye lanterns. <u>A.R.</u>

11. Enlightened one.

12. The Thai word for "east" is "the sun comes out," and the word for "south" is the same as the word for "down."

13. "Stitches" translates an anatomical term referring to the tissues at the rear of the female organ.

14. Literally, "woman who receives."

15. Prolapsis uteri.

16. Hemorrhoids.

17. A Thai term for the female organ.

18. Thai euphemism for the male organ.

19. A slipknot with two loops like a rabbit ear and the two ends of the string spreading outward. A.R.

20. A thornless bamboo.

21. A high rank, usually a child of the king.

22. Literally, the "mother" or "woman" who "raises" or "lifts."

23. Cf. p. 126, footnote 14.

24. See the subject of camphor leaves in my Customs Connected with Death. A.R.

25. Le May, Reginald Stuart, An Asian Arcady: The Land and Peoples of Northern Siam (Cambridge, W. Heffer & Sons, 1926), p. 191. A.R.

26. See my work on ceremonial fences. A.R.

27. See the subject of thɔɔráníisǎan holy water in my Customs Connected with Death. A.R.

28. "Rafters" or "rafter bones" are the pelvic bones on either side of the vagina.

29. Used as face powder.

30. See the section on the color red in my book on Customs Connected with House Building. A.R.

31. The cabalistic design trínisǐmhe will be discussed in a separate section. A.R.

32. Buddhist protective stanzas.

33. In Thai, sǎaj sǐn is the name for the magic thread.

34. "Eight or nine houses" is a Thai idiom which means "far away" and reflects the people's mode of living in the old days. A.R.

35. Lady Monthoo, wife of Thôdsàkan, king of the giants in the Thai Rama epic, is known to all Thai young and old as "Lady Monthoo with only one developed breast."

36. Original parenthesis in English.

37. Encyclopaedia of Religion and Ethics, Vol. 10, p. 465. A.R.

38. Milne, Mrs. Leslie, The Home of an Eastern Clan (Oxford, 1924), p. 279. A.R.

39. Literally, "to be in karma."

40. With kam spelled simply kam, not karma.

41. Probably taken from the little book, Customs of the Palace and Royalty, by the named author, better known as Phájaa Theewaa, the Lord Chancellor.

42. Stevenson, Margaret, The Rites of the Twice-Born (London, Oxford, 1920). A.R.

43. The original is a neat, pithy rhyme.

44. The original is a rhyme similar to the above.

45. The Thai phrase "good thing" is often used to mean "something having magic power," and the author probably intended some of this meaning to be suggested here.

46. An aromatic sedge.

47. Original parenthesis in English.

48. A simple round basket which is inverted over chickens.

49. The best black cotton cloth in Thailand is that dyed with this substance, because the color is unusually fast.

50. The Thai term could also mean blood vessel or tendon.

51. A Thai idiom for happiness, since coolness rather than warmth is desirable in Thailand.

52. These are very common Thai names.

53. Skeat, Walter W. and Charles O. Blagden, Pagan Races of the Malay Peninsula (London, Macmillan, 1906). A.R.

54. Literally, "royal lineage."

55. "First fruits" is given in both Thai and English in the original.

56. A famous reading primer dating from the reign of King Chulalongkorn.

57. Encyclopaedia of Religion and Ethics, Vol. 2, p. 639. A.R.

58. In Thai, "doctor" is mɔ̌ɔ; "midwife" is mɔ̌ɔ tamjɛɛ; and "witch" is
mɛ̂ɛ mɔ́d. Often a single word is expanded by adding another, many
times meaningless word. The word mɔ̌ɔ (doctor) takes the expander
mɔ́d, giving the phrase mɔ́d mɔ̌ɔ, also meaning "doctor."

59. Noted down as Swami Satyanandapuri told me. A.R.

60. Encyclopaedia of Religion and Ethics, Vol. 9, p. 504. A.R.

61. See my book Customs Connected with House Building. A.R.

62. Milne, Mary Lewis, Home of an Eastern Clan: A Study of the Palaungs
of the Shan States (Oxford, Clarendon Press, 1924), p. 184. A.R.

63. The khwǎn is an individual's soul, spirit, morale, or life-force. At
times of crisis the khwǎn is believed to leave, and must be called back.
In many Thai idioms the word khwǎn is best translated as "morale."
The same word is used for the whorl in the hair, and some children have
two khwǎn in this material sense.

64. Candleholders here are flat, leaf-shaped objects of metal, with handles
to grasp, against the side of which the candles are fixed.

65. See my work on offerings. A.R.

66. See the subject of the baaj sǐi in my work on the khwǎn. A.R.

67. A glowing golden skin is a Thai ideal. Turmeric is used to achieve and
enhance this; monks are admired for their golden skin, caused by the
dye in their yellow robes.

68. The original is a neat verse, like a nursery rhyme.

69. See the critique on Hindu customs of the twelve months in Collected
Miscellaneous Writings by H.R.H. Prince Damrong Rajanubhab. A.R.

70. The idiom "cast cloth in the forest" refers to a custom of giving robes, etc. to monks without specifying a particular recipient, by putting them on a tree where they are supposed to be found accidentally by a monk. Here the process is not described but apparently the child is "given" to a monk.

71. See my work on the khwăn rites. A.R.